P9-DMJ-686

WRITING WELL

Books by Donald Hall

Books of Poetry

Exiles and Marriages, 1955
The Dark Houses, 1958
A Roof of Tiger Lilies, 1964
The Alligator Bride: Poems New and Selected, 1969
The Yellow Room: Love Poems, 1971
The Town of Hill, 1975

Books of Prose

Andrew the Lion Farmer, 1959
String Too Short to Be Saved, 1961
Henry Moore, 1966
Playing Around (with G. McCauley et al.), 1974

Edited Works

New Poets of England and America (with R. Pack and L. Simpson), 1957
The Poetry Sampler, 1961
New Poets of England and America (Second Selection) (with R. Pack), 1962
Contemporary American Poets, 1962; Second Edition, 1971
A Concise Encyclopedia of English and American Poetry and Poets (with
    Stephen Spender), 1963
Poetry in English, 1963; Second Edition, 1970
The Faber Book of Modern Verse (New Edition with Supplement), 1965
The Modern Stylists, 1968
A Choice of Whitman's Verse, 1968
Man and Boy, 1968
American Poetry, 1970
A Writer's Reader (with D. L. Emblen), 1976

WRITING WELL

Second Edition

DONALD HALL
University of Michigan

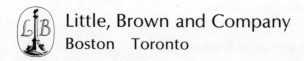

Little, Brown and Company
Boston   Toronto

Back cover photo: Jane Kenyon

Copyright © 1976, 1973 by Donald Hall

All rights reserved. No part of this book may be reproduced in any form or by any electronic or mechanical means including information storage and retrieval systems without permission in writing from the publisher, except by a reviewer who may quote brief passages in a review.

Library of Congress Catalog Card No. 75-36960

Fourth Printing

Published simultaneously in Canada
by Little, Brown & Company (Canada) Limited

Printed in the United States of America

ACKNOWLEDGMENTS

James Agee. Quotation on page 113 from "Southeast of the Island: Travel Notes." Reprinted from *The Collected Short Prose of James Agee* (Boston: Houghton Mifflin, 1969) by permission of Houghton Mifflin Company and Calder & Boyars Ltd.

The Ann Arbor News. Quotation on page 233 from the editorial page of *The Ann Arbor News,* July 4, 1972. Reprinted by permission.

R. P. Blackmur. Quotation on pages 258–259 from "New Thresholds, New Anatomies" in *The Double Agent* by Richard P. Blackmur. Copyright 1935 by Richard P. Blackmur.

John Malcolm Brinnin. Quotation on pages 48–49 from *The Sway of the Grand Saloon* by John Malcolm Brinnin. Copyright © 1971 by John Malcolm Brinnin. A Seymour Lawrence Book/Delacorte Press. Used by permission of the publisher and Macmillan, London and Basingstoke.

John Collier. Quotation on page 221 from *Indians of the Americas* by John Collier. Copyright © 1947 by John Collier, Reprinted by arrangement with The New American Library, Inc., New York, New York.

James B. Conant. Quotation on pages 281–282 from "Athletics: The Poison Ivy in Our Schools" by James B. Conant. Reprinted from *Look Magazine,* January 17, 1961 by permission of Cowles Communications. Copyright © Cowles Communications, Inc., 1961.

Frank Conroy. Quotations on pages 14–15, 144 from *Stop Time* by Frank Conroy. Copyright © 1967 by Frank Conroy. All rights reserved. Reprinted by permission of The Viking Press, Inc. and The Bodley Head Ltd.

Hart Crane. Quotation on pages 258–259 from *The Collected Poems and Selected Letters and Prose of Hart Crane* by Hart Crane. Permission of Liveright, Publishing, New York. Copyright © 1933, 1958, 1966 by Liveright Publishing Corp.

James Dickey. Quotation on pages 227–228 from *Deliverance* by James Dickey (Boston: Houghton Mifflin Company, 1970), pp. 184–186. Reprinted by permission of Houghton Mifflin Company and Hamish Hamilton, London.

David Finn. Quotation on pages 231–232 from *The Corporate Oligarch* by David Finn. Copyright © 1969 by David Finn. Reprinted by permission of Simon and Schuster.

Robert Frost. Quotation on page 256, 257 from "Acquainted with the Night" by Robert Frost. From *The Poetry of Robert Frost,* edited by Edward Connery Lathem. Copyright 1928, © 1969 by Holt, Rinehart and Winston, Inc. Copyright © 1956 by Robert Frost. Reprinted by permission of the publishers, Holt, Rinehart and Winston, Inc. and Jonathan Cape Ltd., and the Estate of Robert Frost.

Germaine Greer. Quotation on pages 283–285 from *The Female Eunuch* by Germaine Greer. Copyright © 1970, 1971 by Germaine Greer. Used by permission of McGraw-Hill Book Company and MacGibbon & Kee, Ltd.

Ivan Illich. Quotation on pages 282–283 from *Deschooling Society* by Ivan Illich, pp. 6–7, 76–77. Copyright © 1970, 1971 by Ivan Illich. By permission of Harper & Row, Publishers, Inc., and Calder & Boyars Ltd.

Oliver Jensen. Quotation on pages 166–167 from "The Gettysburg Address in Eisenhowese" by Oliver Jensen, previously published in *The Territorial Enterprise* and *The New Republic,* June 17, 1957. Copyright © 1957 by Oliver Jensen, Editor of *American Heritage* Magazine. Reprinted by permission of the author.

R. D. Laing. Quotation on page 81 from *Self and Others* by R. D. Laing. Copyright © 1961, 1969 by R. D. Laing. Reprinted by permission of Pantheon Books/A Division of Random House, Inc.

D. H. Lawrence. Quotation on pages 221–222 from *Pornography and Obscenity* by D. H. Lawrence. Copyright 1930 by Alfred A. Knopf, Inc. Reprinted by permission of the publisher, Laurence Pollinger Limited, and the Estate of the late Mrs. Frieda Lawrence.

Mary McCarthy. Quotations on pages 128, 145 from *On the Contrary* by Mary McCarthy. Copyright © 1957, 1961 by Mary McCarthy. Reprinted with the permissioon of Farrar, Straus & Giroux, Inc.

Antonio Machado. Quotation on page 157 translated by Robert Bly in *The Sea and the Honeycomb.* Copyright © 1971 by Robert Bly. Reprinted by permission.

Norman Mailer. Quotation on pages 285–286 from *The Prisoner of Sex* by Norman Mailer (Boston: Little, Brown, 1971). Copyright © 1971 by Norman Mailer. Reprinted by permission of the author and the author's agent, Scott Meredith Literary Agency, 580 Fifth Avenue, New York, New York 10036.

Nancy Winston Milford. Quotation on pages 49–50 from *Zelda* by Nancy Milford, p. 48. Copyright © 1970 by Nancy Winston Milford. By permission of Harper & Row, Publishers, Inc., and The Bodley Head Ltd.

The New Yorker. Quotation on pages 51–52 from Notes and Comments, *The New Yorker,* June 17, 1972, and on pages 52–53 from "Elvis!" Talk of the Town, *The New Yorker,* June 24, 1972. Reprinted by permission; © 1972 The New Yorker Magazine, Inc.

Robert M. Pirsig. Quotations on pages 203–204, 217 from *Zen and the Art of Motorcycle Maintenance* by Robert M. Pirsig. Copyright © 1974 by Robert M. Pirsig. Reprinted by permission of William Morrow & Company, Inc.

Ezra Pound. Quotation on page 34 from "In a Station of the Metro" from *Personae.* Copyright 1926 by Ezra Pound. Reprinted by permission of New Directions Publishing Corporation and Faber & Faber Ltd.

Tracy W. Redding. Quotation on pages 249–250 from *Hoosier Farm Boy* by Tracy Redding (Philadelphia: Dorrance, 1966). Reprinted by permission of the author's estate.

Antoine de Saint-Exupéry. Quotation on pages 214–215 from *Wind, Sand and Stars* by Antoine de Saint-Exupéry, translated by Lewis Galantiere. Copyright 1939, by Antoine de Saint-Exupéry, renewed, 1967 by Lewis Galantiere. Reprinted by permission of Harcourt Brace Jovanovich, Inc., and William Heinemann Ltd.

James Thurber. Quotations on pages 38, 110, 111, 162 from *The Years with Ross* by James Thurber, published by Atlantic-Little, Brown, Boston, Mass. Copyright © 1959 James Thurber. Reprinted by permission of Mrs. James Thurber and Hamish Hamilton, London.

Dan Wakefield. Quotations on pages 92, 143 from *Island in the City* by Dan Wakefield. Copyright 1957, 1958, 1959 by Dan Wakefield. Reprinted by permission of the author.

To Gerard McCauley

AUTHOR'S NOTE

The people from whom I have derived my ideas of style are the writers whose work I have loved. I quote many of them here, so that they may speak in their own voices, and not depend upon the articulation of an admirer. I do not quote them all. I owe my sense of style, as well as some ideas of it, especially to the modern writers I read and imitated when I was young: Ernest Hemingway, Ezra Pound, George Orwell, James Joyce. I do not mean that I am fit to call myself a pupil.

More immediate help came from Charles Christensen and Margaret Zusky of Little, Brown, and from their contacts with numerous teachers who used the first edition in class. The second edition benefits directly from the experience of these people, including Donald Butler, Terrence Collins, Steven V. Daniels, H. Ramsey Fowler, Neita Gleiker, Frederick Goff, Thomas Lux, Russell J. Meyer, Marcia Stubbs, M. Elizabeth Susman, Barbara Wicks, and Peter T. Zoller. Richard Larson, expanding on his review of the first edition in *College Composition and Communication*, provided an additional lengthy critique. Clayton Hudnall has given invaluable assistance, notably in a persuasive argument which resulted in Some Common Problems, and in preparing the instructor's manual for this edition.

In addition, I have profited from correspondence with instructors all over the country, and from conversations with teachers I've met in my travels. Students who have mailed completed questionnaires to Little, Brown have helped me revise this text for future students. I regret that I am unable to acknowledge this help more personally.

I am hugely in debt to Richard Beal, of Boston University, who has helped me to retain my sanity, I am sure at some cost to his own. I am indebted to Lawrence Russ, for considerable assistance, and to David W. Lynch, for adding a second stylistic conscience to my own. Rab Bertelsen has taken charge of the production of this edition with tireless and exact attention. I am indebted to Dorothy Foster, as ever, for reading my handwriting, for typing four complete versions, for patience and accuracy. In addition, Rosemary Yaco has come to my aid in research; and Sharon Giannotta has worked tirelessly to help me make revisions and additions.

CONTENTS

I
WRITING, AND WRITING WELL 1

WRITING TO DISCOVER   1
HONEST AND DISHONEST FEELING   2
EXAMINING THE LIFE   5
REVISING THE MAP   6
THEMES AND REVISIONS   7
SOME PROFESSIONAL WRITING   13
DISORGANIZED WRITING, POMPOUS WRITING   17
LEARNING TO WRITE WELL   18
DAILY WRITING   18
EXERCISES   22

II
WRITING A PAPER 26

GETTING IDEAS   27
ACCUMULATING DETAIL   29
SHAPING THE PAPER   33
   Purpose   33
   Selecting Detail   34
   Beginnings   36
   Middles: Development   40
   Endings   43
EXERCISES   48

III

WORDS   54

THE INSIDES OF WORDS   54
   Words Themselves   54
   No Synonyms   56
   Literalness and Metaphor   59
   Sense Words   59
   Misusing the Insides of Words   61
   Avoiding Self-Deceit   64
   Collecting Words   65
   Words as Blanks   66
   Words and Meaning   66
   Audience and Self   67
   Exercises   68
VERBS   72
   Action, and the Choice of Style   72
   Verbs with Nouns and Adjectives   73
   Verbs with Participles   74
   The Passive Voice   75
   Particular Verbs   76
   Invisible Verbs   77
   False Color in Verbs   78
   Fancy Verbs   79
   Made-Up Verbs   79
   Exercises   79
NOUNS   82
   Particularity and Choosing a Style   82
   Abstract and Particular   84
   Abstractions: Beginnings and Endings   86
   Invisible Nouns   87
   Making Bad Nouns from Verbs   88
   Fancy Nouns   88
   Revising Nouns   88
   Exercises   90
ADJECTIVES AND ADVERBS AND OTHER MODIFIERS   93
   Qualities and Choosing a Style   93
   The Adjective and the Cliché   93
   The Modifier That Weakens the Noun   94

Modifiers as Weak Intensives   95
Automatic Adjectives   95
Nouns as Modifiers   98
Using Modifiers Well   98
Revising Modifiers   102
Exercises   102
ORIGINAL WORDS: COMPARISONS   105
The Need for Originality   105
Overhearing Your Original Self   106
Looking for Original Images   107
Simile and Metaphor   108
Originality and Memory   109
Analogy   110
The Unintended Comparison   111
Looking for Analogies   112
Revising for Comparison   114
Exercises   114

IV
SENTENCES   118

STYLE AND THE SENTENCE   118
PARTS OF SENTENCES   118
TYPES OF SENTENCES   121
Simple Sentences   121
Compound Sentences   122
Complex Sentences   123
Compound-Complex Sentences   124
Incomplete Sentences   124
Exercises   126
CLARITY AND COHERENCE   129
VARIETY OF SENTENCES   130
The Uses of Variety   130
Subordination and Variety: Complex Sentences   131
Long Sentences   133
Punctuation and Variety: Compound Sentences   135
Mixing the Types   138
Revising for Variety and Conciseness   140
Exercises   141

UNITY   146
  The Need for Unity   146
  Grammatical Unity   146
    Misplaced Modifiers. Conjunctions and Unity: Complex Sentences. Agreement. Consistency of Tenses.
  Structural Unity   151
    Parallelism. Emphasis. Balance. Rhythm. Resolution. Concluding the Sentence.
  Unity of Diction   160
    Formality and Informality. Formality Gone Bad. Pompous Language. Formal and Informal Sentence Structure. Informality Gone Bad. Subject and Audience. Mixing Formal and Informal Diction. Revising for Unity.
  Exercises   170

V

PARAGRAPHS   178

USES OF PARAGRAPHS   178
FOCUSING WITH PARAGRAPHS   179
UNITY IN THE PARAGRAPH   181
  Unity and Topic Sentences   183
COHERENCE IN THE PARAGRAPH   186
  Coherence and Consistency   188
  Coherence and the Paragraph: Transitions   189
  Overt Transitions   189
  Repeated Words or Phrases   190
  Parallel Constructions   191
  Transitional Words and Phrases   192
  Implicit Transitions   193
DEVELOPMENT IN THE PARAGRAPH   195
  Some Ways to Develop Paragraphs   195
  Development: Length and Completeness   200
  Development: Order and Clarity   205
  Development: Order and Forcefulness   207
  Revising Paragraphs   209
EXERCISES   209

VI
TYPES OF WRITING 223

EXPOSITION 223
ARGUMENT AND PERSUASION 228
  Clarity in Argument 229
  Reasonableness in Argument 230
  Time for the Opposition 234
  The Order of Argument 235
  Logic and Emotionalism 237
  Common Fallacies in Thinking 238
    Generalizing from a Particular. The Overinclusive Premise.
    Guilt by Association. Begging the Question. Evading the Issue.
    Nonsequitur. Sequence as Cause. The Argument ad Hominem.
    Analogy as Fact. The General Fallacy: Imprecision.
DESCRIPTION 242
NARRATIVE 245
  Dialogue and Quotation 247
AUTOBIOGRAPHY 248
WRITING FICTION 250
WRITING ABOUT WRITING 252
WRITING RESEARCH 260
  Using the Library 261
  The Card Catalogue 261
  Reference Works 263
  Bibliography 265
  Footnotes 266
  A Research Project 269
EXERCISES 281

SOME COMMON PROBLEMS
A Brief Review of Grammar, Punctuation, and Mechanics 289

MAKE WHOLE, CLEAR SENTENCES 290
  Sentence Fragments 290
  Comma Splices 293

MATCH THE PARTS OF SENTENCES THAT NEED
  MATCHING   296
  Matching Subjects with Verbs   296
  Matching Pronouns with the Words They Refer to   298
CONNECT MODIFIERS WITH WHAT THEY MODIFY   301
KEEP THE SENTENCE CONSISTENT   302
KEEP PUNCTUATION CLEAR   304
  End Punctuation   304
    Period. Exclamation Point. Question Mark.
  Commas   305
  Semicolons   309
    Semicolons between Whole Clauses. Semicolons with Series.
    Semicolons with Adverbs as Conjunctions. Semicolons with
    Incomplete Clauses.
  Apostrophes   311
    Possessives. Contractions. Plural of Numbers.
  Quotation Marks, and Punctuating Quotations   312
  Other Marks of Punctuation   312
    Brackets. Colons. Dashes. Ellipses. Hyphens. Italics. Parenthe-
    ses.
KEEP MECHANICS CONVENTIONAL   317
  Abbreviation   317
  Capital Letters   318
  Manuscript Form   319
  Numeral   320
  Spelling   320
    I/e, e/i. Variant Plurals. Dropping a Final *-e* before a Vowel.
    The Final *-y.* Doubling Consonants.

A GLOSSARY OF USAGE AND GRAMMATICAL TERMS   323

AUTHOR AND TITLE INDEX   375

SUBJECT INDEX   381

WRITING WELL

I
WRITING, AND WRITING WELL

WRITING TO DISCOVER

Students write papers and answer questions on tests, scientists write reports on their work, teachers write evaluations of their students, people make lists to remember what they must do, some of us keep diaries to remember what we have done, salesmen write messages from the field to the office, and we write notes and letters to keep in touch with relatives and friends. There are practical reasons for literacy. The reasons for writing *well* are practical also.

But not at first. First, comes the message: "I want milk." Even earlier, "Mmm," to the mother's ear, can mean "I want milk." As our brains grow, our messages become more complicated. We make our verbal messages emphatic by gesture and facial expression, as a guitar solo may borrow some of its rhythmic drive from a drum. Learning to write well is harder than learning to talk, but it can bring pleasures deeper than the satisfaction of immediate needs.

A good writer uses words to *discover*, and to bring that discovery to other people. He writes so that his prose is a pleasure that carries knowledge with it. That pleasure-carrying knowledge comes from

1

self-understanding, and becomes understanding in the minds of other people. It makes the difference between writing and writing well.

Here is a passage from an essay about a short story.

> The usage of these types of image contribute to the overall beauty of the thematic content of this lovely piece.

The writing is pretentious and wordy, but a message comes through. Rewritten well, a message will come through with more information, and more feeling. The first message is swaddled in seven sweaters and three pairs of pants; it can hardly walk. The writer revised the passage.

> These images make the story pleasing to read—you taste the fruit of the orchard, you touch the ripening grape—but also the sensuousness shows us the point of the story.

The rewritten prose names and communicates feeling. A shortened version could have read simply,

> These images contribute to the beauty of the story and its theme.

This version is brief and accurate. It is less pretentious than the first, but it is not good enough. It is dry, and it does not carry the voice of the person speaking. It is a message purified of character and feeling, like a slice of bread purified of nutrition and taste.

The live shape could have taken many forms besides the one this writer gave it. Someone else, writing well about the same story, did it differently.

> This story needs to be read aloud. When you hear the voices of Helen and her husband, gestures and facial expressions seem to accompany the words. I feel as if the author had put invisible stage directions between the lines. The relationship we hear in the dialogue shows the meaning of the story.

One reader saw images, another heard dialogue. Both were eventually able to say what they meant in language that let their own feelings—responses to a work of art, this time—come through with clarity. Writing well is the art of clear thinking and honest feeling.

HONEST AND DISHONEST FEELING

The phrase "honest feeling" implies an opposite, dishonest feeling, which no one admits to, but which we sometimes see clearly enough in others. We all know that many feelings are falsely expressed. We have grown up on the false laughter of television, the fake enthusiasm of advertising, the commercial jollity and condolences of greeting cards, and the lying assertions of politicians. If some falsity has not entered our prose, we are made of aluminum.

We can be false in a thousand ways. We do it with handshakes and we do it with grunts. We do it by saying outright lies, and we do it by keeping silent. But by these examples we imply that we always understand our own falsity. When we fool *ourselves*—which we do frequently—we are in more trouble. We fool ourselves with words that can mean almost anything. How much have we said when we call someone "straight"? We fool ourselves when we avoid blame by using a passive (the table was knocked over and broke) or sometimes by using personification (the glass fell off the table). We fool ourselves by clichés, or trite expressions that have become meaningless substitutes for feeling and thought.

> It's not black and white.
> The situation is very complicated.
> That's more or less what I had in mind.

Clichés are little cinder blocks of crushed and reprocessed experience. Every profession—medicine, law, theater, business in its different disciplines—has its own clichés, and when clichés belong to a particular profession, we call this collection of familiar phrases *jargon*. One set of clichés appears especially at graduations, from primary school through graduate school.

> The future belongs to you.
> The challenge of new . . .
> The most exciting generation of . . .
> Responsibility, good citizenship, service to the community, . . .

One of the great sources of jargon is the university. Here is a paragraph from a prospectus for a Ph.D. dissertation.

> This is not a shocking development, perhaps, since even a cursory familiarity with the history of higher education in the United States reveals a consistently enlarging sphere of concern and influence for colleges and universities whose curricula and programs have expanded to meet a variety of societal needs. It may seem only natural that as during the past three decades higher education has reached an unprecedented magnitude in terms of numbers of faculty and student participants, resources

at its disposal, and social power, higher education as an institution has been wont to take the arts under its protective wing with
a theretofore [sic] unparalleled seriousness of commitment and
ambition.

It took this student years and years to learn to write the jargon expected of him. Every phrase in the passage is a cliché, and the clichés
are held together by the mortar of empty words like "is" and "and"
and "with." But the edifice is all reprocessed garbage.

shocking development
cursory familiarity
the history of higher education in the United States
consistently enlarging sphere
variety of societal needs
only natural
an unprecedented magnitude
in terms of numbers
resources at its disposal
protective wing
theretofore unparalleled

The smoothness of the masonry is exceptional, but the passage is without content and without feeling. The paragraph is "insincere" because
it does not represent a person's feelings. Of course the author did not
intend insincerity, nor did he feel that he was lying. He felt, we can
presume, that he was using the language expected of him.

   We must look closely at the notion of sincerity, or we can use it to
justify its opposite. The worst liars insist—to themselves and to the
world—that they are most honest. Yet sincerity can be a valuable idea,
if we think clearly about it, and sincerity has everything to do with the
reasons for writing well. A man named Peter Elbow, quoted in Ken
Macrorie's excellent book *Uptaught*, says:

I warn against defining sincerity, as telling true things about
oneself. It is more accurate to define it functionally as the sound
of a writer's voice or self on paper—a general sound of authen-
ticity in words. The point is that self-revelation . . . is an easy
route in our culture and therefore can be used as an evasion: it
can be functionally insincere even if substantially true and intimate. To be precise, *sincerity is the absence of "noise" or
static—the ability or courage not to hide the real message.*

The static is the distance between what the words say and what we sense lies behind them. The person with a pose of sincerity fixes us with his eyes, saying, "I am going to be wholly honest with you. I am a bastard. I cheat on my girlfriend and I fink on my roommate. I hate my father because he gave me a car. I hit a blind man once when nobody was looking." The real message: "Love me, I'm so *honest.*"

The distance between the meaning (the apparently stated) and the expression (the really implied) ruins the statement, and prevents real communication between people. In the Ph.D. candidate's passage above, the meaning has something to do with the arts in the American university; the expression is a continual exhibition of academic smoothness; it is a little dance, performed by a well-trained educationist seal. It says, "Look at me. Admit me to your ranks. I am one of you."

We cannot accept sincerity as a standard if we are going to take the writer's word for it. We can take it seriously if we listen to his *words* for it. Sincerity is *functional* (Elbow's word) if we believe it, if we hear the voice of a real person speaking forth in the prose—whether of speech or of the written word. And functional (maybe we should call it "convincing") sincerity comes from the self-knowledge we earn by self-exploration. It is not easy. It requires self-examination, and hard thinking or analysis. It is worth it. Socrates made the commitment: the unexamined life is not worth living.

EXAMINING THE LIFE

By learning to write well, we learn methods of self-discovery and techniques for self-examination. Understanding the self allows us to move outside the self, to read, to analyze, to define. Writing well can be a starting point for all thinking. Self-discovery and self-examination are separate things, though they can happen at the same time. Self-exploration finds what we have inside us that is our own. Of course we are stuffed with clichés—we have been exposed to them all our lives—but clichés are not "our own." We have swallowed everything that has ever happened to us: we dropped the bottle to the floor, at the age of eight weeks, and cried for the loss of it; the telephone did not ring last week, and we cried for the loss of it; the toy shines under the tree, the toy rusts behind the garage; the smell of bacon, the smell of roses, the smell of kittens that have been careless; the flowers and the beer cans emerging from the snow. Everything that ever happened remains on file our heads. As a professor at M.I.T. put it: the human brain is a big computer made of meat.

If the brain is a computer, we are all engaged in learning how to operate it. For the Ph.D. candidate quoted above, the task of writing was simple; he was programmed to write that kind of prose; he pushed the right keys and his brain computer turned out preassembled units of educationist jargon. The commencement speaker, or the student writing home for money, presses other keys for printouts of ready-made pseudo-thoughts and pseudo-feelings. But let us suppose that we are interested in something genuine, the voice without static, the utterance in which expression and meaning are the same. We must learn new ways to use the accumulation of words, sense impressions, and ideas that we keep in the disc-packs of the brain.

Confucius told us to "Make it new." "It" was thinking, feeling, expressing, writing. Only by making it new, each time we speak or write, can we make it true. To make it new does not mean to make it merely novel. One can leave out capitals, change typography, mount new rules of spelling—and still write with clichés or other static. Really to make it new, we must avoid the worn roads of conventional associations; we must find what is uniquely our own voice out of our own experience. Then our words will not make rows of identical houses like the subdivision prose of cliché. "New" is "fresh, genuine, ourselves, our own experience."

It is not, however, the predictable result of spontaneity. Spontaneous writing is a good way to start to learn how to write, and a good way to uncover material you didn't know was in you. One important computer key is a sense of freedom in writing. But then there is the second half of genuine expression, the half that applies the map-maker's self-examination to the new country of self-exploration. This self-examination, leading to revision, allows the writer to communicate knowledge to other human beings.

REVISING THE MAP

Almost all writers, almost all the time, need to revise. We need to revise because spontaneity is never adequate. Writing that is merely emotional release for the writer becomes emotional chaos for the reader. Even when we write as quickly as our hand can move, we slide into emotional falsity, into cliché or other static. And we make leaps by private association that leave our prose unclear. And we often omit steps in thinking, or use a step that we later recognize as bad logic. Sometimes we overexplain something obvious. Or we include irrelevant detail. First drafts remain first drafts. They are the material that we must shape, a marble block that the critical brain chisels into form.

Good writing is an intricate interweaving of inspiration and discipline. A student may need one strand more than the other. Most of us continually need to remember both sides of a piece of writing: *We must invent, and we must revise.* And in these double acts, invention and revision, we are inventing and revising—not just our prose style—but our knowledge of ourselves and of the people around us. When Confucius recommended "Make it new," he meant what Plato called "the examined life." It was a moral position. By our language, we shall know ourselves—not once and for all, by a breakthrough, but continually, all our lives. Therefore the necessity to write well arises from the need to understand and to discriminate, to be genuine and to avoid what is not genuine, in ourselves and in others. By understanding what our words reveal, we can understand ourselves; by changing these words until we arrive at our own voices, we change ourselves; by arriving at our own voices, we are able to speak to others and be heard.

THEMES AND REVISIONS

On the first day of class, the assignment was to write for twenty minutes under the heading, "How I Came to College." Here is an impromptu theme by Jim Beck.

> Education is of paramount importance to today's youth. No one can underestimate the importance of higher education. It makes us well-rounded individuals and we must realize that all work and no play is not the way to go about it, but studies is the most important part, without a doubt. Therefore I decided when I was young that I would go to college and applied myself to studies in high school so that I would be admitted. I was admitted last winter and my family was very happy as was I. Coming here has been a disappointment so far because people are not very friendly to freshmen and everyone has their own clique and the whole place is too big. But I expect that it will get better soon and I will achieve my goal of a higher education and being a well-rounded person.

Repetition at the end of the impromptu gives it some unity. In the lines in which Jim Beck says that "people are not very friendly to freshmen," the reader glimpses Jim Beck and his feelings. But through most of the paragraph, the writer is not being himself. You can tell that he is not being himself because he is sounding like so many other people. Jim Beck is assembling an impromptu from the cliché collection in the why-I-want-to-go-to-college box. When he says "paramount importance," does he really know what "paramount" means? Does he mean that "today's youth" is genuinely different from yesterday's or tomorrow's? And how far into history does "today" extend? What does "well-rounded" mean? Why say "individual" instead of "person" or "people"? "Important" is vague, and saying it twice makes it vaguer. In the sentence of complaint, where the reader briefly senses an actual writer, Jim Beck would have done better to *show* his loneliness in an anecdote, instead of just *telling*.

Later in the term, when he had a free theme, Jim Beck wrote an essay which was not so much a revision of his impromptu as a new start, and which *really* told how he came to college.

The Race to College
Jim Beck

It's horrible now, and I don't know if it will get any better. The only people who pay attention to me are the people who are trying to beat me out for the track team. My roommate is stoned all day and gets A's on his papers anyway. I hate him because he hates me because I'm a jock. My classes are boring lectures and the sections are taught by graduate students who pick on the students because the professors pick on them.

But I remember wanting to come here so bad! Nobody from Hammerton named Beck had ever been to college. Everybody knew the Becks were stupid. This went for my father, who never got through high school, and for my grandfather, who died before I was born, and who was the town drunk. It went for my two older brothers who went bad, as they say in Hammerton. Steve got a dishonorable discharge from the Marines and he works on a farm outside town and gets drunk on Fridays and Saturdays. Curt stole a car and did time at Jackson and nobody has heard from him since. My sister had a three-month baby and the town liked to talk about that.

I was different. Everybody told me I was. My mother told me I wasn't a Beck. My father told me I was going to bring back the family's good name. (I never knew it had one.) In grammar school the teachers all told me how much better I was than my brothers. By the time I was in sixth grade my father and the school Principal were talking about the University.

My father isn't really dumb. Sometimes people look dumb because it's expected of them. He's worked at the same grocery for twenty years, I guess. Now that I made it to the University, he wants to be called Manager, because he's the only man there besides Mr. Roberts who owns it. (The rest of the help are—is?— kids who bag and an old lady cashier.) When I went back for a weekend everybody treated me as if I won the Olympics.

I said the Principal and my father were talking about my going to the University. All through junior high I said I didn't want to go. I was scared. No Beck could do that. Bad things kept happening to my family. My father had an accident and totalled the car and lost his license and for a year we didn't have a car at all. He had to walk home two miles every night pushing a basket of groceries. When I said I would quit school and get a job, everybody jumped on me.

It wasn't that I was an A student. It was just that I tried hard at everything I did. I got B's mostly. Now with B's, the counsellors kept telling me, I could be admitted to the University, but I wouldn't get a scholarship. I needed mostly A's for that, and then when I got to the University I would lose the scholarship if I couldn't keep the grades up. Then my brother Steve, who was a pretty good athlete once, suggested athletics.

I was too skinny for football, too short for basketball, I could barely swim and my school didn't have a swimming team anyway. There is one sport you can practice with no money and no equipment. I started to run when I was in my last year of junior high. It felt good right away. I ran to and from school. I went over to the high school and did laps. The high school coach noticed me and asked me to go out the next year. Running long distances hurts a lot. Sometimes you get a stitch in your left side and suddenly it shifts to your right side. I didn't exactly mind the pain. I studied it. I studied it in order to go the University, the way I studied everything else.

In my Senior year I was all-state and held two high-school records (600 and half-mile) and I had an athletic scholarship to the University. Now I am here, the first Beck to make it. I don't know why I'm here or why I ran so hard or where I go from here. Now that I am here, the race to get here seems pointless. Nothing in my classes interests me. I study, just as I did before, in order to pass the course or even get a good grade. I run to win, but what am I running for? I will never be a great runner. Sometimes when I cannot sleep I imagine packing my bags and going

back to Hammerton. But I can't do that. They would say, "He's a
Beck, all right."

Jim Beck's essay has the two most important features of good writing: it has unity, which means the focus, the point, the coming together of many details; and it has the voice of a real person speaking out of his own experience, using his own language, with a minimum of tired phrases, of borrowed clothing. It has discipline, and it has feeling. Although Jim Beck is discouraged and feels aimless and melancholy, his mind has made an enormous stride toward knowing and being able to present itself. Self-knowledge may feel uncomfortable, but in the end it is more satisfying than self-delusion. He revised, using his own experience in his own language. *And* he was disciplined; he used tighter sentence structure and he found unity in his experience. He learned about himself while learning to write prose.

The same assignment brought forth this theme from Marian Hart:

I always wanted to go to the University because my Dad went here.

I remember how it got started. I had a job as a car-hop in a drive in, an A & W in Flint where I make my home. Business was slack because it was about 3:30 Saturday afternoon so I was talking away with Barb and Karen who were working there too and I knew them from school of course. We had to wear these very tight stretch pants because Boss said it was good for business. A car came in and because it was my turn I picked up a pad and started out for it, then I saw it was my Dad. He jumped out of the car and hugged me. I knew what it was and so did Barb because we were all waiting to hear about admissions. I told him he could open it and he did and that's why he drove out, to tell me. Barb had to wait until she got off, the Boss wouldn't let her go and there was nobody at home to call up.

So! We got here three days ago, in the same car, only loaded to the roof with my stuff. I was petrified with fear. My Dad kept telling me what to do, and then he kept saying he knew it had changed a lot in 25 years. I wished he'd be quiet. My Mom cried. We couldn't find the dorm. Everybody we asked didn't know either. The boys all had long hair and beards and looked exactly the way I expected them too. My Dad hated it. Then when we found my dorm and we found my room my Dad was all out of breath, and mad, and he just pushed the door open with his shoulder and busted in. There was a naked girl standing there, with no clothes on, my roommate (whose very nice, named Terri, but I didn't know that yet) and he made a funny noise and dropped the suitcase and ran back out into the hall.

The theme needs only revision; it needs focusing, understanding, thinking, and care. When you look over a first draft, trying to find ways to clarify it and bring it together, it is wise to ask yourself, "What is this *really* about?" and see if you can come up with an answer. Jim Beck's first paper was about nothing at all—or about trying to say what you imagine the Institution wants to hear. His second paper was about social class, and trying to escape a family social pattern, and the empty feelings of success. Marian Hart's paper is mostly a playful account of her feelings for her father and his for her, with evidence of some jealousy and flirtation.

"I always wanted to go to the University because My Dad went here."

The word "because" begs questions. Probably thousands of high school graduates *don't* want to go to some University precisely because their Dad went there. And this one-sentence paragraph does not really introduce the reader to the action. It does not set up what follows in an intelligible or unifying way. Of course at the same time it is exactly what Marian Hart had to say, and thus is the first clue to the paper's real content. It *was* true that she wanted to go to the University because her Dad went there. But because she has not yet examined the implications of her prose—the literal illogic, and the emotional truth, of her first sentence—she is not ready to write or think with coherence.

Some of the writing is bad. "Where I make my home" is a euphemism for "where I live." (Euphemisms are fancy words for simple things, or soft words for harsh things, like "pass away" for "die.") Barb and Karen are useless details; they add nothing and are there only because they were part of the landscape in the opening anecdote. The story becomes truer when they are omitted, because the outlines become clearer as the mists of futile detail recede. Another detail, about the tight stretch pants, might seem to be irrelevant also, but, unintentionally, this detail is a prelude to her father's arrival. Later the beards and long hair of the boys, and her father's irritation, could seem irrelevant, if you didn't understand that her father is as fond of her as she is of him, and therefore jealous of young male rivals. The chance discovery of a naked roommate provides the writer with the perfect, comic moment in which the embarrassed father drops the suitcases. The materials are abundant, and this is the place to stop. In her first account she ran out of time here, or she would have gone on to have them eating supper at a German restaurant with a dressed Terri, and then waving goodbye as her parents drove off to U.S. 23. Haste saved her from going on too long.

The week after she wrote the impromptu, Marian Hart rewrote the theme for unity and focus. As she learned more about writing and about herself, she returned to it occasionally and rewrote a passage as part of an exercise. Finally, feeling bored with the theme but also determined to finish it once and for all, she rewrote it as a free theme near the end of term.

My Father's Place
Marian Hart

It is about an hour and a quarter from my house in Flint to the dormitory in Ann Arbor. All the way, as we drove here last August to move in, my Dad was talking about the class of 1939. I tried to listen. I had heard him talk about the University since I was a little girl, and since I was a little girl I had wanted to come here to college. But in the car I was shy and frightened. I was going to meet a roommate named Terri who was from Detroit. She would be sophisticated and have long hair. All the boys would be crazy about her. I would be the invisible frump from Flint. My Dad was talking about *fraternities* and *dances!* My God.

I tried to think about happy things. I tried to think about how happy I was, as I sat there feeling stupid and ugly. I remembered how happy I was to be accepted. It was a Saturday last Spring when I was working at the A & W, being a car hop in the stretch pants that the boss made us wear "because it's good for business."

It was a slack time of day, and suddenly a car rolled up, parking across two parking places, and rocking with the brakes put on too fast. I picked up an order pad and headed out, and then I saw that it was our car and that my Dad was jumping out at me waving an envelope and grinning. He didn't have to say anything. We hugged and he called me his sweetheart. The three of us went out to dinner that night and celebrated.

Now my mother was sobbing and my teeth were chattering and my father was talking about *corsages!* I groaned a little, and he said—for the twelfth time—that of course he knew that everything was different now, with student rights and politics and ecology and (he gagged a little) co-ed dormitories. But . . . and he was off again. He was as nervous as I was.

When we drove into town my Dad's composure fell apart completely. He didn't know where he was. We asked directions but everyone else was as lost as we were. The whole place had changed, he said; none of the old landmarks were there. And he obviously hated the new landmarks. Girls with overalls and no bras and bare feet and long hair were throwing frisbees with boys with blue jeans and no shirts and bare feet and long hair and beards. My father's jaw went tight, and from the back seat I could see the tenseness of his neck that happened when he was worried or angry.

We found the dorm. My father carried the four suitcases. I carried a portable stereo and a box of indispensable records. My mother had three garment bags full of clothes which I knew I would never wear. Of course my room was on the third floor. Every time we passed a boy in the hallway my father's neck, which was red with carrying four suitcases, got tenser.

When we got to the door of my room, he didn't set down the suitcases to knock. Puffing and snorting, he pushed open the door with his shoulder and strode in, me and my mother close behind. Then he dropped all four suitcases, crash, and made a weird little noise. I thought: My God, he's having a heart attack. Then I looked past him and saw a girl standing facing him with her mouth flopped open in surprise—Terri, I thought, even then, and she's *not* too beautiful—and stark naked.

Notice how Marian Hart has brought in the essentials of the A & W scene, but kept her unity by judicious repetition: car/car; affection/affection; college/college. Because of these connections, the flashback is not mechanical but organic; it grows naturally out of the scene. The structure seems to take form spontaneously from its material, the way a wildflower grows at the side of the road. Of course this writer worked hard, as all writers must, to seem effortless.

Both of these student writers revised their work by improving their understanding of themselves and their material; and Marian Hart improved by adding unity to her anecdote, cutting unnecessary detail and arranging the rest to give her story dramatic point.

SOME PROFESSIONAL WRITING

The essays were impromptu, and the revisions printed here came two months later. Professional writers often take longer still, and struggle with the same enemies, disunity and evasion. The professional writer differs from the beginner in many ways: he knows that he is likely to fail at first, and why; he is patient, he is adamant, and he expects his writing to be hard work. Comparing professional models and freshman examples is unfair, of course, but we do not compare them to emphasize the distance between the two. We bring in the models to give an idea of a goal, to exemplify and make concrete the standards we can otherwise only talk about; to show and not just to tell.

The best way to learn to write well is to read good prose. Gradually we acquire the manners that make the good writing we admire. It is like learning a foreign language by living daily with a family that speaks it, shopping in it, and listening to television shows with dialogue dubbed into it.

Take this passage of reminiscence from a published book:

> I was twelve when my father died. From the ages of nine to eleven I was sent to an experimental boarding school in Pennsylvania called Freemont. I wasn't home more than a few days during these years. In the summer Freemont became a camp and I stayed through.
>
> The headmaster was a big, florid man named Teddy who drank too much. It was no secret, and even the youngest of us were expected to sympathize with his illness and like him for it—an extension of the attitude that forbade the use of last names to make everyone more human. All of us knew, in the mysterious way children pick things up, that Teddy had almost no control over the institution he'd created, and that when decisions were unavoidable his wife took over. This weakness at the top might have been the key to the wildness of the place.
>
> Life at Freemont was a perpetual semihysterical holiday. We knew there were almost no limits in any direction. A situation of endless, dreamlike fun, but one that imposed a certain strain on us all. Classes were a farce, you didn't have to go if you didn't want to, and there were no tests.
>
> Freedom was the key word. The atmosphere was heavy with the perfume of the nineteen-thirties—spurious agrarianism, group singing of proletarian chants from all countries, sexual freedom (I was necking at the age of nine), sentimentalism, naïveté. But above all, filtering down through the whole school, the excitement of the *new thing*, of the experiment—that pecu-

liar floating sensation of not knowing what's going to happen next.

One warm spring night we staged a revolution. All the Junior boys, thirty or forty of us, spontaneously decided not to go to bed. We ran loose on the grounds most of the night, stalked by the entire faculty. Even old Ted was out, stumbling and crashing through the woods, warding off the nuts thrown from the trees. A few legitimate captures were made by the younger men on the staff, but there was no doubt most of us could have held out indefinitely. I, for one, was confident to the point of bravado, coming out in the open three or four times, just for the fun of being chased. Can there be anything as sweet for a child as victory over authority? On that warm night I touched heights I will never reach again—baiting a thirty-year-old man, getting him to chase me over my own ground in the darkness, hearing his hard breath behind me (ah, the *wordlessness* of the chase, no words, just action), and finally leaping clean, leaping effortlessly over the brook at exactly the right place, knowing he was too heavy, too stupid as an animal, too old, and too tired to do what I had done. Oh God, my heart burst with joy when I heard him fall, flat out, in the water. Lights flashed in my brain. The chase was over and I had won. I was untouchable. I raced across the meadow, too happy to stop running.

Hours later, hidden in a bower, I heard the beginning of the end. A capture was made right below me. Every captured boy was to join forces with the staff and hunt the boys still out., My reaction was outrage. Dirty pool! But outrage dulled by recognition—"Of course. What else did you expect? They're clever and devious. Old people, with cold, ignorant hearts." The staff's technique didn't actually work as planned, but it spread confusion and broke the lovely symmetry of us against them. The revolution was no longer simple and ran out of gas. To this day I'm proud that I was the last boy in, hours after the others. (I paid a price though—some inexplicable loss to my soul as I crept around all that time in the dark, looking for another holdout.)

Frank Conroy, *Stop-Time*

Notice the careful but subtle ordering here. The brief and stark first paragraph, then the characterization of Teddy leading to a generalization, in the last sentence of the second paragraph, which leads us into the rest of the anecdote. The fourth paragraph has a series of examples of "wildness," and then in the fifth paragraph we have the supreme example: revolution. Here, the writer expresses excitement in rhythmic sentences, in images ("lights flashed in my brain"), and in exaggeration that embodies true feeling ("I was untouchable"). But if the anecdote stopped with this excitement, we would have only a good story. Nothing ends with such ecstasy; both the rhythm of storytelling, and honesty to our experience, require that what goes up must come down. "The revolution was no longer simple and ran out of gas." Conroy's prose imitates the state of mind it describes.

Or take another example, from fiction this time, a tiny paragraph only. One of the models of prose style in contemporary literature is Ernest Hemingway, who worked carefully on rhythm and sound. When he was young especially, he studied style and practiced and revised, to learn the way to his own voice. A short story called "In Another Country," about some wounded soldiers in a hospital in Italy during World War I, opens with this paragraph:

> In the fall the war was always there, but we did not go to it any more. It was cold in the fall in Milan and the dark came very early. Then the electric lights came on, and it was pleasant along the streets looking in the windows. There was much game hanging outside the shops, and the snow powdered on the fur of the foxes and the wind blew their tails. The deer hung stiff and heavy and empty, and small birds blew in the wind and the wind turned their feathers. It was a cold fall and the wind came down from the mountains.

Such a simple style! And if you try to imitate it, you are likely to lace one shoe to the other. The grammar is simple, yet the length of sentence and clause—the units of rhythm—varies continually. The vocabulary is simple—the fall, cold, and wind repeated, wind four times in the last five lines—and yet expressive. The effect of the whole is hypnotic or dreamy; the war is around us but we are not in it. Then the paragraph ends with the corpses of animals, described with a loving detail. Look at the word "pleasant"; normally, we might find this word too general, and want to ask *how*, exactly, did you feel? But here, in the emotions of the paragraph, the vagueness is an accurate understatement; it embodies the emotional restraint in this removal from war, the tentative acceptance that "we" are alive, unlike the animals outside the shops and the unmentioned combatants among whom "we" used to count ourselves.

DISORGANIZED WRITING, POMPOUS WRITING

For a perverse sort of fun, let us rewrite the passage in a couple of bad versions. First, a parody (an imitation of a style, for the sake of mockery) of the disorganized writing that most of us start out with.

> September through December, in the fall, at any rate, the war still went on, but we ourselves weren't doing the fighting by this time. It got chilly then in the Italian city of Milan. It started to get dark earlier in the day. When it got dark they turned on the lights. It was nice to look in the windows of stores. There were a lot of dead wild animals outside of the stores. When it snowed it snowed on the animals' fur too. There was a lot of wind and it blew the animals' fur and it even blew the little ones around. It was really cold because the wind was coming down from the mountains, which were cold.

Maybe even this parody is better than the prose most of us write at first because the writer observes real things. Most bad writing omits anything that might be interesting and expressive. The whole paragraph might be reduced to:

> It was fall in Milan, Italy, one year during World War I. It got colder and the days got shorter.

But the short version omits all feeling. You cannot reduce *War and Peace* to a telegram.

Or we could try it in Pompous Institutional Moderne.

> During the autumn, the hostilities continued to ensue, but we no longer engaged in them ourselves. The daily temperature declined in Milan as the autumn continued, and the hours of daylight gradually contracted. When darkness ensued, lights were illuminated. It was altogether agreeable to promenade and investigate the contents of shop windows. There was considerable unrationed meat available at this time, by reason of the prevalence of slaughtered wild animals. Precipitation in the form of snow, as the months progressed, accumulated on the fur of these slaughtered beasts, and the cold breeze that accompanied the snow caused the tails of the animals to wave. Venison was available, as was small fowl. The extreme cold of this autumn is attributable to the fact that the prevailing winds came from the direction of the mountains which, because of their elevation and the snow which had already accumulated thereon, were lower in

temperature than the temperature which normally prevailed in the city.

This last writer, if he existed, might be elected chairman of the board, but he would never excite our feelings, or understand his own.

We learn to write well, if we learn, for good reason. Few of us will ever write with Hemingway's skill, or Conroy's. We don't need to, unless we are writers. But we need to move toward them. If we write, now, with the haphazard chaos of the first parody of Hemingway, or with the pompous institutionality of the second one, we are in trouble, in our heads and our hearts, not just in our writing. If we learn to write well, we will sharpen our wits on the one hand, and point our imagination and expression on the other—both together, or neither at all.

LEARNING TO WRITE WELL

How then do we learn to write well? We can do three things, at least. First, we can read well, which helps slowly, but keeps on helping; second, we can study writing and think about it and discuss it with others; third, and most important, we can write, and rewrite, and rewrite. Because rewriting our own work is most useful, we must have writing to rewrite. Keep your old themes. Keep a notebook. Keep a journal. Keep copies of papers or exams you write for other courses. In this collection of your own prose, you will find ideas for expanding and rewriting. You may notice, the tenth time you reread something, that you have written in order to hide something from yourself instead of writing to discover. After thinking about clichés or paragraph organization or passive verbs, you will find examples in your own prose, and you will see how to revise them.

DAILY WRITING

While you are learning to write, it is a good idea to write something every day. Continually applying pen to paper will ease the work of writing, and will give you a collection of words and sentences in which to look for ideas and for work to revise. Writing is a skill, like an athletic skill, which comes more naturally to some people than to others, but which improves with practice for everyone. Practice is a necessity. Maybe the best method is daily dated entries in a notebook. This notebook sounds like a journal, but for most people a journal is like a diary, and records merely the day's events.

Had pancakes for breakfast. 9 o'clock boring . . .

Little entries that set out our daily schedule do not help us. Better are memories, whole anecdotes, ideas, and queries. Doing daily writing means writing a page or two a day, every day, seven days a week, working rapidly and without trying to impose a direction on it, without conscious control or focus or an attempt at mechanical perfection. Nor should a daily entry be continuous, necessarily. Some days one has apparently unrelated flashes of thought or memory. Some days one seems to have no ideas at all. On such a day, you may let your hand flow over the page with disconnected words and phrases. When Henry Moore, the great English sculptor, sits in front of the television set at night, sometimes he lets his hand wander over a page, "sketching" while he pays little attention; and sometimes ideas start, in this way, which later (with direction, control, focus, and attention to mechanical perfection) become works of art.

Many professional writers keep notebooks. Theodore Roethke, the American poet, left two hundred and seventy-seven notebooks behind when he died. Some entries were lines and images for poems; some were used, some were not. Others were prose notes to himself about writing poetry, and might have been seeds for unwritten essays.

> Get down where your obsessions are. For Christ's sake, shake it loose. Make like a dream, but not a dreamy poem. The past is asking. You can't go dibble dabble in your tears. The fungi will come running; the mould will begin all over the noble lineaments of the soul. Remember: a fake compassion covers up many a sore. . . .

At other times, he made a more conventional journal entry.

> Today, or tonight, I realized finally at the age of 40, for the first time, that it is really possible for me to think, and even get pleasure from the process. Not that my efforts—or effects—are spectacular. Perhaps four consecutive related thoughts at present is the absolute top of my form—and that only just before falling asleep, or just after eating a fine breakfast, when I'm too lazy to write anything down. But still, even this is a beginning. And such excitement!

F. Scott Fitzgerald kept a notebook in which he recorded situations, observations, jokes, and anything else.

> Widely separated family inherit a house and have to live there together.
> . . .

Girl and giraffe.

. . .

Family quarrels are bitter things. They don't go according to any rules. They're not like aches or wounds; they're more like splits in the skin that won't heal because there's not enough material.

. . .

Jules had dark circles under his eyes. Yesterday he had closed out the greatest problem of his life by settling with his ex-wife for two hundred thousand dollars. He had married too young, and the former slavey from the Quebec slums had taken to drugs upon her failure to rise with him. Yesterday, in the presence of lawyers, her final gesture had been to smash his finger with the base of a telephone.

. . .

Hearing Hitler's speech while going down Sunset Boulevard in a car.

. . .

Run like an old athlete.

Daily writing can lead to loosened minds. Our minds are muscle-bound, not by intellect, but by formulas of thought, by clichés both of phrase and of organization. Our minds do not need to remain restricted. A student going into economics wrote this entry in a notebook:

Blue clouds in Arizona. I was hitchhiking last August, at the edge of the desert waiting for a ride that would take me across state. A little tree, a little shade. Sun so hot it melted turtles. Blue clouds of Arizona. Because there were no clouds at all, just blue glaring and turning white toward the sun. Like an egg only a lot brighter and hotter. Got a ride with a truck driver. "Never went to college myself. The war came along and then I had kids, you know. My daughter's at State." Jiggle. Oil. Hot. We had cheeseburgers in an airconditioned diner and I never felt so good in my whole life as when that ice-air hit me. Then the heat outside. Walking into the oven. (cliché.)

There is no point to his story, or maybe no story. No one told him he had to make a point. All he had to do was write a page. He was practicing.

Practice was the first thing for him, sheer practice in putting pen to paper, letting the words follow each other across the page; if the habit of writing remains alien to us, we will never learn to write with any naturalness. Second, he was learning to loosen up. No one was going to correct his spelling, or argue with his logic, or tell him that his clauses were not parallel; he felt free to let the images follow each other loosely by association. Until the last phrase, his loosened mind provided fresh images. But if he had written a string of clichés, nobody was going to bother him about it. Earlier in his notebook, before he trusted himself to loosen up, his prose had been rigid and trite.

Beginning a notebook of daily writing, almost everyone is shy and stiff, as if this private writing were a public performance. One student began her notebook:

> I am not "an emotionalist," if such a word exists. I feel as if I'm taking a step forward in saying that I tend not to be sincere in my writing. From this point forward I shall try to do so. I feel that I'm honest with myself, but when I know that others will read my work I unconsciously become dishonest as I write.
>
> If I were to write a short essay on any topic and hand it to a person to read, I wouldn't stay in the same room while the person read my work. Whether this is because of shyness or embarrassment, or both, I don't know.

Two months later, her prose was less self-conscious and more relaxed, and she seemed to enjoy herself more.

> They try to give something special every week. When I read eggrolls listed on the menu, I thought, great, my favorite thing in the world. But to my dismay, I was shocked at what the Stockwell Cafeteria had done. How could they destroy *my* eggrolls? I bit into one of them and I noticed *black,* inside my eggroll. Shortly later, I discover that *raisons* had been planted in the eggrolls! Raisons! How could they! It seemed that they just sat around saying, "What can we put in the eggrolls to make them terrible? We can't lose our image!" Of all the stupid things. That's enough to start a new war with China!

Nobody leaned over her shoulder, drew a red circle around "raisons," and wrote "raisins" in the margin. Over the term her writing improved, perhaps because she wrote ninety-two pages of daily writing; her spelling stayed about the same.

Everyone who starts daily writing at first fears running out of material. Really, we have enough memory packed away, by the age of eighteen, to keep us writing until we are seventy. We gradually discover tricks that keep the pages coming. We should stop writing while we still have something to say; it is even wise to make an arbitrary rule: stop at the bottom of a full page, even in the middle of a sentence, and write nothing more until the next day. The next day, you will never sit and wait for the words to start.

Many students find that they work best with large categories of reminiscence, writing many pages—weeks of daily writing—on one general subject: my six best friends and their families; fishing trips with my father; Christmas vacation; jobs I have had; my teacher in grammar school; pets; relatives; the Little League; 4–H clubs; fights with my brother; learning to repair my ten-speed bike; my favorite meals; my favorite jokes (one student remembered forty pages of jokes!); and physics for the layman. Some students interested in science and technology try to write about science in a language that nonscientists can understand—a difficult and useful kind of writing.

Daily writing is a means and not an end, however. Unless the writing becomes directed and shaped toward an end, it does not help us to talk to another person. Unity, clarity, effect, and the disciplines of sentence and paragraph—all are necessary to move the message from the writer to the reader. Once we have found an idea or an image or a secret lode of language, then we must learn to shape and control in order to communicate.

We need to learn all about language—choosing words, inventing metaphors, phrases, clauses, and sentences, and constructing paragraphs—before we can establish control over our writing. But of course we must try to make whole shapes, like the revisions by Jim Beck and Marian Hart, from the very beginning, even before we have learned the names of what we do. It makes sense, before we begin to study words, to take a look at what happens when we write a paper.

EXERCISES

1. Write a brief impromptu essay on the events of the first few days in college. Use specific examples or anecdotes. Find some unity or focus to hold your writing together.

2. Write a paper about the English courses you took in high school. What did you do? What did you learn? What did you feel was emphasized? What did you feel was not emphasized enough? Find some unity or focus to hold your writing together.

3. We discover ourselves by the language we use. Write a dialogue, or a conversation, in which two people reveal their characters by their language.

4. Analyze in class the language in this theme. You and your instructor might revise part of it.

My Big Moment

In my humble opinion, after all is said and done, opportunities for people to show what they are made of are conspicuous by their absence at this university. Because of this sad truth, the day I gave my report stuck out like a sore thumb. It was a red letter day. I had spent the entire year at college burning the midnight oil and leading a precarious existence earning my tuition working for a professor who was a veritable mine of information. I was very much interested in the finer things of life. My hope to do things that would make me stand out from the crowd were usually doomed to disappointment. As I wended my way from class to class each day, and then to the job where I put my nose to the grindstone, I often thought that the events in my life at which I could point with pride were few and far between. But today would be different.

Today I, a rank outsider, would be the center of attention. People would realize that I was smart as a whip. They would listen with bated breath. At ten o'clock I stood as scared as a rabbit before the class. Although I was hungry as a bear because I had not eaten breakfast, I was calm and collected. I stood before them and I told the unvarnished truth about Man's mistreatment of Mother Nature. I explained that the powers that be must sit up and take notice of the fast and furious pace of pollution, and that there was a crying need for immediate action. I viewed with alarm the future of society when the purity of the very air we breathe hangs in the balance. When I concluded my few remarks, there was thunderous applause. I could tell I had hit the nail on the head. I was tired but happy. I had hit one out of the ballpark.

5. During a whole waking day, pay attention to yourself, and especially to your feelings. If you feel anger, shame, joy, suspicion, or anxiety, think these feelings through. What brought them about? What events in your life can you associate with these feelings? Did these feelings seem appropriate to your present conscious way of looking at life? Or do they seem inappropriate, not like you? Pick one sequence of examined feelings and write a paragraph about it, avoiding jargon or cliché.

6. In the passage quoted from *Stop-Time* by Frank Conroy, could anything be cut out to give the story greater unity or focus?

7. Read this passage carefully. Try to decide what makes it good writing. Point out how the author achieves her effects.

For many people moving is one kind of thing and travel is something very different. Travel means going away from home and staying away from home; it is an antidote to the humdrum activities of everyday life. a prelude to a holiday one is entitled to enjoy after months of dullness. Moving means breaking up a home, sadly or joyfully breaking with the past; a happy venture or a hardship, something to be endured with good or ill grace.

For me, moving and staying at home, traveling and arriving, are all of the piece. The world is full of homes in which I have lived for a day, a month, a year, or much longer. How much I care about a home is not measured by the length of time I have lived there. One night in a room with a leaping fire may mean more to me than many months in a room without a fireplace, a room in which my life has been paced less excitingly.

Margaret Mead, *Blackberry Winter*

8. Here is another "How I Came to College" impromptu. (a) Criticize it, for language and for structure. (b) Edit it. Rearrange, and rewrite.

Never Too Late

I just got out of the Marine Corps last May and I couldn't get a job. Thats how I came to college.

I guess that sounds dumb but maybe I am. My teachers back in school said I was an underachiever, even back in kindergarten I underachieved at blocks. The sergeant when I went in the Marines said other things I can't put down here.

When I got out I just hung around. School was a drag, I never learned anything, couldn't get interested. What for? I always thought. Also I was, if you pardon the expression, one smartass. When everybody got put on pro by the principal for long hair I had my head shaved and they sent me home for that. My father was mad.

So I never even finished. The Marine Corps was worse than school as far as that's concerned. I hated every minute of it. Some times guys would ask me what I was going to do when I got out and I told them I was going to buy a car. Then they shut up.

I never got to Viet Nam, thank God. When I got out I just watched television for about a week. I bought a used-car and worked on it in the back yard. I looked for work but the only thing I could get was parking cars for a dude restaurant and I said no. People kept telling me to get an education. It's never too late, they kept saying.

The reason I came to college is that I had nothing else to do.

9. Here is a better example of the same impromptu. (a) What makes it better? (b) In what ways could this student learn to improve her writing? Pay attention to mechanics, to focus, and to word choice.

All my life I have known that I would, some day, go off to school. By the end of my senior year in High School I knew where and when I'd be leaving and spent the summer getting used to the idea. But getting used to the idea was all I did—I did not begin to think or worry about what college was really going to be like. I did not spend hours contemplating the importance of "going off into the big wide world." I did not even speculate what things would be like, what if I hated my roommate, what if the work was too hard, what if I'm unhappy. I did not think about specifics, I had told myself that I would have time to get psyched the week before I left.

But a week before the day I had planned to leave, before I had prepared myself I got a phone call from my father. He had to give a lecture at a convention on the west coast in five days. For him to make it we had to leave that day and he would drop me off in Michigan on his way to California. I had one hour to pack. One hour to collect all my belongings and somehow fit them into a car that looked like it could not hold half the things I wanted to take. It happened so fast I did not have time to think, I did not even have time to say goodby to my mother who was out shopping. We left in a hurry leaving behind many things I had forgotten to pack and a small note to my mother that simply said good-by.

If I had more time I'm sure my goodbye to my mother and friends would have been a long, emotional scene. Driving through my town I had no time to look at my Elementary School, my High School, the house of my best friend and get sentimental. It was pouring and concentrating on the driving was all I could do.

The eleven hour drive also left no time for thought. I drove most of the way so that my father could prepare his speech. Every so often he would read parts to me to try them out. Our talk consisted of whether injection-lasers was a hyphenated word or not. (I still don't know.)

Then I was here, in the dorm, with my roommate, in my classes. It seemed as if I had been here all my life and the trauma of leaving home was over. I did not even have time to think about it until later and then I could not even remember how it felt to leave home.

10. Write a page in a notebook, every day, for the rest of the term. Bring your notebook to conferences for your instructor to inspect without correcting. Bring it to class, if your instructor asks you to, with a page or a paragraph marked to read aloud. Discuss in class the problems and rewards of daily writing, giving each other suggestions for subjects, and examples of work.

II

WRITING A PAPER

"Students write papers and answer questions on tests." So I began this book, naming an immediate and practical necessity for the student writer. Then I talked about emotional honesty and self-discovery, matters essential to good writing, and matters that good writing leads to. But in most composition courses the student is asked to write a complete paper at the very beginning, and to write additional complete papers every week or two throughout the term. It is time for some practical advice on writing a paper.

We have looked a little at the complete papers written by Jim Beck and Marian Hart, and have spoken about focus and unity. Now we must investigate how a paper comes to be written, and how it comes to achieve focus and unity. For these students, doubtless their daily writing increased their fluency, and fluency helped them to revise their papers. But daily writing—spontaneous and undirected and uncorrected—"is a means to an end, and not an end in itself." The end is good writing, and the occasion for good writing in a composition class is the paper. The paper is *controlled, disciplined,* and *directed* by the student writer—and generally corrected by a teacher. Both Jim Beck and Marian Hart learned to write papers, something quite different from daily writing.

26

A paper has a purpose. A paper *shows* its purpose, both in its shape and in its statement, or the paper fails. In beginning a paper, we *find* that purpose; in writing the paper, we *make* that purpose *clear* to the outside world.

A paper must support its purpose by detail; it must have sufficient detail, and yet it must not have too much. It must set details into an order that expresses purpose. If we are writing six hundred words, we must find a purpose small enough to be supported adequately in two or three pages of writing. Our first necessity, when we begin a paper, is to narrow the subject down.

To accumulate detail, we can use the dreamlike spontaneity we cultivate in daily writing. But to cut and shape, to narrow and to focus, we need to cultivate other qualities of the mind. We must develop a sense for order and shape, a sense by which we understand the whole paper as several units organized to become one larger unit, and controlled by a purpose to an end.

We must also understand that our whole paper—from our choices of words to our choices of detail for a concluding paragraph—directs itself to the eyes and ears of other people. We do not write for ourselves only. Even the most cloistered poet addresses the Muse. We need to persuade, to inform, to please, to convince, to charm, to arouse, to impress *other people.*

Once we understand that writing is directed elsewhere—and not inward, where we can be sure that a generous interpretation will accept our intentions—then we can understand the function good style fills. We avoid clichés, or extraneous information, or misleading abstractions, or dangling modifiers, or incomplete arguments, *for one reason:* all these flaws, errors, or imperfections block the passage between the writer and the reader.

In further chapters, I will look into the choice of words, the making of sentences, and the construction of paragraphs, and at the different types of writing a student may undertake. But here, beginning a book about writing, we must investigate how the whole paper is made. We must look into a process which will be the student's classroom task throughout the term: writing papers single in purpose, whole and adequate in shape, and clear to an audience.

GETTING IDEAS

Many beginning writers find that getting started is the hardest work in writing. How do you find a starting point for a paper?

It depends on what you are doing. It also depends on the agility of your mind. But however spry or stiff you feel, you can learn to become *more* agile, *more* open, *more* prolific with ideas. If you have been doing daily writing, you have a warehouse of possibilities on the pages that you have accumulated. If you are writing a free theme, you can consult your daily writing for a thought or an anecdote that is apt for expansion. If you are assigned a theme to demonstrate a technique—a type of argument, for instance—you can find a starting point in your daily writing to develop and use.

If you are assigned to write a paper on Sino-Soviet relations, or on why you want to go to law school, or on a Kurt Vonnegut novel, your daily writing will not help you to find an idea. You must accumulate detail, allow ideas to grow from other ideas, and then shape the whole. I will speak more of this shaping later.

If you have no daily writing, and you are assigned a free theme, you have numerous ways of looking for subject matter. Topics come from your own life. For some papers, you can write anecdotal reminiscence. But even when you write exposition, or argument, the subject can come from your own life. If you wish to write an argument, think of recent conversations. Almost everyone gets involved in controversy from time to time. Choose a position to attack or defend, out of something in your own experience. Newspaper articles leave us feeling angry or approving—and are another source of topics for argument. Still lacking ideas, look over letters from home, or remember your last visit there.

But argument or advocacy is not a necessary part of an essay. You may want simply to investigate something. Hearing about how state lotteries proliferate you may want to do research on them and set forth the information in a paper. You may want to write exposition on the safest way to ride a motorcycle, or how to organize a rent strike. Books, television, talk shows, and everything we see in our daily lives—from movies to the way customers and shop clerks behave—can provide the topic for exposition. We must keep our eyes open. When we need to get an idea, we must let our inward eyes move freely over our experiences recent and past. A million topics wait for us.

In January of 1975, an instructor at the University of Michigan assigned a short theme, to be written outside class, as the second paper of the term. Students were to write two hundred and fifty to three hundred words of comparison and contrast, taking their subject at least partly from university life. For instance, the instructor suggested, they could compare living at home to living in a dormitory. But he suspected that this subject would prove too large, too vague, and too inclusive. Maybe they could narrow the topic, and compare sleeping at home with sleeping in the dormitory, or home cooking with dormitory food. Or they could contrast two things at the university: living in a dormitory with living in an apartment; riding a bicycle with driving a car; lecture courses taught by professors with recitations taught by teaching fellows.

The instructor asked for questions. Yes, they could write about something they didn't have direct knowledge of—like living in an apartment—provided the comparison was not too distant; don't compare walking to class with hiking in Switzerland. No, he didn't think a comparison of two beers sounded like a promising paper. Could the student compare tastes so that his audience could tell the difference? Maybe he could compare two bars?

Sharon Rustig returned to her room without a subject. Going over her daily writing, she noticed that on an earlier page she had mentioned her ten-speed bicycle, which she had left home because she feared that it would be stolen if she brought it to Ann Arbor. Now she wished she had brought it anyway. Maybe she could compare having a bicycle with not having one.

ACCUMULATING DETAIL

Normally, an idea comes to us with a few bits of detail attached. For safety, the motorcyclist must wear a helmet and keep his equipment in good repair. During the Easter vacation when we went to Washington, the buses broke down and the cherry trees failed to bloom, Alice Notley had hepatitis, and Mrs. Reade disappeared for two days. A state lottery must distribute x percent of its earnings or people will not support it.

We must do two contrary things with detail. We must accumulate a great deal of it; and we must cut it down to what is essential and useful. First, let us look at ways of accumulating detail; if the next section of this chapter tells us how to cut and to shape, this section should tell us how to gather the material for shaping and cutting.

Paper-writing for most of us goes through many stages. First, we take notes at random, not trying to think in an orderly way, but simply to gather as much possibly useful material as we can. We should *brainstorm*, letting our minds float freely and writing down the memories and associations that swim around us. We should take notes even if we think we will probably never use them. Writing about lotteries, we might associate them with bingo at the church, or with dog racing. Writing about motorcycle safety, we might think of the air bags proposed for automobiles. Probably both ideas will be cut out in the third stage of composition, when we shape the paper. But when we brainstorm, we censor nothing; at this stage, it is impossible to be certain what will fit our paper's shape, because we do not have the shape.

You can write notes freely and loosely, secure in the knowledge that no one but you need ever *read* your notes. Training in daily writing is useful at this stage. Write down what may be silly and what may be pompous; just write. Follow the train of thought even when you have no idea of its destination. Stop, put the notes away, and come back to them later. When you return, you will usually discover that some secret part of your head has been doing homework in the meantime; you will discover a fresh flow of details.

I have been describing the kind of paper that comes from your memory, your thought, and your imagination. Some papers properly take you to the library, or to an interview. You will need facts and figures to talk about state lotteries. You will be doing research, which is another matter. But before you begin research, before you look at your first index, you should brainstorm; you can accumulate speculative notes about what to look for and where to look.

When you have accumulated detail by floating freely, you may find that you can create more detail by scrutinizing what you have written down. Perhaps this scrutiny could be called another stage in writing the paper. Looking over your brief notes, *think* about each one, asking yourself if the one bit of information implies any other. If Mrs. Reade was missing for two days, what were the other teachers on the trip up to? The cherry trees did not bloom; was there any other vegetation? color? smell? By scrutiny and self-questioning—apparently opposite mental acts from the dreamy note-taking of the first stage—you can acquire more detail.

Sharon Rustig began to take notes in her spiral notebook, lining up two columns about bicycles.

Advantages	*Disadvantages*
quickness/save time	get stolen
fun	have to take inside
keep in shape	winter

She ran out of ideas quickly, and felt disappointed. She couldn't get a hundred words out of *that*, much less two hundred and fifty. Besides— she thought, looking at her list—who's going to care about "fun"? What could she write to *show* the fun?

She started to think of other topics, and then she remembered that one of her instructor's suggestions had been the comparison of bicycle with car. Sharon had never considered bringing an automobile to campus, because of the expense. But the expense would be something to talk about, another item on a list. Quickly, she began another two columns, this time about cars.

Advantages	Disadvantages
distance	ecol.
bad weather	money
	insurance
	gas
	parking
	trouble parking

As the list of disadvantages grew, she realized that she had found her topic. She would compare and contrast the advantages of bikes and cars on campus. Bikes were going to win.

A day later, Sharon began to write, in order to see what her ideas looked like when they turned into sentences.

Bicycles or Cars?

At first sight, a car seems as if it ought to be a better deal when you are going to college. Because it's bigger and you can go longer in it. Also because of bad weather. But really bicycles are better because of the ecology and the price of everything. Automobile insurance costs an incredible amount of $. So does gas, and its going up, when the oil producing nations raise the price again next fall. Parking here is expensive also but worse than that its impossible to find any. A friend of mine got his car towed because he had parked it next to a hospital place and paid $30 to buy it back from the garage that the police towed it away.

The trouble with bikes is that they get stolen all the time. If you are careful you can usually prevent this from happening to you. You get a good lock and you make sure that you get it looped through the rear wheel and the chain and you get it locked to something really solid. Also you take it inside although that's a lot of trouble.

> All in all, because of money and ecology, it's better to have a bike than a car.

Sharon wrote her first draft late at night. When she read it in the morning, she crunched it into a ball and threw it at the wastebasket. It missed. Then she picked it up, flattened it out, read it, and made notes in the margin, criticizing herself. "What's 'a better deal' mean?" she wrote after the first sentence; "mixes up two things," she wrote beside her sentence combining ecology and money. Then she took notes from her own paper, arranged them in order, and began again.

> If a student could have either a car or a bicycle at college, she should have a bicycle. There are many reasons for this. First I will tell the advantages of cars and the disadvantages of bicycles, and then I will do vice versa.

She crossed out the paragraph and started again.

> Bikes are better than cars, at least on this campus. Although cars give you protection in winter, and take you greater distances, they cannot compare to bikes for practical daily use.

She had found her beginning.

When Jim Beck wrote "The Race to College," he consulted his daily writing. From the term's beginning, his daily writing had frequently been about his family, and his real feelings about coming to college.

> September 20. I don't know what to write about except I got an E on my class theme about coming to college. God I hate everything about this place and I want to go home so bad I can taste it but if I go home now they'd laugh at me and my parents will want to kill themselves. So I stick it out, right? The trouble with getting so many congratulations on going to college—you have to go to college! I can't remember why they wanted me/I wanted me to go so much . . .

He wrote a page a day, and kept circling back to this subject. Later, he spent five pages talking about his brothers and their failures, and several pages talking about his father's job, interrupted by recollections of a fishing trip, and recollections, too, of his father watching him win a race in a state track meet. Without knowing that he was doing it, Jim Beck was accumulating detail the way many writers do.

Although some writers are able to plan their work ahead, and even outline before they write, most writers have to proceed like Jim; they must write rapidly and without much control, *at first*, in order to accumulate detail, in order to find out what they want to write about. *Then* they must cut, shape, organize, and control.

SHAPING THE PAPER

To write a good paper, you have to organize details in the best order, and you must leave out any details, however attractive, which do not contribute to the whole. The idea of focus, in the first chapter, is perhaps the most important *formal* idea in making a paper.

Purpose

For focus we need *purpose*. When he came finally to make "The Race to College," Jim Beck understood his purpose: to make clear the connection between his background and his drive to go to college, and the troubles that this connection made for him. Sharon Rustig began with the purpose of making her contrast. Now her paper had to show contrast by its form. Beginning with the daily practicality of bicycles, she continued her first paragraph by listing more advantages of bicycles.

> You can pedal to class, lock up outside the door, and carry your books upstairs in ten minutes. If you have an hour between classes, you can go back to your room, if you have a bike. Or you can run downtown to shop and run back again.

She decided that it was time for some contrast, and that the contrast would turn on a paragraph break.

> But with a car, you would get to class later, because you would spend all your time looking for a place to park. When you do park, you have to pay for it, and if you park illegally, sometimes you have to pay a *lot* for it. A friend of mine who's car got towed had to buy it back for thirty dollars.

For the development of the rest of her list of ideas, she went back to her notes. Her next paragraph began,

> But parking isn't the only thing that's expensive about a car . . .

Then in the next paragraph she returned to her favorite vehicle.

> And bikes are not only quick and cheap. They give you exercise . . .

She had one negative thing to say: you had to worry about your bike getting stolen. She didn't see how to work it in, so she made a note to herself in the margin of her draft—"Say about getting stolen"—to remind her when she wrote her final draft.

Selecting Detail

Professional writers often find that they do most of their revision by cutting. They cut details that are irrelevant to their point, they cut details that repeat the same feelings or information that other details have already carried, and they cut explanations of the obvious. Revision is more than omission, but learning what to omit is much of what you need to *finish* a piece of writing. Ezra Pound talks about his experience in writing a poem, and what he says of poetry is also good advice on what we must do continually in prose.

> Three years ago in Paris I got out of a "metro" train at La Concorde, and saw suddenly a beautiful face, and then another and another, and then a beautiful child's face, and then another beautiful woman, and I tried all that day to find words for what this had meant to me, and I could not find any words that seemed to me worthy, or as lovely as that sudden emotion. . . . I wrote a thirty-line poem, and destroyed it because it was what we call work "of second intensity." Six months later I made a poem half that length; a year later I made the following *hokku*-like sentence:—
>
> "The apparition of these faces in the crowd;
> Petals on a wet, black bough."

Writing is acquiring material (the floating on memory, the rapid daily writing) and it is ordering and cutting that material. The writer must be a paradoxical combination of opposites: the big spender and the miser, the nymphomaniac and the virgin, the all-acceptor and the all-rejector. Probably we are more troubled with irrelevant detail when we write out of our own lives than when we write from any other source. Cutting can take place when we try to organize our notes before writing, or it can come later; probably we cut at both stages. When we start to write, it is often hard to know which details are going to prove relevant. Many writers consciously write too much in their first drafts, knowing they do not yet know what will be useful, and knowing that they will later cut for focus and form.

Suppose you describe a particular day. At the end of a vacation, you had a perfect (or perfectly horrible) day. On that Thursday, when you woke up, it was 8:35. You ate scrambled eggs with catsup. These details could be relevant, or they could be mere padding. Cut what does not contribute to the whole. But first, you must have a whole. The point of your paper could be the triviality of your day; a dog barked, the mail was junk, nobody was home when you telephoned your friends. The point is to have a point. Find one—or even make one up. Truth-to-feeling is the point; we are not under oath in a court. If we are remembering a sequence of events—A, B, C, and D—we can rearrange the sequence to make a piece of writing more true to the feeling we want the whole to give. If event B happened second, but in retrospect was the emotional climax, we can *lie* a little, in order to tell the emotional truth. We can use C, A, and D in that order, and save B for last. We are still writing out of our own life. We are telling the truth in the serious sense. Within the limits set by credibility, we can even combine different events into one, or different people into the same character. Suppose in a family anecdote two uncles were moving in and out of a story, doing approximately the same things. In an anecdote, it might well be more shapely and pointed—and just as "true"—to turn them into one person.

To make a point, and to give our writing a shape, we must limit our material. Here we are back to unity again, a notion brought up in numerous forms in this book. If we try to write about a whole summer, we are most likely to write disjointed paragraphs, and be boring and superficial. We should find one event, or one unifying device (a place, a person, an automobile, a time of day, a kind of food) to tie together different details. Contrast can make a glue as adhesive as similarity. We must find the detail and form that combined will embody the summer's spirit.

When Jim Beck decided to make a theme out of his drive to attend college, he knew that he had accumulated detail in his daily writing. In fact, he had too much detail; at first, when he looked over thirty-six pages of undisciplined writing, he felt elated because he had so much to write about; then he felt depressed because he had too much to write about.

Should he tell about his father's parents? Really, the story of their troubles was background to his father's diffidence. Should he tell about his brother Steve's dishonorable discharge? In two pages of daily writing he had told only half the story, but he suspected that Steve's life story contributed to local opinion of the Becks. In a way, it belonged.

Of course *everything* belongs. Everything that ever happened to us contributes to how we are, how we act, and how we feel at this moment. Because Jim Beck had to condense his idea into three pages, he had to narrow his topic. He had to focus on his purpose, to seek out the proper order for this thought. The idea of focus helped him begin to narrow. In this paper, the topic was his personal feelings; he realized that he must concentrate on himself and keep his family at the side, mentioning his parents and his brothers only so far as the detail promoted his purpose.

Right away, he could cut thirty-six pages down to eight or ten. The rest of the cutting came when he chose detail that would be most felt by a reader. He decided that accounts of races by which he won his athletic scholarship would mean little to a reader. He decided with regret to omit an anecdote about a vice principal.

Beginnings

Beginnings of papers, for inexperienced writers, can turn into shapeless horrors. Experienced writers learn to pay special attention to beginnings. One professional says that if he can "find" the first sentence—as if a piece of paper were lying around on a dark shelf of the brain, with the right words on it—the rest of the essay is simple; the door opens, and he finds it easy to construct the house of the essay. But, he says, sometimes it takes him months to find the key.

Most of the time, we lack the months. Some hints about beginnings may help.

We usually overexplain, at the beginning of a paper, and begin too far back. Trying to talk about something that we did last weekend, we may realize that it resembled something we did last summer; then we may realize that last summer's feelings were like the feelings we had at age five when we started kindergarten; or at age three, when we moved to a new town. All these details may be valid, but to include them all would destroy the paper's shape. The bridge into the country of last weekend would be longer than the country itself. With enough self-questioning, we could begin every autobiographical paper with "I was born," or, "My grandparents emigrated from Lithuania in 1905," or, "Life for my peasant ancestors in medieval Turkey must have been difficult." This malady of origins and causes might be called the house-that-Jack-built syndrome.

Long bridges curse not only autobiography; the same malady can afflict all writing. In discussing how World War II began, we can begin with the fall of the Roman Empire. In making up a short story, we can supply causes from our imagination as prolifically as we can supply them from memory in writing autobiography. In assembling a research paper, we can go backward in time, or laterally in comparisons. Wanting to write about ecology, we may pick the disappearing whale as our topic; we can begin with the general topic of man's destroying his environment, narrow it to his destroying animal species, narrow it to his destroying whales, and then narrow it to the decline in the population of one type of whale. The last category is the paper's focus, but if we are not careful we can spend three-quarters of our paper walking the bridge to our topic.

The good, sharp beginning narrows the topic. Begin with something that arrests the reader, and points to the main topic. Reference back (or laterally) can follow if it is necessary, and it can be brief.

> Last weekend I broke up with Ed. I have not felt so lonesome since I moved to a new town when I was four, leaving the friends of my whole life behind me, and knowing no one at all.
> I know other people besides Ed, but I feel as if I didn't. The break-up had been coming for weeks. . . .

Or we can begin *without* an immediate lateral glance.

> Humpbacks are mammals, as all whales are; they breathe into huge lungs, bear live young, which they nurse for the better part of a year, and have vestiges of hair. . . .

In this research paper, the author catches our attention immediately with facts that will interest almost anyone, probably because they interested her and she shows it: "huge lungs," "for the better part of a year."

Editors of magazines sometimes refer to "zingers," which are beginnings (or "leads") to articles, constructed to grab the reader by the hair. *Time* is good at zingers. Here are three opening sentences from one issue.

> The United States was founded on a complaint.

> When the young Chinese woman heard a mysterious voice asking, "What's under your pillow?" she felt sure that the answer was a "biological radio apparatus" put there by a special agent who suspected her of crimes against the state.

> Professor Jürgen Zerche was lecturing on political science one day this spring when a band of some 70 young leftists barged into his classroom at the Free University of Berlin and began shouting curses at him.

All immediately involve our interest, and none has a preamble. One begins with a startling short sentence, the other two with arresting anecdotes.

Much serious writing begins with what we might call a quiet zinger, something exciting or intriguing and at the same time relevant to the material that follows. When Homer begins the *Iliad,* about the anger of Achilles and its consequences, the first word in the long poem means "rage." Here are the beginnings of three books.

> On top of everything, the cancer wing was Number 13.
>> Alexander Slozhenitsyn, *Cancer Ward*

> Who does not know Turner's picture of the Golden Bough?
>> J. G. Fraser, *The Golden Bough*

> Harold Ross died December 6, 1951, exactly one month after his fifty-ninth birthday. In November of the following year the *New Yorker* entertained the editors of *Punch* and some of its outstanding artists and writers. I was in Bermuda and missed the party, but weeks later met Rowland Emett for lunch at the Algonquin. "I'm sorry you didn't get to meet Ross," I began as we sat down. "Oh, but I did," he said. "He was all over the place. Nobody talked about anybody else."
>> James Thurber, *The Years with Ross*

In this last example, the first sentence is a conventional way to introduce a biographical memoir. Then Thurber shifts abruptly to anecdote, showing (not telling) in his first paragraph how important and fascinating Ross was to his staff. This showing points to the book's focus.

At other times and in other kinds of books, a definition of the subject may be essential before we can begin.

> In its widest possible extension the title of this book—*Adventures of Ideas*—might be taken as a synonym for The History of the Human Race. . . .
>> A. N. Whitehead, *Adventures of Ideas*

Whitehead builds a swift bridge into his topic.

Purpose and context determine the kind of beginning. But in any piece of writing, the beginning focuses our writing, it requires special attention, and requires brevity and incisiveness. We *need* some information quickly; information which may be pertinent but not wholly necessary should be suppressed; information which is both pertinent and necessary, but which might make a tedious beginning, can often be put off until later in the essay, when its relevance becomes obvious and it ceases to seem tedious.

One kind of opener is often boring, the overt announcement of what is to be done: "I am going to show that the government of the United States is split into three branches, the executive, the legislative, and the judicial." Papers may be constructed analytically, by delineating parts, but they should show and not tell. The paper that begins with the sentence above will generally develop by taking a paragraph each for the three branches, and end, as boringly as it began, "I have shown that the government of the United States is comprised of the executive, the legislative, and the judicial branches." It is essay structure for people who have difficulty following the story line of Mighty Mouse.

We already saw Sharon Rustig starting her paper. Jim Beck, once he had discarded the thought of beginning with his grandparents, tried several opening sentences.

> When I was daydreaming about college it scared me, but I didn't have any idea how I would hate it. I thought that it might be too hard but I never suspected that it would be horrible. It's horrible now, and I don't know if it will get any better. . . .

> Since I first came to the university, I haven't slept more than four hours in a row. . . .

> When I arrived in this town for orientation at the end of August, the first thing I saw was a bunch of Hare Krishnas. . . .

Giving up on getting the beginning right in his first draft, he went on to the rest of his paper. When he looked at his draft the next day, he decided to start with the third sentence of his first attempt,

> It's horrible now, and I don't know if it will get any better.

principally because he thought it would arouse curiosity; it was a bit of a zinger.

Middles: Development

Beginnings and endings are obvious points of attention when we concentrate on shape, on narrowing, and on focus. But obviously, the passage from beginning to ending must create an order that is lucid and expressive. Revising her theme, Marian Hart achieved unity and shape by omitting unnecessary details and ordering the necessary ones. Remarks on unity, sequence, and coherence in Chapter V, Paragraphs, will indicate standards for the mini-essay, the paragraph, that apply to the maxi-paragraph that is the essay. Remarks in that chapter, on transition within the paragraph apply to transition *between* paragraphs also, and therefore to the flowing development of the whole essay. For further attention to developing the paper, see Coherence in the Paragraph, pages 186–195, and Development in the Paragraph, pages 195–209.

The middle is the matter. *The shape we give the essay,* like the motion in the paragraph, *is the structure formed by our thought.* Most of the time, our matter determines our manner—or it ought to. An anecdote or a historical summary or an exposition of process must use chronological order. In an argument that advances a thesis, the essay's order seldom depends on chronology. Instead, it is an order of persuasion—accumulating detail, proceeding by logic, and using various forms of persuasion or argument.

Focus itself depends on order or development. A different order of ideas can make a different statement, even when the ideas or details remain the same. In a reminiscence, if we begin with pleasant associations and move to horrid ones, we leave the reader with a negative impression; if we move from horrid to pleasant, we are liable to leave the reader feeling positive. We could accumulate identical details for each paper, but make a different impression by our organization. There are "insides" to the order we give details, as well as to words and syntax. One student wrote, in a history paper:

> The rainfall in the Southern provinces is approximately two inches a year. On the average. What this means is that most years the country people starve in a drought; one year in five, they drown in a flood. However, the combination of a surviving Indian ritual, and a local brand of Roman Catholicism, keeps the people remarkably cheerful and content.

For the same assignment, writing from the same source, another wrote:

Indian rituals which still survive, combined with a peculiar in-
digenous Catholicism, keep the natives of the South apparently
contented. However, the climatic conditions are deplorable. The
rainfall averages two inches a year. This means that the peasants
parch for several years in drought, and are drowned in floods the
next one.

Both students' notes for this passage were, approximately:

Catholicism and Indian stuff
happy
infant mortality
rainfall
floods
starvation, drought

The two students were heading in different directions—the first toward
an expository essay on daily life in the tribe, the second toward an
argument for public works such as irrigation and flood control—but
they started from the same information, which they organized or
pointed in different ways.

Notice that neither student used the detail about infant mortality in
this sequence of details. It was not directly related to religion, or to the
economy of water. Because it was not a part of the movement of the
passage, it was irrelevant to it. When we shape into our paper the
details we have accumulated, we will find that we have to cut many of
them.

The development in Jim Beck's paper is deceptively simple. He
started with a paragraph telling us how much he hated college, with
details to make sure the reader understood the feeling.

It's horrible now, and I don't know if it will get any better. The
only people who pay attention to me are the people who are
trying to beat me out for the track team. My roommate is stoned
all day and gets A's on his papers anyway. I hate him because he
hates me because I'm a jock. My classes are boring lectures and
the sections are taught by graduate students who pick on the
students because the professors pick on them.

But this would not be news. Lots of people are unhappy in college. He
then constructed his second paragraph to make a contrast to the first.

He not only told us how much he wanted to come to college, but gave us reasons why.

> But I remember wanting to come here so bad! Nobody from Hammerton named Beck had ever been to college. Everybody knew the Becks were stupid. This went for my father, who never got through high school, and for my grandfather, who died before I was born, and who was the town drunk. It went for my two older brothers who went bad, as they say in Hammerton. Steve got a dishonorable discharge from the Marines and he works on a farm outside town and gets drunk on Fridays and Saturdays. Curt stole a car and did time at Jackson and nobody has heard from him since. My sister had a three-month baby and the town liked to talk about that.

In the third, fourth, and fifth paragraphs, his writing made us understand his separateness from the rest of his family, and from his home town—and then the easy and appropriate order of chronology began to organize the paper. Jim spent a paragraph speaking of athletics in general, to move on to his own ambitions as a runner, and he had carried us with him—right up to the paper's conclusion—with ease and clarity.

> I was different. Everybody told me I was. My mother told me I wasn't a Beck. My father told me I was going to bring back the family's good name. (I never knew it had one.) In grammar school the teachers all told me how much better I was than my brothers. By the time I was in sixth grade my father and the school Principal were talking about the University.
>
> My father isn't really dumb. Sometimes people look dumb because it's expected of them. He's worked at the same grocery for twenty years, I guess. Now that I made it to the University, he wants to be called Manager, because he's the only man there besides Mr. Roberts who owns it. (The rest of the help are—is?— kids who bag and an old lady cashier.) When I went back for a weekend everybody treated me as if I won the Olympics.
>
> I said the Principal and my father were talking about my going to the University. All through junior high I said I didn't want to go. I was scared. No Beck could do that. Bad things kept happening to my family. My father had an accident and totalled the car and lost his license and for a year we didn't have a car at all. He had to walk home two miles every night pushing a basket of

groceries. When I said I would quit school and get a job, every-body jumped on me.

It wasn't that I was an A student. It was just that I tried hard at everything I did. I got B's mostly. Now with B's, the counsellors kept telling me, I could be admitted to the University, but I wouldn't get a scholarship. I needed mostly A's for that, and then when I got to the University I would lose the scholarship if I couldn't keep the grades up. Then my brother Steve, who was a pretty good athlete once, suggested athletics.

I was too skinny for football, too short for basketball, I could barely swim and my school didn't have a swimming team any-way. There is one sport you can practice with no money and no equipment. I started to run when I was in my last year of junior high. It felt good right away. I ran to and from school. I went over to the high school and did laps. The high school coach noticed me and asked me to go out the next year. Running long distances hurts a lot. Sometimes you get a stitch in your left side and suddenly it shifts to your right side. I didn't exactly mind the pain. I studied it. I studied it in order to go to the University, the way I studied everything else.

Endings

Endings are nearly as important as beginnings, and the same cautions apply. We often make them too long, summarize facts that are already obvious, reargue a point already established, say abstractly what we have shown concretely—and by all these methods dilute the intensity our conclusion should have. Our endings often drag and decline into blank space, dwindling instead of concluding. This diminishment is bad organization. Usually the dwindling can be cut, just as most bridges at the beginning can be removed. If the dwindling qualifies the conclusion, the qualification can come before the conclusion.

There are exceptions. In a long and complicated argument, we may be pleased to find a succinct summary at the end of the author's argument. It is like seeing an aerial photograph of country we have just walked through. But the short paper—the kind in which we are most interested in this book—rarely profits from summary and often withers by it. We should point the whole essay toward the last sentence, and when we have written it, stop writing. Often we conclude an essay—and then continue writing. The essay writer must develop the confidence to let the facts and arguments stand by themselves without epilogue. People who moralize at the end of a story, or summarize at the end of an argument, are the same people who kill jokes by explaining them. In a short paper about an experience she had while babysitting, a student concluded:

> After that third phone call, the breathing, and the hanging-up, I sat huddled in a big chair and shaking, waiting for the Bakers to come back. For a while I turned out the lights, thinking that a dark house might not seem so inviting to any fiend prowling around. But the darkness scared me.
>
> It was about three-quarters of an hour before they came back. In that time, I thought through everything I could do if I was attacked. I could scream—but the neighbors were all away. I could run—but then I was leaving Ginnie. My mind went over and over everything. I even started to wonder which dress I ought to be buried in.
>
> When I heard the car stop I was petrified. But then I heard Mrs. Baker saying something when she opened the garage door. My heart slowed down. When they came in, I told them all about the phone calls, my parents being out of town, the houses dark next door. I guess I thought they'd give me a medal.
>
> Instead, they looked puzzled.
>
> "Why didn't you call *us?*" said Mrs. Baker.
>
> Then I realized that I had been dumb to sit there scared in the dark, waiting for the breather to knock down the door, with the telephone number written on the pad beside the phone. While the phone had rung three times, I had simply become more and more panicked, and I had never thought of the easiest thing to do. I must have been too scared. Well, I thought, that's one mistake I won't make again.

Here, the essay dwindles like an explained joke. She might have ended it,

> "Why didn't you call *us?*" said Mrs. Baker.

Or, if she had wanted to add another idea, and a detail, she might have extended herself for one sentence.

> I began to wonder if I had enjoyed my fear so much that I forgot the pad of paper beside the telephone which had a phone number on it.

At any rate, her paper would have improved if she had crossed out her last paragraph.

Usually we should conclude a topic without seeming to draw attention to the conclusion. Part of the paper's unity is the resolution it comes to, all details organized toward an end, a coda felt by the reader. Paradoxically, this resolution can be violated by obviousness. Anything that feels tacked on destroys a sense of unity. E. M. Forster begins "What I Believe" with a paradox that takes our attention: "I do not believe in belief." After six or seven pages, he is able to move smoothly into his conclusion, which resolves and completes all that has gone before, at the same time including new material.

> These are the reflections of an individualist and a liberal who has found his liberalism crumbling beneath him and at first felt ashamed. Then, looking around, he decided there was no special reason for shame, since other people, whatever they felt, were equally insecure. And as for individualism—there seems no way out of this, even if one wants to find one. The dictator-hero can grind down his citizens till they are all alike, but he can't melt them into a single man. That is beyond his power. He can order them to merge, he can incite them to mass antics, but they are obliged to be born separately and to die separately and, owing to these unavoidable termini, will always be running off the totalitarian rails. The memory of birth and the expectation of death always lurk within the human being, making him separate from his fellows and consequently capable of intercourse with them.
>
> Naked I came into the world, naked I shall go out of it! And a very good thing too, for it reminds me that I am naked under my shirt. Until psychologists and biologists have done much more tinkering than seems likely, the individual remains firm and each of us must consent to be one, and to make the best of the difficult job.

When you write with E. M. Forster's skill and fluency, you have forgotten categories like beginnings and endings—because you have learned them so well.

When Jim Beck first drafted his paper, he had no title and he had no ending. His last paragraph trailed off.

> Sometimes when I cannot sleep I think about going back to Hammerton but I can't do that. Sometimes I think about getting a gold medal in the Olympics. Both of them are happy dreams except that I *know* I'm not Olympic class and if I went home it would be a disgrace to everybody. So all I am doing is sticking it out and hating every minute of it and hoping that things will get better some time.

Then he saw that he had a title by taking his actual running and turning it into a metaphor standing for his drive to get to college. Next he saw that by cutting and shaping his original last paragraph, he could make the paper's ending have power for the reader, and refer back to the beginning without being obvious about it.

> In my Senior year I was all-state and held two high-school records (600 and half-mile) and I had an athletic scholarship to the University. Now I am here, the first Beck to make it. I don't know why I'm here or why I ran so hard or where I go from here. Now that I am here, the race to get here seems pointless. Nothing in my classes interests me. I study, just as I did before, in order to pass the course or even get a good grade. I run to win, but what am I running for? I will never be a great runner. Sometimes when I cannot sleep I imagine packing my bags and going back to Hammerton. But I can't do that. They would say, "He's a Beck, all right."

When Sharon Rustig had finished blaming cars for being expensive and impractical while praising bikes for being cheap and efficient and healthy, she had one major topic left over. She had saved her best for last, where she could compare the ecological values of car and bicycle. Starting with convenience had led her to the problem of parking, which had led her to the expense of cars: the ecological argument was delayed to the end—which was lucky, because it allowed her to end with the emphasis supplied by her major reason.

She drafted her final paragraph, and slept on the paper, and on the evening before it was due, wrote her final draft. She turned a personal anecdote into a generalization, because she thought it made better argument. She looked for the right word instead of the approximate one. She checked punctuation and spelling. She even found a place where she could mention bicycles being stolen. She typed it up, proofread it—and this is the theme she handed in:

Two Wheels are Better Than Four
Sharon Rustig

Bikes are better than cars, at least on this campus. Although cars protect you against bad weather, and take you on long trips, they cannot compare with bikes for practical daily use. You can pedal from dorm to class, lock up outside the door, and back-pack your books upstairs—ten minutes from bed to classroom! If you have an hour's break between classes, you can go back to your room instead of wasting your time hanging around the hallways. Or you can zip downtown and do an errand and zip back to your next class.

But with a car, you would get to class half an hour late, be-cause you couldn't find a place to park. If you park legally, you feed a meter. If you park illegally, you feed more than that. If your car is towed away from a no-parking area, you may pay as much as thirty dollars to get it back again. And not only parking is expensive, in connection with cars. Automobile insurance if you are student age will cost you about two hundred dollars a year. Gasoline has become expensive and is liable to get more so by the end of the year.

Bikes are better, not only because they are more efficient in getting you from place to place, and not only because they are cheaper, but because they're good for your body. They give you good exercise, especially if you live on a hill. Most students don't do much exercise, and just sit around getting flabby, so a bike is good for your health as well as everything else. The only bad things about bikes are their habit of getting stolen, but this works out for health too. You toughen up your neck muscles by riding around with a ten pound bike chain for a necklace.

But I haven't said the most important reason that bikes are better than cars. Cars use up petroleum which is in short supply. Bikes use up nothing but the bike riders' excess fat. Car exhaust pollutes the atmosphere and causes respiratory diseases. Bicy-cles exhaust nobody except the rider. Ecology makes the final reason why a bike is better than a car.

Sharon had written her three hundred words.

Of course it's impossible to use Sharon's experience as a model for everyone. We are all different, and we need to find our own ways to write well. The only rules to make, for someone writing a paper, are abstract ones: clarity, coherence, wholeness, development, and adequacy. Whether we write autobiography like Jim Beck, or exposition like Sharon Rustig—or whatever else—these general standards must apply. Each paper we write is a separate, personal attempt to reach these goals.

EXERCISES

1. In class, imitate collectively how we choose a subject and narrow a topic. Here are some general subjects, which can be narrowed into topics.

> the arms race
> the plight of the aged
> the Saturday-night special
> wiretapping
> legalization of marijuana

Some of these topics are broader than others. All can be narrowed further.

2. (a) Work up on your own an idea that might be developed into a theme. (b) Accumulate details. (c) Organize details into a possible order, eliminating those which seem irrelevant. (d) Bring all material to class. One student at a time can read his materials for general discussion. Or the instructor may want to collect the materials and mimeograph some of them to use in the next class meeting.

3. In class, brainstorm details for a paper on a recent local controversy. Then try to organize the details using the blackboard. Or take the details home, elaborate and organize them for the next class.

4. Analyze these passages for the order and relevance of the details used.

> a. By the early years of the 1890s, German firms had become notably prosperous. In one decade, Hamburg-Amerika alone had carried half a million passengers to New York—half again as much as either Cunard or White Star. The German companies basked in Imperial favor, were staffed by brilliant, ambitious executives and, as time would tell, competitive to the point of madness. The motto on the Hamburg-Amerika house flag was indicative: *Mein Feld ist die Welt* ("My field is the world").
>
> The "noble example" of Germany in its surge to the forefront of maritime power had rallied the waning hopes of sea-minded Americans, and led directly to Congressional support for the rehabilitation of the American Line. "Germany has a scant foothold on the deep sea,"

said one patriot, "and none of the splendid nautical traditions of America. What the empire has done, the republic can do more readily. No race like ours with a grasp upon two oceans and the mingled blood of Viking and pioneer can long be cheated of its birthright."

Kaiser Wilhelm himself was caught up in the nobility of it all. After a short cruise on one of the great ships he wrote a letter to his mother. "Any man who, standing on the deck of a ship with the starlit firmament of the Almighty as his canopy and the boundless seas as the only object of his vision," said His Imperial Highness, "takes occasion to question his conscience, to weigh his responsibilities, and to contrast them with his inclination to do good and keep in the path of righteousness, will not hesitate to pronounce a sea voyage a salutary thing for himself and those depending upon him."

To put an end to the dominance of rivals like the *Campania* and the *Lucania* and to halt the leapfrog way in which Cunard alternated with White Star in claiming the fastest speed, the longest menus and the most ornate grand saloons, the North German Lloyd Company adopted Prussian measures. They went to the Vulcan shipbuilding company in Stettin with a simple, stark proposal: build us the fastest ship in the world and we'll buy it; give us anything less, and you can keep it.

John Malcolm Brinnin, *The Sway of the Grand Saloon*

b. But the Dolphin House was not grand. Hermione and I settled in, for what we thought would be a weekend, and developed, in fact, to be eighteen months, with the occasional relief of a day in the city. The head waiter, who had been born in Constantinople, actually carried our bags. Dinner that first night was exquisite. We bathed in the cool glow of a '45 Château Lafite-Rothschild which I had all but forgotten. The quarters, however, were shabby.

A walk on the beach, after lunch the next day, revealed that we had unknowingly chosen a coast that resembled, in uncanny ways, our native Dalmatia. Sigurd was to join us in a fortnight. How pleased he would be!

Hermione and I played jacks until tea, a lively American game which we had picked up during a visiting lectureship in Seattle. Tea was mediocre, as breakfast had been. We noticed that Americans were good at the more obvious things, but lacked expertise at the small ones. When did we ever see toast cut with elegance, in all this wide land?

Hermann von Kreicke, *The Migrant Swan*

c. In a rather pathetic attempt to keep her home, Scott had sent her Compton Mackenzie's book *Plasher's Mead* to read. But she didn't like it: "Nothing annoys me more than having the most trivial action analyzed and explained." She said the heroine was "ATROCIOUSLY uninteresting" and maybe she'd save the book and try to read it again in rainy weather. But she also tipped her hand more than she may have intended, for in the same letter she told him, "People seldom interest me except in their relations to things, and I like men to be just incidents in books so I can imagine their characters—" Everything, it seemed, had to revolve around her, her perceptions, her games, or she was not interested and refused to play. Certainly that letter carried a note of warning about herself, if Fitzgerald had been in any condition to receive it. But he was not. He knew the terms, they were remarkably like his own, and that exquisite egotism drew him even more completely to her.

But what he did not fully perceive, perhaps because Zelda did not, was the uncertainty within his girl. For, as worldly as she loved to seem to be, as reckless and ebullient as she was, Zelda knew nothing first hand of any world other than the protected Southern one of provincial towns and families who knew one another and were kin. For all her banter, New York, chic and fabulous, must have seemed as remote to her as the Orient.

Nancy Milford, *Zelda*

d. But the real failure of the theater, the real evidence of its prevailing shallowness, its lack of standards, of convictions, of courage (and of course the lack of convictions helps account for the lack of courage), has to do with what functions, not as a mass but as a class medium. The true, deep failure emerges when one has got past the anonymous faces in the audience at a run-of-the-mine opening night, when one has got past the irrelevant name of the playwright, the unfamiliar names of the backers. The true, deep failure emerges on the most high-toned of opening nights, on the Social Register and Café Society personalities in the audience; on the Dun-and-Bradstreet names of the backers; on the immensely relevant name of the playwright, and the producer, and the director, and the star. Here what passes for good taste, what preens itself as sophistication, is not only graciously pleased to be represented but couldn't be paid to stay away.

Louis Kronenberger, *Company Manners*

5. Revise this beginning:

Every Easter we drove to my great Aunt's house in Troy to eat a ham for Easter dinner. Even when my father was a little boy, they had gone to Troy for Easter. Sometimes it would snow and we would be late. Once we blew a tire about half way, and the spare was soft, and we took at least an hour and a half to get it fixed.

Last year was my Senior year in high school, and my great aunt thought graduating from high school was a big deal, so I knew I would get a lot of attention when I got there. We have to pack because we actually stay over Friday and Saturday nights. Fortunately, for some reason, I packed my tennis shoes and my jeans. If I hadn't, I wouldn't have been able to play touch football decently, I wouldn't have wound up in the emergency ward, and I wouldn't have met Linda.

6. Which of these beginnings are interesting, and which seem potentially boring? Why?

a. When the United Nations met in September, its members were already agitated, anxious, and almost apoplectic.

b. The origins of the missile crisis are already well-known to the informed reading public.

c. Bang!

d. When I was born I lived in Cleveland. Then my family moved to Akron when I was two years old. After that we moved to Muncie, Indiana . . .

e. The goat had three eyes.

7. Here are two small articles from *The New Yorker*'s "Talk of the Town." What do you think of the beginning, endings, details, development, shape, and conclusions?

a. Within the last half-dozen years, the mockingbird, moving north into New England and multiplying, has progressed from the status of welcome stranger and curiosity to that of nuisance. Bird people who first found the invasion from the Southland a romantic affair are beginning to group the mockingbird, in their emotions, with such long-established non-favorites as the starling and the blue jay. The main trouble is that once a mockingbird establishes itself in a territory, with its full repertoire of imitations, the amount of time left open for legitimate songbirds to make themselves heard is limited. Even the other species of mockers retire from the scene. The thrasher, which used to enliven two or three days each spring with its madcap torrent of high-branch mimicry, tends to avoid the territory. The catbird sits mute. Unlike the thrasher and the catbird, the first of which used to join riotously, the second modestly, in the song of other birds, celebrating their talents with some affection, the mockingbird sings occlusively. For their first few years in the North, the mockingbirds seemed to have left behind their habit of singing at night. But last year they began occasional night sessions, and this year they have developed regular midnight-to-dawn routines in imitation of the killdeer, the meadowlark, the cardinal, and the oriole. The mimic is shutting the authentic music-makers out of their own songs, if not by monopolizing their singing time, then by giving their songs back to them so crudely that they become discouraged from producing the pure thing.

b. A lot was wrong with Elvis Presley's first-ever New York appearance, at Madison Square Garden last weekend. Somebody in the Presley organization misjudged the desires of the crowd, and as a result Elvis was preceded by a standup comedian called Jackie Kahane. No doubt Mr. Kahane's patter knocks 'em dead in Vegas, but New York is not Vegas and the Garden is not a night club. "Kids today . . ." said Mr. Kahane gamely, and lamely, as the audience clapped in unison. "I have a kid. Everything this kid eats turns to hair." He was finally booed off the stage. There was fault to find with Elvis's own performance as well. Instead of a rhythm section to back him up, he had a twenty-three-piece orchestra, a six-man rock band, and an eight-member chorus—a bit too much insurance, even for the Garden. The program was rigidly arranged and planned, allowing for little in the way of spontaneity, and it consisted largely of romantic ballads and sugary, easy-listening songs. The classics that most of the audience had come to hear—"Heartbreak Hotel," "Don't Be Cruel," "Hound Dog"—occupied only fifteen minutes of a fifty-minute program. The blandness was conceptual as well as musical, as when Elvis sang a non-controversial medley of "Dixie," "All My Trials," and the "Battle Hymn of the Republic." The gyrations that made the man famous were seldom in evidence. Instead, he offered a repertoire of stereotyped actions and heroic poses.

Oddly, none of this made any difference. The audience was ecstatic throughout. (It would have been ecstatic even if Elvis had sung nothing but Gregorian chants.) During the intermission before Elvis's appearance, our companion, a young woman who still has her Elvis scrapbook packed away in a trunk somewhere, told us a story that made it all quite comprehensible. "When I was twelve years old," she said, "I was riding in the car with my mother and brother, and a song called 'I Want You, I Need You, I Love You' came on the radio. I immediately felt a certain twinge. My mother said, 'This is that Elvis Presley they're all talking about. I don't see what all the fuss is about.' My brother said the same thing. I just sat on the back seat and didn't say anything. You see, I *did* know what all the fuss was about."

The lights went down, the orchestra struck up what used to be called "Thus Spake Zarathustra" and is now called "The Theme from '2001,'" the audience began a full-throated scream, and Elvis appeared. He looked magnificent. His coal-black hair was fuller and drier than in days of old, and he wore a fantastical white costume studded with silver. He strolled back and forth on the stage, accepting the plaudits of the crowd like a Roman emperor. He looked like an apparition, and this was appropriate, because he has been a figure of fantasy for seventeen years. As the performance went on, it became impossible to avoid the conclusion that he is a consummate professional. He never cut loose, but he did not have to. The slightest gesture of his hand, the smallest inclination of his head set off waves of screams from the favored direction. The greatest ovation, except for the one that attended his initial appearance, came when he went into the first of his old songs, "Love Me." "Treat me like a fool," he sang. "Treat me mean an' crool, but love me."

Throughout, Elvis maintained a certain ironic distance from it all, sometimes engaging in a bit of self-parody. At the beginning of "Hound Dog," for example, he posed dramatically on one knee, said, "Oh, excuse me," and switched to the other knee. But he manifestly enjoyed the audience's enjoyment, even as he indicated with a smile here and a gesture there that it all had less to do with him than with their idea of him. On our way out, we asked our companion if she had liked the show. "It was bliss," she said, "I haven't felt so intensely *thirteen* since—well, since I was thirteen."

8. Here are some exercises and questions about Sharon Rustig's drafts, and her final paper. (a) Go through her first complete draft (on pages 31–32) and correct it, as if you were the teacher and this were a paper submitted to you. (b) Later on page 32, Sharon tries two beginnings. What is wrong with the first one? Why is the second one better? (c) Notice the changes between the next-to-last draft printed (on pages 32–33) and the final draft. Are the changes improvements? Why? (d) How could the final paper be improved? Look at diction, mechanics, and organization. What in her writing should Sharon try to improve?

III

WORDS

THE INSIDES OF WORDS

Words Themselves

The Gospel According to St. John starts, "In the beginning was the Word." When we construct the world of our own prose style, we begin as St. John does. It may seem difficult, at first, to think of words apart from contexts; "salt" does not stand alone; it is part of "salt and pepper," or "please pass the salt." Words seem like drops of water in a stream that has its own wholeness and its own motion. But when you write well, each word is accurate and honest and exact in itself, and contributes its special history to the wholeness of the stream of meaning.

The writer must be able to feel words intimately, one at a time. He must also be able to step back, inside his head, and see the flowing sentence. But he starts with the single word. He starts with tens of thousands of these units, and he picks among them. He may end by writing a passage like this account of man's first sleep on the moon:

> It was almost three-thirty in the morning when the astronauts finally prepared for sleep. They pulled down the shades and Aldrin stretched out on the floor, his nose near the moon dust. Armstrong sat on the cover of the ascent engine, his back leaning

54

against one of the walls, his legs supported in a strap he had tied around a vertical bar. In front of his face was the eyepiece of the telescope. The earth was in its field of view, and the earth "like a big blue eyeball" stared back at him. They could not sleep. Like the eye of a victim just murdered, the earth stared back at him.
                    Norman Mailer, *Of a Fire on the Moon*

Until the end, this exposition seems simple and straightforward. Simple and straightforward it is, with the power of visual exactness, "his nose near the moon dust," and the unexpected detail, "a strap he had tied around a vertical bar." Norman Mailer cements each word in place exactly and inevitably, with the help of rhythm and sentence structure. For now, just look at how he prepares the last, emotional image by related words.

This passage, and much of Mailer's book, is about man and machine. The machinery is sophisticated, complex, overwhelming. Men are frail in comparison. The language begins to embody this idea, by repeating the names of parts of the body: "nose," "back," "legs," "face." We have become accustomed to the jerking motions of the puffed-up spacesuits, as if we are watching robots. Now suddenly we see "nose" and "face." We might be a mother looking at a sleeping child. From "face" we move to the most vulnerable and necessary of sense organs, the "eye," first by way of a telescope's "eyepiece," then by a visual comparison, easy to follow, of the earth to a "big blue eyeball," which stares. We have departed from the astronauts' bodies, and moved onto metaphorical bodies. Then, because the eyeball stares, we can leap to the emotional crux: the earth is dead, murdered as it were by the astronauts who leave it behind for another planet, beginning the exploration outward, into the stars. Mailer makes his point not by telling us about it overtly, but by his control of language, his understanding of the insides of words, so that the movement from "nose" to "face" to "eyepiece" and "view" to "victim just murdered" has an inner and emotional necessity.

All the warm night the secret snow fell so adhesively that every twig in the woods about their little rented house supported a tall slice of white, an upward projection which in the shadowless gloom of early morning lifted depth from the scene, made it seem Chinese, calligraphic, a stiff tapestry hung from the gray sky, a shield of lace interwoven with black thread.
                    John Updike

These sentences begin a short story called "The Crow in the Wood." Updike exercises the possibilities of our language in rhythm, in variety of sentence structure, and in observation that is dreamy and precise at the same time. He does it with words. Instead of looking at everything he does, let us look at a few of the words that stand out. "Adhesively" is a word we all know, from the noun or adjective "adhesive," as a longer way of saying "glue" or "sticky." Here the snow "fell" "adhesively." Snow really cannot fall like glue, and so we have something apparently inaccurate; yet it is right, because the context prepares us. It is a "warm night"; the snow will be damp. And "adhesively" rather than "stickily" in this context shows that the snow is not merely gooey to the fingers, but will actively adhere to something. "Adhesively" by its unusualness draws the right attention to itself.

Then look at the word "slice," " . . . every twig . . . supported a tall slice of white. . . ." Most of us would have said something about snow "piling" or "accumulating" on branches. But "a tall slice of white," besides being pleasing to the ear, is a brilliant image; the sharpness of "slice," together with the image of whiteness, nearly dazzles the eye. With the word "slice" is an unspoken "knife," just out of sight. And I think we have a moment's vision of an upright piece of white-frosted cake.

We could pick many more words for praise, in the passages from Mailer and Updike, and maybe for blame as well, which we will look into later. But the excellence here is perhaps like all excellence. These writers are *original, as if seeing a thing no one has seen;* yet they report their vision in a *language that reaches the rest of us.* For the first quality the writer needs imagination; for the second he needs skill. Without both qualities, he could not write the passage. Imagination without skill makes a lively chaos; skill without imagination, a deadly order.

No Synonyms

To appreciate the word—the "eyepiece"/"eyeball," the "slice," the "adhesively"—the writer and the reader must first realize that no words can be synonyms. Some words are close to each other in meaning, close enough to reveal that they are not the same. The writer must know not just the surface definitions of words; he must go deeper, and realize the families of contexts into which words have extended their associations—like "slice" with "knife" and even "cake." These families are the connotations of the word, and the associations we make with their denotation; "pepper" is not a connotation of "salt" but it is an association of it. Since the writer uses the whole family, it does not matter that he discriminates connotation from association. But he must know the insides of words; he must be a friend of the family.

The verbs "to emulate," "to imitate," and "to ape" may be listed as synonyms in a dictionary—and they are synonyms, by definition—but when we use them in a sentence they carry slight differences in meaning. "To emulate" sounds fancy; also it usually implies that the imitation involves self-improvement. "To imitate" is neutral, except that everyone knows that an imitation is not the real thing; inferiority shadows the word. "To copy" is mostly to reproduce exactly, though like "to imitate" it states a lack of originality. "To ape" is to mimic, and to be comical or mocking about it. If you wanted to say that a young pianist imitated a famous virtuoso, but you carelessly used the word "ape" instead of "imitate," you would grant his style the grace of a gorilla. Context is all; the inside of a word must reinforce or continue the force built by the context. When a sportswriter wrote that another middle linebacker aped Dick Butkus, he was being witty.

Dictionaries of synonyms and other books, especially *Roget's Thesaurus*, list words that resemble each other. The experienced writer can sometimes use a thesaurus to joggle his brain, to find not a "synonym" but the *right* word. He will be aware of the insides of the words he discovers. The thesaurus can be useful, not for supplying words never heard before (we know words only when we have met them in sentences; some dictionaries supply examples of words in use) but to remind the writer of words known in the past, but not remembered when needed.

Sometimes an unsophisticated writer finds disaster in such a book. A thesaurus supplies us with words that *resemble* each other, but we must recognize the *differences* between them. When I look up "imitation," in my pocket *Roget*, I find under Verbs:

> imitate, copy, mirror, reflect, reproduce, repeat; do like, echo, re-echo, catch, match, parallel; forge, counterfeit.

> mimic, ape, simulate, impersonate, act, etc. *(drama)*, 599; represent, etc., 554; parody, travesty, caricature, burlesque, take off, mock, borrow.

> follow in the steps (or wake) of, take pattern by, follow suit [colloq.], follow the example of, walk in the shoes of, take after, model after, emulate.

The editors separate the verbs into three categories, which ought to help the cautious writer, but it is difficult sometimes to defend the sorting-out. Why does "forge" or "counterfeit" belong among the closer synonyms in the first group, and "emulate" among the phrases in the third group? Why is "represent" among the comic or belittling words? Putting "ape" with "travesty" and "parody," however, reminds us of the comic insides of "ape." The beginning writer should certainly be wary of a thesaurus, because if he believes in synonyms he could produce a prose that means something wholly different from his intention.

> I walked in the flowers that bordered the garden, sniffing the sweet airs of spring.

could become,

> I peregrinated in the flowerets that flounced the orangery, sniffing the saccharine ventilation of the vernal equinox.

Spoken by W. C. Fields, the second version could be perfect for its context. As an example of how people misuse a thesaurus, it is exaggerated.

Using dictionary synonyms, you can test your sensitivity to the insides of words. Put the adjectives "false," "fake," "phoney," "insincere" with the noun "laugh." Everyone has heard laughs that were unreal, laughs for the sake of flattery, laughs that express the laugher's nervousness, or laughs at jokes that are not funny. If we wrote a description of such a laugh, we might want to write, "His laugh was false," or "His laugh was fake," or "His laugh was phoney," or "His laugh was insincere." Each time the exact meaning, depending on the context found in the story or the essay, would differ. "His laugh was false" sounds direct and serious, a stern and objective judgment. "His laugh was fake" sounds harsher, a strong indictment of the laugher; it implies that the falseness was deliberate. "His laugh was phoney" tells us more about whoever wrote the phrase. The choice of "phoney" over "false" or "fake" or "insincere" makes the speaker imply something like, "I am relaxed enough to be slangy." On the other hand, "His laugh was insincere" sounds pompous in its moral judgment—partly pompous, partly naïve.

These attempts to name the associations that words gather, without the context that paragraph or essay bestows, are speculation; but, whatever the context, the words would all be different. Slightly, but genuinely different.

Literalness and Metaphor

Another way to become sensitive to the insides of words is to take them as literally as you can. When you read, "Fog enveloped the city," try seeing a gigantic gray-brown envelope enclosing Los Angeles. You can see some silliness in literal images—but it is a silliness that can increase your sensitivity to whole words. Puns help too, working through the ear. Literal-mindedness, like all exercises that can improve your writing, can improve your reading as well.

Literal-mindedness exposes mixed metaphors, careless phrases comparing things that are comic or gross or inappropriate when we bring them together. Mixed metaphor usually happens when a writer uses clichés—the kind called dead metaphors—without noticing their original meanings. Sometimes people write, "The door yawned open"; the would-be comparison of door to mouth is dead from overuse. Sometimes people write, "The door beckoned," and the dead metaphor has the door turn into a hand that gestures an invitation. Once a student wrote in a paper, "The door yawned and beckoned." Two clichés make a mixed metaphor, if we are reading the insides of words: first the door is a huge, gaping mouth; suddenly an arm materializes between rows of teeth, and motions us to enter.

When we take words literally, we respond to metaphor. We see the fog *compared* to an envelope. A metaphor is a comparison made without being stated. We *state* a comparison as a simile—"like a big blue eyeball"—and we *make* a comparison when we leave out "like" or "as." Hamlet in his soliloquy wonders if he should "take arms against a sea of troubles." It is futile to fight with the ocean. The futility is what Shakespeare had in mind. If you take the words literally, as they come, you can see something like an armored knight wading into the surf and slashing at the waves with his sword. The image shows an emotion that the abstract word (futility) would only name. The picture—which we receive by literal reading—gives us the emotion, without losing the idea of futility that the picture expresses.

Sense Words

Words that carry feeling most strongly are pictures and smells and touches and tastes and noises. The more sensuous words are, the more they reach us and move us. We see how Updike embodies feelings of cozy shelter, and of precise observation of the outside world, by using images, not by using words that *tell* us how to feel (like "cozy") or that abstract ideas from actions (like "observations"). We see Mailer giving us an exact visual image of the astronauts trying to sleep on the moon.

We feel the astronauts' cramp and discomfort because of the images; he need not say "cramp" and "discomfort." In the next paragraph, Mailer writes about the failure to sleep, and he writes ideas, but he uses images as well.

> It used to be said that men in the hour of their triumph knew the sleep of the just, but a modern view might argue that men sleep in order to dream, sleep in order to involve that mysterious theater where regions of the unconscious reach into communication with one another, and charts and portraits of the soul and the world outside are subtly retouched from the experience of the day.

"Theater," "charts," "portraits . . . retouched"—Mailer uses images to make his concept clear by a comparison. Not *all* writing can be sensuous and figurative, but *most* writing can be. Of course it is always possible to be safe and boring by stating only the facts, without images and feelings. Mailer could have said that the astronauts arranged themselves to go to sleep but couldn't, perhaps because so much had happened that day. Updike could have said that when his characters woke up, they discovered that it had snowed while they slept.

Sense words carry feeling, and they fulfill purposes appropriate to different kinds of writing: for Mailer, the sense words embody a speculation; for Updike, they convey sensation that will soon body forth fiction to the reader's imagination. For Jane Addams, in this passage from *Twenty Years at Hull House*, images explain a scene at the same time as they express outrage over poverty in Victorian London:

> . . . On Mile End Road, from the top of an omnibus which paused at the end of a dingy street lighted by only occasional flares of gas, we saw two huge masses of ill-clad people clamoring around two hucksters' carts. They were bidding their farthings and ha'pennies for a vegetable held up by the auctioneer, which he at last scornfully flung, with a gibe for its cheapness, to the successful bidder. In the momentary pause only one man detached himself from the groups. He had bidden on a cabbage, and when it struck his hand, he instantly sat down on the curb, tore it with his teeth, and hastily devoured it, unwashed and uncooked as it was. He and his fellows . . . were huddled into ill-fitting, cast-off clothing, the ragged finery which one sees only in East London. Their pale faces were dominated by that most unlovely of human expressions, the cunning and shrewdness of

the bargain-hunter who starves if he cannot make a successful trade, and yet the final impression was not of ragged, tawdry clothing nor of pinched and sallow faces, but of myriads of hands, empty, pathetic, nerveless and workworn, showing white in the uncertain light of the street, and clutching forward for food which was already unfit to eat. . . .

Notice that our sense of outrage, almost without exception, comes from the images chosen; we are not *told*, except when she writes "that most unlovely of human expressions"; we are *shown*. If Jane Addams used only abstractions like "degradation" and "extreme poverty," we could forget them easily; we do not forget the man who devours the cabbage "unwashed and uncooked," or the hands clutching at inedible food.

Misusing the Insides of Words

Just as we can learn to embody feelings by being aware of a word's whole family and by using language that appeals to the senses, so we can misuse words to fool ourselves and other people. The poet W. B. Yeats wrote, "The rhetorician would deceive his neighbors,/The sentimentalist himself." Sentimentality means faked or exaggerated feeling, not genuine emotion. Usually, the rhetorician who wishes to deceive others must first become a sentimentalist who deceives himself. In the advertising business, it is well known that you have to *believe* in your product; so that grown people ride the commuter trains believing that Hotz is superior to all other cold breakfasts. To con others, you begin by conning yourself, or you end that way.

Some propagandists deceive by will. The dangerous con sets out to change minds by slanting words to *seem* objective and yet to carry a disguised subjective content. News magazines (*Time, Newsweek, U.S. News and World Report*) often convey subtle editorial comment within their reporting. Newspapers do the same, though editors try to keep the editorials editorial, and the news objective. The controversy was raised again in the seventies on the objectivity, or lack of it, in the news media; even when you appear objective, you can select with bias. One photograph of candidate Y looks flattering; another makes him look like an ass.

We will never destroy bias, but we can attempt to learn to see bias, and not be deceived by reporting that is really editorializing. A few years back, one news magazine was blatant in its support for one presidential candidate over another. It said so editorially. And in its "news" stories it used the associations of words. Candidate A, they said, "in his rumpled suit slouched into the gleaming limousine." Candidate B, on the other hand, "strode smiling into his black sedan."

Now a sedan may sound expensive, but it may also seem to suit the dignity required of a candidate for high office. "Gleaming limousine" is more lavish, more gloatingly rich. "Rumpled suit" and "smiling" are obvious contrasts. The most telling use of the loaded word is the contrast between "strode" and "slouched." Who would vote for a man who slouched when he could pick one who strode instead? Yet in all fairness, can we say that the *news* in each sentence is different? In Dick and Jane language, the sentence would read, "The man got in the car." The rhetoricians of the news magazine, playing upon the separation between meaning and expression, flash us the sign: "Vote for B!" Because they pretend to objectivity, their use of sense words to influence opinion is dishonest and underhanded.

They seem to be doing it consciously, though no one can ever be sure of someone else's consciousness. More dangerous uses of loaded words, for anyone who wishes to be honest, are the words we kid ourselves with. We use euphemism to persuade ourselves that one thing is really another; a janitor still cleans floors, but it sounds more lofty to be a custodian. When we say that someone is "wealthy," we are avoiding the plainer word "rich," which has acquired overtones of vulgarity. If a real estate agent shows you a two-room shack converted from a chicken coop, he does not call it a "house," he calls it a "home." A Cadillac is never a "used car"; it is "previously owned."

Often, a euphemism is more abstract or general than the plain word. The euphemism not only sounds fancier (mortician/undertaker; route salesman/milkman) but it has less color or imagery. Apparently, Americans are especially prone to euphemism. H. L. Mencken, in *The American Language*, gave some historical background.

> The tendency to engaud lowly vocations with names presumably dignified goes back to the Revolution, and has been frequently noted by English travelers, beginning with Thomas Anburey in 1779. In 1784 John Ferdinand Dalziel Smyth observed that the smallest American shopkeepers were calling their establishments *stores,* which indicated a large place to an Englishman. "The different distinct branches of manufacturers," he said, "such as *hosiers, haberdashers, clothiers, linen drapers, grocers, stationers,* etc., are not known here; they are all comprehended in the single name and occupation of *merchant* or *storekeeper.*"

By 1846 the American barbershop had begun to be a *shaving salon,* and by 1850 a photographer was a *daguerrian artist.* By 1875 barbers were *tonsorial artists* or *tonsorialists,* and in the early 80s presentable saloonkeepers became *restauranters* or *restauranteurs.* By 1901 the *Police Gazette* was carrying on a campaign for the abandonment of the lowly *bartender* and the adoption of either *bar clerk* or *mixologist.* . . .

But euphemism is not only comical. We employ euphemism, frequently, when we want to conceal something real. When we have a tomcat castrated, we hesitate to admit that we have cut off his testicles, or even castrated him; we have had him "altered." We have a tooth "extracted"; it would be more painful to have it "pulled." The rhetoric of the Vietnam War was full of abstract euphemisms. "Pacification" meant shooting people; we learned that we destroyed villages in order to "save" them; "Vietnamization" meant using Asians for killing Asians, and withdrawing Americans. A "relocation center" looked very like a concentration camp. We used the word "incursion" to avoid calling an invasion an invasion. We used "waste" rather than "kill," perhaps because even in war we need euphemisms to con the conscience. "Terminate with extreme prejudice" was a high-sounding expression for an order that could have been expressed in one word: kill.

Politics and political acts of destruction always bring forth the worst in our prose, as we struggle to justify ourselves. Hitler euphemistically labeled his genocide of Jews "the final solution." One of the finest essays on style is George Orwell's "Politics and the English Language"; he says, writing in the forties:

> Millions of peasants are robbed of their farms and sent trudging along the roads with no more than they can carry: this is called *transfer of population* or *rectification of frontiers.* People are imprisoned for years without trial, or shot in the back of the neck or sent to die of scurvy in Arctic lumber camps; this is called *elimination of undesirable elements.* Such phraseology is needed if we want to name things without calling up mental pictures of them. Consider for instance some comfortable English professor defending Russian totalitarianism. [George Orwell was British, and was writing after Stalin's execution of the Kulaks and the mass murders of the Soviet purges of the late thirties.] He cannot say outright, "I believe in killing off your

opponents when you can get good results by doing so." Probably, therefore, he will say something like this:

"While freely conceding that the Soviet regime exhibits certain features which the humanitarian may be inclined to deplore, we must, I think, agree that a certain curtailment of the right to political opposition is an unavoidable concomitant of transitional periods, and that the rigors which the Russian people have been called upon to undergo have been amply justified in the sphere of concrete achievement."

Meanwhile, the bullet enters the back of the head. Always be suspicious—as Orwell advises—when the words do not call up a picture. "Terminate with extreme prejudice" does not call to mind the prisoner bound, blindfolded, kneeling, the pistol at the back of his head, the sound, the rush of the body forward, the splatter of brains and blood.

Avoiding Self-Deceit

Sometimes, then, we use abstractions or euphemisms to avoid or suppress feeling. And sometimes we use words of the senses in dishonest ways, not so much to evade feeling as to twist it. "Slouched" and "strode" are both verbs of action that make us see. We must know in ourselves, by using our brains and our sensitivity, whether the difference between two images is literal description or an emotional nudge disguising itself as objective description. We do not complain that emotions *show;* we complain that the emotions are *disguised.* We do not object to laughter or to anger. We object to laughter that hides anger, expressing gaiety while it means hostility. We can learn to sense the falseness in language—our own or others'—as we learn to sense falseness in a gesture or a facial expression.

If we ourselves have strong opinions or biases, we must try to correct for the veer of our own wind, both in reading and writing. If we react instantly to a cliché like "the military-industrial complex," we are not thinking about it, and we can manipulate ourselves or be manipulated by others. We must become aware of our habits of opinion. We need not alter our convictions; we need only open them to the air—and to our own conscious minds. When we hear a phrase like "iron-curtain countries," we must not respond like an automaton to a pressed button but like a human being, and decide what the phrase means, if it means anything, in its current context.

The more intense our convictions, the more vulnerable we are to self-deceit. Knowing ourselves comes first: if we understand our feelings, we are forewarned of our vulnerability.

Collecting Words

We must watch our words to see if we are using them with respect for honest expression. It helps to love words, and a love of words is something that we can develop. The growing writer finds pleasure in becoming a word collector, picking up, examining, and keeping new words (or familiar words seen suddenly, as if for the first time) like seashells or driftwood. Think of the richness in "hogwash," or the exact strength in "rasp." English is thick with short, strong words. You can collect words from books, of course, but you can also find them in speech; a sense of lively speech adds energy to the best writing. A writer listens to speech—others' and even his own—with a greedy ear. Primitive people and children love words as things in themselves and collect them as ornaments. To become a better writer, rediscover some of the pleasure from words-as-things that you had in your childhood but have probably lost along the way. You patrol the miles of speech looking for words like "flotsam."

Dictionaries can help, too. A thesaurus or a list of synonyms has the limitations mentioned earlier (pages 57–58). Brief dictionaries have brief definitions, and though they may light up a dark patch in our reading, they often give such a limited definition for the word, so void of context, that we may misuse it when we try to say it in a sentence. Good-sized college dictionaries carry more information, and can be a pleasure to read. The more information, the better. Some time, when you are in the library, take down from the shelves one of the thirteen volumes of the *Oxford English Dictionary* and browse a little. The English poet and novelist Robert Graves says only one book is indispensable to the writer's library: the OED. In the thirteen volumes, the editors collect almost all the words you are likely to come across (except for very new words, and words that at the time of publication were considered unprintable), but it is not the completeness that makes it so valuable. It is the contexts. In the OED, the editors tried to supply the earliest example for each shade of meaning of every word.

Suppose we look up the word "vegetable." More than three columns of small print chronicle the life of the word, which began as an adjective meaning "having the vegetating properties of plants; living and growing as a plant or organism endowed with the lowest form of life." The earliest example is 1400. The poet Lydgate, a couple of decades later, wrote of the wind (spelling modernized): ". . . that is so comfort-able/For to nourish things vegetable." When Andrew Marvell wrote "To His Coy Mistress" two and a half centuries later (1678), he used the adjective in the same way: "My vegetable love should grow/Vaster than empires and more slow." Six examples (complete with small context) come between Lydgate and Marvell.

Meanwhile, the noun "vegetable" got started in 1582, when an author named J. Hester spoke of "the Hidden Vertues of sondrie Ve-gitables, Animalles, and Mineralles." The reader can discover thirty-six contexts for the word vegetable as a noun from 1582 into modern use—and many shades of meaning. If you take pleasure in words, you will find your sensitivity to the insides of words increasing the more you know the history of words. So much of our history, external and internal, global and psychic, is coded into our words. The more you know, the more you respect the integrity of the word; integrity means wholeness; a word's wholeness includes all its possibilities: its family, its insides.

Words as Blanks

A frequent failure in our language, spoken or written, is our use of words that can mean anything the context requires. These words are like blanks for the reader or listener to fill in. Words of vague praise or blame—"lovely" and "terrible"—are frequent blanks. "Great." "Ter-rific." What does "lovely hair" look like? Is it red or blonde or white or black or brown? Long or short? Liveliness is specificity. Vogue words are usually blanks also. "Dig," "heavy," "cool." "Fink" was popular a few years ago as a vogue word of contempt, no more precise than the "jerk" or "creep" of earlier generations. Yet once "fink" meant some-thing exact: a man employed to join a labor union and spy for bosses. Words of complex history suddenly come into fashion and lose all color.

Words and Meaning

Words used as blanks get in the way of writing and thinking and feeling. Words mean things only by our agreement. If we start using "April" to mean "sunset" or "anything pleasant," it will not be of use to us any more. Our agreements about words are coded into dictio-naries, which of course change, as the words shift gradually in meaning because of historical change and the literary genius that adapts old words to new conditions. Our agreements about words are also coded into the dictionary from which we really make our sentences—the dictionary (the computer) of the brain. This mental collection is even more complicated and useful, for our writing, than the dictionary on the shelf. The thirty thousand associations of the word "April" are there to be used in the right way at the right time. The inside of a word is a huge room of possibilities, limited—because "April" does not include "August" or "catsup" for most of us—but multiple: flowers and showers, Easter, spring, seeds, vacation from school, Chaucer and Browning and "the cruellest month" for readers of poetry, ploughing or manure-spreading for farmers.

Someone might associate April with catsup or cats or soup or a girl in the first grade called April. These associations are private; the few phrases I listed at the end of the last paragraph are public or general. A moment's thought will usually reveal to the writer, at least in revision, whether he is using a word privately or generally. "Tulips like catsup" would be a grotesque and inappropriate simile for most of us—despite the real color—though it might be a spontaneous expression of the writer who privately associated April with catsup. Any writer must learn to suppress the highly private, because writing must get through to an audience; you are talking to someone besides yourself; you have climbed out of the pure autism of the crib, and are trying to make human contact.

Audience and Self

But we must also remember, in choosing words, that "an audience" is not "everyone." The larger the audience we try to reach, the fewer associations we can take for granted, and the more circumscribed our room of possibilities. If we are writing for a big newspaper, we probably do not assume that most of our readers associate April with Chaucer, Browning, and Eliot. An idea of audience is crucial to our choice of words. Everyone makes this sort of choice in conversation: we use words with our best friend that we do not use with our grandmother; if we hitch a ride with a white-haired man wearing a blue suit, our words probably are different from those we would use if the driver wore sunglasses, bell-bottoms, and long hair. If our vocabulary stays the same, chances are that we are being hostile in the sacred name of honesty.

In writing we make the same choices. If we write a letter to the college newspaper, we choose the words from a pool different from the one we use when we write a thank-you letter to an aunt. The term paper in business administration requires a vocabulary different from the one we need for a term paper in literature.

The difficult, necessary task is to adjust your vocabulary to your audience with tact, humility, and appropriateness—but without hypocrisy, without being false. Sometimes it is merely a matter of common sense. If you are writing for an audience from the southern hemisphere, you must remember that April connotes autumn and leaves falling, not green and seeds sprouting. But common sense is easy, compared to the difficulties of learning the difference between appropriate tact and gross hypocrisy. When Jim Beck wrote his first essay, the one about "well-rounded individuals" and so on (on page 7), he was writing *for* an assumed audience, and *against* himself. Probably at that moment he did not believe that he could write with honesty for an audience that was a teacher. Probably Jim Beck had no vocabularies to fall back on at that moment but that of high-minded hypocrisy, and that of the boys in the locker room or the dorm, which can be just as hypocritical and one-sided as graduation oratory. By learning to write with more respect for himself, for his own feelings told in his own words, he learned to write with honesty, and to face things with honesty. By becoming aware of the insides of words, he learned a lot about the insides of Jim Beck; and he learned to make the inside outside—to *write*.

EXERCISES

1. Here are three lists of words similar in meaning. Discuss the varieties of meaning within each list.

ostentatious, showy, conspicuous, exhibitionistic;
preserve, maintain, keep up, support;
disease, illness, sickness, infirmity, disorder, indisposition, malady, debility.

2. Using a thesaurus, rewrite this passage by substituting a "synonym" for each of the words. (See the example on page 58.)

I remember sitting with my foot up on pillows on the edge of my bed in my room, gazing at my freckled face in a hand mirror. My face embarrassed me most of the time and I couldn't get a comb through my mass of unruly, tangled red hair.

Shirley MacLaine, *Don't Fall off the Mountain*

3. Look past these thesaurus words, and find the proverb:
   a. It requires an entirety of species to fabricate a cosmos.
   b. Precipitousness occasions depletion.
   c. The sum total of matter which scintillates is not necessarily bullion.

4. Make up new euphemisms for the following professions, events, or actions.

goaltender in hockey, food server in a cafeteria, bookseller;
final exams, Mother's Day, Veterans Day;
tackling a quarterback from the blind side, cheating on a quiz, asking for money.

5. Collect five words that interest you, and write a paragraph about each of them, as if you were writing the catalogue for an exhibition of paintings or a museum of dinosaurs.

6. Find a word used as a blank (see page 66). Find the original meanings in the dictionary. Read the word's history in the *Oxford English Dictionary*. Write a note on the decline of the word.

7. In these paragraphs, underline the words that the author uses most brilliantly—the way John Updike uses "adhesively" or "slice"—and defend your choices in class:

a. As the waves roll in toward Lands End on the westernmost tip of England they bring the feel of the distant places of the Atlantic. Moving shoreward above the steeply rising floor of the deep sea, from dark blue water into troubled green, they pass the edge of "soundings" and roll up over the continental shelf in confused ripplings and turbulence. Over the shoaling bottom they sweep landward, breaking on the Seven Stones of the channel between the Scilly Isles and Lands End, coming in over the sunken ledges and the rocks that roll out their glistening backs at low water.

Rachel Carson, *The Sea Around Us*

b. The top of the hill, pasture for one straggly cow, was clear of brush except for patches of dark juniper, in spreading flat circles ten feet across. Around the tumbled stone walls tall pines and maples held off an advancing army of small gray birch. At one side, by the bouldery path that had once been a town road, a little family graveyard lay on slightly tilted ground. A deer trail ran right through it, bright and twisting between the slate stones, and a birch had fallen and rotted out of its bark, leaving a print like a white hand.

Thomas Williams, *Town Burning*

8. Underline the sense words in this passage from a magazine article. How effective are they? Does the author have the insides of words under control?

A blinding splendor sparkling in lazy rhythm to the whine of retarding jet engines welcomes you to Mexico City. The surreal glow seems to extend to the end of the world and it's not hard to believe some ten million persons are rising for the day, hustling in the brilliant carpet of light below.

Before the plane has touched the runway, dawn explodes. Sentry volcanoes glisten in rainbow hues—imperfect cones turned upside down, slowly shifting their color from black, to grey, to crystalline sugar frost. Below them, smog clouds—modern mad children of our times—begin to drift in peaceful motion as a soft light invades the aircraft and stirs its sleepy passengers.

Sergio Ortiz, "Mexico" *(Playgirl)*

9. Underline examples of euphemism in these passages from a speech about the public relations business:

So confident were we that a breakthrough was imminent that it became popular to think of changing our name from public relations specialists to communications specialists.

. . .

What is new is the role the public relations consultant is beginning to play in relation to the social crises which no one foresaw 10 or 20 years ago. In these new assignments—which represent a small but rapidly growing part of his business—he is no longer primarily a communicator: he is a sort of moderator whose job it is to try to prevent the crisis from getting out of hand. He may still use the same tools, but the measure of his performance is not how effectively he gets his clients' message across, but how successful he is in avoiding a flare-up which can stop the machinery of his clients' business, how he can help his clients conduct their business in a way that is responsive to the new demands made by concerned scientists, environmentalists, consumerists, minority leaders, underprivileged segments of the community, the young generation.

David Finn, "Modifying Opinions in the New
Human Climate" *(Public Relations Quarterly)*

10. Whatever your own convictions, look in these passages for loaded language, euphemism—the use and misuse of language in general. Underline whatever seems underhanded, and discuss in class.

a. During 1974, expenditures for industrial air and water pollution control at GM facilities totaled $74 million, not excluding expenditures for research and development and operating costs. Because of recent E.P.A. rules promulgated as part of the water and air pollution control and solid waste disposal laws, GM and industry in general may be faced with additional substantial capital expenditures over the next three to five years. There is concern that some mandated time schedules may be unachievable, and that some requirements for control systems may be questionable on a cost/benefit relationship. GM will actively pursue its stated goal of compliance with all applicable pollution control laws—but at the same time will do what it can to ensure that such control is economically justifiable in relation to the anticipated benefits.

From "1974 General Motors Report on Programs of Public Interest"

b. The Great Lakes, which hold one-fifth of all the fresh water on the surface of the earth, have become heavily contaminated. Hundreds of millions of gallons of industrial pollutants are discharged into Lake Superior and flow on into Lake Huron. Lake Michigan drains a huge complex of industries. Lake Erie is described as a "chemical sink." Most of the lake's fish, once a rich harvest, have been killed. In the slow-moving lake water, contaminants have settled to the bottom. Thus, although clean-up efforts are now beginning, experts are far from sure that the lakes can be reclaimed even if further pollution can be halted.

John Perry, *Our Polluted World*

c. The coal companies propose to extract North Dakota's lignite over the next few decades by strip-mining—the environmentally notorious method of removing all the earth from atop the seam rather than removing the coal from under the earth via tunnels They are offering to sign coal-mining leases at royalty rates that have drawn the interest of prosperous farmers.

Ben A. Franklin, "What Price Coal?" *(The New York Times Magazine)*

d. The world needs nuclear energy. The fossil fuels—coal, oil and natural gas—are being consumed at an alarming rate. Many experts believe that by the end of this century half of the world's supply of electric power will come from nuclear stations.

Nuclear fuels are highly concentrated. Operation of a coal-fueled Fermi-2 would require about 3,650,000 tons of coal a year. As a nuclear plant it will consume about 1.25 tons of nuclear fuel annually.

The basic difference between a nuclear and a fossil-fueled power plant is the heat source and method of generating steam. From there on the process is similar to conventional plants: Steam goes to the turbine which spins the rotor of the electric generator. The spent steam is condensed back into feed-water which goes back to the reactor where it is again turned into steam.

Another difference is the very large investment in control, safety and environmental protection systems. If one system fails there is another, and yet another, to take charge and correct the situation. Every effort is made to design, fabricate and construct nuclear plant facilities to the highest quality standards. No other industry has a safety record to match nuclear power.

The Nuclear Way, "Building Fermi-2"
(from a publication by Detroit Edison)

e. We also learned from fallout, how little was known about the risks incurred by large populations exposed to radiation or toxic substances. Before the advent of nuclear energy, medical experience with the internal effects of radiation was very limited, based largely on the fate of several hundred unfortunate women who in the 1920's had used their lips to point up brushes for applying radium-containing luminous paint on watch dials. Standards of radiation exposure were set on the assumption that, at some minimal level, the body would experience no harm at all from radiation, and the AEC used these standards in order to support their claim that fallout was "harmless" to the population as a whole. Later, when it was realized that unlike industrial workers, the general population is unable to escape exposure (for example, by quitting a job) and includes especially susceptible individuals such as children and the aged, the "acceptable" limits were reduced to about three percent of their original value. Finally, experiments show that *every* exposure to radiation, however small, carries with it *some* risk, in the form of genetic damage or cancer . . . .

Barry Commoner, *The Closing Circle*

f. *How large is the risk from normal radioactive discharges?* As explained in Sections 2, 3, and 4, the allowable exposure to the general public from nuclear power plants is limited by Federal regulations to less than one mrem/year. The effects of radiation resulting from nuclear power plants are undetectable. However, making very conservative estimates based on the effects of large doses of radiation, the public risk from allowable exposure limits (which are greater than actual exposures) is less than one in 10 million persons per year.

Nuclear Power and the Environment:
Questions and Answers (published by
the American Nuclear Society)

VERBS

Action, and the Choice of Style

Verbs act. Verbs move. Verbs do. Verbs strike, soothe, grin, cry, exasperate, decline, fly, hurt, and heal. Verbs make writing go, and they matter more to our language than any other part of speech.

Verbs give energy, if we use them with energy. We could have said, "Verbs are action. Verbs are motion. Verbs are doing." But if we had written the sentences in this second way, we would have written dull prose. We could have gone even further into dullness, and written, "Verbs are words that are characterized by action."

Try to use verbs that act. Yet we must realize what this advice implies. The implications involve commitment to a kind of thought that will not always be possible; and so the exhortation is relative and not absolute; sometimes you will need to write verbs that are less than active. If there are no synonyms, also there are no two sentences that mean the same thing but are different only in style. A change in style, however slight, is always a change in meaning, however slight. Is it, therefore, *possible* to make a stylistic generalization at all? Does it mean anything to ask people to use active verbs, when sometimes active verbs will not mean what people wish to say? The vagueness or approximateness in some weak constructions may represent accurately a reservation in the speaker's mind.

The generalization remains possible, with explanation and with room for exception. Both explanations and exceptions will follow in the sections on verbs and nouns, but let us start with a general explanation. Passives and weak verbs most of the time evade precision and commitment. Examples follow, in which weak verbs add static to statement, and in which passives avoid being wrong by evading definite statement. These habits fuzz our prose with bad brain fuzz. To recommend, in a book on style, that we use active forms of active verbs, is to recommend energy and clarity, definite statement and commitment.

Verbs with Nouns and Adjectives

Usually, a single verb is stronger and better than a strung-out verb-and-adjective or verb-and-noun combination. People say, "I am aware of this fact," or even, "I am cognizant of this situation," when they could have said, "I know it." In these examples, we have a weak verb and adjective followed by a noun that means little, but appears to end the sentence, to give the verb an object. The phrases mean something different from "I know it," but the difference in meaning is mere pomposity. "I am aware of the fact" differs from "I know it" because it shows us that the speaker thinks well of himself; he sounds like a professor trying to put down another professor who has tried to put him down. "I am cognizant of the situation" is so pompous it may sound ironic; it would usually fall from the lips, or leak from the pen, of someone diffident about his intellectual status, like a television executive.

Look out for the verbs be/is/are and has/have combined with nouns and adjectives. See if you do not gain by using the verb itself, clear and clean. "He looked outside and became aware of the fact that it was raining" revises easily into "He looked outside and saw that it was raining" or, more simply, "He looked outside. It was raining." Instead of "We had a meeting," try "We met." The meaning is different, slightly, but if the second phrase is accurate, we save three syllables and add energy to our prose; when we cut to the essential motion, we add vitality. Less is more, in prose as in architecture. Instead of "They were decisive about the question of . . . ," try "They decided to. . . ."

Now "to be decisive"—if we look at the insides of words—means something quite different from "to decide." The person who "is decisive" has vigor and intellectual intensity; he cuts through the uncertainties that surround a question, and makes a choice firmly and quickly. If you are describing a committee meeting in which, after long discussion, the members reached a consensus or took a vote and decided to do something, "they decided" is the clearest phrase to use. "They reached a decision" wastes words, probably; it does imply that it took some work "to arrive at the decision," which by itself would imply more ease, and less struggle, than "reached." If you feel that the meaning requires "reached" or "arrived," you must use the accurate word. But, certainly, in writing about the committee meeting described above, "they were decisive about . . ." would be misuse of words. They weren't decisive at all. They decided. Most of the time, when we use a wordy noun/adjective-verb phrase, we are merely trying to *sound* more complicated. Most of the time, the shade of meaning in "reached" or "arrived" is not needed. We use the longer phrase just to *seem* to be considering fine points. The sensible rule: Use the shorter, more direct verb ("they decided") except when the longer variation has a precision that your meaning requires. "They talked for two days about lowering the voting age, without coming to a conclusion. Then Senator Jensen returned from a junket. He spoke briefly. He was decisive. The measure carried by a two-thirds majority."

Verbs with Participles

The same advice applies to phrases that use verb forms ending in -ing (present participles). "They were meeting to discuss" can often become "They met to discuss," and "He is clearing his throat" becomes "He clears his throat." But the participle is different in meaning—it makes a different sort of time—and therefore it can be useful when we mean it. "She'll be comin' 'round the mountain" has more incipient motion in it than "She'll come 'round the mountain." Participles imply continuing action. Just be sure that you *intend* the difference, and are not just lazy. Apparently the mind finds it easier to be pale than to be colorful. Or maybe the mind finds it easier to avoid the extra vocabulary of verbs, sticking to "be" and "has" with nouns and adjectives. Whatever the reason, when we add little words like "is" and "has" to participles, adjectives, and nouns, usually we thin our prose into impalpability.

The Passive Voice

When most writers use the passive, they usually subtract meaning from their prose. We say, "a message was received," instead of "they" (or "I" or "you" or "he" or "she") "received a message." We suppress identity, which is a particular, and we put hazy distance between implied subject and definite action. The passive voice avoids responsibility, as we sometimes claim that "a dish was dropped in the kitchen," rather than name the dropper. It diminishes a sentence by omitting a doer. It can be politically useful: "Napalm was dropped yesterday on structures in a fire-free zone near the DMZ." Sometimes we use the passive from diffidence, or modesty, or false modesty, or all three. It waters the soup. We sound as if we wrote labels for medicine bottles. "Doses may be administered three times daily. Dosage recommended for adults is. . . ." So a depressed writer on a gray day, describing a scene, might say, "The tree was observed to be an elm. Leaves were seen falling. It was assumed that the season was autumn." Scientific prose uses the passive by convention, establishing an impersonal tone. Sometimes writers on nonscientific subjects achieve a pseudoscientific tone by using the passive.

Occasionally the passive is right, or unavoidable. Passives are used in a textbook whose author advises against passives.

> The author uses passives in the text.
> The text uses passives.
> Passives are used in the text.

In some contexts, the third sentence might be best. The second is most terse, but it involves a metaphor—the text must be compared to a person, if it *uses* something—which may weaken it. The first correctly says that the author does the using, but it would be intrusive in some contexts to state the subject when the subject is perfectly obvious; it would be overexplained, and wordy. It might be better to use the passive to avoid these other troubles, as the least of three evils.

Sometimes the passive is useful because we do not know the identity of the doer. The passive (especially if it is rare) can imply this ignorance, which may be part of the meaning of the sentence. Suppose this were the start of a story:

> He walked into his bedroom. Clothes lay in heaps on the floor. Dresser drawers lay upside down on the rug, their contents scattered.

It is a description of a scene, most of it in the active voice, with inanimate objects (clothes, dresser drawers) doing active things (lay, lay upside down). It is terse, but it implies no reason for the scene, and no response to it. The active voice in this passage is less meaningful than the passive would be:

> He walked into the room. Clothes were heaped on the floor. Dresser drawers were dumped on the rug, and their contents had been scattered.

The scene is the same. We still don't know who did it. But the passives (after the first sentence, which is active) imply that someone else, unknown, has done the damage. They only *imply* it, they do not *state* it, but the implication is real, and further implies some shock on his part. We sense that the second and third sentences are versions of what happens in his mind as he enters the room: "I've been robbed!" To make this last sentence active would sound artificial: "Someone has robbed me!" It would sound as if the writer were taking as *absolute* the injunction to avoid the passive, which is only a sensible, general rule.

Good writers use the passive for variety in sentence structure, too. Rarely, but they do. In a paragraph about two groups taking opposite sides on an issue, in which the sentences all have the active voice, the author looking for stylistic variety might insert a sentence, "Arguments were put forward, on both sides, which would make a goat blush." When you decide to use a passive for variety, only be certain that you are not using it for any of the reasons that make passives bad: diffidence, false modesty, evading responsibility, or imitating scientific respectability.

Particular Verbs

I have been writing all along as if there were two classes of verbs: strong ones and weak ones. Of course language is more complicated than that, and not only because sometimes weak is better than strong, as I have argued. Some strong verbs are stronger than others. "He moved" is stronger than "he was in motion." But in a context that admits it, we might say with greater strength, "he crept," or "he slid," or "he hurtled." We would almost always want to say "he crept" rather than "he moved, creeping." (A difference of meaning might, once, make the second phrase useful.) The first verbs I listed in the paragraph that starts this section are general verbs: do, move, act. The second series is particular, and more colorful. Energy lies often in small shades of difference, rather than in opposites like "she was in motion" and "she slithered."

Invisible Verbs

In the first chapter, we read academic jargon from the prospectus for a Ph.D. dissertation. Later in the prospectus, the candidate wrote a sentence in which he particularly misused verbs; in fact, he managed to write almost *without* verbs.

> Illustrative of what Kornhauser means by constraint imposed on professionals in organizations are the findings of Leo Meltzer in a survey of 3,084 physiologists in the United States.

The sentence has no strong and active verbs. "Means" is the closest. "Illustrative" is an adjective substituted for a verb. "Imposed" is a past participle that suppresses responsibility. "Are" is boring.

To rewrite the sentence in a language not far from the original, but with more vigor and clarity, we can simply cut and rearrange.

> Leo Meltzer questioned 3,084 physiologists in the United States; his findings illustrate Kornhauser's contention that organizations constrain professionals.

Maybe "surveyed" is more accurate than "questioned," but "surveyed" smells of jargon.

The last phrase of this revision may not mean what the original author had in mind. Did he mean that the institution imposed the constraint, or that something else, unnamed, chose people in organizations, rather than others, to impose restraint on? The ambiguity in the original passage is real, and serves no function; it is merely unclear. The second version is clearer, though without context it still raises questions. What is this constraint? What desires are held back? Does the author mean "constrain" as restraint or as compulsion? Does he mean all organizations—like YMCA's, universities, corporations, fraternities, bridge clubs, and nations— or specifically professional ones, like the American Association of University Professors, the Modern Language Association, or the American Medical Association? Clarity comes from vigor combined with detail. Verbs are the most vigorous parts of speech; by particularity, they add to detail.

False Color in Verbs

The search for particularity and color can become obvious, and the prose look silly. In the examples that follow, the faults do not lie in the verbs alone, but in the whole style. Verbs are at the center of the action in our prose, however, for good or for ill. In the play, *The Owl and the Pussycat,* a would-be novelist reads the first page of his manuscript to the girl who has invaded his apartment. When he starts by saying the sun "spat" on his protagonist, she flies into a rage. So should we. Men's action magazines are full of Methedrine prose, violence done to language in the name of violence. In a recent thriller called *A Clash of Hawks,* the author's second sentence reads,

> The 200-foot-high derrick was a black, latticed steel phallus raping the hot, virginal blue sky.

Tough writing is not the only kind of bad overwriting. Maybe pretty writing is worse. It is Liberace prose, and it can rely on verbs for its nasty work, too.

> Songbirds trilled out my window, vines curled at the eaves, and Spring drenched the day with gladness.

Often a beginning writer tries to make the verbs in dialogue too specific: "he whimpered," "she snapped." Almost always it looks too strenuous. We should use "said," or nothing at all, most of the time. The trick is energy with appropriateness. We may need to learn to do too much before we can learn to do it right. Newly wakened to verbs, one student wrote this passage in his next theme:

> The train slammed to a stop in the station. Steam vomited from all apertures. Passengers gushed through the barriers and hurtled into the night.

It was a useful exercise, because the student was searching through his mental dictionary for energetic verbs. The color was more vivid than the actions colored, like photographs in advertisements for food. Steam gushing out at the base of an engine is not *like* vomiting; "vomiting" is too sick and unpleasant and bad smelling a word; the writer uses it only for its power, and not for what it contributes to the picture. Though the general advice—to choose color over pallor, energy over lethargy—holds true, one matter overrides all others, in any discussion of style, and that is appropriateness: context is all.

Fancy Verbs

Some verbs are too fancy for normal use. Writers use them when they think their prose ought to wear fancy clothes. "Depict" is usually inferior to "paint" or "draw" or "describe." "He depicted a scene of unparalleled magnitude." (W. C. Fields/thesaurus talk again.) Maybe that means "he painted a big picture," or "he told a good story," or half a dozen other things, but its real meaning is its would-be fanciness. It is a sentence admiring itself in the mirror. "Emulate" would usually be fancy for "copy," "ascertain" for "make sure," and "endeavor" for "try."

Made-Up Verbs

Then there are the made-up words, neologisms, which sound fancy to the people who use them. When we are tempted to say "finalize," we would do better to say "end" or "finish." In general, we should avoid verbs made of an adjective and an -ize; "personalize" is another. Advertising and politics have created many crude verbs, sometimes using nouns as bases instead of adjectives; not long ago, we had to learn to pronounce "Vietnamization." Some good old English verbs end in -ize. "Scrutinize," deriving from the noun "scrutiny," is a useful verb. "Finalize," on the other hand, is used to sound fancier than "finish" or "end," to give false complexity to a simple act. Therefore it is bad style, pretending to be something that it isn't, a form of euphemism. The writer should search the language for the simplest and most direct way of saying and expressing, never making up a new word when an old one will do.

EXERCISES

1. Underline the weak verbs (verb-noun or verb-adjective or verb-participle combinations, invisible verbs, verbs lacking particularity) in these sentences. See if you can substitute strong verbs for those underlined. When you make a substitution, does the meaning of the sentence vary? Can you think of reasons for preferring the weaker verb combinations in any of the sentences?

a. She made the observation that German had been her minor in college.

b. We have endeavored to reach a conclusion that will be satisfactory.

c. We were just starting to sing when the door opened.

d. The committee has been meeting every day for a month.

e. I am trying to be healthy so that I will be playing tennis when I have arrived at eighty.

f. We had gotten around to the subject of getting good grades and got into an argument.

g. A different way of expressing the same idea is that having no commitment to activity we are engaged upon a course of activity lacking purpose.

h. We were in action right away, moving out into the field on our stomachs until we got to the river.

2. Here are five sentences containing passives. Underline the passive verbs, and then consider if any are necessary or useful passives. When the passive is objectionable, consider the reasons for objection, and revise the sentence so that passive becomes active.

a. Arabella was understood by her neighbors to have cornered the market in soybean futures.

b. People committed to excellence are sought after in the business community.

c. At the picketing sites on North Campus, GEO members were not allowed to use the restrooms.

d. My canoe tipped over, I was thrown out into the water, and I saw the MacDonalds ahead of me.

e. Remembering August with Emily in Poughkeepsie, and rereading her letter which arrived this morning, I gradually realized that I had been deceived.

3. Here are some fancy verbs. Find simpler verbs that would usually do better.

masticate
cogitate
commence
expectorate
perspire

4. Here is a list of verbs chosen for varieties of tone and degrees of color. With each of them, find alternatives, near synonyms, which might work better in a specific context. For an example, remember the differences between emulate/imitate/copy/ape discussed on pages 57–58. Make up a context for each of the verbs—listed and discovered—in which the verb feels appropriate.

> clutch
> exterminate
> rattle
> cook
> act

5. Look through your own writing—old themes or daily writing— and find a paragraph that can be improved by strengthening the verbs. Copy out the old version, and revise it. (You will find yourself changing other words as well as verbs; but pay closest attention to verbs.)

6. Here are five passages of prose. Underline the verbs, and discuss in class the quality of each verb.

a. John was the son of a prostitute and a naval officer. He lived with his mother until he was six, when he was transferred to his father's care. He was transported into a completely different world. His father, who had not married, sent him to a public school where he did well until, unexpectedly, he failed his university entrance exam. Thereupon he was drafted into the Navy, but failed to become an officer. His father, who was a very exacting man, had been somewhat upset by his son's failure at university level, but was much more upset by his failure to become an officer, and it drew from him the remark that he did not think he could be his son at all. When, in the next few months, John disgraced himself as a sailor in a number of ways, his father told him plainly that he was not his son any more, and that he now knew he never had been. He formally disowned him.

During his early months in the Navy, John was noted to get into states of anxiety, and it was on the grounds of anxiety neurosis that he had been turned down as an officer. Subsequently, however, his behaviour earned the label of psychopathic delinquent, and it was out of keeping with his "character" hitherto. When his father disowned him his deviance escalated to what was called an acute manic psychosis. His basic premise had become: *he could be anyone he wanted, merely by snapping his fingers.*

R. D. Laing, *Self and Others*

b. And she lifted her hands and danced again, to annul him, the light glanced on her knees as she made her slow, fine movements down the far side of the room, across the firelight. He stood away near the door in blackness of shadow, watching, transfixed. And with slow, heavy movements she swayed backwards and forwards, like a full ear of corn, pale in the dusky afternoon, threading before the firelight, dancing his non-existence, dancing herself to the Lord, to exultation.

D. H. Lawrence, *The Rainbow*

c. A machine gun lashed at him from across the river, and he ducked in his hole. In the darkness, it spat a vindictive white light like an acetylene torch, and its sound was terrifying. Croft was holding himself together by the force of his will. He pressed the trigger of his gun and it leaped and bucked under his hand. The tracers spewed wildly into the jungle on the other side of the river.

Norman Mailer, *The Naked and the Dead*

d. The service shall be delivered in the following manner: Immediately before commencing to serve, the Server shall stand with both feet at rest behind the base line, and within the imaginary continuation of the center mark and side line of the singles court. The Receiver may stand wherever he pleases behind the service line on his own side of the net. The server shall then throw the ball into the air and strike it with his racket before it hits the ground. Delivery shall be deemed complete at the moment the racket strikes the ball.

How Service Is Delivered, Official Tennis Rules

e. Weighing the half-pounds of flour, excluding the scoop, and depositing them dust-free into the thin paper sacks held a simple kind of adventure for me. I developed an eye for measuring how full a silver-looking ladle of flour, mash, meal, sugar or corn had to be to push the scale indicator over to eight ounces or one pound. When I was absolutely accurate our appreciative customers used to admire: "Sister Henderson sure got some smart grandchildrens." If I was off in the Store's favor, the eagle-eyed women would say, "Put some more in that sack, child. Don't you try to make your profit offa me."

Maya Angelou, *I Know Why the Caged Bird Sings*

NOUNS

Particularity and Choosing a Style

If verbs supply the energy that makes prose go, nouns are its body. Without nouns, nothing would be doing the going. Nouns are the simplest parts of speech, the words least tricky to use. Nouns are the names of things, "things" in the broadest sense: table, elm, Nancy, rain, noun, Centerville, nation, hunger, nine o'clock.

Many of the generalizations that apply to verbs apply to nouns also. We prefer as a rule the specific, the sensuous, the strong, the simple, and the colorful over the abstract, the general, the polysyllabic, and the fancy. We prefer "elm" to "tree," "Nancy" to "girl," and "nine o'clock" to "evening." The more particular the noun, the clearer the pictures we make, and the more accurate we can be in representing feelings. When a student wrote,

> I remembered a group of flowers that grew on some land near a relative's house . . .

he changed it to,

> I remembered a patch of daisies that grew on a meadow near my Cousin Annie's farm . . .

and the particularity is all gain. The first example was not bad style, but it was pale prose. The second by comparison is vivid.

But we generalize "as a rule," and we must express reservations. Sometimes the more general noun is more accurate and honest than the specific one. From a distance, you see "a man" or "a woman," not "a sophomore" or "a mechanic." "Town" may be more appropriate, in the right context, than "Centerville," though it is less specific. We must keep in mind the injunction to be specific; but, as ever, we must be wary that our injunctions do not lead us into absurdity. A student revised some daily writing into,

> On Tuesday afternoon, October thirteenth, I read a sentence half-way down the first page of *War and Peace* which . . .

Maybe in a particular context, such extreme specificity would be useful, but usually it would sound overly precise.

Also, we must remember again that the advice to cultivate one kind of style, at the expense of another, means thinking or seeing things in special ways. *A change in style, however slight, is always a change in meaning, however slight.* For some types of writing, like a scientific summary, or a paper in philosophy, an injunction to "Be particular!" and "Avoid abstraction!" is worse than useless; it is destructive.

> The existence theorem states, "To prove the existence of a something one must first present evidence of that something and its existence acceptable to other minds." The nonexistence theorem states, "As long as one assumes the nonexistence of a something one will assume that the signals from the something

either do not exist, are noise, are created in another human mind, or come from some mindless process in nature." Therefore, if an unknown mind without a visible, detectable body sends signals, we ignore them, repress memories of having received them, attribute them to noise, or attribute them to a mindless but systematically varying source, or say that they are the results of faulty operation of the observer, i.e., projections from the observer's own mind.

> John Cunningham Lilly, *The Mind of the Dolphin*

Lilly is writing a vigorous argumentative prose, which must be abstract. So must books about prose style, for that matter.

The wise advice is simply to be as particular as the context allows us. Too often, we are vague and general, when we would say much more by discovering the concrete. Instead of saying,

> When it got cold the animals looked for shelter.

we could convey much more by a particularity.

> In October there was frost; the sheep huddled in one corner of the barn for warmth, the cattle in another.

Abstract and Particular

Degrees of difference separate the noun at an extreme of abstraction from the noun at an extreme of particularity. S. I. Hayakawa, adapting Alfred Korzybski, speaks of moving up a ladder of abstraction, climbing from the most particular level, gradually discarding particularities, and arriving into the thin air around the highest abstraction. His example is clear.

> 1. The cow known to science ultimately consists of atoms, electrons, etc., according to present-day scientific inference. Characteristics ... are infinite at this level and ever changing. This is the *process level*.
> 2. The cow we perceive is not the word, but the object of experience, that which our nervous system abstracts (selects) from the totality that constitutes the process-cow. Many of the characteristics of the process-cow are left out.
> 3. The word "Bessie" ... is the *name* we give to the object of perception of level 2. The name *is not* the object; it merely *stands for* the object and omits references to many of the characteristics of the object.

4. The word "cow" stands for the characteristics we have abstracted as common to cow_1, cow_2, cow_3, . . . , cow_n. Characteristics peculiar to specific cows are left out.

5. When Bessie is referred to as "livestock," only those characteristics she has in common with pigs, chickens, goats, etc., are referred to.

6. When Bessie is included among "farm assets" reference is made only to what she has in common with all other saleable items on the farm.

7. When Bessie is referred to as an "asset," still more of her characteristics are left out.

8. The word "wealth" is at an extremely high level of abstraction, omitting *almost* all reference to the characteristics of Bessie.

The number of rungs on this ladder is limited only by our ingenuity, but I think we can most usefully distinguish three main degrees—the abstract, the general, and the particular. These notions are always relative, and can always be expanded. Within "the particular," we can subdivide into greater or lesser particularity. Take "animal, dog, spaniel." One might go further into particularity by adding a proper noun, or age, or color, or by naming a breed of spaniel—all requiring more words. One might go higher in generality to "organism" or sideways into scientific classification with "quadruped." These three-somes can be quite relative. We can list three words which are all abstract but which become more nearly specific: "emotion, love, lust." The writer could use "lust" not as one of the seven deadly sins, but as an embodiment of the general "love"; he might have said "desire" or "eros," but "lust" seemed clearer.

The more abstract a noun, the more difficult it is to use well. Words like "emotion" (or "love," for that matter) or "courage" or "hatred" or "responsibility." To make these nouns work, you must provide a context with anecdote or analogy; you must put flesh on the bones. Usually an adjective in front of an abstraction does not do the work. The abstraction is lazy, retrieved by the writer from the attic of Big Ideas, and the adjective strives to do all the work; but adjectives themselves often are weak, and so we have two weaklings failing to budge the door that one strong noun could burst open. "Love" is thin and airy; it is pretty, but what is it about? Our affection for a pet salamander? The grandfather for his granddaughter? Bert's obsession with the character of Charles Dickens? Mark and Nancy in the Oldsmobile? Married affection? "Love" is a grab bag of possibilities, only a bit less abstract than "emotion" or "feeling." If we modify it with the adjective "intense," we narrow its possibilities a little, but we do not really localize it. If we speak of "young love," we are more particular—and yet we move toward cliché. Many clichés are adjective-noun combinations in which the adjective is a desperate, though habitual, attempt to rescue a bland abstraction with a particular adjective; "blind faith," for example.

Abstractions are usually lazy. The writer finds it easier to label the general category of a feeling than to search out the particulars that embody the feeling. Sight, taste, smell, touch, hearing carry feeling from writer to reader—not concepts. (And most writers using abstractions, we notice instantly, are not using concepts as a philosopher does, but vaguely and inaccurately.) Usually, we talk best about "love" when we do not use the word at all. If we use "Nancy," and "Centerville," and "a 1969 Pontiac," and "rain," and "nine o'clock," and connect them with strong verbs, the reader may know what we mean by the big hazy word "love"—in this time and in this place.

"Time" and "place" are abstractions. Are they used appropriately here? Sometimes the abstract affords a setting for the concrete, as a black velvet background shows up diamonds. In other contexts, instead of "time" and "place" we would want to use more specific words— steering wheel, September, elm, Long Lake Road.

Abstractions: Beginnings and Endings

An abstraction can be explained by a context or an anecdote. Some abstraction or generalization is necessary to any conceptual or argumentative writing. Only fiction, poetry, and autobiography can be free of it, and they do not always stay free. When we revise an essay, we should look most carefully to eliminate abstractions at two points—beginnings and endings. Frequently, we introduce a subject with an abstraction, "I am going to tell a story that illustrates inequality," and then we tell a story that illustrates inequality. If the illustration is clear, the introductory abstraction was unnecessary; what is more, it was probably distracting. When you announce that you are going to tell a funny joke before you tell it, you take the humor away. Let the idea of inequality arise in the reader's mind—by name or not—from your anecdote, and it will be much more powerful. Telling the reader the meaning of what he is going to hear bullies him; he is likely to resist.

Similarly, we often trail off an anecdote with an abstraction. Having told a perfectly clear story, we end, "which is an illustration of the inequality so prevalent today." Don't nudge your reader in the ribs, saying, "In case you didn't get it, this is what I mean." We summarize abstractly because we lack confidence in our own writing, and in the reader's intelligence. Of course some stories need interpreting; they are therefore usually less valuable material. If the road is clear, do not put up road markers; they are good only for stumbling over.

Invisible Nouns

So far, we have been talking about degrees of particularity and color, and we have admitted that some prose needs abstractions. The Preacher could not have said, "All is vanity," if there had been an enforced commandment against abstractions. But some nouns are almost always useless. These nouns are invisible. When someone says, "The snow is gray in color," What is the phrase "in color" doing? It doesn't do anything for meaning or particularity. Maybe it has a connotation that reflects on the speaker, though not on the snow. Maybe it contains a message informing us that the speaker is precise, academic, and pompous.

Words like "nature" and "character," which have perfectly good uses, turn up invisibly in pale prose. Probably the snow was gray in color because of the urban nature of the environment, and the frigid character of the weather.

We use invisible nouns with adjectives—much as we use invisible verbs like "be" and "do" and "has" with adjectives or nouns—to make a sentence *sound* grander than it really is, or because we lack the vocabulary. Whatever the reason, we abuse the language. Some other nouns we render invisible: "sense," "kind," "action," "situation," "respect," "regard," "case," and "element." Look at this piece of prose from the annual report of a large corporation:

> The President is pleased to report that, despite the unusual nature of the fiscal situation in the past twelve months, earnings have risen substantially above the margin foreseen by the Treasurer's Report of March, 1971. In a marketing sense, the profitable character of the corporation proved itself under trying circumstances.

"Circumstances" is another invisible noun—at least invisible as it is used here.

Making Bad Nouns from Verbs

The sensible writer chooses the plain noun, if it is adequate, over the fancy one, and he chooses the old noun rather than making up a new one. On page 79 I mentioned the verb "finalize," which had been wrenched out of an adjective: it has been wrenched further into a noun: now and then we run across "finalization," when "end" or "finish" or maybe "finality" would do. Bad stylists know no limits. "Scrutiny" is a fine noun; "scrutinize" is a necessary and traditional verb. But recently a young man wrote on an application form that he submitted documents "for your scrutinization." The word means nothing more than "scrutiny"; it must have sounded more respectable to this writer.

Or maybe his vocabulary failed him. He remembered the verb "scrutinize" but forgot the noun "scrutiny." So he made up a new noun out of the verb. When you are tempted to make a new noun from a verb, go to the dictionary first. You know "unify"; when tempted to create "unifization," go to the dictionary and you will find "unity" and "unification"—and clarity, and a more eloquent prose.

Fancy Nouns

Reading bad prose, we find thousands of examples of pomposity or fanciness, either neologisms like "scrutinization," or polysyllabic alternatives to simple words, like "domicile" for "house" or "cessation" for "end." These words parallel verbs like "masticate," substituted for "chew." The fanciness may arise from diffidence or ignorance or pretension or whatever. The result is the same; fanciness separates the thing described and the mental act of perceiving it. Feelings keep their distance. It is by fancy abstractions and by clichés that Orwell's Communist professor is able to discuss without feelings the murder of innocent people.

Revising Nouns

In revising, we should look for the lazy abstraction, as well as the invisible noun, the neologism, and the merely fancy noun, and remove them when we find them. Removing them leaves a hole, which we can fill with other nouns, or with phrases, to specify and bring down to earth the airy word we started with. Lazy abstractions are like clichés and jargon—and the three are usually discovered together—because they are instantly available to the tongue; they lie heaped together with clichés in the foreroom of the brain; we do not have to search for

them with our intelligence, or dream for them with our imaginations.
Here is a passage from a paper.

> Financial problems were coming to a head in my family last
> spring and we didn't know if my sister and I could have the
> benefit of higher education. Then my grandfather got the sur-
> prise of his life when a large amount of money came his way
> when he least expected it. He got a sum from the VA which he
> didn't know was coming him. Through his generosity, we were
> enabled to arrange payment for tuition.

As usual with faulty prose, the faults do not lie in one part of speech
alone. Some hunks of cliché are ready-made—"coming to a head,"
"financial problems," "benefit of higher education," "surprise of his
life," "when he least expected it," "arrange payment"—and combine
with a dozen other signs of lazy thinking and evasion of feeling. Think
of the emotional reality—the anxiety, the jubilation in a family—which
these phrases obscure with their familiar haze. Instead of "financial
problems," let us forget euphemism and talk about being in debt, or
having no money, or losing a job, or payments coming due; *anything*
more particular. The ultimate particularity would probably sound as
cold as a balance sheet (outstanding indebtedness $27,429.31; assets
. . .) but we know a median lies between the bland, evasive euphemism
of "financial problems" and the sterile figures. The median is actual
circumstances and anecdotes; the median is stronger than the extremes.

Certainly "go to college" or "go on in school" is preferable to "have
the benefit of higher education." Then instead of speaking generally of
"surprise"—an abstraction that takes the surprise out of surprise—why
not show it happening? Have the grandfather opening the envelope, or
picking up the telephone. Use dialogue. Or use some new analogy to
express his feelings, instead of a useless cliché. He could be as surprised
as someone who finds a pearl in his clam chowder. How much is "a
large amount of money" or "a sum"? Both seem genteel evasions for
saying a specific figure, like "a check for $5,000." But perhaps it seems
crass to the writer to name the figure. Then at least some phrase should
qualify the idea of numbers, so that the reader can place the figure
between five hundred and five million dollars, or judge the amount of
money by what it can do: ". . . received a check for enough money to
send us both through school."

The phrase "through his generosity" includes an unnecessary, labeling abstraction. We do not need to be told that he is generous. When we are bullied with the notion, we resist it. Maybe the old man just wants to boast that his grandchildren go to college. Then the last part of the paragraph has a pair of general nouns and a fancy verb in place of simpler and more natural language. It is pretentious to write "we were enabled to arrange payment for tuition" when we could write, "we were able to pay for college."

The student, in fact, revised the passage into:

> My family was so far in debt last spring that we didn't think my sister and I could go to college. My father had borrowed money to get a fish and chips franchise, and lost it all in six months. My sister and I both took jobs in the summer. I was working twelve hours a day in the mill, and when I came home at night I was so mad and tired I just drank beer and watched the box. Then my grandfather telephoned my father and I saw my father suddenly start crying. The VA had just sent my grandfather a check he didn't know was coming, and it was enough to pay for us both. That night, we bought a bottle of Four Roses.

He changed verbs and other parts of speech, but the revision of his nouns is most useful of all.

EXERCISES

1. Write a paragraph with a highly abstract title—"love," "idealism," "education," "boredom," naïveté," "courage"—which does not contain the title word, but which embodies a particular occasion of the word. Read your paragraph aloud in class, and see if the class recognizes the abstraction.

2. Take each of these nouns and find two other words to go with it, one more general and one more specific. If you can't find a word, use a short phrase.

rodent	cat
student	butter
lily	book
day	spaghetti
business	sports car

3. Collect four or five clichés that combine an abstract noun with an adjective, like "blind faith," "basic need," and "conflicting desires." See how many you can find alternative words and phrases for, always realizing that a different context will require a different substitute for each of these filler phrases. Thus, "basic needs" in seven

contexts might well be revised into seven distinct phrases. Provide brief contexts, if you need them for clarity.

4. In these sentences, underline the nouns that fail by invisibility, imprecision, fanciness, neologism, or over-abstraction. Invent substitutes that improve the sentences.

    a. I chewed the food without swallowing it.

    b. What is the nature of your complaint?

    c. Religion, says Harvey Cox, has undergone privatization.

    d. When I think about my high school, I remember the love I felt for my Spanish teacher and the other feelings I felt for other people.

5. Underline the nouns in these passages, and label each as abstract or general or particular, according to the context. In class, compare your results with those of other students. Be prepared to argue. These distinctions are often tenuous, but discussing the distinctions will sharpen your eye for the insides of words.

    a. Cultures, likewise, are more than the sum of their traits. We may know all about the distribution of a tribe's form of marriage, ritual dances, and puberty initiations, and yet understand nothing of the culture as a whole which has used these elements to its own purpose. This purpose selects from among the possible traits in the surrounding regions those which it can use, and discards those which it cannot. Other traits it recasts into conformity with its demands. The process of course need never be conscious during its whole course, but to over-look it in the study of the patternings of human behaviour is to re-nounce the possibility of intelligent interpretation.

                Ruth Benedict, *Patterns of Culture*

    b. We may therefore entertain the hypothesis that formal logic and the law of contradiction are the rules whereby the mind submits to operate under general categories of repression. As with the concept of time, Kant's categories of rationality would then turn out to be the categories of repression. And conversely, "dialectical" would be the struggle of the mind to circumvent repression and make the uncon-scious conscious. But by the same token, it would be the struggle of the mind to overcome the split and conflict within itself.

                Norman O. Brown, *Life Against Death*

    c. It was formerly the custom in our village, when a poor debtor came out of jail, for his acquaintances to salute him, looking through their fingers, which were crossed to represent the grating of a jail window. "How do you do?" My neighbors did not thus salute me, but looked first at me, and then at one another, as if I had returned from a long journey.

Henry David Thoreau, "On the Duty of Civil Disobedience"

d. At 15,000 feet, its best operating height, the Kittyhawk IA could fly at a maximum speed of only 354 mph and climb to that height in 8.3 minutes, a longer time than the AGM2 Zero took to reach 20,000 feet. Empty weight was 6,350 pounds, normal loaded weight 8,280 pounds, which was the load carried into combat without drop tank or bombs, and maximum permissible weight was 9,200 pounds. Service ceiling was 29,000 feet. The IA climbed best at lower altitudes, but its best rate was only about 2,100 feet per minute at 5,000 feet.

Pacific Hawk

e. One Hundredth Street was dark, filled with life. I turned off Second Avenue into the street, searching for Number 321. I passed the people, and they were dark too, as seemed appropriate for those who lived in this block. For a moment I imagined that if white men lived here very long, they too would turn dark, by laws as irrefutable as the one that would make them dark if they lived on the beach in Florida—except that here the darkness would not be caused by the sun but by the lack of it.

I passed the dark scar of a vacant lot, blistered with refuse, and came to a building that looked like most of the others. The number was 321. I pushed through the door that was patched with raw board where glass once was, and started up the steps. There were voices, in Spanish, and sounds of frying. An odor like dead cats possessed the stairway. On the third floor I knocked at the door of the front apartment, and one of the girls greeted me.

Dan Wakefield, *Island in the City*

f. In 1945, the 45,000 dead at Sétif could pass unnoticed; in 1947, the 90,000 dead in Madagascar could be the subject of a simple paragraph in the papers; in 1952, the 200,000 victims of the repression in Kenya could meet with relative indifference. This was because the international contradictions were not sufficiently distinct. Already the Korean and Indo-Chinese wars had begun a new phase. But it is above all Budapest and Suez which constitute the decisive moments of this confrontation.

Frantz Fanon, *The Wretched of the Earth*

g. It is a very small office, most of it taken up by a desk. The desk is placed smack in front of the window—not that it could have been placed anywhere else; this window looks out on the daylight landscape of Bergman's movies. It was gray and glaring the first day I was there, dry and fiery. Leaves kept falling from the trees, each silent descent bringing a little closer the long, dark, Swedish winter. The forest Bergman's characters are always traversing is outside this window and the ominous carriage from which they have yet to escape is still among the properties. I realized, with a small shock, that the landscape of Bergman's mind was simply the landscape in which he had grown up.

James Baldwin, *Nobody Knows My Name*

6. In the passages just quoted: (a) Discuss each author's use of verbs, and how it suits the nouns he uses. (b) Can you find places that might be improved? Try improving one phrase in each passage.

ADJECTIVES AND ADVERBS AND OTHER MODIFIERS
Qualities and Choosing a Style

Modifiers—adjectives, adverbs, participles, and sometimes other words—give quality to nouns and verbs. "The *huge, green* lion"; "leapt *slowly.*" Adjectives and adverbs *modify* nouns and verbs. Participles and sometimes nouns work in the same way: "the *grinning* lifeboat," "the hypothesis *constructed* on Thursday," "*rock candy* mountain," "*mouse* music." Used well, modifiers create distinctions in meaning, and add particularity to the particular. They discriminate and add precision.

But modifiers give us the greatest trouble of all parts of speech. The beginning writer, especially when he tries to write colorfully, may stuff his style into obesity with a diet of fat adjectives.

Overuse or misuse of adjectives and adverbs—*even particular ones*—makes prose weak and lethargic. Because they are qualities rather than actions or things, adjectives and adverbs are inherently weaker parts of speech. Yet once more, choosing a style *means* something. A *change in style, however slight, is a change in meaning, however slight.*

To choose vigor in writing is usually to work with fewer modifiers. A few great writers, like Faulkner, use as many adjectives as any beginner—but use them well, and with great originality. Most of the best writers use them sparingly and then make them count. We are not saying that adjectives are unimportant to writing. They are important. But verbs and nouns carry the sentence; if they take charge properly, they liberate adjectives, adverbs, and other modifiers to do their proper work, to make the exact final discriminations necessary to honesty and fullness of meaning.

The Adjective and the Cliché

In our minds we associate adjectives and nouns in pairs. Our minds are not only computer dictionaries, they are junkyards of cliché. If we think "grass," we probably think "green." We move in worn tracks. If we think "snow," we think "white." These weary associations are not really thinking; they are automatic responses to stimuli. The more ourselves we can be, the less we will resemble a machine. If we remember more closely the grass and the snow we are describing, we will describe it precisely, out of our own memories, not out of the sad memory bank of other people's words. We might find an unexpected adjective for grass that is accurate for the grass at that place and that time. We might think of "harsh grass." Or we might not describe the grass at all, or we might describe it in a clause or in a whole sentence. But we must avoid the description that repeats familiar association. Only the distinct particular takes our attention. Green snow is news.

Other nouns summon their cousin adjectives by bookish associations. The word "sentinel," for many of us, carries with it the adjective "lonely"; "the lonely sentinel" is a cliché. Some of these combinations become comical from overuse or inherent absurdity, like "inscrutable Oriental." Others have sources not so bookish: "responsible citizen," "gracious living." Whenever you use an adjective that sounds habitual to its noun, try omitting the adjective, or recasting the phrase. In avoiding cliché, we have to *think*. We have to decide what we mean by a phrase like "fundamental truth."

The Modifier That Weakens the Noun

An adjective gives us the noun's quality or type: *white* snow. An adverb relates to a verb in the same way: he grinned *happily*. But each of these examples would be bad style in most contexts. In each, the modifier diminishes the word it should strengthen. "Snow" is whiter than "white snow." "Snow" is white in the brain's computer-dictionary, so why do we need to color it in our sentence unless we are suggesting its opposite? To say "white snow" must bring to mind snow that is gray with dirt. At a moment in a description, this suggestion might be just what the writer wanted: "White snow fell, that morning, on the trash of the old city." The contrast is part of the meaning; "white" takes its place, modifying "snow," because of the later words "trash" and "city." But most of the time, when a writer adds "white" to "snow," he subtracts from his sentence. He adds "white" in an uneasy search for particularity; he lacks confidence in the insides of the word "snow." The adjective overinsists on a quality already firm in the word.

If we know that the character grinned, must we be told that he "grinned happily"? It can only bring to mind that he *might* have been grinning unhappily, which is a nasty thought; the author reassures us that this supposition is not so, but without the reassurance, there would have been no supposition.

A beginning writer often goes through stages with adjectives, and different people have different problems with them. With some beginners, all adjectives are predictable.

> It was a long trip from the high mountains of the frozen north to the desert wastes of sunny Arizona, but it was highly educational and well worth while.

Or remember Jim Beck's original theme on going to college.

> Education is of paramount importance to today's youth. No one can underestimate the importance of higher education. It makes us well-rounded individuals and . . .

The problem is not primarily adjectives and adverbs, but thinking (or not thinking) in the old tracks.

Modifiers as Weak Intensives

We misuse adjectives and adverbs as weak intensifiers. We say "she moved gracefully" when we might say with more gusto that "she danced" or "she swept" or "she glided." We use vague adjectives in place of specific ones or in place of clauses that could add color and precision. We say "a tremendous amount"—when "amount" is vague and "tremendous" is a weak and unspecific intensifier—or "really huge," when we might say "ten million" or "as long as a supertanker." Here the specific number or the comparison carries color; the precision is one of feeling, not of dimensions.

Automatic Adjectives

Another misuse of adjectives and adverbs, a more advanced or sophisticated misuse, appears in writers when they suddenly appreciate bright colors in writing, and appears frequently when we begin to write stories and poems. In this misuse, the symptom is not cliché but multiplicity. Nearly every noun carries its adjective, like a tote bag, and every verb wears an adverb for a cape. The style is flashy and overdressed. Here is part of a poem from a creative writing class.

> I woke suddenly from a ghost-ridden dream
> of old women, to find myself wandering vaguely
> on the far edges of the raw city where white skulls tipped crazily
> in the western sky, and dirty children ran by
> to the cave shelters of abandoned cars . . .

The lines are improved by mechanically stripping them of modifiers. Is anything lost? Yes. "Abandoned" is necessary to the emotion in "abandoned cars." If it is merely "cars" that are "shelters," they could be comfortable, middle-class vehicles in which one drives to the supermarket with one's mother. The "abandoned" makes the children take "shelter" in something like a dump.

Certainly "old women" is different from "women." The phrase is altered by leaving out the adjective; perhaps we should restore "old." But the other modifiers are well exterminated. "Suddenly" does nothing but make the line move less quickly. "Ghost-ridden" does little to intensify "dream," and what it does, the later image of the skulls does better; also, hyphenated adjectives are usually bad; John Heath-Stubbs, an English poet, says that one should always be cautious of hyphenated names: it means that the lineage of one of the families is not too sound. In "ghost-ridden," what does "ridden" mean? Is the author really using the insides of the word? Does he know what the inside *is*?

"Wandering" includes "vaguely" the way "snow" includes "white." "Edges" are necessarily "far." "Raw" seems to add something to city, and perhaps the author would want to keep it, but the word adds little to the poem except a harshness that is better expressed elsewhere (in "skulls tipped" and "children ran by to the shelters of abandoned cars"). And it adds a metaphor that connects with nothing else in the poem. When you call a city "raw," you are making a metaphor; since cities are not culinary objects; they are in reality neither "raw" nor "cooked." When we call a city raw we are comparing it to a steak or a carrot or an egg; "uncooked" is an inevitable inside of the word "raw." But nothing else in the poem comes from the kitchen. The metaphor in "raw" is dropped, unused because the author was unaware that he was using a metaphor. He was using "raw" conventionally, as in "raw deal" and "raw material"—without paying attention to its insides. In a poem, the experienced reader absorbs the insides, and is disturbed by the dead and unfulfilled metaphor. Let us omit the adjective "raw."

"Skulls" are "white" enough without calling them so. If skulls are tipping in the sky, we don't need an elbow in our ribs commenting "crazily." This adverb appears to specify the action "tipped"—but would you be able to distinguish between a skull that was tipping crazily and one that was tipping sanely? Really, "crazily" describes nothing; it testifies only to craziness in an image that is already crazy.

"Western" in the context created by these lines adds nothing to speak of. West is sunset and death, perhaps, but here it is mostly a pretty noise and a useless specificity. "Dirty" does nothing for "children" that is not done better by verbs and nouns (and by the "abandoned" modifier in the spare version). "By" together with "to" is overly prepositional, wordy. And "cave" adds an image or a metaphor that clutters the final line. It is harsh and moving to find that "shelters" for these children are "abandoned cars." This juxtaposition elicits the emotion. To compare (by way of an adjective) the shelters to caves is to confuse the feeling, and to drag in another world of comparisons, like cavemen, Neanderthals, and fur clothing.

Here the general noun "shelter" seems to me to work better than the more specific noun "cave," which is used as an adjective. But a good argument could support choosing "cave" over "shelter," making the last line, "to the caves of abandoned cars." We could argue that the associations of "cave" include darkness, and that the primitive world (cavemen) makes a strong contrast with the automobile. Whichever word you prefer, "cave" or "shelter," one thing seems clear: either word by itself is better than two words together—"cave shelter," or "sheltering cave," if we wanted to write it that way. The modifier belongs to the same world as the noun—caves are like shelters are like caves—and so adds nothing but the slight confusion of its difference. The noun alone is preferable, here as everywhere, unless the modifier adds something new to a noun that is already precise.

The poet was at a stage in his writing when he used a modifier automatically with every noun and verb. The modifiers were not predictable; the author was past the stage of clichés, or, more accurately, he was at a stage where he could cut them out before he brought his work to class. But he was diffident about his nouns and his verbs. His nouns and his verbs were doing their jobs well, but he lacked confidence in them. And so, to protect the poor things, he sent each of them to kindergarten with an adjective holding its hand.

When he revised it, the poem read:

> I woke from a dream
> of old women, to find myself wandering
> on the edges of the city
> where skulls tipped
> in the sky, and children ran
> to the shelters of abandoned cars . . .

Here only two modifiers remain from the thirteen in the original version. Certainly the spare revision is better writing, and it was accomplished wholly by deleting modifiers.

Nouns as Modifiers

In the phrase "cave shelter," "cave" was a noun used as a modifier. English uses participles and nouns as modifiers—"sheltering cave," as well as "cave shelter"—with the same dangers, and the same opportunities, which attend plain adjectives. Use them with the same cautions in mind.

It is an advantage of the English language that its grammar is not rigid. In some languages, a noun would have to undergo respelling before it could be used as an adjective. English has a reputation among languages for adaptability and looseness. It can accept change. And because it accepts change, in speech and writing, the writer or the speaker can make shades of meaning more precise. Using nouns as modifiers, he can say "house party," "religion committee," "death wish."

He can also say "this type grammar," or—as in Bergen Evans' example of tediously multiplied nouns-as-modifiers—". . . he absconded with the River Street fire house Christmas Eve party funds." Because English lacks rigidity, it is subject to chaos and disorganization. "Type" is frequently a filler-noun, and when we use it as a modifier we make even less sense with it than we normally do. With Bergen Evans' example, as with too many sentences that are seriously intended, the proliferation of nouns as modifiers creates heaviness and awkwardness.

Be careful when you use nouns as modifiers. Sociologists are guiltiest of abusing this device. One hears of the "city group research effort." By the time one reaches the third of these noun-modifiers, one begins to feel afloat in a sea of possibilities. What will go with what? It is as if one were suddenly cast adrift in a Chinese sentence, with no inflexions, and with no connectives, and with no tense or number. Instead, confine yourself to one or two noun-modifiers in a row.

Thus phrases are often two nouns that might eventually become one compound noun, like "rain storm" or "wheel barrow" becoming "rainstorm" and "wheelbarrow." When the combination is more unusual, you have the opportunity to make an original contribution. The precedents include such a great phrase as Gerard Manley Hopkins' "Carrion Comfort."

Using Modifiers Well

Ernest Hemingway is known for using adjectives and adverbs sparingly. Let us look once more at the passage that begins "In Another Country."

In the fall the war was always there, but we did not go to it any more. It was cold in the fall in Milan and the dark came very early. Then the electric lights came on, and it was pleasant along the streets looking in the windows. There was much game hanging outside the shops, and the snow powdered on the fur of the foxes and the wind blew their tails. The deer hung stiff and heavy and empty, and small birds blew in the wind and the wind turned their feathers. It was a cold fall and the wind came down from the mountains.

Hemingway says, "the war," not "the long war" or "the distant war" or "the bloody, maiming, killing, useless, horrid, revolting war." He uses "always" and "any more" as adverbs in his simple predicates. "Cold" is an adjective in the second sentence; "electric" is necessary to lights, at a time when electric lights were new; in a country at war they seemed especially unwarlike; "pleasant" is an adjective as restrained as the verbs "was" and "go." Then the eye of the paragraph turns away from restrained thoughts of war, and looks at the dead animals that substitute for dead soldiers; right away the verbs and nouns become stronger and more particular: "game," "shops," "powdered." Then the adjectives, exact and strong, come marching in: "stiff and heavy and empty." The last is especially vigorous. The adjectives used sparingly are used strongly and well.

Let us apply the same standards to the passage quoted before from a story by John Updike.

All the warm night the secret snow fell so adhesively that every twig in the woods about their little rented house supported a tall slice of white, an upward projection which in the shadowless gloom of early morning lifted depth from the scene, made it seem Chinese, calligraphic, a stiff tapestry hung from the gray sky, a shield of lace interwoven with black thread.

Updike is sometimes condemned by critics for overwriting, for self-indulgence in description, for too much prettiness. Can you find anything here to back up such a charge? We can admire a writer, or a passage of his writing, and still find flaws.

What good does the word "secret" do us? It adds a little to the meaning—a kind of coziness—but to me the word seems there mostly to be pretty. I would like the line better if it read, "all the warm night the snow fell so adhesively. . . ." "Warm" is connected to "adhesively," but "warm" would be stronger if as an adjective it were more isolated; if the next noun, "snow," did not carry its adjective also. Then later, in one phrase after another, each noun takes one adjective, and although each adjective is defensible in itself, the effect is monotonously pretty: "tall slice," "upward projection," "shadowless gloom" "early morning." The mixture tastes too sweet. Rearranging clauses, putting an adjective after a noun instead of before it, putting two adjectives with one noun and none with the next—any number of minor reworkings could improve the passage.

The modifier in exposition or argument can help you or hurt you, just as in poetry and fiction. E. B. White, in a brief essay on schools, says that he always went to public ones; by contrast, he says, "my wife was unacquainted with public schools, never having been exposed (in early life) to anything more public than the washroom of Miss Winsor's." The sentence includes several modifiers—"unacquainted," "public," "exposed," "early," and "public" again—and yet it has vigor and clarity. The words express light disdain for the snobbism that White associates with private schools. The verb phrase "was unacquainted with" is preferable to alternatives like "knew nothing about" because "acquainted" is a word we use in social contexts: "No, I am not acquainted with that person." In the small world of White's sentence, the past participle wears a monocle and looks down at the peasants. "Exposed (in early life)" suggests that public schools are a contagious disease, like measles. And the parenthesis "(in early life)" has a mock formality that agrees with the medical metaphor.

But the adjective with which White plays the best trick is "public," which he uses twice: "anything more public than the washroom of Miss Winsor's," "Public" then becomes associated with public lavatories; we wrinkle our nose in disdain. At "Miss Winsor's"—the name sounds snobbish—of course the lavatory would be spotless and relatively private. What's more, it would not be a lavatory, john, W.C., or even bathroom; it would be a "washroom." By a *turn* on the adjective "public"—from schools to implied lavatories—White makes his point most clearly.

In expository prose, adjectives usually narrow a noun's generality, to make the statement more specific. But if we do not watch ourselves carefully the adjective drifts into one of its characteristic errors. Here is a passage of exposition from a student theme.

> If you approach the shore of a rocky island, in your kayak, you
> must paddle slowly and cautiously. Even a gentle breeze may

crush the kayak against a sharp rock, and sink the traveler, his vehicle, and all his very precious equipment.

Let us examine the modifiers. "Rocky" is necessary. "Slowly and cautiously" might become only "cautiously," because "slowly" seems included in the idea of caution. Later, "sharp" is useful, to make the threat more particular. But "very precious" is not so useful; is the equipment any more precious by being called so? Does "very" do anything at all? The sentence would end more vigorously as three nouns in a series: ". . . the traveler, his vehicle, and his equipment."

Earlier, one adjective made a palpable cliché, "gentle breeze." Yet the writer clearly wants, and needs, to tell us that the winds that would cause this accident need not be gale force. "Why not use 'gentle breeze' " says the beginning writer, "since 'gentle breeze' is exactly what I mean?" But the problem is not "what I mean," but "what gets through"; the problem is communication. "Gentle" together with "breeze" simply repeats a commonplace, and the reader is unmoved. We would do better simply to alter the expectation slightly, and speak of a "faint breeze," "slight breeze," or "tiny breeze."

Or take another passage, this time by a professional writer.

> The November meeting at the Union League Club was widely reported in the press, which saw evidence of high enthusiasm and sober purpose in the proceedings. A period of feverish activity now ensued. Legal documents were drawn and redrawn (mostly by Choate), potential trustees were sounded out, and advice was solicited. On January 31, 1870, the first board of trustees was elected. The ingredients of this twenty-seven-man founding board were predictable—a pomposity of businessmen and financiers, a clutch of lawyers, a nod of city officials, and a scintillation of writers and architects; less predictable, perhaps, was the inclusion of four practicing artists—the painters John F. Kensett, Frederick E. Church, and Eastman Johnson, and the sculptor J. Q. A. Ward.
>
> Calvin Tomkins, *Merchants and Masterpieces*

Usually a careful writer, Tomkins sounds fatigued. Commonplace combinations of adverb and verb, or adjective and noun, make much of the prose tedious, wordy, and wasteful: "widely reported," "high enthusiasm," and "feverish activity." The clichés of color are there too: the "ingredients" of the "board" were "predictable." Other modifiers are decent qualifications, like "*November* meeting," and "*legal* documents." The author moves into color and vivacity through strong nouns, "a clutch of lawyers, a nod of city officials, and a scintillation of writers and architects."

Revising Modifiers

When you revise your prose, question the need for every adjective and adverb. Can I do without these modifiers? Does the noun (like "postulate" in "basic postulate") or the verb (like "run" in "run quickly") do the job without the modifier? Or can I find another exact noun or verb to do the job in one word? Do I avoid a succession of adjective-noun combinations, the monotonous pairs? Do I fall into cliché by joining two words that are commonly used together? Do I, on the other hand, use the modifier when I need it, to make the discrimination, or to add the color, which makes the sentence expressive?

EXERCISES

1. Here are five simple nouns and five simple verbs. Make up ten sentences, using one of the words in each, in which you use an adverb or adjective that would not be a normal association. But let your context make the modifier work. If "snow" were the word, you might speak of "warm snow" as Updike does, and make it work by a word like "adhesively."

cut	sand
scramble	humility
search	concern
waver	hut
bask	scholar

2. In these sentences from student themes, underline adjectives and adverbs that are useless, either because they are redundant (like "white snow" or "basic postulate") or because they are vague intensives (like "very cold").

a. The cat slinks quietly into the room, its sharp claws ready for instant combat.

b. It was a very long examination, with huge one-hour questions to answer completely, and I didn't have the slightest idea how to prepare for it.

c. Whenever a large supertanker approaches a coastal port, concerned environmentalists take special notice.

3. In these passages from student themes, underline all modifiers. Then see if you can improve the passages by cutting some of the modifiers, or by substituting new modifiers for old ones.

a. Traveling is a great way to learn history. After seeing important places like Bunker Hill and the Smithsonian Institute, national history takes on new and significant meaning.

b. Twenty-four separate and distinct pieces of glass in a metal frame make windows that open outward and dull the landscape with layers of dirt. The factory metal window frame is rusting through the yellow, chipped, peeling paint.

c. Side by side, the swimmers skimmed across the water like swift hydroplanes. The crowd was frantic as it cheered the racing swimmers on.

4. Underline adverbs and adjectives in these passages of published prose. Can you criticize the authors' use of modifiers?

a. Suppose there were no critics to tell us how to react to a picture, a play, or a new composition of music. Suppose we wandered innocent as the dawn into an art exhibition of unsigned paintings. By what standards, by what values would we decide whether they were good or bad, talented or untalented, successes or failures? How can we ever know that what we think is right?

For the last fifteen or twenty years the fashion in criticism or appreciation of the arts has been to deny the existence of any valid criteria and to make the words "good" or "bad" irrelevant, immaterial, and inapplicable. There is no such thing, we are told, as a set of standards, first acquired through experience and knowledge and later imposed on the subject under discussion. This has been a popular approach, for it relieves the critic of the responsibility of judgment and the public of the necessity of knowledge. It pleases those resentful of disciplines, it flatters the empty-minded by calling them open-minded, it comforts the confused. Under the banner of democracy and the kind of equality which our forefathers did *not* mean, it says, in effect, "Who are you to tell us what is good or bad?"

Marya Mannes, "How Do You Know It's Good?"

b. Far out along the autumn plain, beneath the sloping light, an immense drove of cattle moved eastward. They went at a walk, not very fast, but faster than they could imaginably enjoy. Those in front were compelled by those behind; those at the rear, with few exceptions, did their best to keep up; those who were locked within the herd could no more help moving than the particles inside a falling rock.

James Agee, "A Mother's Tale"

c. To sabotage a nuclear power plant and cause release of its radioactivity would be very difficult. It would require an intimate knowledge of the plant design and construction, its operational controls, and its protective systems. The fail-safe design and control interlocks of the plant would thwart all but the most expert attempts. While a determined group of saboteurs might gain access to the plant and do considerable damage to the reactor, it is unlikely that they would be able, in the limited time available, to produce an exact chain of multiple failures necessary to release large amounts of radioactivity to the environment. The hazard from sabotage exists as a result of a complex society in which many vital services are centralized. The saboteur could more easily attack food, water, or communication services with at least equally disastrous results.

Nuclear Power and the Environment: Questions and Answers (published by the American Nuclear Society)

d. Nick looked at the burned-over stretch of hillside, where he had expected to find the scattered houses of the town, and then walked down the railroad track to the bridge over the river. The river was there. It swirled against the log spiles of the bridge. Nick looked down into the clear, brown water, colored from the bubbly bottom, and watched the trout keeping themselves steady in the current with wavering fins. As he watched them they changed their positions by quick angles, only to hold steady in the fast water again. Nick watched them a long time.

Ernest Hemingway, "Big Two-Hearted River"

e. Personal consideration of various and sundry matters of considerable importance have led numerous observers to ultimately conclude that the final end of Western civilization is certainly closer to a realistic possibility than might earlier have been tentatively assumed.

f. Fishing is one of man's oldest occupations and fish stories entered folklore very early. Poets and nature fakers added their touches to marine superstitions that persist to our day. The popular press still cannot resist unsubstantiated stories of sea monsters.

When the helmet diver appeared a century ago, the saga gained the ultimate dramatic ingredient, a human hero to descend and give battle to the fiends. Their sanguinary engagements have been portrayed by dry writers ashore. The lonely, hardworking divers may be forgiven for their silent endorsement of the sagas. Indeed the helmet diver, imprisoned in his casque, and almost always working in filthy harbors and channels, is unable to determine whether an interference with his air pipe is caused by a giant squid or a rotted spar. Doubt leaves room for interpretation.

Jacques Cousteau, *The Silent World*

g. We were camping in the oasis. My companions were asleep. The tall, white figure of an Arab passed by; he had been seeing to the camels and was on his way to his own sleeping place.

I threw myself on my back in the grass; I tried to fall asleep; I could not; a jackal howled in the distance; I sat up again. And what had been so far away was all at once quite near. Jackals were swarming round me, eyes gleaming dull gold and vanishing again, lithe bodies moving nimbly and rhythmically, as if at the crack of a whip.

Franz Kafka, "Jackals and Arabs"

h. Braggioni sits heaped upon the edge of a straight-backed chair much too small for him, and sings to Laura in a furry, mournful voice. Laura has begun to find reasons for avoiding her own house until the latest possible moment, for Braggioni is there almost every night. No matter how late she is, he will be sitting there with a surly, waiting expression, pulling at his kinky yellow hair, thumbing the strings of his guitar, snarling a tune under his breath. Lupe the Indian maid meets Laura at the door, and says with a flicker of a glance towards the upper room, "He waits."

Katherine Anne Porter, "Flowering Judas"

5. You might make more exercises out of the eight examples above. Here are some possibilities. (a) Discuss in class the modifiers in each passage. (b) In each passage, look at the verbs and nouns. Are they used well? (c) In example d, put an adjective with every noun that lacks one, and an adverb with every verb. Make the additions as apt as you can, and see what you have done. (d) Try to rewrite passage a or b, omitting adverbs and adjectives. How much, and what, do you lose?

ORIGINAL WORDS: COMPARISONS
The Need for Originality

When we put words together—adjective with noun, noun with verb, verb with object—we start to talk to each other. We begin to show our original selves, or we show a dull copy of someone else's original. Originality is clarity and vigor. A source of originality in language is forms of comparison—simile, metaphor, and analogy. In order to talk about metaphoric writing and originality, we must go over some old ground again.

Formulas or clichés or trite expressions substitute for the originality that each of us can master. A girl who was mourning the death of her grandfather wrote, starting her first theme of the term, "A tragedy recently occurred at my ancestral home." In conference, the girl wept over the death, she was pale, her hands shook. Her body showed her wretchedness, but her prose showed her reading of a weekly country newspaper. No grief was in her phrasing, only the set phrases of head- lines or lead sentences in obituaries. Perhaps the formulas came to her pen so that she might avoid the pain that comes with real feeling. Or perhaps they came because she did not know the difference, in words, between the formula that communicates nothing, and the originality that communicates feeling. "A tragedy occurred" is a formula that denies the tragic. Compare "a catastrophe was averted" and "a blessed event took place"; they all communicate a journalistic source; but also they all deny feeling, not *only* by being familiar (reminding us of the source) but by being passive or fancy.

A phrase becomes a formula or a cliché not just because it is used so commonly, but because it prevents feeling. The phrase "rain fell" is more common than "a tragedy occurred," yet we do not think of it as a formula because we do not use it to keep feelings down. A psychiatrist described clichés as "the lies we tell ourselves, that we *want* to hear." When the student wrote, "A tragedy recently occurred at my ancestral home," she was not lying overtly, or intending to lie. It was not like saying that she did not chop down a cherry tree when she really did. The lie was internal, the lie of using language to avoid difficult reality, the lie of euphemism.

Overhearing Your Original Self

Listen to yourself as you daydream, or think idly. Are you reciting newspaper formulas or greeting card verse? If you overhear yourself, in your own head, thinking trite sentimentality about your love, something is wrong with your loving.

In general, trying to *overhear* yourself is a good idea. On some days, you can listen to the dreaming voice easily; on other days it seems mute; it is more likely that you are deaf. The dreaming language is clichés sometimes, sometimes puns or phrases with crazy originality. Sometimes the voice hums the tune from a song; when you remember the lyrics a coded message is there, like "Eleanor Rigby" when you are feeling lonely or abandoned, or when something inside you feels that you will be lonely soon. The puns and crazy phrases are codes too. Look at them closely. They have information for you. They are spoken by your original self, looking for attention from your conventional self, which is the self trained by parents and school and television to think like a train on a track. The crazier the phrase, the more devious the pun, the more deep the source in the self. When the dreaming voice talks in cliché, it is the train track getting in the way of the real voice, because the real voice would tell us the truth we would find painful.

Overhear yourself to know yourself. Then you can farm your daydreams for original verbal images that express feeling. The crazy image and the pun do not make good writing in themselves—though often they can be the leaping-off point in daily writing—but they do give clues to feelings that the conscious mind can follow. Here is an unrevised passage from a student's daily writing.

> I was taking out the garbage this morning and I heard (in my head) Fanny Davis's voice talking. She has a funny way of talking, Englishy but not really, and I knew it was her. She was saying, "I like to use the word 'to intimate' without any regard for its actual meaning." I kept stuffing the garbage bags into the cans, wondering why I made that up, and why I chose Fanny's voice. It's always sounded affected to me. But that wasn't the sort of thing she says. She talks about her family and the home on the lake up North and going skiing in Switzerland. I was feeling blue. Bob had gone to New York and I knew that Sally was there, his old girl friend, and I worried about that. Then I started laughing, right at the garbage, because I saw that "to intimate" and "too intimate" are close, but "to intimate" is a long way from the meaning of "too intimate." I was blue because I was too close to Bob, and I could get hurt. I think I chose Fanny because she always seemed totally sexless.

The girl had uncovered something—which she almost knew already—by overhearing a daydream pun and by figuring it out. We may start dreaming; we end up thinking. Now she might be ready to examine her feelings about Bob, or her feelings about her feelings.

Looking for Original Images

We can try to activate the daydreaming mind. We will not always succeed. The girl who wrote the paper beginning "A tragedy occurred" was never fully able to write about her grandfather. But her writing and her self-knowledge improved. In her daily writing she returned to the subject many times. The week after her initial theme, she wrote, "A month ago my grandfather died," and went on for a few rather dry sentences. Though the prose was colorless, it was much more honest than tragedies occurring at ancestral homes. Still, it had no images, no pieces of *sense*.

Later, thinking about things she could associate with her grandfather, she wrote about "farm implements" that were "unused" and "hanging on the wall of the barn." Then she changed "farm implements" to "rake and hoe." Then she revised the sentence again and added an image that could come only from the imagination extending itself into the unseen but the probable. "His hoes and rakes hang from pegs in the barn. Spiders will spin webs there while the iron turns red with rust." She had farmed the dreaming part of her head, which imagined the barn, with a selective intelligence, and wrote two sentences that, in their detail and their associations, began to embody her melancholy and loss.

Simile and Metaphor

Images are groups of words that give an impression to the senses. Most images are visual, but we can also make images of taste, touch, hearing, and smell. Images communicate feelings and locate them firmly, really talking from writer to reader. Comparisons in simile and metaphor mostly use images, and become ways for us to show emotions.

Similes are comparisons that use "like" or "as," little words that announce a comparison. Metaphors omit the announcement. We write, "Her face bloomed with affection," and the word "bloomed" compares the girl to a flower; the face-flower is pretty, it is coming into its maturity, and it is associated with spring or summer. The writer may wish to go on talking about the girl in similes that use garden images. Perhaps her dress "rustles like leaves" and her skin is "as soft as petals." The difference between similes and metaphors is small—a signal is there or not there—but it is real; the simile, because it announces itself, is more reasonable, more conscious of what it is doing.

For clarity, we must distinguish this brief comparison from the word "comparison" as it is used later in this book, when we discuss comparison and contrast as structures to be used in argument and exposition; also, we must distinguish it from the grammatical sense—the "comparison of adjectives." A comparison between the gross national products of Greece and Turkey, or between "less" and "least," is not like comparing an old cheese to an untidy hog.

The new, verbal comparison—simile, metaphor, and analogy—is our most original act of speech; the originality comes from the dreaming part of the self. Although we cannot always manufacture metaphors at will, we can learn to be *alert* for comparisons, and we can stimulate their coming. The dead grandfather's funeral happened during a thunderstorm. When the girl tried to write about it, she encountered the trite associations of thunderstorms and death. She began simply.

> The funeral was 2 p.m. He was laid out in the front parlor, which was always closed except for weddings and funerals. Fifty people were there, some crowded into the parlor, others backed into the

> living room. The minister talked a little and read scripture. Then
> the sky turned dark.

The prose is simple and direct but it lacks energy. "The minister talked a little and read scripture" would probably be better if it included direct and indirect quotation. "Then the sky turned dark." *How* dark? How did you *feel* about the sky turning dark? We have the sense reading this prose that the feelings (formerly denied and lied about in journalistic clichés) are still restricted, held back, reserved.

Suppose the sky turned "as dark as" something. If it turned "as black as the ace of spades," we would be nowhere. What does the ace of spades have to do with her grandfather or her feelings? Even if she had told us the old man was a poker-playing farmer, the simile is so hackneyed that no one will see the black of the playing card when she says it. The useful comparison will be new and will relate to the context: to her memories of the man, to the funeral, to the idea of death. To say "the sky turned as dark as the soot from a factory chimney" would seem inappropriate; what would a factory have to do with a farm? "The sky turned black as my grandmother's dress" would be a better direction; but maybe that's too black, or the texture is wrong. Or she might want to compare it to something she remembers and associates with the dead farmer: "The sky turned black, like inside the barn after milking." "The sky turned dark as a blueberry."

Sometimes one phrase will not be adequate. You want your comparison to go on longer than that. "The sky turned dark. I could see a black round storm cloud coming. I remembered leaning over the open well, staring down into the round black eye of the water." Here, we find a comparison within the comparison; the water is an "eye," and the reader alert to the insides of words will reconstruct the dead metaphor: "the eye of the storm"—and revive it—although (or because) the author has not stated it.

Originality and Memory

To find the right comparison, we must draw on memory and daydream; imagination newly combines old things remembered; it is always present, and often hard to discover. Memory is crucial to our writing, thinking, and feeling. By scrutiny of the retained past, we begin to understand and to express that understanding. In the floating world, we connect feelings in the present to feelings about the past. We express these connections mostly by comparisons. In the uniqueness of each of us, we can find something that the sky grew as dark as.

Analogy

We use the word analogy for a comparison that makes or illustrates a point, and usually takes longer to say than a metaphor or a simile. An analogy can be extended into a whole essay; ministers' sermons are sometimes analogies—life is like the hundred-yard dash: birth is the starting gun, the tape is death, God is the judge. A whole book, or system of thought, can be based on analogy. Oswald Spengler, in *The Decline of the West,* at the beginning states an analogy, that a civilization is an organism, is born, grows old, and dies; then he writes a long book to make a factual case for his analogy.

Analogy often works best within a unit no longer than the paragraph. Frequently, it illustrates the sense in which an abstraction is intended. Analogies may make points; they don't prove them; they show how you feel, or they clarify your use of an ambiguous or all-inclusive word; "love" and "hate" are two of the vaguest words going. Suppose we were tempted to support the stick-figure philosophical assertion, "Love is better than hate." We would not get far with such a proposition, because it is too vague for support, but we would at least put eyes and ears on our stick figures if we went on, "It is a meadow in the country compared to an alley of garbage and broken glass."

An analogy often runs through a paragraph like a thread in tweed, not separated into patches of assertion followed by comparison, but interwoven. James Thurber wrote this paragraph about working with the editor of *The New Yorker,* Harold Ross:

> Having a manuscript under Ross's scrutiny was like putting your car in the hands of a skilled mechanic, not an automotive engineer with a bachelor of science degree, but a guy who knows what makes a motor go, and sputter, and wheeze, and sometimes come to a dead stop; a man with an ear for the faintest body squeak as well as the loudest engine rattle. When you first gazed, appalled, upon an uncorrected proof of one of your stories or articles, each margin had a thicket of queries and complaints—one writer got a hundred and forty-four on one profile. It was as though you beheld the works of your car spread all over the garage floor, and the job of getting the thing together again and making it work seemed impossible. Then you realized that Ross was trying to make your Model T or old Stutz Bearcat into a Cadillac or Rolls-Royce. He was at work with the tools of his unflagging perfectionism, and, after an exchange of growls or snarls, you set to work to join him in his enterprise.

Thurber begins by announcing his subject, "Having a manuscript under Ross's scrutiny," departs from it for the rest of a long sentence, returns to the manuscript for a sentence, then in the final three sentences develops his analogy, makes it funnier, and makes his point about Ross as an editor. He makes points by contrasts: "mechanic" not "engineer"; not "automotive engineer" but "guy." And he makes it by developing his analogy into impossibility (repairing a Model T into a Cadillac), and developing it out of all touch with reality; the customer joins with the mechanic to rebuild his torn-up machine. The analogy expresses feeling, it is witty, and it is a pleasure to read. Consider this alternative, omitting the garage and substituting abstraction and generality for analogy:

> Having a manuscript under Ross's scrutiny was an edifying if terrifying experience. He was a skilled editor, not an academic, but a practical man. When you first gazed, appalled, upon an uncorrected proof of one of your stories or articles, each margin had a thicket of queries and complaints—one writer got a hundred and forty-four on one profile. You beheld all your work torn apart, and it seemed impossible to put it together. Then you realized that Ross was trying to make ordinary prose into prose of the highest order. He was using his editorial skills with unflagging perfectionism, and, after an exchange of growls or snarls, you set to work to join him in his enterprise.

This eviscerated version is slightly shorter in words, but the cutting loses rather than gains: the paragraph diminishes in energy and expression.

The Unintended Comparison

With analogy as with other forms of comparison, you must be wary of the dead, the mixed, and the inadvertently comic. Often a writer will trap himself in an unconscious analogy expressing an attitude that he really feels but denies to himself. The comic disparity is as slapstick as a top-hatted man with his trousers missing. Here is an English critic, writing about American music in the London *Times Literary Supplement*. He writes in attempted praise of American energy and vitality, but other messages come through his bad prose.

> The American composer is neither enriched nor shackled. He had nothing to start from but old rags and bones of European culture that, imported to a new environment, soon lost their

savor. Then gradually, in the pulping machine of a polyglot society, the rags and bones began to acquire a taste of their own.

Look at the main analogy, rags and bones. When they were imported
here, they "soon lost their savor." Did the gentleman actually expect
rags and bones to taste good? His idea of the American stew expresses
his distaste by an analogy to eating the product of something like a
paper factory: ". . . in the pulping machine . . . the rags and bones
began to acquire a taste of their own." This writer expressed his
feelings, but he expressed feelings he didn't know he had. He appears
to believe that he *likes* American music, but something unacknow-
ledged inside him is holding its nose.

To express a feeling without examining it is worthless. Originality
combines opposites: we dream—with our eyes open; we are inspired—
then we scrutinize and revise. Scrutiny provides the motive for revision. We need to look into words—to see the connection between "rags
and bones," "savor," and "taste"—and we will sometimes discover
feelings we had not wished to acknowledge. Then we can revise ourselves or our prose or both. We must float on daydream and memory
for new words, and then put the new words under scrutiny again. Only
by developing all these mental abilities can we begin to be honest. The
paradox is that to be sincere we must struggle; we must struggle to be
spontaneous, and then struggle to revise, refine, and order our spontaneity. To speak our most intimate selves we must revise.

One way to cultivate our sensitivity to the insides of words is to
develop an ear for the unintended comparison. (The unintended comparison is often an overt, and sometimes extended, version of the dead
metaphor.) On a Monday-night football broadcast, Howard Cosell said
of a new quarterback that he "walked in the wake" of a great prede-
cessor. Here, the unintended comparison approaches blasphemy.

Looking for Analogies

An analogy can be thought out, on purpose, more easily than the lone
metaphor, which, to most writers, seems a gift from the god within us,
an inspiration. Suppose you are discussing what can make a love affair
succeed. Suppose you decide that it takes a lot of work. The word
"work," itself a metaphor nearly dead, can lead you into analogy.
What kind of work is it like? Is it like a nine-to-five job? You can make
an analogy in the negative: "This work is no nine-to-five job." Is it like
building a house? Rebuilding a destroyed city? Making the sets for a
play? Being a skilled mechanic or an automotive engineer? What kinds
of buildings, businesses, roads, cars?

The liveliest prose moves from analogy to analogy without strain. It takes practice to learn how to invent, and practice to learn when to stop inventing. When analogy shifts abruptly, the effect is usually ridiculous, and comic writers can use these sudden shifts to their advantage; if in one sentence you compare tennis with big game hunting, do not compare it in the next sentence with knitting unless you want a laugh. Often a sentence or a paragraph of general summary or narrative separates passages of differing analogies, keeping them from clashing.

One more example of comparisons brings imaginative combinations of words to Brooklyn, New York. The author is expressing complex feelings about its space.

> Manhattan is large, yet all its distances seem quick and available. Brooklyn is larger, seventy-one square miles as against twenty-two, but here you enter the paradoxes of the relative. You know, here: only a few miles from wherever I stand, Brooklyn ends; only a few miles away is Manhattan; Brooklyn is walled with world-travelled wetness on west and south and on north and east is the young beaver-board frontier of Queens; Brooklyn comes to an end: but actually, that is, in the conviction of the body, there seems almost no conceivable end to Brooklyn; it seems, on land as flat and huge as Kansas, horizon beyond horizon forever unfolded, as immeasurable proliferation of house on house and street by street; or seems as China does, infinite in time in patience and in population as in space.
>
> The collaborated creation of the insanely fungoid growth of fifteen or twenty villages, now sewn and quilted edge to edge, and lacking any center in remote proportion to its mass, it is perhaps the most amorphous of all modern cities; and at the same time, by virtue of its arterial streets, it has continuities so astronomically vast as Paris alone or the suburbs south of Chicago could match: on Flatbush Avenue, DeKalb, Atlantic, New Lots, Church, any number more, a vista of low buildings and side streets of glanded living sufficient to paralyze all conjecture; simply, far as the eye can strain, no end of Brooklyn, and looking back, far as the eye can urge itself, no end, nor imaginable shore; only, thrust upon the pride of heaven, the monolith of the Empire State, or different mode of life, and even this, seen here, has the smoky frailty of a half-remembered dream.
>
> James Agee, "Southeast of the Island: Travel Notes"

Though portions here may be overwritten—I have my doubts about
"is walled with world-travelled wetness" as a way to say "borders the
ocean"—there is imagination and order in the connected comparisons.
Look at the order of sizes: Brooklyn, Kansas, China; then from an
adverbial peak, downward: "astronomically vast as Paris alone or the
suburbs south of Chicago." Look at the body metaphors, perhaps coming from the phrase "the conviction of the body": "arterial,"
"glanded," "paralyze." Look at the brief analogy with a quilt in the
second paragraph. The energy and import of this prose derive from
simile, metaphor, and analogy.

Revising for Comparison

First, check your sentences to make sure that you are controlling the
comparisons you make. Make sure that you do not inadvertently turn a
quarterback into a deity, or an art form into a bad smell. Second, see
that you have not made cliché comparisons that no longer function,
like "black as the ace of spades."

Then do the more difficult. *Add* simile, metaphor, and analogy.
Most of us in our first drafts lack energy and feeling. Our prose resembles the pale version of Thurber, after the analogy was deleted. The
prose is too plain to reach the reader with excitement and precision.
Float on memory and daydream to invent; scrutinize with critical
intelligence to cut and to improve. Ask yourself if your invention is
new, if it is appropriate, if it does not clash with anything else. In a
paragraph of exposition, *think* if you can clarify by analogy. What was
it *like*, to have your prose edited by Ross? What was it like, the day
your grandfather died?

EXERCISES

1. In the passage by James Agee, how useful are the phrases or
words, "beaver-board," "fungoid," "glanded," and "smoky?" How do
they work or how do they fail?

2. Using different colors of pen, underline words in the Agee passage—verbs in red, nouns in blue, and modifers in green. Notice how
the parts of speech work together. Notice how the metaphors and
other comparisons contain all parts of speech.

3. Here are some clichés that began life as new metaphors. Can
you figure out how each of them might have started? Invent a new
metaphor that communicates what the cliché fails to communicate.

toe the line
an axe to grind
chip on his shoulder
pick a bone with you
heart-to-heart talk

4. Here are seven common comparatives. Taking any three, write sentences in which you make a new simile.

as long as
as bright as
as wet as
as green (or any color) as
as sour as
as good as
as heavy as

5. In these passages, underline forms of analogy, metaphor, and simile. Choose three examples that you particularly like, and explain your reasons for preferring them.

a. But the thing that really tormented them was the thought of those two old-age pensioners living in their house, usurping floor-space, devouring food, and paying only ten shillings a week. I doubt whether they were really losing money over the old-age pensioners, though certainly the profit on ten shillings a week must have been very small. But in their eyes the two old men were a kind of dreadful parasite who had fastened on them and were living on their charity. Old Jack they could just tolerate, because he kept out-of doors most of the day, but they really hated the bedridden one, Hooker by name. Mr. Brooker [the landlord] had a queer way of pronouncing his name, without the H and with a long U—"Uker." What tales I heard about old Hooker and his fractiousness, the nuisance of making his bed, the way he "wouldn't eat" this and "wouldn't eat" that, his endless ingratitude and, above all, the selfish obstinacy with which he refused to die! The Brookers were quite openly pining for him to die. When that happened they could at least draw the insurance money. They seemed to feel him there, eating their substance day after day, as though he had been a living worm in their bowels.

George Orwell, *The Road to Wigan Pier*

b. I lay down on a solitary rock that was like an island in the bottom of the valley, and looked up. The grey sage-brush and the blue-grey rock around me were already in shadow, but high above me the canyon walls were dyed flame-colour with the sunset, and the Cliff City lay in a gold haze against its dark cavern. In a few minutes it, too, was grey, and only the rim rock at the top held the red light. When that was gone, I could still see the copper glow in the piñons along the edge of the top ledges. The arc of sky over the canyon was silvery blue, with its pale yellow moon, and presently stars shivered into it, like crystals dropped into perfectly clear water.

Willa Cather, *The Professor's House*

c. The average American judge, as everyone knows, is a mere rabbinical automaton, with no more give and take in his mind than you will find in the mind of a terrier watching a rathole. He converts the law into a series of rubber-stamps, and brings them down upon the scalped skulls of the just and unjust alike. The alternative to him, as commonly conceived, is quite as bad—an uplifter in a black robe, eagerly gulping every new brand of Peruna that comes out, and converting his pulpit into a sort of soap-box.

H. L. Mencken, "Mr. Justice Holmes"

d. . . . Women have served all these centuries as looking glasses possessing the magic and delicious power of reflecting the figure of man at twice its natural size. Without that power probably the earth would still be swamp and jungle. The glories of all our wars would be unknown. We should still be scratching the outlines of deer on the remains of mutton bones and bartering flints for sheepskins or whatever simple ornament took our unsophisticated taste. Supermen and Fingers of Destiny would never have existed. The Czar and the Kaiser would never have worn their crowns or lost them. Whatever may be their use in civilised societies, mirrors are essential to all violent and heroic action. That is why Napoleon and Mussolini both insist so emphatically upon the inferiority of women, for if they were not inferior, they would cease to enlarge.

Virginia Woolf, "A Room of One's Own"

e. Manson's greatest work of magic, however, was the transformation of Charles Denton Watson. When they met Watson in the spring of 1968 at Dennis Wilson's house, Watson was a swinger dating a stewardess from Chicago. The family was proud that it could create a change in Tex Watson, the holder to this day of a Texas high hurdles track and field record. Watson dressed mod. He looked mod. He had a wig shop. He was strictly now. But they erased the swinger from him. Years later, when he was down to 110 pounds, weeping in his cell, covered over with a blanket, just before they shipped him to the Atascadero nut hatch, he was truly now. No past—time burnt—books burnt—past burnt. All bridges melted with dope and fervor. All time factors in the now. The now of Charlie.

Ed Sanders, *The Family*

f. A gentleman is one who cultivates disadvantage. He will not positively pursue it. But he takes little prudential or evasive action when it comes. There is laziness in your true gentleman, a streak of recumbency. But also fastidiousness: the dividends of the world—honors, power, earned fortune—come greasy. A man may win the game but stay grimy to his elbows. There is something about defeat, material setback, even personal betrayal by those one trusted that leaves one clean. At its purest, gentility is dated. It goes, perhaps unfairly, with camel's-hair coats and shooting sticks, with talc and loyal setters. The entire code was a feature of England before 1914, when caste was firm and private incomes were adequate to the many small defeats, impracticalities, covert ostentations, and boneheadednesses that made up a gentleman's non-career. Both the men and the manner were largely wiped out in the muck of world war. This was indeed the supreme imposition, the disadvantage least to be flinched from. But now and again the sandy mustaches, the pale, astonished eyes of the true gents still haunt the imagination.

George Steiner, "Gent," *The New Yorker,* February 12, 1972

g. But his position was weak. Like a cougar, the army was constantly perched above him, ready to pounce.

John Gerassi, *The Great Fear in Latin America*

IV

SENTENCES

STYLE AND THE SENTENCE

A sentence is a group of words with a period, exclamation point, or question mark at the end. But no definition of the sentence is likely to help us much in writing one. Sentences happened first, the spoken kind; grammarians named them later. We learn sentence structure by speaking and listening, by reading and writing, more than we learn by studying types of sentences. Still, after studying we can listen harder, read more closely, speak more eloquently, and write more clearly. We can learn to *vary* the style of our sentences to express our feelings and ideas, and to hold the reader's interest; at the same time, we can learn to *control* that style to make a satisfying whole, and to make our meaning clear to the reader. To *vary*, and to *control*. A paradox in style: we must have variety and sameness, combine unity and diversity, in the same group of words.

PARTS OF SENTENCES

Before we go into the types of sentences, we will need to know the names of the parts of sentences.

The *subject* of a sentence is the noun, or noun substitute like "who," about which we say something, or ask a question.

118

> The *frogman* dove.
> The *theory* was valid.
> *Who* committed this brutal crime?

In this sentence the *simple subject* is "woman," and the *complete subject* is "the woman in the blue house by the river":

> The woman in the blue house by the river wrote bizarre sentences on the walls.

Another basic division in a sentence is the *predicate*. The predicate is the verb along with its modifiers and complements. The predicate is what the sentence says about the subject; most often, the predicate is the action that goes on in the sentence. In these sentences, the simple predicates are in italics:

> The frogman *dove*.
> The theory *was* valid.
> Who *committed* this brutal crime?

The *simple predicate* in the next sentence is "wrote"; the *complete predicate* is "wrote on the walls with invisible liquids."

> The woman in the blue house wrote on the walls with invisible liquids.

Objects come in three forms: direct objects, indirect objects, and objects of prepositions.

The *direct object* is the part of a sentence that the predicate acts upon. Here, the direct objects are in italics.

> She designed the *atomic reactor*.
> The president washed the *dishes*.
> *What* did the elephant say?
> Tell them *where we're going*.

An *indirect object* usually comes before a direct object, and tells us to whom or for whom (or to what or for what) the predicate acts.

> She gave the *team* a case of beer.
> Sam wrote *her* a new song.

Most of the time, the indirect object replaces a prepositional phrase using "to" or "for."

> She gave a case of beer *to the team*.
> Sam wrote a new song *for her*.

In these last two sentences "team" and "her" are *objects of prepositions,* nouns or noun substitutes that a preposition relates to another
word or word group. Here are more prepositions followed by objects.

> To be defenestrated is to be thrown *out a window.*
> Dick the Bruiser was barred *from the premises.*

A fourth construction has two objects, in which the second modifies or
describes the first. The second, or *complementary object,* is in italics.

> They made her *bartender.*
> He called her a *humbug.*
> Margaret painted the tree *purple.*

With linking verbs like "is" and "become" and "appear," we find the
subjective complement.

> They were *pretty.*
> The house looked *old.*
> Herbert became *senile.*

A *phrase* is a group of words which work together as a unit, but
which lack a subject and a predicate. These phrase-units work together
in several ways:

Prepositional phrase	The bat *in the attic* is not a vampire.
Verbal phrase	More and more people *will be buying* sub-compact cars as gasoline prices rise.
Infinitive phrase	Hockey fans tend *to enjoy violence.*
Gerund phrase	*Establishing a fascist state* requires ruth- lessness and ambition.
Participle phrase	*Doubting the medical assumptions of his time,* Pasteur sought further knowledge about what causes disease.

On the other hand, a *clause* is a group of words, used as part of a
sentence, which contains a subject and a predicate. A clause may be
main (or independent) or *subordinate* (or dependent). A *main clause*
can be a simple sentence in itself.

> The thin dog barked.

A *subordinate clause* is not a complete sentence by itself, and may be
used as a noun, as an adjective, or as an adverb.

Noun clause	*Whether the new league will flourish* is a question that no one can answer with certainty.
✓Adjective clause	The cricket, *which appeared to be wearing a tiny tuxedo,* did not answer his naive questions.
Adverb clause	She ordered the troops to attack *when it became apparent that to delay any longer would be suicidal.*

Each of these last two clauses is a *modifier*. A *modifier* is any word, phrase, or clause that functions as an adjective or adverb.

> The bat in the attic is not a vampire.

Here the prepositional phrase "in the attic" does something to, *modifies*, "bat," telling us *which* bat. If we say, "the vampire bat is in the attic," then the word "vampire" is an adjective that modifies "bat."

> The vampire flew slowly around the room when he assumed the form of a bat.

Here we have three modifiers, all acting as adverbs. One modifier tells us about the way the vampire flew: the single word "slowly"; then a prepositional phrase tells us where: the vampire flew "around the room"; then a subordinate clause, "when he assumed the form of a bat," tells us when it happened. Manner, place, and time.

Now that we have the names of parts, we can examine types of sentences.

TYPES OF SENTENCES

Simple Sentences

A sentence is "simple" as long as it remains one clause, containing one predicate. "John laughed" is a complete, two-word sentence, simple and common in its structure: subject/verb. We could add modifiers, "Big John laughed loudly," or a preposition, "John laughed at her," and the sentence would remain simple.

A sentence can be quite long and yet still be simple. This sentence is simple, but elaborates the predicate with prepositional phrases:

> Neal *runs / with his wife / at Waterman Gymnasium / before classes.*

A subject can be long, too.

> *The ape-man in the gray loincloth, a wooden spear in his hand,*
> *attacked.*

Or the verb can be elaborated.

> The ape-man *attacked swiftly, with a sharp cry, from behind the*
> *rocks.*

Or we can have a direct object, and the object can be elaborated.

> The ape-man attacked *the sluggish warriors, those intruders tired*
> *from their lengthy searching.*

Or the simple sentence can have all its parts elaborated and remain simple.

> The ape-man in the gray loincloth, a wooden spear in his hand,
> attacked the sluggish warriors swiftly from behind the rocks, the
> boulders shining in the hot sun.

The basic sentence is still "The ape-man attacked," though by this time we have more definition for each of the parts, more information, and too many adjectives.

Compound Sentences

A compound sentence has two or more main clauses, each containing a subject and a predicate, each describing an action complete in itself. The clauses in the compound sentence are joined by a connective—"and," "but," "or," or "nor"—or by a semicolon or colon.

> The economy stagnates and prices rise.

> We can lower the price of admission or we can stage fewer plays.

> He never went to the snake house again; he had been revolted
> by the alligator.

The clauses in each of these sentences are independent. Each sentence could become two sentences, with a minimal change of meaning.

> The economy stagnates. Prices rise.

> We can lower the price of admission. We can stage fewer plays.

> He never went to the snake house again. He had been revolted
> by the alligator.

In the compound sentence, notice that the two complete clauses are nearly equal in importance, or *coordinate*. A compound sentence, of course, can have more than two parts.

> Lolich pitched a curve, the runner on first sprinted toward second, and Veryzer ran to cover the base.

But a string of coordinate clauses is usually boring.

> There was more crime in the street, the criminals were running around free, the judges were letting people go, nobody was safe in the streets, criminals were out on bail, murderers were on parole, and nobody did anything.

Complex Sentences

If, however, one part of the sentence depends on the other—if the one is the cause of the other, for instance—we have a complex rather than a compound sentence. We call the clause that depends upon the other, for explanation or completion, the *subordinate clause*. A complex sentence would be,

> *Because the economy stagnates,* high prices find few buyers.

The first clause in this sentence is subordinate.

We can vary sentences even when we keep to simple clauses and compounds of equally complete clauses. The complex sentence provides further variety, and allows us additional conciseness and precision. Clauses introduced by relative pronouns, "that," "which," or "who"—sometimes called *relative clauses*—are subordinate to a main clause; they depend on it.

> Do you remember the face of the man *who sold you this ticket?*

> The crowd suddenly turned on the King *who had betrayed them.*

In other sentences, we attribute cause or sequence, and we do it by a conjunction like "because" or "after."

> *Because the Girl Scouts had proved to be unscrupulous,* the neighbors burned the cookies they had purchased.

> *After the movie ended,* everyone in the audience went. ?

We have many other conjunctions that can introduce subordinate clauses, each with its own precise meaning to be used by the careful writer—like "although," "after," "if," "since," and " when."

Compound-Complex Sentences

Frequently, we combine compound and complex sentences, using at least two main clauses and one subordinate clause.

> I was late *because George had come over unexpectedly,* and I drove as fast as I could.

> The young heiress jumped under the covers *when her uncle walked in wearing his gorilla suit,* and she refused to come out.

> *If you had only proofread the article more carefully,* Mr. Crumbly would not have been so insulted, and we wouldn't have this lawsuit on our hands!

In each sentence the clause in italics is subordinate; the main clauses are in roman type.

Incomplete Sentences

Another type of sentence commonly used is the incomplete sentence, or fragment. The incompleteness is for lack of a subject or of a predicate. "John laughed" is a brief complete sentence. Neither "John" nor "laughed" would be complete by itself, but we could use either of them alone in context.

> She thought about whom she might ask to the picnic. Harry? Harry was too grubby. John? John.

> When she saw him she covered her mouth and, though she tried to suppress it, laughed. Laughed. He could not believe it.

But the more common incomplete sentence is a phrase or a clause of several words.

> The essay by Ellsberg shows great control of sentence variation. Like the variety in the first paragraph.

The incomplete sentence is informal. In a more formal prose, other ways could have been found to work "like the variety in the first paragraph" into a long sentence. We use the incomplete sentence also with many common phrases like "No comment," "Not at all," and "Of course."

Although the incomplete sentence, or sentence fragment, occurs frequently in good informal prose, the beginning writer does well to avoid using sentence fragments entirely, until he has learned to control the varieties of sentences.

Most of the time, most student writers make sentence fragments accidentally, without noticing that their sentence lacks a main verb. Often it is the most ambitious sentence that wanders off into incoherence. Here is a vagrant sentence from a theme.

> As a result of American military incursion into Indo-China, which was begun in a gradual and secretive way just beyond the bounds of public awareness, and which was modeled on the French attempts that had failed consistently, with heads of state of any interested foreign countries bribed and enormous amounts of economic and military aid being given to the pseudo-leaders, and the American politicians continuing to conceal the true purposes and the true nature of our interests.

By the time this student came to the fifth clause of this huge sentence fragment, he had forgotten the place he started from. The sentence confuses us, and remains incomplete. What *did* happen "as a result of the American military incursion into Indo-China"? Proofreading and patient revision could have prevented this problem. A probable soluton here would be to rewrite the sentence fragment as two or three shorter, complete sentences. In prose, the first rule is clarity.

Another possible danger in incomplete sentences is that they tend to avoid committing themselves. If we take notes on a history lecture, using fragments rather than sentences, we may look at them a month later and read something like, "Too many wars. Bad economy." Unless we remember the context, these phrases may leave us puzzled. They could imply that the number of wars, at some time in history, destroyed a nation's economy. Or they could imply that bad economy created the wars. Or both. With neither a verb nor the expected order of subject and object to complete the action, the meaning is left vague. Of course it is exactly the ambiguity—not having to make up our mind—which appeals to the part of our mind that likes to absolve itself from responsibility.

> The recession put everybody out of work in Flint. All those rich people in Cadillacs driving past the homes of the unemployed.

Here the sentence fragment avoids responsibility for making connections, and leaves the meaning unclear. Are the rich people responsible for the unemployment? Should the rich people take detours to avoid the workers' parts of town?

We must remember, at the same time, that a writer *can* consciously control the sentence fragment, *when he knows what he is doing*. If the diction in the prose is informal enough, the sentence fragment is yet another possible variation in rhythm and structure. It isolates a fragment in time, because the period creates a pause longer than the pause inserted by a comma or a semicolon.

> We were going to be consumed by fire once more, and once more the world would let it happen. As usual. What was true yesterday will be true tomorrow.
>
> Elie Wiesel, *A Beggar in Jerusalem*

Only be careful to use incomplete sentences in an informal context, and deliberately, like Elie Wiesel, to establish pause and emphasis. A careless writer may make clauses into sentences (with periods and capital letters) without purpose, and with choppy results.

> He was a writer. Which is a difficult profession.
> She looked tall. Although she was really only 5'3".

Avoid this sort of thing. These sentences need to become complex, with commas.

EXERCISES

1. In these sentences, identify subjects, predicates, objects, indirect objects, and objects of prepositions:

   a.   The Empire State Building is no longer the tallest building in New York.

   b.   When we sent the Marines after the Mayaguez, we gave the Cambodians a hard time.

   c.   Which of the fifty states spends least on education?

2. In these sentences, identify phrases as prepositional, verbal, infinitive, gerund, or participial:

   a.   Remembering the tradition of the Old South, Rhett was unable to dishonor his name.

   b.   The Senator from Arkansas tried voting the way he felt.

   c.   In the morning, the sun will be drying the dew off the grass.

3. Identify the clauses in these sentences as main clauses or subordinates. Are the subordinates used as nouns or as modifiers?

   a.   She rose when he walked through the door, and when he spoke she turned her back.

b. The jury, which was white and male, took twenty minutes to arrive at a decision.

c. Although brown rice is highly nutritious, people cannot live on brown rice alone.

4. Identify each of these sentences as simple, compound, complex, compound-complex, or incomplete:

a. Because Margaret had brought the elephant into the house, Sandy had to take her sculptures down to the basement.

b. Lost in thought, she didn't hear the thunder begin in the mountains far off, or feel the wind starting to blow harder.

c. Rose ordered an apricot sour although she had been drinking daiquiris, and winked at her companion as she did.

d. This sentence, for example.

e. Rocking back and forth on her heels, the professor lectured.

f. Although the rainfall is minimal, irrigation waters the valley and nourishes the corn.

g. Whenever Goebbels heard someone speak of culture, he reached for his gun.

h. Australopithecus reasoned, he cooperated, he hunted in large bands, and he used tools.

i. Larry went up for the jump shot and Dave leaped to block it.

j. The man in the Foster Grants strolled down the crowded street, a beret on his head, a cane in his hand.

k. Always cheerful, Mr. Sputter the mailman smiled, although a German shepherd hung by its teeth from his sleeve.

l. Without hesitation, thinking only of the trapped ocelot, Branny dashed through the rising flames.

m. He grabbed the chicken feathers and threw them off the cliff, screaming and dancing all the while, although the rites were not yet due to begin and he, a crazed poet, was forbidden to take part.

5. Here are five contexts, each including an incomplete sentence. Which of them succeed, and which of them fail? Revise the failures into successes.

a. Henry Moore was born in 1898, in a country not known for sculpture since the Middle Ages. Son of a coal miner, raised in Yorkshire, trained to be a teacher, when Moore learned that he could attend an art school on an ex-serviceman's grant.

b. Nevertheless, advocates of strip mining persist in their rhetoric. We hear of "vast untapped natural resources." It makes strip mining sound like pouring a glass of beer. Instead of like destroying the earth.

c. When I came back from Canada, my friends were all tanned. Everybody. I looked like a pale dime in a pile of rich, copper pennies. And I felt like ten cents.

d. They looked up and saw it. The second stage of the launch vehicle.

e. Whenever the Congress decides to tangle with the president, and the people need tax relief or something of that order of magnitude, although the country needs immediate help, and the newspapers are all complaining, except that nothing ever gets done.

6. In these paragraphs, find the type of each sentence. You can also use these paragraphs to review phrases and clauses.

a. Familiarity has perhaps bred contempt in us Americans: until you have had a washing machine, you cannot imagine how little difference it will make to you. Europeans still believe that money brings happiness, witness the bought journalist, the bought politician, the bought general, the whole venality of European literary life, inconceivable in this country of the dollar. It is true that America produces and consumes more cars, soap, and bathtubs than any other nation, but we live among these objects rather than by them. Americans build skyscrapers; Le Corbusier worships them. Ehrenburg, our Soviet critic, fell in love with the Check-O-Mat in American railway stations, writing home paragraphs of song to this gadget—while deploring American materialism. When an American heiress wants to buy a man, she at once crosses the Atlantic. The only really materialistic people I have ever met have been Europeans.

Mary McCarthy, "America the Beautiful"

b. When I slide under a barbed-wire fence, cross a field, and run over a sycamore trunk felled across the water, I'm on a little island shaped like a tear in the middle of Tinker Creek. On one side of the creek is a steep forested bank; the water is swift and deep on that side of the island. On the other side is the level field I walked through next to the steers' pasture; the water between the field and the island is shallow and sluggish. In summer's low water, flags and bulrushes grow along a series of shallow pools cooled by the lazy current. Water striders patrol the surface film, crayfish hump along the silt bottom eating filth, frogs shout and glare, and shiners and small bream hide among roots from the sulky green heron's eye. I come to this island every month of the year. I walk around it, stopping and staring, or I straddle the sycamore log over the creek, curling my legs out of the water in winter, trying to read. Today I sit on dry grass at the end of the island by the slower side of the creek. I'm drawn to this spot. I come to it as to an oracle; I return to it as a man years later will seek out the battlefield where he lost a leg or an arm.

Annie Dillard, *Pilgrim at Tinker Creek*

7. Looking into your daily writing, or old themes, find and copy examples of these: (a) A simple, complete sentence. (b) A compound sentence. (c) Three complex sentences of two clauses, in which you use different conjunctions. If you do not have three examples, revise until you do. (d) A compound-complex sentence. (e) An incomplete sentence.

CLARITY AND COHERENCE

In a moment, we will look into ways of using *variety* to construct sentences, and then into *unity*. Variety and unity are the two poles, and the world of the sentence spins between them.

But something counts more than either unity or variety, something so fundamental that we may not think of it, yet as necessary to good writing as matter to the universe. Our sentences must be understandable, and to be understandable they must hang together. *Clarity* and *coherence* are needed in writing at all levels—from words, to sentences, to paragraphs, to themes, to whole books. We start pursuing clarity when we choose the right word; when we bring that word together with a second word, we begin to pursue coherence. In the larger unit—the paper or the ten-volume history of the world—we make meaning by the *shape* that we give the assembled whole.

We first discover clarity and coherence, most obviously, in the next-to-smallest unit, the sentence. We must make clear sentences before we can make clear paragraphs or clear themes. Variety and unity are ways of making clarity and coherence; we name our goals before we enumerate ways to reach these goals.

One way of trying to define a quality—something as abstract as "clarity," as "coherence"—is to take a look at its opposite. Here is an obscure and incoherent sentence.

The attention brought to Campus Management's mismanagement of its rental property at 410 Observatory makes a convincing case for the need of a strong and active tenants' organization in Ann Arbor.

From an editorial, *The Michigan Daily*

When we try to rewrite this sentence, we run into difficulty, because before we revise, we need to know what the writer wants to say. What does he mean when he asserts that "attention" itself "makes a convincing case . . ."? Perhaps he confuses two ideas. (In another chapter, we will look into logic, and speak about clarity as it relates to methods of thought. See pages 230–244.) Maybe the meaning is something like this: "When we see how this property is mismanaged, we realize that we need a strong and active tenants' organization in Ann Arbor."

Here is another.

> It seems to be delivering a message right up to the end, but to decipher it, one has to dig deep within his subconscious and then he may not be sure of the nature of the manner in which it has affected him.
>
> From a theater review, *Ann Arbor News*

It is hard to rewrite phrases like "the nature of the manner." Maybe this sentence could become two sentences. If we put a period after "within his subconscious," then we could make a sentence like, "Even then, one may not be sure of how the film-makers have done their digging."

Or take a sample from a student theme.

> All these shortages are eventually going to put people in a position which forces them either to take some type of action that will level off the population somewhere, or people are slowly going to make life difficult for the whole human race.

All these examples have faults in punctuation and grammar—but they come to one common result: the sentences are unclear. The writers were unable to use the language to make their own thoughts clear to another person.

When you read in this book advice on not misplacing modifiers, or on avoiding the comma fault or the sentence fragment, remember that the goal is not mere correctness, but clarity and coherence. The goal is making contact with other people.

VARIETY OF SENTENCES

The Uses of Variety

By using different sentence types, we can vary the speed and style in our prose. We must vary our sentences to keep the reader interested and involved. Monotony destroys attentiveness; if the reader sleeps, our clarity is wasted. Also, we can draw from our store of sentence variations to fill the need for subtle expression, and with our knowledge of sentence possibilities increase the range and conciseness of expression. The means are not separate from the ends. *A change in style, however slight, is a change in meaning, however slight.* You will find meanings that you cannot express, cannot convey, unless you can find in your box of varied sentence structures the shape you require.

Subordination and Variety: Complex Sentences

Subordinate phrases and clauses, used as modifiers, and without connectives, can save us words, and strengthen our sentences. These subordinates give our prose density and variety.

In the *absolute construction,* we omit the connective and the verb, or sometimes a preposition, and modify directly and clearly. The absolute construction is in italics.

> *Day done,* he raised his pitchfork to his shoulder.

Here we have cut from "When day was done," or a longer construction.

> *The desk ordered, pencils sharpened, paper blank,* he was ready for a day of combat with the English language.

> The fullback twisted and plunged, *his legs pistons, his head an iron wedge.*

A construction much like the absolute is the adjective with a prepositional or comparative phrase.

> Spring air, *thick with odor of lilac,* moved through the gardens of Montgomery.

Similar in effect is the *appositive,* a construction that identifies the word preceding it.

> Joe, *the mailman,* said hello.

The appositive is more simply adjectival than the adjective with prepositional phrase, and briefer than clausal versions: "Fred the horse thief walked in" is more concise than "Fred, who is the horse thief, walked in." In relative phrases not in apposition we can also omit words when the relationship is clear without them; when they can be omitted, they should be. Any unnecessary word, in writing, makes it more likely that the reader will become bored and inattentive. Say,

"The flowers she picked were lying on the newspaper," not "The flowers that she picked. . . ." This device is often useful in expository prose. "He had taken a position that was both unworthy and untenable" becomes more forceful when we say, "He had taken a position both unworthy and untenable."

The participle is also helpful. Participles are verb forms used as adjectives, *usually* ending in -ing, -ed, or -en.

> *Breathing* heavily, he plopped down on the bench.

"Breathing" modifies "he."

> The *broken* umbrella was afraid of the rain.

"Broken" modifies "umbrella."

> *Impressed* by her credentials, Mr, Jefferson stroked his *unshaven* chin, muttering, "Yes, yes, just what we have in mind."

"Impressed" modifies "Mr. Jefferson," and "unshaven" modifies "chin."

We can frequently use participles in modifying phrases in place of whole subordinate or independent clauses, saving words. Participles past or present:

> Tiring of the game, Hamilton took out his doughnut cutter.

> Tired of the game . . . etc.

The versions above are briefer than these alternatives:

> Hamilton was tired (tiring) of the game. He took out his doughnut cutter.

> Hamilton was tiring (tired) of the game, and he took out his doughnut cutter.

> When he tired of the game, Hamilton took out his doughnut cutter.

Notice how syntax, like words, has insides. Each arrangement makes a gesture of meaning. The final example, with its subordinate clause beginning with "when," is an alternative to the participle many writers prefer. It is more precise. "Tired of the game, Hamilton . . ." doesn't definitely connect the tiredness and Hamilton's act. It implies a connection, but doesn't state it. "When he tired of the game, Hamilton . . ." states the order in which things happened: "At the moment when he tired, he. . . ." Although it is not logical to assume that, because one event follows another, the first caused the second, we usually assume so unless we are told not to. But if we wanted to emphasize causation, we could use another conjunction, "Because he was tired of the game, Hamilton. . . ." In many contexts, the "because" might seem overinsistent, or bullying. If we write that a person's best friend has stolen his wife, ruined his business, turned his friends against him, and hired someone to kill him, it is enough to say, "Bill had grown to hate his former friend." If we write, "Because Bill had done these things, he had grown to hate his former friend," we have wasted the reader's time. He is likely to feel insulted, because we have estimated his intelligence so slightingly. We have no way of deciding, without context, what form of the sentence would be best. In relaxed, informal writing, the participle might feel right. But the participle leaves questions for the reader, questions that conjunctions like "when" or "because" would answer The writer has to decide, with each sentence, how much, and with what precision, to tell the reader.

For advice on punctuating complex sentences, see pages 307–308. Also see the discussion of dangling participles on pages 301–302.

Long Sentences

In the most controlled prose, in the long sentences made by writers being formal, clause follows clause, the sentence is compound as well as complex, and absolutes, participles, and appositives combine with prepositional phrases—a combination of combinations that includes, balances, and ultimately unifies.

If we took the sentence above and reduced it to one complete clause for each idea, we might end with something like this:

> Some prose is highly controlled and the sentences are long. This happens when the writer is being formal. There are many clauses. The sentence can be compound and it can also be complex. The sentence can also include absolutes, participles, appositives, and prepositional phrases. This combination makes the sentence inclusive. It gives it balance, and it gives it unity.

Seven sentences, in this version, and fifty-nine words. The earlier version was one sentence, and forty-four words. The gain in brevity is trivial, but the shorter version is more accurate. It is more accurate by its use of subordination, not only in bringing form and content into agreement, but by making direct syntactic connections instead of continually stopping the flow of sense and picking it up again with a pronoun.

But the example is made up for the occasion. Here are some sentences from writers at work. Auden is defining the sea as symbol in religion and in literature.

> The sea, in fact, is that state of barbaric vagueness and disorder out of which civilization has emerged and into which, unless saved by the effort of gods and men, it is always liable to relapse.
> W. H. Auden, *The Enchafed Flood*

This sentence starts slowly, with "in fact" and "state of," but ends with a flourish. Auden carries us up the hill, as far as the phrase "and into which," and then holds us at the summit for a while with "unless saved by the effort of gods and men" before he takes us downhill to resolve the main thought. The parallelism between the prepositions and relatives "out of which" and "into which" finds its action in the exact verbs "emerged" and "relapse," interrupted, with precise syntactic sense, by the "unless" clause that separates the relative and the verb in the final clause. We might try once more to supply a version of the sentence as someone else might have written it.

> The sea literally depicts a state of being that is barbaric. Also, it is vague, and it does not have any order in it. Civilization is what has come out of the sea. Civilization is always liable to go back into the sea. But civilization is saved by the efforts of gods and men. Or it has been so far, anyway.

Let us find more long sentences, graceful and agile.

> In the early morning the distant image of Cannes, the pink and cream of old fortifications, the purple Alps that bounded Italy, were cast across the water and lay quavering in the ripples and rings sent up by sea-plants through the clear shadows.
> F. Scott Fitzgerald, *Tender Is the Night*

The passage begins and ends with prepositional phrases ("In the early morning . . . through the clear shadows") and in between are more of them, and adjectives, and a varied use of verbs: "bounded, cast, lay quavering." The verbs, which follow each other in time, have as subject the three phrases and clauses before—an elaborated subject, which includes the verb "bounded" as well as nouns and adjectives. Then we move into more prepositions and nouns, another verb, preposition and noun, preposition, adjective, and noun. At the center stand the verbs that carry the sentence. The prose is ornate and well-ordered, but not so formal as the prose of some historians and essayists. Here is a whole paragraph, beginning with a simple sentence.

> Perhaps Philip had not made up his mind either. The English had given him provocation enough: Drake's impudent raid down the Spanish coast and across to the West Indies, Leicester's army in the Netherlands, the worsening fate of the English Catholics for whom, ever since his marriage in England, Philip had felt a special responsibility. The Pope exhorted him to act, the English exile begged him to hurry, and among his counsellors the war party was in the ascendant. It may be that Philip was only making haste slowly because, as he had once written, in so great a matter it was better to walk with leaden feet.
>
> Garrett Mattingly, *The Defeat of the Spanish Armada*

Here is classic prose that is vigorous and formal at the same time. Try to recast the second sentence into simple sentences. Notice the colon used to imply that something follows which had been announced by the phrase before the colon. Notice how Mattingly starts listing provocations with a long compound subject, varies into a short subject, and then concludes with a long subject ending with a subordinate clause. After this long, complex sentence, the historian varies the pattern by writing a three-part compound and ends with a longer complex sentence.

The long, complex sentence lends itself to organizing things that are related to each other, like events in history, plots of stories, or arguments with several parts.

Punctuation and Variety: Compound Sentences

We use a comma, generally, when the two independent clauses in a compound sentence are long.

> The man wore a green bandana around his neck, but his wife wore a Brooks Brothers suit and a black silk tie.

Short compound sentences, however, need no commas. "He was fat and she was thin." The contradiction inside "but" often suggests a comma's pause, but it is a matter of ear, of judgment, rather than of rule. "He was thin, but he was tall" draws more attention to the speaker's insistence on two opposed ideas than does the same sentence without a comma, "He was thin but he was tall," which seems more matter-of-fact, more conversational. Context determines choice.

Compound sentences are loosely held together; a semicolon can substitute for the connective "and." The semicolon implies the close relationship between two clauses, which "and" also implies, but the semicolon makes a different rhythm, by substituting a pause for a connective word. It is a useful variation, and it feels more formal. Avoid tacking together loose compounds, correlative clauses all in a row. Prose that repeats the same loose structure comes to feel too lax. We are all familiar with the speaker who cannot pause.

> I saw her and she was carrying a kitten and it had a crooked tail and I think it was part Siamese and . . .

Some of the same boredom afflicts us when the writer multiplies compounds.

> I saw her and she was carrying a kitten. It had a crooked tail and it was part Siamese. The cat was making tiny squeaks and struggling in her arms. She smiled and then she let out a shriek. The cat had clawed her and jumped out of her arms and run away.

It is easy enough, without radical change, to introduce variety; we vary the type of sentence, using some subordination, and we vary the punctuation in the compound sentences.

> When I saw her she was carrying a kitten with a crooked tail. It was part Siamese. The cat struggled in her arms, making tiny squeaks. She smiled. Then she shrieked. The cat had dug its claws into her, jumped out of her arms, and run away.

Without variety we will be bored. But the variety we choose can be more or less expressive. In this small anecdote the action in the last sentence may be best expressed by the three loose clauses, which were there in the original version; however, the long compound has more effect when it follows the two short sentences—two periods make the rhythm choppy with pause—than it had when it followed other compounds. It is like coming from a dark theater into daylight; the light is brighter because we are used to darkness. In a small way, the grammar and the rhythm add to the feeling, or the expression, which is the meaning.

When we join two or more clauses in a compound, we use a connective word or a semicolon, except on rare occasions when we join brief clauses by commas. The classic example is Caesar's "I came, I saw, I conquered," in which the commas make the pauses appropriately brief. Periods—"I came. I saw. I conquered."—make too much space between these clauses. Remember that if the clauses are long, a comma willl not hold them together by itself. We need a comma *and* a connective, or a semicolon. In

> The hair fell to the floor of the barbershop, the man with the broom was dozing in the corner.

the comma is misleading. The sentence could be two sentences, with a period and a capital letter. Or a semicolon could take the place of the comma. Or we could insert the word "and" or "but" after the comma. The distinction between "long" and "short" in this advice is vague, and must remain so. It is clear that in clauses as brief as,

> John blushed, Sara wept, Linda shrieked, the whole class erupted at once.

the commas work. In the bad barbershop example above, the comma would not work. When you come to clauses of middling size, you must decide. It could be,

> I climbed the hill, Susan climbed with me.

or

> I climbed the hill; Susan climbed with me.

We might well prefer a subordinate phrase—"I climbed the hill, Susan with me." No rule will decide among these arrangements. Context and tone should decide. The writer sould first be aware of the alternatives, and should refine his sensivity to the differences.

The insides of syntax and punctuation show themselves in slight differences in meaning. The first version above is rapid and idiomatic and informal. The semicolon in the second example increases the pause slightly, and the formality considerably. The period makes the longest pause, and creates a choppiness, perhaps even a Dick-and-Jane tone—that boring monosyllabic simplicity we remember from learning to read in the first and second grades. (All comments on the implication of these forms are speculative; a context could make the choppiness rhythmically satisfying.) The final example is the loosest, the most lax; it is not so grammatically informal as the first, but it is closest to loose speech. The first example, by omitting the connection, is a tighter unit.

We have been talking as if "and," "but," or "or" either took a comma or didn't, depending on how long the clauses were, or on whether the sense would benefit from a pause. Sometimes when the clauses on each (or either) side are long, we may want to use the semicolon, so that we can take a longer breath, yet still indicate a close relationship by keeping the two clauses in the same sentence.

> The block was dilapidated, gray, the houses raw and the sidewalks sprouting grass; but he knew he was home.

This semicolon before the connective is more common with "yet" and "so." We can write,

> The lion was sleeping in the corner of the cage, yet his feeder approached him warily.

But we are more likely to use the greater pause.

> The lion was sleeping in the corner of the cage; yet his feeder approached him warily.

When we use adverbs as connectives—words like "however," "therefore," and "consequently"—we always use a semicolon.

> The lion stirred awake in the corner of the cage; consequently, his feeder threw down the pail of food and ran away.

Notice that the adverb connective takes a semicolon in front of it and a comma after it. Or we can make the two clauses into separate sentences.

Much good style, for variety as well as for accuracy to feeling, mixes sentences that are complex and compound, simple and loose, short and long, and incomplete.

Mixing the Types

We can manipulate the types of sentence we use for variety, and to create an expressive effect, to establish a mood, or to emphasize a point. Here are some examples. Keep in mind that the passages get their effect not by the sentence structure alone, but by the whole apparatus we build into them—words and ideas. Sometimes, for the sake of sense or mood, we may manipulate our phrases to achieve more regularity than variety.

> In a little house on the mountain slopes above Delphi lived an old woman with her witless son. The house consisted of a single room; one wall was the mountainside itself, and always dripped

with moisture. It was really not a house at all, but a ramshackle hut which herdsmen had built for themselves. It stood quite alone away up in the wild mountain, high above the buildings of the city and above the sacred precincts of the temple.

Pär Lagerkvist, *The Sybil*

The sentence structure here is simple and stable. The construction is uncomplicated and regular. All the sentences except the first are regular in word order, beginning subject/verb and continuing evenly, without parenthetical expressions, or phrases set off by commas, or any other complications in the syntax. The syntax is as undisturbed as the scene. The sentences are medium in length, and similar in length, establishing a rhythm that reinforces the stability and simplicity in the scene described. We participate in the rhythm of untroubled isolation. That rhythm is established, even more, by the uniform length of the main phrases within the sentences. If we listen to ourselves reading the passage we will find that natural pauses divide the phrases in this way:

> In a little house on the mountain slopes above Delphi/
> lived an old woman with her witless son./
> The house consisted of a single room;/
> one wall was the mountainside itself,/
> and always dripped with moisture./
> It was really not a house at all,/
> but a ramshackle hut which herdsmen had built for themselves./
> It stood quite alone away up in the wild mountain,/
> high above the buildings of the city/
> and above the sacred precincts of the temple.

It has enough variation to avoid monotony. But on the whole, the even length contributes not only stillness to the scene, but our sense of the narrator's calm, unemotional objectivity.

The following passage from Norman Mailer's *The Armies of the Night* exhibits different sentence construction, with different effects:

> So it became a rite of passage for these tender drug-vitiated jargon-mired children, they endured through a night, a black dark night which began in joy, near foundered in terror, and dragged on through empty apathetic hours while glints of light came to each alone. Yet the rite of passage was invoked, the moral ladder was climbed, they were forever different in the morning than they had been before the night, which is the

meaning of a rite of passage, one has voyaged through a channel of shipwreck and temptation, and so some of the vices carried from another nether world into life itself (on the day of one's birth) may have departed, or fled, or quit; some part of the man has been born again, and is better, just as some hardly so remarkable area of the soul may have been in some minuscule sweet fashion reborn on the crossing of the marchers over Arlington Memorial Bridge, for the worst of them and the most timid were moving nonetheless to a confrontation they could only fear, they were going to the land of the warmakers.

In this passage the long, driving, complicated sentences, with many clauses, make us feel high energy, involvement, and enthusiasm. The long sentences will not let the reader relax, but drive us forward with the marchers. The syntax suggests the struggle in the rite of passage. It twists and turns, struggling forward, stopped momentarily by parenthetical expressions ("on the day of one's birth"); by repetitions ("a night, a black dark night"); and by subordinate clauses ("which is the meaning of a rite of passage"). The relentless speed is impressive; notice the reliance on commas; we have no place to take a long breath except at the period, and perhaps a medium-long one at the semicolon. Whereas Lagerkvist, in the passage quoted earlier, used regular, short sentences to give fictional events a dispassionate sense of objective reality, Mailer uses long sentences and complex, forceful syntax to bring the strongest subjectivity to real events.

Revising for Variety and Conciseness

Look over your writing for the construction of sentences. Ask yourself if you vary enough to avoid monotony, if your variations are as expressive as they might be, and if your informal sentences are appropriate and sufficiently precise.

Also, see if you can be more concise. To revise for conciseness often requires conjunctions and complex sentences. Conciseness and precision go together. We ramble on, in our first drafts or in our daily writing, assuming connections and causes but not stating them. If we try to make our prose more concise, by writing complex sentences with precise conjunctions, we often discover that what we wanted to imply does not really derive from what we said. So this device of revision—by adding the conjunction—becomes another way of testing, and achieving, the identity of expression and meaning. Precision of time and cause is a responsibility that the loose or compound sentence may evade. In an earlier example, a tiny revision illustrated a small gain in brevity and responsibility.

> I saw her and she was carrying a kitten. It had a crooked tail . . .

became

> When I saw her she was carrying a kitten with a crooked tail.

Maybe the greatest change here is in the tone; the writer seems to be controlling something, not merely rattling on.

Here is a passage from a theme in which the writer dumps things together without showing relationships. He wastes words by repetition, and he wastes the power in those words by poor organization.

> The building was still burning and firemen couldn't put it out. An hour or so went by. The National Guard looked nervous and young. They drove around in their jeeps with their guns. They tried to look tough. We didn't know if their guns were loaded or not. They were scary just because they had guns but they looked scared themselves. They were about the same age as the students. Yet they were guarding them.

Because the relationship between remarks is often vague in this passage, we could not rewrite it with certainty unless we knew facts, or the feelings the author tried to express. Reading the passage, we may doubt that the student had arranged the facts in his mind with clarity, or had understood his feelings. Later, he revised the passage, and his sentence structure accounted for much of the improvement—though as with writing always, the *whole* assembles everything we label as parts (punctuation and verbs; metaphors and participles) and of things that we cannot label.

> As we watched the building burn for hours, the firemen standing by helpless, we became aware of the patrolling jeeps of the National Guard, young men the same age as the students they were guarding, young men who tried to act tough but looked as frightened of their guns as we were.

The gain in economy and vividness is great, and so is the gain in clarity of thought and feeling.

EXERCISES

1. Scrutinize these sentences, from student themes, for clarity and coherence. Rewrite each of them. If you have to, make assumptions about the writers' intended meanings.

a. It is hard for a graduate student to hold down both a teaching position and work for their degree.

b. He takes one student, Mike, who says he can trust anyone and also that he only has acquaintances and no friends since when is unclear.

c. When a friend of mine, Robert Olds, who I had known for years converted to Christianity in high school and I began to resent him.

2. Make the following sentences more concise.

a. When he had finished eating the birthday cake, he stretched out on the sofa.

b. The magnetic pole, which is not the same as the North Pole, governs the compass.

c. United States Customs destroys tons of food every year. These fruits and meats are illegally imported.

d. A vacuum-cleaner salesman, who was nearly seven feet tall and who smiled continuously, fell down the cellar stairs.

3. Revise the following passage to introduce varied sentence structure. Use variation not just for its own sake, but to make the writing more precise. Remember that commas, semicolons, colons, and periods are aids to rhythm, and therefore to meaning, to expressiveness, and to clarity.

Every man who worked on the docks had to wear a hard hat. He also had to wear heavy canvas gloves. The hats protected the men from falling objects. Sometimes crates fell into the hole. Sometimes steel beams were swung down to the dock on cables. There was danger of metal splinters and serious abrasions. These dangers were increased because the longshoremen might work for 12 hours straight. They might work from 6 P.M. to 6 A.M. Some of the men also had jobs during the day. And many of the men drank heavily. This was because they got depressed. Sometimes there would be a shipment of whiskey. The men might pretend to have an accident. They would let a crate fall. It would break open. They would stash the unbroken bottles. And they would hide them. They would drink some when the officials were not around. The officials were paid by the shipping companies. They didn't want to be blamed for missing goods.

4. Find and identify, in the passage you made from exercise 3, a subordinate clause, a main clause, an appositive, a participle, and an adjective with a preposition. If you cannot find one of each, revise the passage.

5. Revise the following passage into one complex sentence. You will have to make your own assumptions about causal and temporal relationships. Do more than one version if you can see different meanings.

It was raining. It was about seven o'clock the next morning. The jeeps sloshed through the street outside the window. We couldn't sleep. We had breakfast. We all felt hungry. All there was was some beans and brown bread left over. We felt better. The sun came out about nine o'clock.

6. Rewrite the sentence by F. Scott Fitzgerald (page 134) or the paragraph by Garrett Mattingly (page 135) as a bad example, with repetitive sentence structure, wordiness, pallor, and lethargy.

7. Try to write one long, silly sentence using as many devices as possible; try to make it compound and complex, with an appositive, a participle, an adjective with a prepositional phrase, and whatever else you can get into it. Then dismantle it and change it into a short passage with a more reasonable sentence structure and more than one sentence.

8. Analyze these passages, finding the structure in each sentence, and noticing the variety of sentences within the same paragraph. Praise or find fault, as you see fit.

a. Down the hall in Apartment 2 the reporter found a very "strong case." There were holes in both the floor and the ceiling, big enough for the biggest rats. Cockroaches crawled up the kitchen wall. A curtain divided off a section of the room for a bedroom, and out from it peeked an old woman. She smiled at the visitors and watched them with interest. Isabel Sánchez, the head of the house, was pointing out some more ratholes. A teen-age girl sat staring at a television set whose screen was filled with a constantly wavering, almost undistinguishable cowboy movie, spoken in Spanish. The reporter walked to the kitchen to watch the cockroaches, and observed that some dishes were sitting on the table that contained the remains of rice and beans.

Dan Wakefield, *Island in the City*

b. The greatest sea power in Europe and the greatest land power faced each other in war. The stake was the leadership of Europe. Each was fighting to strengthen her own position at the expense of the other: in the case of the sea power to hold her widely separated empire; in the case of the land power to challenge that empire and win one for herself. Both, as the war began, were uneasily conscious that an important and even decisive factor might be an Asiatic nation, enormous in extent of territory, which had a foothold in Europe and was believed by many to be interested in watching the two chief Western powers weaken and perhaps destroy each other until in the end she herself could easily dominate Europe.

Edith Hamilton, *The Greek Way*

c. The young officer, to whom this seemed a matter of routine, continued to give his orders, in accordance with the general directions of his Group Commander, in a calm, low monotone, and the three reinforcing squadrons were soon absorbed. I became conscious of the anxiety of the Commander, who now stood still behind his subordinate's chair. Hitherto I had watched in silence. I now asked: "What other reserves have we?" "There are none," said Air Vice-Marshal Park. In an account which he wrote about it afterwards he said that at this I "looked grave." Well I might. What losses should we not suffer if our refuelling planes were caught on the ground by further raids of "40 plus" or "50 plus"! The odds were great, our margins small; the stakes infinite.

Sir Winston Churchill, quoted in *The War in the Air*

d. The universe and everything in it constitutes God. The universe is a gigantic human organism and man is a tiny image of it, a toy replica of God. Because he is a miniature of the universe, by a process of spiritual expansion a man can mystically extend his own being to cover the entire world and subject it to his will. It is because all things are aspects of one thing that all things are grist to the magician's mill. The complete man, who has experienced and mastered all things, has vanquished Nature and mounted higher than the heavens. He has reached the centre where man becomes God. The achievement of this is the Great Work, the supreme magical operation, which may take a lifetime or many lifetimes to complete.

Richard Cavendish, *The Black Arts*

e. Many women have given their lives to political organizations, laboring anonymously in the background while men of far less ability managed and mismanaged the public trust. These women hung back because they knew the men would not give them a chance. They knew their place and stayed in it. The amount of talent that has been lost to our country that way is appalling.

Shirley Chisholm, *Unbought and Unbossed*

f. There under a spotlight, two Oriental gentlemen in natty blue suits were doing some amazing things with yo-yos. Tiny, neat men, no bigger than children, they stared abstractedly off into space while yo-yos flew from their hands, zooming in every direction as if under their own power, leaping out from small fists in arcs, circles, and straight lines. I stared open-mouthed as a yo-yo was thrown down and *stayed down,* spinning at the end of its string a fraction of an inch above the floor.

Frank Conroy, *Stop-Time*

g. The American does not enjoy his possessions because sensory enjoyment was not his object, and he lives sparely and thinly among them, in the monastic discipline of Scarsdale or the barracks of Stuyvesant Town. Only among certain groups where franchise, socially speaking, has not been achieved, do pleasure and material splendor constitute a life-object and an occupation. Among the outcasts—Jews, Negroes, Catholics, and homosexuals—excluded from the communion of ascetics, the love of fabrics, gaudy show, and rich possessions still anachronistically flaunts itself. Once a norm has been reached, differing in the different classes, financial ambition itself seems to fade away. The self-made man finds, to his anger, his son uninterested in money; you have shirtsleeves to shirtsleeves in three generations. The great financial empires are a thing of the past. Recent immigrants—movie magnates and gangsters particularly—retain their acquisitiveness, but how long is it since anyone in the general public has murmured, wonderingly, "as rich as Rockefeller"?

Mary McCarthy, "America the Beautiful"

9. **Examine these passages to discover the way in which the sentence structure and variation express the content:**

a. Shortly, everybody in Coach House Road was aware that Eli Peck, the nervous young attorney with the pretty wife, was having a breakdown. Everybody except Eli Peck. He knew what he did was not insane, though he felt every inch of its strangeness. He felt those black clothes as if they were the skin of his skin—the give and pull as they got used to where he bulged and buckled. And he felt eyes, every eye on Coach House Road. He saw headlights screech to within an inch of him, and stop. He saw mouths: first the bottom jaw slides forward, then the tongue hits the teeth, the lips explode, a little thunder in the throat, and they've said it: Eli Peck Eli Peck Eli Peck Eli Peck. He began to walk slowly, shifting his weight down and forward with each syllable: E-li-Peck-E-li-Peck. Heavily he trod, and as his neighbors uttered each syllable of his name, he felt each syllable shaking all his bones. He knew who he was down to his marrow—they were telling him. Eli Peck. He wanted them to say it a thousand times, a million times, he would walk forever in that black suit, as adults whispered of his strangeness and children made, "Shame . . . shame" with their fingers.

Philip Roth, "Eli, the Fanatic"

b. And then the Arab drew his knife and held it up toward me, athwart the sunlight.

A shaft of light shot upward from the steel, and I felt as if a long, thin blade transfixed my forehead. At the same moment all the sweat that had accumulated in my eyebrows splashed down on my eyelids, covering them with a warm film of moisture. Beneath a veil of brine

and tears my eyes were blinded; I was conscious only of the cymbals of
the sun clashing on my skull, and, less distinctly, of the keen blade of
light flashing up from the knife, scarring my eyelashes, and gouging
into my eyeballs.

Albert Camus, *The Stranger*

UNITY

The Need for Unity

W. B. Yeats, the poet, said that a finished poem made a noise like the
click of the lid on a perfectly made box. Prose makes the noise too,
only less loudly and clearly than poetry. A good passage of prose
combines its variety into a final unity, resolving rhythm, emotion, and
idea into a pleasing whole.

Unity and variety need each other. They are the two poles, and the
world spins between them. Without variety, there is nothing to be
unified. Identically constructed sentences strung together in a row
have the unity of chicken wire. Dick-and-Jane has this unity, which is
perhaps why we want to leave first grade for second. Paragraphs of
sequent compound sentences are similarly boring. But variety without
unity is dissatisfying, a disorder that partakes of the lack of focus
discussed in Chapters I and II. As the whole essay must include a sense
of resolution, of summing up, of everything coming together—so must
smaller units, down to the paragraph, the long sentence, or the sequence of varied sentences.

Grammatical Unity

The good prose already quoted has examplified unity in agreement,
consistency, and coherent conjunctions. I bring such grammatical
matters together in this section because they can help to unify and
clarify our sentences.

Misplaced Modifiers. Placing modifiers properly is essential to unity
in content and construction. We must always be careful that a clause
does modify the word that its position makes it appear to modify. The
dangling participle, with its often comic effect, destroys unity.

Being six years old and rusted through, I was able to buy the car
for a song.

Arranged in this way, the clause "being six years old and rusted
through" modifies "I"; it implies that "I" was six years old and rusted
through. Here the best solution would be a subordinate stating cause.

> Because it was six years old and rusted through, I was able to buy the car for a song.

A similar mistake is the dangling appositive noun phrase.

> A good teacher, his superiors saw to it that he was promoted.

But this would imply that "his superiors" were "a good teacher." Solutions:

> He was a good teacher; his superiors saw to it that he was promoted.

> Because he was a good teacher, his superiors saw to it that he was promoted.

Yet another kind of misplaced modifier is the dangling participle introduced by a preposition.

> On achieving the age of twenty-seven, his parents threw him out of the house.

(The author may have *intended* the parents to be twenty-seven, and expelling a small child; but we would know that much from the context.)

Or the dangling phrase can be adjectives.

> Tall and strong, the job was easy for him.

There is a prevalent dangling adverb.

> Hopefully, this book will be done by late July.

Does the book really hope? The simplest rewriting would be,

> I hope this book will be done by late July.

In all such misreferences, ambiguity is a possible problem; the reader may not be able to tell what we really *did* mean. We lose clarity, we lose coherence. Even if our *intended* meaning is apparent, however, the laxity behind the misapplied language is a flaw, and cannot be excused as informality. The reader is appalled by the frayed edge left by misapplied order. The disunity itself is unpleasant.

Conjunctions and Unity: Complex Sentences. When we make complex sentences using words that imply sequence or cause or other forms of subordination, our sentences will be whole and solid only if the context supports the idea implicit in the conjunction. For this unity, we must use conjunctions *responsibly;* the duty is frequently violated. Writers violate it often because they omit something; their conjunction appears illogical, when, with all the information, the conjunction would make sense. If we read,

> The work was hard; however, John was an extraordinary worker.

the word "however" is illogical. The hardness of the work should not be a potential contradiction of John's ability. If we read,

> The work was hard; however, the pay was good.

"however" functions logically: pay as compensation for difficulty. The first sentence omits something like this:

> The work was so hard it was difficult to imagine anyone doing it; however, John was an extraordinary worker and therefore he could do it.

Here the protestations in the second half of the sentence ("however . . . extraordinary") balance the extremity of the first half ("so hard it was difficult to imagine anyone doing it"). The two parts of the sentence go together, and the conjunction earns its place.

A beer commercial (the brand changed) has an interviewer ask a man,

> "As a lawyer, what do you think of Fitz's?"

The relationship between the two parts of the sentence is mysterious. The possibilities of sentences in this pattern are without limit. We could say, "As a retired major-league relief pitcher, would you tell me the median rainfall in the Canary Islands?" Really, the beer commercial hides a meaning; it only appears to be as pointless as the parody of it. Its illogic conceals a social statement. Other beer commercials in the series include women who don't find beer drinking unfeminine, a black man who identifies himself as a professional artist, and several working-class males. The lawyer finds his way into the series to imply that beer-drinking is acceptable among rich chaps too. He likes beer best after sailing all afternoon in his catamaran. Beer, then, is *not* just lower-class, white, and male, and the interviewer means something by his weird sentence. But what he means, he is not allowed to say: "We want to show that the upper-class, professional, chic sailing types drink Fitz's. You are a lawyer who sails. Do you like Fitz's?" Information is suppressed, and the result is, "As a lawyer, what do you think of Fitz's?"

Sometimes when we assert a cause we make our prose more vague.

> Because it was raining she did not go to work.

A low-pressure area of ambiguity spreads out from this sentence. Does it imply that whenever it was raining she did not work, perhaps because she was a house painter? Or does it imply that the rain keeps her home from work because she likes to garden in the rain? Or does it imply that on this day, when it was raining, she impulsively decided not to work? Information has been omitted. We are given a sentence that states causation but leaves us with a hundred questions. The complex sentence's apparent tightness dissolves because, with information omitted, the parts do not fit logically. Two simple sentences, making fewer claims, would be more satisfying here.

> It was raining. She decided not to go to work.

Contiguity implies connection, but, without further information, the accurate dim contiguity is better than the speciously clear "because."

When we first discover the intricacies of the complex sentence, we sometimes abuse our conjunctions in order to vary for variation's sake, and we can turn out some remarkable prose. Here is a passage someone wrote for an exercise in the complex sentence.

> While the sun was hot, the day was not warm, for the month was May, which, in the year that I am remembering, turned cold, because of a lowering of the temperature.

Except for a sag at the end, the sentence *sounds* all right; but if we examine it, it leaves us with so many questions that we get snagged on every fourth word. This example is extreme, but subtler misuses of conjunctions are common; they make disunity as we search for complex unity. Or, as in the beer ad, they distort meaning for a rhetorical purpose. Advertising people and politicians can misuse syntax, to deceive us, as much as they can deceive us by abstraction or euphemism. And so can we deceive ourselves.

Agreement. With errors in agreement, as with misplaced modifiers, ambiguity is possible. But the stylistic disunity is perhaps more distressing than the ambiguity. Agreement is grammatical consistency. Singular noun goes with singular verb, plural noun with plural verb.

> The *boy* with the purple cougar *was* bowlegged.
> The *boys* with the purple cougar *were* bowlegged.

Errors in agreement are common when we use indefinite pronouns. "One," "none," and distributives like "each," "every," "everybody," "nobody," and "everyone"—all take singular verbs. Here are typical errors.

> Everyone says they had a good weekend.
> None of the machines work.
> Everybody had their tennis racket with them.

Common speech accepts most of these errors in agreement; but the most unified style rejects them. We should write:

> Everyone says he had a good weekend.
> None of the machines works.
> Everybody had his tennis racket with him.

We should write *he* and *his,* to be correct in grammar. Grammar in this standard use of "he" and "his" may, however, conceal sexism. No one has yet found an alternative that fails to seem confusing or awkward, like "Everyone says they had a good weekend." For some of us, surely, an awkward style is preferable to the bias implicit in correctness.

Perhaps we can only insist that everyone should *know* the traditional rule; then, if we wish to break the rule, we will know what we are doing and why we are doing it.

Consistency of Tenses. The tense, or time, is the form by which a verb signals past, present, or future. Similarly, we should stick to one verb tense in describing one action. An account of something that happened to us usually sounds best in the past tense, but occasionally fits the present. Summarizing a book, we use either tense, often the present. But it is not choosing past or present that matters most (context decides, as ever); it matters most that we stick to the tense we start with. In careless writing, we drift back and forth without noticing it.

> The maple turned red in September, a bright range of reds from near-gold to near-Chinese. The sky is blue, and the maples show fiercely against it, making the colors more deep. On October the first frost came, and. . . .

The second sentence should take the past tense, to agree with its neighboring sentences. On rare occasions, and usually at a paragraph break, we can change tenses. A leisurely description moves into sudden action, and a break from past to present signals this change. Be careful if you try this device; and know that you are doing it.

Structural Unity

Many attributes that give stylistic finish and polish come from the organization of the sentence, rather than from diction. Ranging from the definable *parallelism* to the intangible *rhythm,* these structural attributes are harder to define than the grammatical unity that is obligatory in good prose.

Parallelism. Parallelism generally belongs to formal prose, and frequently appears in informal prose as well. Parallel constructions are phrases or clauses within the same sentence that repeat the same word forms (nouns, verbs, adjectives, and the like) in the same order to perform the same function.

> He quit the job because the boss was cruel, the pay was meager, and the work was dangerous.

> the boss was cruel / the pay was meager / the work was dangerous

After the conjunction, each subordinate clause follows the pattern made by article/noun/past tense verb/predicate adjective. Parallelism is not a grammatical necessity, like agreement. It helps us to manage sentences, and to *clarify* grammar. It is a matter of clarity and symmetry, not of correctness.

We use parallelism most obviously when with pairs of words we introduce the parallels: "both/and," "either/or," "neither/nor," "not/but," "not only/but also," "first/second/third." The sentence beginning with one member of these pairs should pivot on the other; also, the parallel clauses should be syntactically parallel. Do not write,

> Not only did he run into the fire, but also wearing no shoes.

This nonparallel construction is comprehensible, but it feels stylistically lax. These clauses are not parallel because the second uses a participle instead of the active verb in the first clause. We could rewrite it.

> Not only did he run into the fire, but also he wore no shoes.

In writing many clauses together, it is common but confusing to depart from parallelism and destroy unity.

> His reasons were: first, the overwhelming size of the debt; second, that the company was ill-managed; third, having so little leisure in such a job.

The sentence can be rewritten in numerous ways; for instance,

> His reasons were: first, that the debt had grown huge; second, that the firm was ill-managed; third, that the job afforded little leisure.

The parallelism would remain the same—and we would still want parallelism—if we dropped the enumerations.

> His reasons were that the debt had grown huge, that the firm was ill-managed, and that the job afforded little leisure.

The briefest way to write the sentence would be to make parallels in the predicate subordinate to one "that," by using the verb "to be" once and then understanding it elsewhere in its absence.

> His reasons were that the debt was big, the firm ill-managed, and the job onerous.

The more concise the sentence becomes, the more formal the prose.
With "either/or," "not only/but also," and similar correlative expressions, be sure that by position in the sentence you make the words correlate the same parts of speech in each clause. We frequently misplace our "eithers" and "onlys." We say,

> Either she committed the crime or someone else did.

and we are right. This "either" and this "or" correctly refer to "she" and "someone else." But too often we say,

> Either she ironed all morning, or she watched television.

Because the verbs are being related, the sentence should read,

> She either ironed all morning or watched television.

Here are other ambiguous uses followed by clear ones.

> Either the professor was asleep or drunk.
> The professor was either asleep or drunk.

and

> They not only ran to the grocer, but also to the florist.
> They ran not only to the grocer, but also to the florist.

In making a list, either use an article or a preposition once, at the beginning of the list, or use it throughout.

> The soup, spaghetti, lamb, and salad . . .

or

> The soup, the spaghetti, the lamb, and the salad . . .

but not a mixture.

> The soup, spaghetti, the lamb, and salad . . .

Not for formal prose, at any rate. For rhythm and emphasis, in informal prose, or in a poem, one might depart from parallelism and profit by the departure.

When one or more prepositional phrases contain several words, parallelism always repeats the preposition. It says,

> Through wind, through sleet that stung his cheeks, and through snow . . .

not

> Through wind, sleet that stung his cheeks, and snow . . .

When you use long clauses, introduced by parallel conjunctions, repeat the conjunction. With long clauses, we need the repetition for clarity. In short clauses, we can omit them after the first.

> Although day was done, and night approaching, he kept on ploughing.

But

> Although the sun had gone down more than twenty minutes ago, and although shadows thickened in the field, he kept on ploughing.

Also, use parallel parts of speech. Verbs go with verbs in a parallel, nouns with nouns, and adjectives with adjectives. This parallelism begins with lists:

> From a distance, he looked tall, gray, well-dressed, and a foreigner.

Instead of "a foreigner," which is a noun, the sentence should fulfill its unity with the adjective "foreign." A common departure from parallelism pairs a participle and an infinitive.

> He talked to prove he was intelligent and showing off his cultural background.

This writing is stylistically inconsistent, jarring the ear like an untuned piano. We should say,

> He talked to prove he was intelligent and to show off his cultural background.

Two participles would be stylistically acceptable, but the infinitives make a more vigorous sentence.

Another frequent lapse in parallelism is to omit a "to" when infinitives follow each other. In formal prose, we preserve the infinitive "to" even when simple verbs follow each other. We do not say,

> To see, want, and buy is the essence of the American consumer.

We say,

> To see, to want, and to buy is the essence of the American consumer.

The longer the clause, the more upsetting it is when we omit a "to."

> His desires were few: to live on the ocean, to spend at least a portion of each day sketching the sea-birds, to sleep alone, and cook for himself only.

Unity departs when the "to" is omitted before "cook." Yet in informal prose, and speech, we occasionally do something that resembles our practice with articles and prepositions; the "to" remains with the first infinitive, and is understood with the rest.

> He wanted to move back, get a job, buy a convertible, and drive through town in style.

As with the rule on prepositions and articles, the word "to," once omitted after the first use, may not slip back in again.

Constructions on two sides of coordinates should agree. If we find ourselves writing,

> Either he was rotten or a badly misunderstood young man.

we should improve it by keeping the parts of speech parallel.

> He was either rotten or badly misunderstood.

Sometimes we make sentences like this one:

> He hoped that she would come and she would wear the blue dress.

The first clause uses "that" and the second violates unity by omitting it. The sentence should read,

> He hoped that she would come and that she would wear the blue dress.

The word "that" can safely be omitted entirely, when no parallel clause is used. "He hoped she would come" by itself is fine, but when "he hoped" more than one clause, we need parallel "thats." In the single clause, follow your ear.

Emphasis. Since emphasis works to construct a sentence firmly, emphasis promotes unity. When we use emphasis well, we make a unity between sentence structure and meaning and between sentence structure and appropriate emotional tone. Repetition, contrast, and order are three means of emphasis.

Parallelism is emphatic, and parallelism is a form of *repetition.* Where the politician's speech as a whole gathers speed by repeating a phrase, like "and what is your answer to *this*, Mr. President?", so the sentence gathers firmness by repeating parts and structures. The repetition creates dramatic heightening, like quickening drumbeats on a movie sound track.

> We must agree that *the present administration is* bankrupt, *that it has* no cash reserves of the spirit, *that its morale is* a total liability.

Balance, our subject in the next section, also contributes to emphasis.

Varying sentence types can also become emphatic (and thus variety can lend its power to unity) when we shift suddenly from one sort of sentence to another. This is *contrast.* Most commonly, we see a short sentence provide emphasis after several long sentences.

> We cannot agree that the Cabinet has been ineffective, because as far as we can tell the Cabinet does not exist. If it exists, will someone please tell us if it has met? For we have been unable to discover when it meets, or where, or with whom in attendance, or if the President knows his own Secretaries by name. We think he doesn't.

By *contrasting sentence types* we build emphasis into the developing of the paragraph.

Careful development in the sentence can contribute emphasis. This is emphasis by *order*. For emphasis, we put the most important words in the sentence at the beginning or at the end—and mostly at the end. (See Concluding the Sentence, pages 159–160.) If a sentence has three parts, which we could score from one to three from least to most interesting, the emphatic sentence probably would be 2, 1, 3; it could be 3, 1, 2, and it could be 1, 2, 3; it could not end with 1 and remain emphatic.

When the sentence saves the most crucial or dramatic part for last, we call it a *periodic* sentence We postpone the most important part of a sentence—often the simple predicate—by using clauses or phrases or parenthetical remarks, in order to build suspense and gain attention. Sentence structure promises that something is coming, but holds it back, teasing the reader, so that the resolution comes with power.

> That the spring was late this year, that the dogwood never bloomed and that the flowers struggled wanly out of the garden, all of these failures must have contributed to the moment when Frederick, suddenly and without warning, shot his wife.

When we have several details or ideas to present in a sentence, the emphatic order is the *crescendo*. If one of the details is a surprise—something that may seem out of place, but really belongs there—it should come last. Otherwise the order is simply the order of intensity.

> After the flood, we saw great willows uprooted, houses ripped from their foundations and drifted against canyon walls, and the swollen bodies of the dead.

> The president has tricked the workers, ignored the military, soaked the rich, and plundered the poor.

Departures from an emphatic order destroy unity by appearing fortuitous. A periodic sentence feels constructed and planned, sturdier than a loose sentence, which trails off into "many other instances of this kind." An emphatic order makes us feel control, not randomness. It is one more device contributing to the click of the box.

Balance. Balance and parallelism are related; both have to do with repetition. Both can create emphasis. But parallel construction is a matter of maintaining equal grammatical structure, and balance has to do with getting the sentence parts, each with its own weight, where they fit. Balance is style, it is not grammar, nor can it be described grammatically. A balanced sentence is one in which the main parts of the sentence have approximately the same rhythm and importance. A balanced sentence need not have *two* parts in balance; it may have three or four or more. Balance is similarity and *sense;* parallelism is similarity and *structure.* Balance is a less precise matter than parallel construction.

> In his day, Frank built model airplanes of balsa wood and went to the movies on Saturday; / now, at the same age, Jim cruises around in his own car and flies to New York for the weekend.

> Fred said it was dangerous, / but Bill insisted on going.

These sentences have balance but do not have precisely parallel construction. For accurate expression, and without ambiguity, they depart from exact parallelism. Of course balance and parallelism are not necessarily exclusive. Not only are they similar in the unity they create, but both can work in the same sentence.

> The Grogs wanted only to share and be reconciled; the Kogs wanted only to kill or be killed.

Balance and parallelism give emphasis to a sentence and help us to remember it. Many proverbs and epigrams employ them for these reasons.

Here is parallelism without balance.

> We are to have what we have as if it were loaned to us and not given; to be without proprietary rights to body or soul, mind or faculties, worldly goods or honors, friends, relations, houses, castles, or anything else.
>
> Meister Eckhart

Balance without parallelism:

> People possess four things
> that are no good at sea:/
> anchor, rudder, oars, and
> the fear of going down.
>   Antonio Machado

Balance and parallelism:

> The foxes have their holes and the birds have their nests; but the Son of Man has no place to lay his head and to rest.

Extreme balance and parallelism, as in wise sayings:

> The old pine-tree speaks divine wisdom; the secret bird manifests eternal truth.
>
> Zen proverb

Rhythm. Rhythm and resolution, which we name together because they seem related, are more difficult to define or exemplify than any other words used in this book. By rhythm we mean sounds pleasingly arranged, the sort of emphatic arrangement we might wave our arms to accompany, or want to tap our feet to. The Hemingway passage quoted on page 16 succeeds by its rhythm. Here is another example of superb rhythm, quite different from Hemingway's, more lush and energetic.

> Witches, werewolves, imps, demons and hobgoblins plummetted from the sky, some on brooms, others on hoops, still others on spiders. Osnath, the daughter of Machlath, her fiery hair loosened in the wind, her breasts bare and thighs exposed, leaped from chimney to chimney, and skated along the eaves. Namah, Hurmizah the daughter of Aff, and many other she-devils did all sorts of somersaults. Satan himself gave away the bride, while four evil spirits held the poles of the canopy, which had turned into writhing pythons. Four dogs escorted the groom.
>
> Isaac Bashevis Singer, "The Gentleman from Cracow"

Rhythmic pleasure is essential to the resolutions that make good style, but rhythmic effects cannot be separated from the meanings in the words embodying the rhythm. Look at the examples elsewhere in this book of carelessly constructed sentences, for instance on pages 3–4, 7, and 166–167. In these examples we can feel the difference between prose that is strong in rhythm and resolution, and prose that is weak in rhythm and resolution.

I suspect that a writer's ear is his most subtle, and possibly his most valuable, piece of equipment. We acquire a good ear by reading the great masters until their cadences become part of our minds. The stored memory of a hundred thousand sentences becomes the standard of the writer's own ear.

Resolution Resolution is the art of ending a thing so that the reader feels satisfied. Resolution partakes of sound, sense, feeling, and emphasis. The periodic sentence, holding back its emphasis until the end, is an obvious method of achieving resolution. Here is another periodic sentence.

> Without schooling, without friends, without money, without the accent that is necessary for success in Britain, he arrived in London.

This device is so pointed that we cannot do it often, and must usually rely on more subtle resolutions. No rules can govern resolution or rhythm, only example and exhortation, because each click of the box is improvised. The more we know the materials that make style, the more extensive our ability to improvise. Look back at F. Scott Fitzgerald (page 134) and see the slow, rising beginning, the calm plateau at the verbal center, and the slow, peaceful descent at the end. Then contrast it with quicker-moving, informative prose by Garrett Mattingly (page 135). Each sentence is its own little dance, in which variety arrives at unity by way of improvisation; and each sentence relates to each other sentence as part relates to part, so that the paragraph is a round of dances that become one dance.

In talking about rhythm and resolution, we are not so much covering new material as looking at old material from another point of view. Asking you to practice rhythm and resolution is asking you to write well.

Concluding the Sentence. I have been speaking—in Emphasis, and in Resolution—about ending the sentence well. No sentence can have resolution if it trails off in flatness or emptiness. Let us look at some common failures. In conversation, and in unedited writing, we frequently start a sentence with high energy and then collapse when we try to conclude it: we have a subject, but we haven't the faintest notion for a predicate. We say,

> The increase in heroin consumption in the early seventies

because we are worried. But we don't know exactly what to say about it, so that we reach around for a predicate filler, to end our sentence.

> is a matter of the utmost importance,

or

> requires our immediate attention,

or

> is an aspect of contemporary life that must concern us all.

Sometimes a writer will string such sentences together—all strong subjects with weak predicates.

> The increase in heroin consumption in the seventies is of paramount concern to us all. Firm international controls are of the utmost necessity. The identity of heroin-producing nations is a matter of public knowledge. The destruction of crops at their source is one way of dealing with the problem.

Each sentence achieves the art of falling. These dancers trip on their skirts. The writer has a partial idea—like a sentence fragment—but makes it into a pseudo-complete sentence with trite predicates. The mind that writes such sentences seems to be disorganized, or lazy about organizing. The unresolved, trailing-off sentences communicate a vacuum. Yet with a little attention, the writer could have talked plainly, with decent whole ideas, and an attendant fullness.

> The increase in heroin consumption in the seventies requires international controls to destroy the crops at their sources in the heroin-producing countries.

We used only a third of the words, in this version, and the sentence is unified.

Formulas for ending sentences are like other verbal formulas. All formulas are to be avoided, but some are more destructive than others. The filler predicate is certain to destroy any possibility of a satisfactory coda, an ending that satisfies us by its rhythm and resolution.

Unity of Diction

Earlier, we called some words "fancy," and we have alluded to formal and informal styles. Now, in a chapter on the sentence, it will be wise to consider the levels of diction, the tones of voice our prose can aim for. We think of them now, as we consider unity in sentences, because consistency of tone is another means of holding our writing together, another means to unity. Logically, diction could be part of other chapters, but this place seems most convenient, because unity of diction begins inside the sentence.

Formality and Informality. Choosing a level of diction, as I mentioned in Words (pages 67–68), means *tact.* You do not use the same vocabulary, sentence structure, or organization of thought on contrasting occasions. The doctor delivering a paper to his colleagues writes a formal and scientifically exact prose; the same person, writing an alumni newsletter, writes a relaxed and conversational prose. If one style wandered for a moment into the opposite prose, we would have disunity.

> The amino acids were observed to disappear from the patient's urine which was a helluva note.

or

> "Pa" Barker writes that he and his child bride have settled into suburbia where they are expecting obstetric surgery.

The alumni note could be an attempt at humor. Much humor depends upon disunity. More examples will follow presently.

Of course "formal" and "informal" are relative, and many points fall between the extremes. We must think about three things: first, what distinguishes formal from informal; second, the occasions requiring or suggesting different tones; third, how much unity of tone is appropriate to an essay or a story, and how much variety it will tolerate, accept, or enjoy.

It will be good to start with formal and informal prose writings as touchstones, or concrete reference points for our abstractions. For formal prose, look at this passage from Ecclesiastes in the King James translation of the Bible. The King James Bible always combines vigor and formality.

> I returned and saw under the sun, that the race is not to the swift, nor the battle to the strong, neither yet bread to the wise, nor yet riches to men of understanding, nor yet favour to men of skill; but time and chance happeneth to them all.

Or look at this contemporary passage of literary criticism:

> But to make the modern world possible in art is not the same, as Lawrence would have insisted, as making life possible in the modern world. The myths that Mr. Eliot is at such pains to parallel are, almost without exception, not acceptable to Lawrence. They were, indeed, the very things that made living his life all but impossible. He chose, both as an artist and as a man, not to manipulate myths but life itself. It is this that stigmatizes him as a dangerous heretic. He was, in fact, anarchy compounded, which may explain, if not justify, the element of panic in Mr. Eliot's attack that leads him into such unwarranted abuse.
>
> Wright Morris, *The Territory Ahead*

For informal prose, here is a passage from James Thurber's *The Years with Ross.*

> Ross began as a dice shooter in the AEF, and ended up with a gambling compulsion. Nobody knows how many thousands of dollars he lost in his time at poker, backgammon and gin rummy, but it ran way up into five figures. He finally gave up sky's-the-limit poker, but would often play all night in Reno or Colorado, on his trips West, in games where the stakes were only a dollar or so. He must have won at poker sometimes, but I don't think he ever really got the hang of the game; certainly he didn't bring to it the intuitive sense he brought to proofs and manuscripts. He once told me about what he called the two goddamdest poker hands he had ever seen laid down on a table. "One guy held a royal flush, and the other had four aces," he said. When I asked, "Who got shot?" he looked puzzled for a moment and then said, "All right, all right, then, it was a straight flush, king high, but I've been telling it the other way for ten years." His greatest gambling loss occurred in New York, in 1926, when he plunged into a poker game with a tableful of wealthy men. He got off to a lucky start, and was two thousand dollars ahead and going to drop out when one of the players said, "Winners quitters, eh?" Ross, who was drinking in those days, stayed in the game, kept on drinking, and lost thirty thousand dollars.

The more formal the prose, as a rule, the more complicated the sentence structure, and the more pronounced the parallelism.

In diction, formal prose avoids the slangy, the colloquial, or the novel. A writer attempting a formal style sometimes falls into temporary informality because he cannot think of the appropriate word; because his vocabulary is inadequate, or because he is too lazy to look for the word. Writing a research paper on exports from a small nation, we want to imply that the minister of the treasury lacked financial integrity; but "lacked financial integrity" is a pompous formula. What do we say of him? If we call him "a crook," we will intrude an alien vocabulary upon this paper. The slang is like an error in tact. The best solution is to say something particular, and avoid the generality. Perhaps we can say that he was convicted of taking bribes.

In a more informal context, "crook" might be just the right word, bringing in a slangy touch of roughness, a little asperity. Tact is all. And it is like social tact, which is often called hypocrisy. When you see an old friend for the first time in six months, you may call him all sorts of names that you would not use in front of your priest's sister. When you are introduced to the Rumanian ambassador between the acts of the visiting ballet, you do not use the same epithets you would use with your old friend; you are more apt to say something original, like, "How do you do, Mr. Ceascu?" If you called him "you old son of a bitch" (which is no more original, of course), you would have a social problem.

Formality Gone Bad. We can help to define our terms by looking at what they are not. The virtue of informality can slide into the vice of obscurity, wasted words, or vague terms. The virtue of formality can wiggle in a hundred directions into the many vices of pomposity, fanciness, pretense, jargon, and meaningless abstraction. George Orwell turned a good formality into a horrid one by rewriting the passage from Ecclesiastes that I quoted earlier. In this parody, his modern version is the High Abstraction of academic sociology in particular. Orwell takes,

> I returned and saw under the sun, that the race is not to the swift, nor the battle to the strong, neither yet bread to the wise, nor yet riches to men of understanding, nor yet favour to men of skill; but time and chance happeneth to them all.

and turns it into,

> Objective consideration of contemporary phenomena compels the conclusion that success or failure in competitive activities exhibits no tendency to be commensurate with innate capacity, but that a considerable element of the unpredictable must invariably be taken into account.

Orwell's parody, which would pass for good prose with many people, sounds untouched by human hands, like a monstrous frozen dinner fabricated from sawdust and boiled crayons.

Some years earlier, Sir Arthur Quiller-Couch did a parody of part of Hamlet's "To be or not to be . . ." soliloquy. Quiller-Couch's parody is not sociological jargon in particular. His parody collects a little anthology of typical modern faults in formal writing, formal attempts ending in pomposity and verbosity. As in Orwell's parody, the result is the abstract and the general rather than the metaphorical and the particular. Here is the Shakespeare, and then the Quiller-Couch.

> To be, or not to be: that is the question:
> Whether 'tis nobler in the mind to suffer
> The slings and arrows of outrageous fortune,
> Or to take arms against a sea of troubles,
> And by opposing end them? To die: to sleep;
> No more; and by a sleep to say we end
> The heart-ache and the thousand natural shocks
> That flesh is heir to, 'tis a consummation
> Devoutly to be wish'd.

> To be, or the contrary? Whether the former or the latter be preferable would seem to admit of some difference of opinion; the answer in the present case being of an affirmative or of a negative character according as to whether one elects on the one hand to mentally suffer the disfavour of fortune, albeit in an extreme degree, or on the other to boldly envisage adverse conditions in the prospect of eventually bringing them to a conclusion. The condition of sleep is similar to, if not indistinguishable from, that of death; and with the addition of finality the former might be considered identical with the latter: so that in this connection it might be argued with regard to sleep that, could the addition be effected, a termination would be put to the endurance of a multiplicity of inconveniences, not to mention a number of down-right evils incidental to our fallen humanity, and thus a consummation achieved of a most gratifying nature.

Neither the Orwell nor the Quiller-Couch parody can be called formal. Because of their imprecision, they could be called sloppy, though never informal; imprecision is a quality in most bad prose, whether it is formal or informal in its intent. These parodies are in a stiff prose style that *passes for* formality among many writers.

Pompous Language. We use pompous language to paint over a reality we wish to evade. Earlier, I mentioned euphemisms; sometimes, whole sentences are euphemistic. The airline has the flight attendant say, "Would you care to purchase a cocktail?" instead of, "Do you want to buy a drink?" because the second sentence sounds crass, plain, and barmaidish. For the same reasons, "beverage" is often substituted for "drink." These words are fancy substitutes for plain talk, and we use them (or they are used on us by commerce) for deceit. They are a vice to which formality is put. But they are not genuinely "more formal." "Wealthy" is not more formal than "rich," it is just more fancy. "Rich" is not slang; it belongs in the most formal discourse. It is plain, and formality can include plainness without disunity, as it cannot include slang without upsetting its wholeness of tone. Think of the difference between "crook" and "rich." And think of the difference between "tool" and "implement." Like "rich," "tool" is plain, and perfectly suited to formal discourse; "implement" is polysyllabic and general, and often a pompous alternative to "tool."

Formal and Informal Sentence Structure. The question "Do you want to buy a drink?" is neither formal nor informal in itself. "Would you care to purchase a cocktail?" is pompous. "Want to get sloshed?" is slangy, which is not the same as informal. We could use "Do you want to buy a drink?" in a context that was either formal or informal, because its words are plain. Informally:

> The girl came down the aisle looking tidy and cheerful. In back of the makeup and the hair, which looked as if it would break off in chunks if you touched it, perhaps there was a living girl, somebody with a name like Eileen or Carol. She wanted to say, "Do you want to buy a drink?" But the airline had enamelled her talk along with her hair. "Would you care to purchase a cocktail?"

Or, more formally:

> When you arrive at the age of fifty, your ability to choose has narrowed, and you find yourself at the narrow end of the funnel, blocked from expanding or wandering, focused instead on one bleak point at the bottom of the page. When you were young, you questioned: Do you want to be an actor, or a poet? Will you live in London, New York, or Paris? Now you are no longer young: Will you eat lobster for dinner? Do you want to buy a drink?

The difference here is *more* a matter of sentence (and paragraph) structure than it is of vocabulary. It includes words also, but except that fancy euphemisms are excluded from both camps, the difference in vocabulary is relative. "Tidy" and "cheerful" could go in either passage. The idiomatic gesture of "along with," in the first passage, is relatively informal; perhaps "as well as" would be the formal equivalent. "Chunks" has an informal sound. But the sentence structure in the second passage—complex, pointed, controlled—mainly accounts for its greater formality.

Informality Gone Bad. The fault typical of informal prose, when it goes bad, is incoherence. It does not hang together. (Pompous formal prose, or jargon, at least *seems* to hang together.) Here is a journalist's parody of what the Gettysburg Address would have sounded like if President Eisenhower had delivered it.

> I haven't checked these figures but 87 years ago, I think it was, a number of individuals organized a governmental set-up here in this country, I believe it covered certain Eastern areas, with this idea they were following up based on a sort of national independence arrangement and the program that every individual is just as good as every other individual. Well, now, of course, we are dealing with this big difference of opinion, civil disturbance you might say, although I don't like to appear to take sides or name any individuals, and the point is naturally to check up, by actual experience in the field, to see whether any governmental set-up with a basis like the one I was mentioning has any validity and find out whether that dedication by those early individuals will pay off in lasting values and things of that kind.
>
> Well, here we are, at the scene where one of these disturbances between different sides got going. We want to pay our tribute to those loved ones, those departed individuals who made the supreme sacrifice here on the basis of their opinions about how this thing ought to be handled. And I would say this. It is absolutely in order to do this.
>
> But if you look at the over-all picture of this, we can't pay any tribute—we can't sanctify this area, you might say—we can't hallow according to whatever individual creeds or faiths or sort of religious outlooks are involved like I said about this particular area. It was those individuals themselves, including the enlisted men, very brave individuals, who have given this religious character to the area. The way I see it, the rest of the world will not remember any statements issued here but it will never forget how these men put their shoulders to the wheel and carried this idea down the fairway.
>
> Now frankly, our job, the living individuals' job here, is to pick up the burden and sink the putt they made these big efforts here for. It is our job to get on with the assignment—and from these

deceased fine individuals to take extra inspiration, you could call it, for the same theories about the set-up for which they made such a big contribution. We have to make up our minds right here and now, as I see it, that they didn't put out all that blood, perspiration and—well—that they didn't just make a dry run here, and that all of us here, under God, that is, the God of our choice, shall beef up this idea about freedom and liberty and those kind of arrangements, and that government of all individuals, by all individuals and for all individuals, shall not pass out of the world-picture.

Oliver Jensen, "The Gettysburg Address in Eisenhowese"

And here, in case you do not remember it, is Lincoln's formal original.

Fourscore and seven years ago our fathers brought forth on this continent a new nation, conceived in liberty, and dedicated to the proposition that all men are created equal.

Now we are engaged in a great civil war, testing whether that nation, or any nation so conceived and so dedicated, can long endure. We are met on a great battlefield of that war. We have come to dedicate a portion of that field as a final resting-place for those who here gave their lives that that nation might live. It is altogether fitting and proper that we should do this.

But in a larger sense, we cannot dedicate—we cannot consecrate—we cannot hallow—this ground. The brave men, living and dead, who struggled here, have consecrated it far above our poor power to add or detract. The world will little note nor long remember what we say here, but it can never forget what they did here. It is for us, the living, rather, to be dedicated here to the unfinished work which they who fought here have thus far so nobly advanced. It is rather for us to be here dedicated to the great task remaining before us—that from these honored dead we take increased devotion to that cause for which they gave the last full measure of devotion; that we here highly resolve that these dead shall not have died in vain; that this nation, under God, shall have a new birth of freedom; and that government of the people, by the people, for the people, shall not perish from the earth.

The parody is twice the length of the original, yet doesn't convey any more information. In fact, it is much less specific—substituting nebulous phrases like "this big difference of opinion, civil disturbance you might say" for clear and simple ones like "a great civil war." The sentences wander and repeat themselves ("It was those individuals themselves, including the enlisted men, very brave individuals . . .").

It would be easy to continue listing the faults, because they were planted deliberately. But it is more important here to notice how they change the effect the statement makes. The writing is so diluted and drifting that we don't feel the speaker cares for the subject itself; we don't believe that he is genuinely moved. One common fault that helps to create this impression is repeating pointless qualifications like "I think," "I believe," and "I would say." Many people mistakenly think that such qualifications make writing more informal and natural. But these personalisms are understood without being said, and they make one feel that if the speaker (or writer) is so hesitant and tentative about speaking his mind then he is probably not certain of it.

Be wary of becoming careless in trying to be informal. Carelessness is partly a matter of vagueness of words: "individual," which is jargon for "person," is vaguer than "person" or "people." But it is also lacking sentence and paragraph structure, trailing off at the ends of sentences, lacking resolution and emphasis. Series of simple and compound sentences that bore us are usually careless; parts do not mesh into a whole; there is no consistency. If you write with some respect for variety and unity—if you write with a sense of shape and finish—you will avoid such failings, and inhabit some point along the line that stretches from formality to informality.

Subject and Audience. We choose a level of diction to fit subject and audience. We know, before we think it over, that a recollection of family reunions will be more informal than an essay advocating that the post office be abolished. Content and circumstance determine permissible areas on the line from formal to informal, and will determine whether we choose "crook" or "criminal" before we come to it. If a student remembering junior high school writes,

> After a month of missing wallets and empty purses, we decided that somebody in the classroom was a crook.

we read along easily, and the slangy word is vigorous at the end of the sentence. If the student had written,

> After a month of missing wallets and empty purses, we came to the conclusion that someone in the classroom was a criminal.

we would find the style ponderous—"came to the conclusion that"—

and serious to the point of comedy. "Criminal" is a heavy word for petty thievery in the junior high.

On the other hand, if the student, in an essay on the traffic in heroin, wrote,

> In 1975, an investigation organized by Interpol showed that high officials in three Mediterranean countries, in which opium grew, in which opium was refined into heroin, and from which illegal shipments started for the United States, were crooks making vast profits by virtue of their public positions.

the word "crooks" would be inappropriately informal, in a sentence so formal in diction and structure. "Criminals" would be the better word.

We must learn to look for errors in tact when we revise; we must look for the low word in the high place, and for the high word in the low place. When we have used the wrong word or construction, we can revise it out. If we write "crook" because we cannot think of "criminal," we can consult the dictionary. If we fall into repeated compound sentences in a formal context, we can complicate some of them. If in a modest piece of prose, we find that we have slipped unwittingly into polysyllables and long, complex sentences, we can simplify. But in order to learn to revise we must learn what to look for.

Mixing Formal and Informal Diction. We would write more easily if we could think of prose as either informal or formal, as if nothing lived between the poles. But most good prose lives in the temperate regions on either side of the equator. The informal essay enjoys an occasional periodic sentence, or unusual word. The formally deft argument uses a sudden colloquialism with charm and wit.

A sentence by E. B. White exemplifies the mixture a witty writer can make. White has been talking with appropriate disdain about a pamphlet on writing that, among other things, admonishes us, "Whenever possible, personalize your writing by directing it to the reader." "Personalize" is a slimy word. As White says, "a man who likes the word 'personalize' is entitled to his choice, but we wonder whether he should be in the business of giving advice to writers." The word is used commercially to mean an imprinted name, "personalized stationery" for instance, and does not mean "to make personal" or "to direct toward another person." White's comment, after he quotes the advice, is the sentence,

> As for us, we would as lief Simonize our grandmother as personalize our writing.

The mini-analogy expresses White's feeling: it would be monstrous to "personalize our writing." He compares the offensive diction to an unnatural act. At the same time, he uses a cunning and *personal* oddity of diction. The plain way to say the sentence is, "we would as soon Simonize our grandmother," but White uses the old-fashioned "as lief." And "lief" nudges against "Simonize," the old-fashioned word against the trademark. The bizarre mixture of dictions—the *dis*unity—makes its point.

So the mixture of dictions can be expressive as well as comic. Often it is chiefly comic. W. C. Fields' polysyllables are comic because he uses high words in low matters—or for low purposes, like conning people.

Revising for Unity. Unity brings us much to consider in revision. Go over your prose, thinking of it as something that ought to be as whole and as shapely as a clay pot or an automobile fender. Maybe a little less shiny and symmetrical than an automobile fender.

Look for rhythm and resolution, paying special attention to the ends of your sentences. Look for parallelism, emphasis, and balance. Repair any grammatical disunity that may have crept in. Look for places in which your tone shifts for no good reason, and make repairs.

EXERCISES

1. Rewrite these phrases, to give them emphatic unity, or to remove errors or ambiguities:

a. Without knowing which one was best, the chocolate-covered one appealed to me most.

b. Having arrived at the airport fifteen minutes ahead of schedule, my friends were nowhere to be seen.

c. A genius at seven, his parents were worried about his relationships with second-grade classmates.

d. Hopefully, some of these exercises are simple.

e. Everyone wore levi jackets with their names printed on them.

f. While the sunset was beautiful, the aroma of the garden was more beautiful still.

g. In Zambia, Russia, Poland, and in Venezuela . . .

h. When the game was over, when the stands emptied, when the popcorn was swept up, and the lights were extinguished, a vast silence overtook the stadium.

i. Intelligent, pretty, sympathetic, a good friend, Jane was known to everyone in the dormitory.

j. She danced to prove she didn't care, and implying she did.

k. He answered that he didn't care what she did, that he was furious with her, and he would never speak to her again.

l. Either you come inside, or get a spanking.

2. **Destroy the grammatical unity in these sentences by misplacing modifiers, creating dangling participles, undoing agreement of different kinds, and by any other devious means you can invent:**

a. When the *Titanic* set sail, the world waited for a new speed record for an Atlantic crossing.

b. Too many cooks spoil the broth.

c. Climbing Mt. Everest, breaking the four-minute mile, the English of that Coronation year seemed to be true Elizabethans.

d. Sheila sighed, and reached into Dan's pocket to find her handkerchief, which was not there.

e. Nervous pacing in their hallway, Roger and Marie looked over the narrow island of their universe, crammed with the minute details of their deadly life, suspended now in a moment of terror.

3. **Decide whether each of these sentences has balance, parallel construction, both, or neither:**

a. Let him who seeks cease not in his seeking until he finds; and when he finds, he will be troubled, and if he is troubled, he will marvel, and will be a king over the All.

The Gospel According to Thomas

b. Only when you have no thing in your mind and no mind in things are you vacant and spiritual, empty and marvelous.

Zen Buddhist saying

c. He who knows does not say; he who says does not know.

Lao-Tzu

d. But logic does not always win popularity, and a man who points out the gloomy end of things can hardly expect to gain popular esteem.

Robert L. Heilbroner, *The Worldly Philosophers*

e. A common opinion prevails that the juice has ages ago been pressed out of the free-will controversy, and that no new champion can do more than warm up stale arguments which everyone has heard.

William James, "The Dilemma of Determinism"

f. Another odd feature of the human landscape in these climactic years is that both sides claim to be moved by the purest impulses of human brotherhood.

I. F. Stone, *The Haunted Fifties*

g. Let the actor for the time being keep to himself, store up his emotions, his spiritual materials, his reflections about his part, until his feelings and a definite, concrete, creative sense of the image of his part have become crystallized.

Constantin Stanislavski, *Creating a Role*

h. I think a nation such as ours, with its high moral traditions and commitments, has a further responsibility to know how we became drawn into this conflict, and to learn the lessons it has to teach us for the future.

Alfred Hassler, *Saigon, U.S.A.*

i. A self that consisted of conventional lies, shams, self-deceptions, memory images, a self just like that of other people, grew in me again but behind and above it stood a greater and more comprehensive self which impressed me with something of what is eternal, unchanging, immortal and inviolable and which ever since that time has been my protector and refuge.

Karl Jaspers, *General Psychopathology*

j. My father and mother were certainly of vital importance, not only in themselves but because they created a world for me to revolt against.

Ingmar Bergman, *Four Screenplays of Ingmar Bergman*

4. Write three balanced sentences without parallel construction, three with parallel construction but without balance, and three with balance and parallel construction.

5. Revise a page or two from your daily writing, keeping in mind unity, emphasis, parallelism, balance, rhythm, and resolution. Not only avoid disunity, but employ unity for the sake of expression.

6. Revise this passage so that it has a more satisfying rhythm:

The old man lived in the gloomiest part of the forest. He had a house there. It was made of crude bricks. All kinds of trees grew around the house. There were oaks, fir trees, and kinds that had no name. They shut out the sun. Only scattered patches and changing shapes of sunlight showed on the ground. The old man didn't mind. He had lived in the city for many long years. He had grown to hate the neurotic scurrying about. And the hypocritic smiles and cement-block faces.

He loved the peaceful and sensuous darkness. He felt at home in it. He loved the freedom that the darkness gave to his imagination. He spent hours sometimes filling the darkness with memories, with images, and with fantasies. He filled it with the bodies of beautiful women. He filled it with the faces of kindly young men. He filled it with seas that held treasures and monsters. His demons terrified him sometimes. But it was exciting at the same time. And after a while he couldn't tell if he was telling stories to the darkness; sometimes he thought the darkness was telling the stories to him.

7. Revise these sentences so that they are resolved more meaningfully, more specifically:

a. The Vietnam War was a conflict which was a matter of the utmost importance.

b. *Moby-Dick,* a masterpiece of the nineteenth century, is a great piece of writing.

c. The dark-haired girl that he had only glimpsed before was very attractive.

d. If David and Susan don't manage to compromise somewhat they'll have trouble.

e. The dog was strangely reserved, almost sinister; Dan didn't like it much.

f. The two of them were excited and pleased with their new car; it performed well.

g. The murder of the senator was a senseless and tragic act.

h. In the face of the increasing violence in our city drastic measures must be taken.

i. We must try to write better.

j. Racial hatred in this country affects all of us.

8. Looking into sources available to you (textbooks, magazines, newspapers, college catalogues) find five sentences in which the writer uses a pompous or fancy construction in place of a possible plainer one. Rewrite for plainness, and speculate on the reasons behind the pomposity.

9. Rewrite these sentences as simply as possible. Cut out all the pretentiousness.

a. He couldn't comprehend how the thermostat mechanism was to be operated.

b. The general voiced the personal opinion the defoliation was a reasonable measure in a police action such as this.

c. Your utilization of the word "sensuality" is improper.

d. That wedge is merely a portion of the circle's entirety.

e. We subscribe to the belief that negligence on your part was responsible for the damage incurred by our apartment's furnishings.

f. My lower appendage does not have a great deal of mobility, confined as it is by the plaster cast.

g. She doesn't minister to my emotional requirements for affection with a great deal of conscientiousness.

h. His investment in the emotional complex of their relationship, which had been ongoing for somewhat over five years, was minuscule.

i. Due to private considerations the precise nature of which I cannot reveal I will not be adopting the course of action you proposed as a substitute for my own.

j. The culinary offerings of this establishment are not of a very high quality.

10. Rewrite this passage as clear informal prose, without wasted words:

I was walking on down by the Forum and I saw this guy I know whose name is Caius Marcellus. He looks all shaken up and I wondered why, so I asked him. He could hardly talk he was so upset. He said, "Caesar's been murdered!" I was so shocked I couldn't believe it. He told me how it happened, that Brutus, Cassius, and some other guys tricked him and got him when he wasn't looking. They stabbed him all over, shouting that he was a tyrant and that it was for the good of the people. As he was telling me this stuff, we saw a big crowd and we heard a lot of noise from the direction of the steps of the Senate. And we saw Marc Antony getting up on the steps and making motions like he wanted the people to be quiet.

11. Write ten sentences, five formal and five informal, in which one word stands out as being inappropriate to the diction in the sentence. For instance, "The senator, having risen to the platform with difficulty, stated that he believed the measures the Senate had taken in the recent crisis, despite their intentions, were crummy."

12. Does the word "wealthy" belong in the passage quoted from Thurber on page 162? Why?

13. Take this passage from Ecclesiastes, or this Shakespearean speech, and make a parody like those done by George Orwell and Sir Arthur Quiller-Couch.

And I hated all my labour wherein I laboured under the sun, seeing that I must leave it unto the man that shall be after me. And who knoweth whether he will be a wise man or a fool? Yet will he have rule over all my labour wherein I have laboured, and wherein I have shown myself wise under the sun. This also is vanity.

Now my co-mates and brothers in exile,
Hath not old custom made this life more sweet
Than that of painted pomp? Are not these woods
More free from peril than the envious court?
Here feel we not the penalty of Adam,
The season's indifference, as the icy fang
And churlish chiding of the winter's wind,
Which when it bites and blows upon my body
Even till I shrink with cold, I smile, and say
This is no flattery; these are counsellors
That feelingly persuade me what I am.
Sweet are the uses of adversity,
Which, like the toad ugly and venomous,
Wears yet a precious jewel in his head.
And this our life, exempt from public haunt,
Finds tongues in trees, books in the running brooks,
Sermons in stones, and good in everything.

As You Like It, II, 1

14. Use the clause or sentence, "he never wanted to write again," in two paragraphs, one formal and the other informal.

15. Make two paragraphs, one using the word "phoney," and one the word "insincere." Keep a unity of tone in each paragraph.

16. In these passages, analyze diction and structure for formality and informality. Be prepared to find some mixture.

a. With the passing of the last natural frontier—that series of horizons dissolving westward—the raw-material myth, based, as it is, on the myth of inexhaustible resources, no longer supplies the artisan with lumps of raw life. All of it has been handled. He now inhabits a world of raw-material clichés. His homemade provincial wares no longer startle and amaze the world. As a writer he must meet, and beat, the old world masters at their own game. In his "Monologue to the Maestro," Hemingway states the problem in his characteristic manner.

There is no use writing anything that has been written better before unless you can beat it. What a writer in our time has to do is write what hasn't been written before or beat dead men at what they have done. The only way he can tell how he is going is to compete with dead men ... the only people for a serious writer to compete with are the dead that he knows are good. ...

With this credo the Portrait of the Artist as a Young American is permanently revised. The provincial is out. The dyed-in-the-wool professional is in. Not only do we have to meet the champ, we have to beat him.

> Wright Morris, *The Territory Ahead*

b. A dramatic necessity goes deep into the nature of the sentence. Sentences are not different enough to hold the attention unless they are dramatic. No ingenuity of varying structure will do. All that can save them is the speaking tone of voice somehow entangled in the words and fastened to the page for the ear of the imagination. That is all that can save poetry from sing-song, all that can save poetry from itself.

> Robert Frost, *Selected Prose of Robert Frost*

c. "Omit needless words!" cries the author on page 17, and into that imperative Will Strunk really put his heart and soul. In the days when I was sitting in his class, he omitted so many needless words, and omitted them so forcibly and with such eagerness and obvious relish, that he often seemed in the position of having short-changed himself, a man left with nothing more to say yet with time to fill, a radio prophet who had outdistanced the clock. Will Strunk got out of this predicament by a simple trick: he uttered every sentence three times. When he delivered his oration on brevity to the class, he leaned forward over his desk, grasped his coat lapels in his hands, and in a husky, conspiratorial voice said, "Rule Thirteen. Omit needless words! Omit needless words! Omit needless words!"

> E. B. White, *The Elements of Style*

d. So Elvis Presley came, strumming a weird guitar and wagging his tail across the continent, ripping off fame and fortune as he scrunched his way, and, like a latter-day Johnny Appleseed, sowing seeds of a new rhythm and style in the white souls of the white youth of America, whose inner hunger and need was no longer satisfied with the antiseptic white shoes and whiter songs of at Pat Boone. "You can do anything," sang Elvis to Pat Boone's white shoes, "but don't you step on my Blue Suede Shoes!"

> Eldridge Cleaver, *Soul on Ice*

e. Every adult, whether he is a follower or a leader, a member of a mass or of an elite, was once a child. He was once small. A sense of smallness forms a substratum in his mind, ineradicably. His triumphs will be measured against this smallness, his defeats will substantiate it. The questions as to who is bigger and who can do or not do this or that, and to whom—these questions fill the adult's inner life far beyond the necessities and the desirabilities which he understands and for which he plans.

Erik Erikson, *Childhood and Society*

f. This is a society which has little use for anything except gain. All is hacked down in its service, whether people, ideas, or ideals. The writer, say, who achieves some entrance into the mainstream of American letters is almost immediately in jeopardy of being stripped of his insight by the ruffians of "success." A man who writes plays and poems, for instance, is asked to be a civil rights reporter, or write a dopey musical—if he is talked about widely enough—if not, there is no mention of him, and perhaps he is left to rot in some pitiful mistake of a college out in Idaho. A man who writes or makes beautiful music will be asked to immortalize a soap, or make sounds behind the hero while that blond worthy seduces the virgins of our nation's guilt. Even a man who is a great center fielder will still be asked to kick up his heels at Las Vegas.

Leroi Jones, *Home*

V

PARAGRAPHS

USES OF PARAGRAPHS

The paragraph is the next-to-largest unit we deal with. We move from words, to sentences, to paragraphs, and finally to the whole essay or story. The paragraph is a small box of sentences, making a whole shape that is at the same time part of another whole, It is a miniature essay itself, with its own variable structure.

In that bible for stylists, *Modern English Usage*, H. W. Fowler writes, "The purpose of the paragraph is to give the reader a rest." I called the paragraph a mini-essay; it is also a maxi-sentence: the blank space at the end of the paragraph, before we indent and begin a new one, is like a period ending the sentence, only longer. Paragraphs punctuate, not by a mark but by arrangement on the page. Paragraphs, like sentences, tell us that something completes itself. The paragraph tells us that we have come to the end of a group of statements composing a larger statement; now the reader must pause a moment, and see what the paragraph was doing.

Look at the preceding paragraph. Its organization is only one of many possible, but it is a common one. It begins with a quotation from Fowler, which announces the purpose of the paragraph. Then the paragraph and the sentence are compared. Fowler does not make this comparison, but in the paragraph the comparison is picked up from

178

Fowler's word "rest." In the last sentence I suggest the function that "rest" fills. The paragraph elaborates and supports the first sentence, and the pause at the end should fulfill the function ascribed to it in the paragraph itelf.

Paragraphs rest the eye as well as the brain. Unbroken print leaves no landmarks for the eye that wanders and returns; we sometimes find ourselves using a finger to keep to the correct line. Though context gives us other reasons for longer or shorter paragraphs, paragraphs are useful as visual aids to comfort in reading. Those little indentations are hand- and footholds in the cliff-face of the essay.

FOCUSING WITH PARAGRAPHS

Paragraphs become units of thought and feeling. The content makes the paragraph, and paragraphs become ways of organizing our complexity (for ourselves and for others) into units we can comprehend. When we set out to write an essay, one breakthrough comes when we see which part belongs with which part. We take tiny pieces, and assemble them into larger units, and assemble the larger units into the focused paper. The middle stage is often the paragraph. It associates detail into order; it concentrates; it begins to narrow our focus. We may start with notes like these (from an autobiographical essay):

> summer I was eight
> Robert Kennedy's assassination
> Martin Luther King
> going hunting with my uncle
> gun laws
> the bounty on hedgehogs
> Oswald's mail-order rifle
> my .22
> killing the baby hedgehogs
> how I felt afterward
> my uncle and World War II
> 4th of July parade
> Vietnam

The order of the whole essay is in question, but first, we must associate smaller units with each other. If these notes are on file cards, we can simply make piles of them. Each pile would be a potential paragraph. If the notes are listed on a piece of paper or in a notebook, the writer can try associating one with the other by lettering and numbering each item, linking like to like with the same number. The most obvious order might start with the summer, the assassination, and the gun laws; then move for contrast to hunting with the uncle, with the anecdote; then end by contrasting attitudes of World War II veterans with those of young men later brought up on wars in Southeast Asia. Or a different order might start with this generalization, and end more dramatically with the anecdote. Any order is arbitrary, but some orders are better than others. I wish to show here not so much a *best* ordering of the whole, as a useful, preliminary sorting of material into units, small collections of notes, which may turn out to be paragraphs. For instance:

B_2	summer I was eight
B_3	Robert Kennedy's assassination
B_1	Martin Luther King
D_2	going hunting with my uncle
C_2	gun laws
E_1	the bounty on hedgehogs
C_1	Oswald's mail-order rifle
D_1	my .22
E_2	killing the baby hedgehogs
E_3	how I felt afterward
A_2	my uncle and World War II
A_1	4th of July parade
A_3	Vietnam

This way is only one of many. It is the second ordering suggested earlier, A through E. The units represented by the capital letters are not necessarily single paragraphs. Maybe A would be two paragraphs—first a description of the American Legion parading, the uncle puffing along in step, and then an ironic comparison between the attitudes of veterans and youths, or even possibly a comparison of the wars themselves. The items grouped under E—the anecdote about killing baby hedgehogs and the consequent feelings—might take several paragraphs. But the *order* would be:

4th of July parade
my uncle and World War II
Vietnam

———

Martin Luther King
summer I was eight
Robert Kennedy's assassination

———

Oswald's mail-order rifle
gun laws

———

my .22
going hunting with my uncle

———

the bounty on hedgehogs
killing the baby hedgehogs
how I felt afterward

Many a beginning writer, or a writer who has not learned to paragraph, might write the essay following the order in which the notes
originally appeared. The result would be chaos, moving back and forth
in time by random association. That is the way we talk, thinking of
points afterward and crying, "Oh, I forgot to say . . . !" But writing is
harder, and takes better organization. The paragraph is our middle
unit of organization between sentences that incorporate raw data and
the finished, shapely essay. In developing explanation or narration, the
rest or the hand-hold lets the reader know that a limited subject has
been dealt with, finished or put on hold, and that we now move to
another topic—perhaps arising from the last one, perhaps in contrast to
it, different certainly. The paragraph becomes a semantic unit. It
carries meaning. The look of it on the page makes a statement; it tells
us that a topic, or a detachable unit of an argument, or that an event,
or a detachable unit of an event, is complete here. As even commas
and sentence structure create meaning in our prose, the paragraph,
well-used, makes a statement to the reader.

In order to make statements with paragraphs, we must be able to
construct good ones. The paragraph must have *unity,* and for unity we
often require a *topic sentence.* The paragraph must have coherence
within itself, and a series of paragraphs must cohere to form the essay;
coherence requires *transitions.* Finally, we must learn to *develop* the
paragraph until it is adequate in its fullness and in its *length,* and until
it presents its material in the best possible *order.*

UNITY IN THE PARAGRAPH

In pursuing *unity* of thought and of feeling, the paragraph must contain nothing extraneous. The writer must omit the odd fact which
happens to be true, but which is irrelevant to the topic. The odd fact
violates unity, and distracts the reader.

> We never had enough time to eat lunch in high school: half of the time I'd get a stomachache from hurriedly wolfing down the food. The food was lousy, anyway. We complained to the administration, but it didn't do any good. We were often held up in getting into the cafeteria because the lunchroom helpers were slow in getting the tables and the food ready. Then, if you were one of the people who got in toward the end, you would have to wait a long time in line. Sometimes the jocks, who acted as lunchroom police, would hold you up, too, trying to bully you into buying a football schedule.

The sentence about the food being lousy doesn't fit here; it is a digression from the topic, "We never had enough time to eat lunch in high school."

We must remain alert, to maintain a unity of subject matter in our paragraphs, because the associations in our thought constantly lead us into irrelevance. When we begin to write about a subject, our mind drifts from one thought to another, by personal association. We ramble, we appear disorganized, because our impressions are unified *only* by personal association. Because the reader does not share our private memories and feelings, he cannot see the connections we make—and we fail to make contact with the reader. Here is an example from a student theme.

> All of the recent concern over the slaughter of whales whose species are nearly extinct has reminded me of my childhood interest in whales and other wild animals, especially animals who prey. I was particularly fascinated by the killer whales, which travel in packs like wolves, often attacking larger whales. They will tear off the lips and tongue first, their favorite parts. But man has been almost solely responsible for the dangerous depletion of some of the whale populations, such as the blue whale. Still, I can remember the fear that animals like puff adders, tarantulas, and sharks could inspire in me as a child. So I wonder if, in certain cases, we aren't being hypocritical for blaming the people who actually live in lands inhabited by animals like tigers and wolves for killing them. We might be just as frightened and irrational as they are. But that still doesn't make it right.

The thoughts in this paragraph make connections for the writer, but not for the reader. The writer jumps from the threat to whale populations to his childhood interests, then to the habits of killer whales, to questions of man's rational and irrational fears of predatory animals. To write a unified paragraph, he would have to decide what the topic of his paragraph ought to be, and then stick to his decision. We cannot expect readers to be patient with a rambling, disorganized paragraph, nor can we expect them to read our minds, and recognize an order that is personal to the writer.

Exposition and argument need especially careful paragraphing, because the writer must carry the reader's mind along a path that leads to understanding or agreement. Paragraphs in argument or exposition are mini-essays in themselves. They deal with one topic, or with closely related data, or with an integral segment of a topic. The paragraph is homogeneous. It is orderly—and we must remember that there are many varieties of order. (See Some Ways to Develop Paragraphs, pages 195–200.)

Unity and Topic Sentences

Probably the most common construction involves the topic sentence, which brings to the paragraph not only order but also unity. Often, a paragraph begins with a sentence that announces the topic and an attitude toward it. Several sentences follow to explain, elaborate, or enumerate examples or analogy supporting the topic sentence. Then a final sentence draws the elaboration to a conclusion, in a way that leads to the next paragraph. Here is a paragraph that begins with a topic sentence.

> *At the end of the Second World War, the university moved from the periphery to the center.* The university would unlock all the secrets of nature and train all the people needed to turn discoveries into weapons and money. It would lead the way to national power and prosperity and would see to it that we got there before the Russians. From a hotbed of radicalism the university became overnight the central factory of the knowledge industry, which was to be the foundation of our future. At the same time, the educational system, with the university at the top, became the national screening device through which individuals were to be put in the proper productive relationship to the national program of power and prosperity.
>
> Robert M. Hutchins, "How Should a University Administrator Respond to Radical Action?"

Many variations upon this order are possible. Variations are also desirable, because a long essay composed of paragraphs equal in length and identical in construction would be boring. Sometimes a topic sentence is not present, or is understood or implied, in much the same way as a transition can sometimes be understood. A writer may just have mentioned that he spent a day in the town of Omaha. He might follow it with a paragraph.

> The visitor can enjoy the aroma of the stockyards. He can watch the rich sit at their clubs, drinking gin next to pools of chlorine, beside flat golf courses. The visitor can walk up the sides of ugly buildings on dry Sundays. He can watch grass grow, at least in early spring and early fall. He can listen to the medley of transistor radios in several parks. He can try sleeping for a week or so, until he is able to leave.

He needs no topic sentence; we already know what the topic is. The topic is the place, and the paragraph has unity because we can see that every sentence describes an activity possible in this place.

Sometimes we find a topic sentence ending the paragraph, as a summary. We can create drama or tension by starting with the arguments and details, and building to a conclusion.

> With Whitaker's facts and the facts of the subscription lists before us, we seem to have arrived at three facts which are indisputable and must have great influence upon our enquiry how we can help you to prevent war. The first is that the daughters of educated men are paid very little from the public funds for their public services; the second is that they are paid nothing at all from the public funds for their private services; and the third is that their share of the husband's income is not a flesh-and-blood share but a spiritual or nominal share, which means that when both are clothed and fed, the surplus funds that can be devoted to causes, pleasures or philanthropies gravitate mysteriously but indisputably toward those causes, pleasures and philanthropies which the husband enjoys, and of which the husband approves. *It seems that the person to whom the salary is actually paid is the person who has the actual right to decide how that salary shall be spent.*
>
> Virginia Woolf, *Three Guineas*

Notice how this structure involves us. We are pulled into its movement by the suspense, not knowing exactly where the argument will lead us. The author seems to carry us with her, and our ideas seem to arise from the material, just as hers do.

For the opposite effect, look back at the paragraph quoted from Robert Hutchins. Paragraphs that begin with topic sentences differ greatly, in rhythm and in tone, from paragraphs that end with them. Hutchins tells us our destination as we start; he begins with his primary idea, and then fleshes it out.

The Hutchins and Woolf paragraphs have different purposes, which make their different structures appropriate. Hutchins wants to inform and explain; it makes sense for him to let us know just where we stand as soon as possible, to give us a sure basis from which to proceed. But Woolf wants to persuade us to share not only her ideas but her sympathies. It makes sense for her to keep us off balance at first, and to involve us in the accumulating fabric of her thought and feeling.

We should vary the place we put our topic sentences not only for variety's sake, but to use the place best suited to our purpose, Sometimes the topic sentence can come in the middle of a paragraph.

> We hesitated before we stepped into the garden, so overwhelmed were we by the odor of flowering quince. And the garden took our breath away with its little benches and follies, as well as its panorama of verdure. *Our host, as generous as he was wealthy, introduced us to his avocation.* He gave us a tour of hardy perennials, and a private introduction to borders of annuals. He walked with us among flowering shrubs, among palm trees, among avocados and figs. Our nostrils flared with tropical recollection.
>
> Hermann von Kreicke, *The Migrant Swan*

Sometimes we even find the topic sentence at the end of the previous paragraph. The paragraph break serves almost as a colon.

> In general, chronology is the most satisfactory organization. *However, we must not rely on it alone.*
>
> We would reduce our psychological world to the order of the clock. We would become slaves of "then" and "afterwards." . . .

The first two sentences in the second paragraph elaborate the negative topic sentence which ends the first paragraph, but which could have introduced the second paragraph just as well.

We have been talking mostly about exposition and argument. In narrative and descriptive writing, topic sentences often change the scene, introduce signposts in complicated country. Here are some sentences that could be lead-ins.

Finally, he thought it was time to return.

The weather turned fine.

When they turned the corner, the street changed abruptly.

Election night began with a bad omen.

When he heard footsteps outside in the darkness, he turned off the oil lamps and reached for his gun.

The final chapters seem pointless.

In argument or exposition, the topic sentences have the flavor of philosophical propositions. For instance:

When a man needs help, he must know where to turn.

The nineteenth-century politician's Biblical oratory is no longer effective.

The paragraph is a unit of sense, a discrete idea or topic.

When we revise our prose, it is useful to look into our paragraphs for topic sentences. We do not demand that every paragraph have one— but the *idea* of a topic sentence is an *idea* of focus and unity, and therefore essential to clear and forceful prose. We consider the topic sentence of a paragraph—overt or implicit, at beginning, middle, or end—to consider if the paragraph is sufficiently unified.

COHERENCE IN THE PARAGRAPH

Frequently, in unfinished writing, a sentence seems extraneous or irrelevant when it should not be; the writer has a use for the information, but he has been unable to build it smoothly into his thought. If a fact genuinely does not belong in a paragraph, it causes disunity. If it only *seems* not to belong, it causes incoherence.

The writer must learn how to blend his information so that it coheres in a meaningful whole: the relationship between the sentences must be clear, and the paragraph must seem a *whole*, not just a collection of individual sentences. Here is a paragraph, from some daily writing, which has little coherence.

I had been having severe headaches and frequent dizzy spells. I was terrified of doctors. I went to the health clinic. I waited three days. It was the time of finals and I was very busy. I saw a doctor. He prescribed some pills. The problems continued.

It is impossible to tell what the relationships are between the bits of information related here. Did the speaker wait three days before or after going to the health clinic? Did he wait because of his fear of doctors or because he was busy? Was he busy studying for finals, or did he hope to be busy with other things during that time? Not only is the sense confused, but the rhythm is irritatingly choppy. Here is a revised and more coherent version of the passage.

> I had been having severe headaches and frequent dizzy spells, but I hesitated to go to the health clinic because I was terrified of doctors. It was the time of finals and I was busy studying for them, so I made the excuse to myself that I didn't have time and that there was nothing the matter with me, just fatigue. Finally, I went, although I waited three days before making an appointment. I saw a doctor, and after he examined me he prescribed some pills. But despite the medication, the problems continued, even after I'd been taking the pills for two weeks.

Notice that the writer has achieved much of the coherence, in this revision, with conjunctions and subordinate clauses. Although most facts remain the same, the author has given the reader much more information.

We achieve coherence, in our writing, when our paragraphs answer the questions that they raise in the reader's mind. If we merely write,

> I was terrified of doctors. I went to the health clinic.

the reader is going to ask, "If you're so afraid of doctors, what compelled you to go?" If we don't answer the invisible question, the paragraph will lack coherence, and the reader will be frustrated or confused.

Similarly, when we make a general assertion, we create the expectation that we will defend it. The reader expects us to justify or explain a statement like, "The public was responsible for the war's continuation," or "Statistics show us that cassettes will eventually drive out the eight-track." The reader does not, presumably, know as much as we know about our chosen subject; we must give the detail, background, statistics, reasons, or explanations that our audience requires and expects of us. We write exposition to deliver information or ideas to other people.

We establish another type of expectation when we use an extended metaphor to enliven and organize a paragraph. Here is a passage from a theme.

> The beast of civil war lay outside the sheepfold, and its roaring could be heard within the gates. At first its voice, as it had begun to slink out of the foothills, had been low and faint. Then, as it drew nearer to the town, the explosions of large artillery shells had been its approaching steps, and the different pitches of the voice—the snarling of machine guns, the howls of mortar shells—had grown distinct. Now the beast clawed at the walls and breathed heavily on the gates with its mouth aflame. The sheep within huddled together, knowing their throats would soon feel the enemy's teeth, knowing the shepherd had fallen asleep.

The extended metaphor compares the enemy to a predatory beast, the city to a sheepfold, and its citizens to helpless sheep. The metaphor makes another kind of coherence, which we would violate if we shifted metaphors in the middle of the paragraph.

> . . . At first its voice, as it had begun to slink out of the foothills, had been low and faint. Then, as it drew nearer, the infernal machine could be heard stomping out death on the plain with the press of bombs, and the different sounds—the grinding of machine gun fire, the chunking of mortars—had grown distinct. Now the beast clawed. . . .

Coherence and Consistency

We should know a few more mechanical ways in which coherence can be maintained on the paragraph. We should stick to the time of a verb tense. It is easy, if we let our minds wander, to begin writing a passage or paragraph in one tense and then switch to another. We may begin in the present tense to be dramatic, and then slip into the past tense because the events described actually occurred in the past.

> He sits on the dock, his feet bare on the warm wood, his eyes half-closed in the hot sun, daydreaming about women in black silk dresses. Suddenly he felt a violent tugging on the pole, and a long shape thrashed in the water ten feet away.

Or we may begin in the past tense and abruptly shift to the present tense, without realizing it, because we want greater immediacy.

> He sat on the dock, his feet bare on the warm wood, his eyes half-closed in the hot sun, and daydreamed about women in black silk dresses. Suddenly he feels a violent tugging on the

pole, and sees a long shape thrash in the water only ten feet away.

In rare instances, when skillfully done, a shift in verb tense can serve a purpose—but almost always such shifts are only mistakes that proof-reading should correct.

Another common violation of coherence is to shift pronouns within a paragraph. If we start with "we," we should not switch to "you." We must be careful, if we have chosen to use the formal "one," that we do not fall back into "I."

> But if *one* has experienced the mystical conversion described by adepts in almost every culture in the world, *one* may still fall back into the old dualities and pettinesses. But once *we* have felt that stronger intensity of being, *you* can never again remain sat-isfied with less. The ghost of that experience haunts *us* like a dead loved one.

Coherence and the Paragraph: Transitions

Transitions are essential to the coherence of paragraph and paper. You might expect to find this topic with Sentences, or with The Essay, but I put it here because transitions happen *within* the paragraph as a way to move from one sentence to another, or *between* paragraphs, as a way of moving from topic to topic while keeping the essay whole. *And transitions are essential to coherence in paragraph and paper.* A prose insufficient in transitions is nervous and obscure. It leaps from subject to subject, without stated or implied connection. The connection re-mains in the writer's mind.

Overt Transitions

Often a transition needs to be obvious, to carry the reader along our passage of thought, to make sure we don't lose him. Perhaps we are making an overt contrast. To draw attention to the contrast, we say, "on the one hand/on the other hand"—which is trite but hard to avoid. Or we use the context of our discussion: "Although most transitions are best left implicit, some are properly overt." Overt transitions are often ideas or actions in conflict, when the essay's meaning depends upon fully exploiting the reality in that conflict. Or if we are piling detail upon detail, we might want to use a transition that calls attention to our multiplicity: "not only . . . but also." Prose that explains, reasons, or argues frequently uses overt transitions. In this example, the transi-tional phrases are in italics:

> This attitude makes him a kind of "Pop automatist," *and he is heir to other aspects of Surrealism as well.*
>
> *Unlike most of the Surrealists, however,* and unlike their succsssors in the "messy" vein, for instance, Oldenburg is not dependent on juxtaposition for effect. *Like all the Pop artists* he takes his objects whole and unadorned. *But unlike most of them,* he has never made the complete transition from rough to pristine handling. . . .
>
> Lucy R. Lippard, *Pop Art*

Repeated Words or Phrases

One way to achieve continuity of thought within a paragraph (or between paragraphs), to make transitions between sentences and between statements, is to repeat words or phrases. One of the simplest of these devices, so simple that we might not think of it as one, is repeating pronouns. We use it for both economy and continuity.

> But towards Aumeister the paths were solitary and still, and *Aschenbach* strolled thither, stopping awhile to watch the lively crowds in the restaurant garden with its fringe of carriages and cabs. Thence *he* took *his* homeward way outside the park and across the sunset fields. By the time *he* reached the North Cemetery, however, *he* felt tired, and a storm was brewing above Föhring; so *he* waited at the stopping-place for a tram to carry *him* back to the city.
>
> Thomas Mann, "Death in Venice" (italics added)

But you should be careful when using a repeated pronoun, because if it is repeated too often it can become monotonous. You can get variety by occasionally using the name the pronoun refers to; Mann, in the story from which I've just quoted, uses "Aschenbach" every now and then instead of "he" or "him." You can also use constructions like "His nose itched" rather than "He felt his nose itching" to avoid using "he" too much. A writer also has to make sure that the reader knows what each pronoun refers to. If we say "Mr. Cortazar saw that the man was following him closely; he stared at him," it is not clear who is doing the staring. Here we may need to be more explicit: "Mr. Cortazar saw that the man was following him closely; Mr. Cortazar stared at him."

Any word or phrase, not just pronouns, can be repeated to make effective transitions if it is important to the meaning or the emotional tenor in the passage.

If we once accept the premise that we can build a better world by using the different gifts of each *sex*, we shall have two kinds of freedom, freedom to use untapped gifts of each *sex*, and freedom to admit freely and cultivate in each *sex* their special superiorities. We may well find that there are certain fields, such as the physical sciences, mathematics, and instrumental music, in which men by virtue of their *sex*, as well as by virtue of their qualities as specially gifted human beings, will always have that razor-edge of extra gift which makes all the difference.

. . . .

This has meant that men had to be willing to choose, win, and keep women as *lovers*, protect and provide for them as *husbands*, and protect and provide for their children as *fathers*. It has meant that women have had to be willing to accept men as lovers, live with them as wives, and conceive, bear, feed, and cherish their children. Any society disappears which fails to make these demands on its members and to receive this much from them.

But from men, society has also asked and received something more than this. For thousands of generations men have been asked to do something more than be good *lovers* and *husbands* and *fathers*, even with all that that involved of husbandry and organization and protection against attack. . . .

Margaret Mead, *Male and Female* (italics added)

If we want to avoid monotonous exact repetition, we can use variations (near-synonyms) for the key words in some places.

His *sculptures* seem like men and women stripped naked. They are *works of art* that seem to lack all artifice, *plastic creations* which, in their emotional if not in their physical presence, have the feeling of natural, organic creations.

These methods are commonly used for transition *between* paragraphs as well.

. . . and the importance of spatial form in *modern* literature.

Modern thought, as well, has used the metaphor of dimensionality. . . .

Parallel Constructions

We can repeat structures as well as words. Parallel constructions (see Parallelism, pages 151–155) can fulfill a need for transition that is not only structural and logical, but emotional; passages with parallel sentences can work like sentences with parallel phrases, to produce a dramatic effect, or to maintain emotional tension.

> Today, now that he is no longer among us, who can replace my old friend at the gates of this kingdom? Who will look after the garden until we can get back to it? . . .
>
> Albert Camus, "Encounters with André Gide"

> We describe how the poor are plundered by the rich. We live among the rich. Live on the plunder and pander ideas to the rich. We have described the torture and we have put our names under appeals against torture, but we did not stop it. (And we ourselves became torturers when the higher interests demanded torture and we became the ideologists of torture.) Now we once more can analyze the world situation and and describe the wars and explain why the many are poor and hungry. But we do no more.
>
> We are not the bearers of consciousness. We are the whores of reason.
>
> Jan Myrdal, *Confessions of a Disloyal European*

Parallel constructions that repeat part of a phrase are common and useful transitions, especially in exposition and in argument.

> . . . and they never decided whether they were Bulgarians or Americans, rich or poor, artists or dilettantes.
>
> And we, on our part, could not decide whether they were heroes or frauds. . . .

Transitional Words and Phrases

We use many transitional phrases to establish the relationship between sentences and between paragraphs, and to prepare the reader for shifts in subject or meaning. The most common are words like "and," "but," "or," and "for." Some are words of sequence and time—"meanwhile," "afterward," "before"; of qualification—"again," "also," "nonetheless"; and of reasoning—"for example," "because," "therefore." Although we often try to avoid phrases like these in fiction or narrative, they are useful and often essential to exposition or argument. Their very commonness and simplicity make them valuable to clarify a sequence of thought. These paragraph openings use common phrases to accomplish transitions; they are taken from *The Naked Ape* by Desmond Morris:

> *Up to this point* I have been concentrating on the social aspects of comfort behaviour in our species . . .

> *In addition* to problems of keeping clean, the general category of comfort behaviour also includes . . .

> *Because* of his exploratory and opportunist nature, the naked ape's list of prey species is immense . . .

> *For the next major category,* that of parasites . . .

> *In order to* find the answer to this question we must first assemble some facts . . .

We commonly use comparison and contrast for transitions, especially in criticism and analysis. The means of transition are relatively simple. We can describe one of the objects for examination in one paragraph and then, in a following paragraph, compare and contrast traits of the other. When we turn to the second object, we often begin with one of the transitional phrases that make for comparison or contrast, like "similarly," "in the same vein," or "however," "on the other hand," "in contrast," or "contrary to."

> Freud gave a picture of the unconscious mind as containing primarily memories and the remnants of suppressed desires. He saw the sexual drives as being the foundation of the unconscious.
>
> Jung, *on the other hand,* claimed that Freud's depth psychology wasn't deep enough, that there was another aspect of the unconscious which contained spiritual drives as important as the sexual drives. . . .

Remember that even in expository prose it is better to leave out well-worn phrases *if the sense is just as clear without them.* Many times, we can cut out the obvious direction signals, and rely on implicit transition.

Implicit Transitions

Some of the most obvious clues to transition—within the paragraph or between paragraphs—are words of sequence, like "therefore," "later," "so," "then," and "next." They are so obvious that it is pleasant to do without them, if we can.

The order within the paragraph can itself be a means of transition. It gives the paragraph motion; it gives a reason for one sentence follow-

194   *Paragraphs*

ing another: left to right, down to up, smaller to larger; or other sorts of order: color to shape, spring to summer to fall to winter; or orders of ideas: from more obvious to less obvious; from less complex to more complex. These motions are clear enough in themselves to allow the movement from the subject to subject without explicit directions. We need not say "after spring came summer" within a paragraph, unless we are writing for people we can presume unaware of the order the seasons follow. We would be more likely to move from rain and early flowers to the longest day of the year, to hot sun and to swimming and to no school.

Between paragraphs, sometimes the rest itself acts as transition. We take a breath, and we pivot on the pause. It shows that we are moving from one grouping to another. We don't always have to be reminded that we are moving. Sometimes we do, and sometimes we do not. Develop *tact* for transitions. Develop a sense also for the *multiple means* of transition. A good writer uses implicit, overt, parallel, repetitive—and many other forms of transition, and uses them in rapid sequence as he moves through his paragraphs, and from paragraph to paragraph.

Suppose we catalogue everything in a boy's pockets. The next paragraph could begin, "Therefore, his pockets bulged as he walked, and he bumped into tables when he passed them. In fact, he bumped into almost everything. . . ." The paragraph could go on about his clumsiness. But the "therefore" at the beginning is unnecessary. It is obvious, if I have made a catalogue of twenty items, that these items bulge out his pockets. Transition can be found in image. No reader need be led by the hand so carefully. The paragraph break could read like this:

> He had on his person two rubber bands, a golf tee, two notes from a teacher, a bottle cap, and a gray-brown handkerchief.
>
> His pockets bulged as he walked, and he bumped into tables when he passed them. In fact, he bumped into almost everything.

The word "his," referring to an antecedent in the previous paragraph, holds the two paragraphs together.

Transitions are a glue that holds parts together. You need enough, or the parts will fall apart. But if you have too much, you will see the glue instead of the parts. The space between the catalogue and the bulging pockets is a sort of invisible glue—but it holds, because we have sense enough to know that the objects listed cause the bulging. The next transition, from pockets to clumsiness, is less obvious and more necessary. It takes more doing. The only thing that bulging pockets share with clumsiness is that the little boy possesses both of them. Of course we could use a generality for a transition.

> . . . a bottle cap, and a gray-brown handkerchief.
>   In fact, he was generally rather gross and clumsy. He bumped into everything. . . .

This transition would work, but it is not elegant. It is obvious and general. Suppose in the next paragraph we want to talk about his table manners, do we say again that he was "gross and clumsy"? No, we have used these words up. The stylish transition happens without drawing attention to itself. We move from pockets to bumping into things by picturing the boy bumping into tables with his fat pockets, and then we do a turn on the word "bumping" and we are off into a new subject before the reader knows it. He has been led from one subject to another by the elbow, as a kindly person helps a blind man across the street. But if we have done the job well, the reader does not feel the guiding fingers touch his arm.

DEVELOPMENT IN THE PARAGRAPH

Once we pass beyond the single sentence, we become involved in development and its problems. We discussed development in earlier sections of this chapter, when we mentioned using topic sentences to achieve unity, and explaining general statements to achieve coherence. The requirements of unity and coherence overlap with the requirements of development. As we must develop paragraphs to substantiate generalizations, so we must develop paragraphs to make our associations clear to the reader. Eventually, as we go over development, we will need to investigate length and order. But first, we must list methods for developing paragraphs.

Some Ways to Develop Paragraphs

One can develop a paragraph in countless ways. No list can be comprehensive. But looking at some methods of paragraph development can help us to see the range of possibilities. The type of development we choose—the *how* in the paragraph—depends on the material we are using—the *what* in the paragraph. If we are listing Paraguay's annual imports, we develop by listing, and not by comparison and contrast. *The container takes its shape from what it contains.* One of our tasks in organizing a paper is to find the means of development that is *most appropriate to our material.* We have mentioned chronology, and we have mentioned spatial contiguity. We may organize a paragraph also to *describe:*

> At Rajghat, a few hundred feet from the river, a fresh pyre had been built of stone, brick, and earth. It was eight feet square and about two feet high. Long, thin sandalwood logs sprinkled with incense were stacked on it. Mahatma Gandhi's body lay on the pyre with his head to the north. In that position Buddha met his end.
>
> Louis Fischer, *Gandhi: His Life and Message for the World*

The first sentence tells us generally where the place is and names materials. Then the author gives us the size of the thing and then more sight and smell connected with it. Finally, he gives us the significance of the thing described.

Or to list:

> Now the leadership elements of the Democratic Party began to filter through the suite of the nominee in a parade that was to last the rest of the day, to assist him in making up their mind. First of the big-city leaders to arrive was David Lawrence of Pennsylvania. Following him came the New York crowd—Wagner, Harriman, DeSapio and Prendergast; then William Green of Philadelphia; then DiSalle of Ohio; then Bailey and Ribicoff of Connecticut; then all the others.
>
> Theodore H. White, *The Making of the President 1960*

First, White tells us what sort of men they are whose names will follow, and then the occasion that brought the men together, and then the names.

Or to *compare* and *contrast:*

> In other respects, the film follows Hearst's career with mixed fidelity. The plot adjustments are significant. Both Hearst and Kane were only children, born in 1863, and both were expelled from Harvard. Hearst's father and mother were not, like Kane's, poverty stricken boardinghouse keepers. George Hearst was a well-to-do farmer's son, whose silver strike at the Comstock lode made him a millionaire, and whose later interest in the Homestake Mine still further increased his massive fortune; he became a senator and earned a respected place in the American Dictio-

nary of Biography. In the film these parents are left a deed to the Colorado Lode by a defaulting boarder, Fred Grange, and the Kane fortune is thus founded not by the acumen and push of a paternal figure but by blind chance.

Charles Higham, *The Films of Orson Welles*

Comparison and contrast works when we talk about relationship or conflict, and not merely separate facts about two or more subjects. Here, the first sentence states the mixture that is the paragraph's topic, and the rest of the paragraph gives examples of each ingredient in the mixture. Notice that the paragraph, when it contrasts and compares Hearst's life with Kane's, carefully maintains the order in which it first mentions them: Hearst-Kane. This order helps to avoid confusion, and makes for coherence.

Or to *define* and *elucidate:*

> For eros is the power which *attracts* us. The essence of eros is that it draws us from ahead, whereas sex pushes us from behind. This is revealed in our day-to-day language when I say a person "allures" me or "entices" me, or the possibilities of a new job "invite" me. Something in me responds to the other person, or the job, and pulls me toward him or it. I participate in forms, possibilities, higher levels of meaning, on neurophysiological dimensions but also on aesthetic and ethical dimensions as well. As the Greeks believe, knowledge and even ethical goodness exercise such a pull. Eros is the drive toward union with what we belong to—union with our own possibilities, union with significant other persons in our world in relation to whom we discover our own self-fulfillment. Eros is the yearning in man which leads him to dedicate himself to seeking *arête,* the noble and good life.
>
> Rollo May, *Love and Will*

We are presented with a definition at the start, but the idea is so large that it calls for further explanation. The paragraph expands and builds upon that original definition, until the author brings to his audience an adequate understanding of the word defined.

Or to make clear by *elaboration* or *rephrasing:*

> The "duende," then, is a power and not a construct, is a struggle and not a concept. I have heard an old guitarist, a true virtuoso, remark, "The 'duende' is not in the throat, the 'duende' comes from inside, up from the very soles of the feet." That is to

say, it is not a question of aptitude, but of a true and viable style—of blood, in other words; of what is oldest in culture; of creation made act.

Federico Garcia Lorca, "The Duende:
Theory and Divertissement"

Here, since the word names something more spiritual than intellectual—something harder to define than a concept—the author does not try so much to define and to elucidate as to name and rename, to offer description and metaphor, until we begin to comprehend the intangible.

Or to *analyze:*

> The nature of the inequality needs, however, to be understood precisely. The smaller firm will invest more adequately and thus produce more economically if it has the security of a contract on which it can reliably survive. The larger firm derives no advantage from negotiating a price lower than that at which the smaller firm can continue to supply the product. A contract that is so unfavorable or so inflexible that it destroys the small firm is self-defeating. The effect of power emerges in the way price is graded to need. The larger firm can calculate the income that the smaller firm requires for survival and minimal satisfaction of its affirmative purposes, and it does so as a matter of course. The small firm can make and enforce no similar calculation on the larger firm. The consequence is that a smaller firm doing business with a larger one will almost always have its returns more nearly at the necessary minimum than the larger firm doing business with the smaller one.
>
> John Kenneth Galbraith, *Economics and the Public Purpose*

We analyze when we need to explain or to demonstrate the mechanism inside a process or an act. We tell how it works rather than what it is. Here the author announces the need for better understanding, and then reasons step by step to show that larger firms have a bargaining advantage over smaller firms.

Or to *make an assertion and give reasons:*

> The country is vastly indebted to him [Louis Brandeis] for his creative work in the field of labor relations. in dispelling misunderstanding between management and labor, and in making collective bargaining an effective instrument for industrial

peace. He successfully arbitrated or conciliated many labor dis-
putes. In 1910 he was arbiter of a serious strike in the New York
City garment trade. Not content with settling the immediate
dispute, he devised the famous "protocol" for the permanent
government of labor relations in the industry, with provision for
the preferential union shop, for a Joint Board of Sanitary Control,
and for a continuing Board of Arbitration composed of repre-
sentatives of the public as well as of the employers and the
union. The procedures thus developed and successfully tested
served as a model in other industries. For several years he served
as impartial chairman of this board of arbitration.

Irwin H. Pollock, The Brandeis Reader

The writer begins with a contention, and then substantiates it by
reciting information upon which he bases it.

Or to *make a statement and then give relevant facts:*

Gandhi recognized that the whites in South Africa thought
they needed protection against a majority consisting of Negroes
and Indians. The province of Natal, in 1896, had 400,000 Negro
inhabitants, 51,000 Indians, and 50,000 whites. The Cape of Good
Hope Colony had 900,000 Negroes, 10,000 Indians, and 400,000
Europeans; the Transvaal Republic 650,000 Negroes, 5,000 Indians, and 120,000 whites. In 1944, the five million Negroes hopelessly outnumbered the million and a quarter whites.

Louis Fischer, Gandhi: His Life and Message for the World

This last category resembles the one before it, except that "facts" (or
statistics) take the place of "reasons," which are arguments based on a
value put on events.

Even in the examples chosen, these methods are not exclusive. One
paragraph may use more than one method, or one method may involve
another. "Relevant facts" usually come in "lists." In this next paragraph, the author develops the paragraph primarily by an assertion
followed by reasons, and his final sentence is a list.

If conventions epitomize the mythology and legendry of
American national politics, then Chicago epitomizes the convention city. For one hundred years, ever since the nomination
of Abraham Lincoln at the Wigwam, it has been the favorite city
of political convention-goers. Counting notches for fourteen
Republican and nine Democratic national conventions in the

last twenty-five quadrennials, Chicago can boast that here were first named all the following Presidents of the United States: Lincoln, Grant, Garfield, Cleveland, Harrison, Theodore Roosevelt, Harding, Coolidge, Franklin D. Roosevelt, Truman and Eisenhower.

Theodore H. White, The Making of the President 1960

Notice that in these quoted paragraphs the progress within the paragraph is the motion of thought. The exact detail, the example that locates the general in the particular, the comparison, the logical steps—these motions develop the thought and unify the paragraph at the same time. Paragraph development makes coherence.

Development: Length and Completeness

We need here to talk about paragraph length. Our paragraphs will vary in length, rarely following a set rule. The length must be *adequate,* first; we must take the time and space to flesh out our arguments, to justify our contentions, to explain our theories, or to describe our characters. We have seen about this need for completeness in Coherence in the Paragraph, but we must repeat it here. We must never forget that the reader is another person, who must be given reasons if he is to be persuaded of our opinions, and must be given details if he is going to see what we see. We must not simply assert, "President Smith is the worst, most dishonest president we've had," and then propose to circumscribe his power. We must be told *why* he is so bad. We need reasons, facts, arguments, details—*adequate* to the assertion. We must develop the paragraph, to make our assertion coherent.

On the other hand, it is possible to say too much, to accumulate too much detail, so that our writing loses force. We must keep in mind what is important and what is not. We must give reasons, but we must not give every reason we can think of. We must give only so many as we need to make our point. With too many reasons the reader will be bored, or will feel bullied.

To decide whether our detail is adequate—neither too little nor too much—we must develop judgment and tact; we must look at what we've written not only as a writer, but as a reader.

Since adequacy always depends on context, it's useless to lay down rules for paragraph length. Different kinds of writing, however, usually need paragraphs of different lengths. The more formal the writing, usually the more lengthy the paragraphing. In narrative and fiction, we use paragraphs with more varied lengths, and in informal writing our paragraphs shorten. Newspaper writing breaks up the solid column of print by making a paragraph out of every sentence or two.

In exposition, or in writing up research, we may move from topic to topic by long paragraphs that introduce a subject—a step in the presentation—elaborate it, enumerate it, explain it, or conclude it. We may frequently write paragraphs as long as a typewritten page. If the paragraphs get much longer, we should cut them down. We can always find a place at which we can make a break that is not wholly arbitrary, and give the reader a rest. One argument could make a six-page paragraph, but it would be tiring to read. If we look back at it, we can find the steps in the argument. We can break between one step and another, even though the pause in reasoning is small. In a long description, we can break between one part of the subject and another. Talking of a barn, we can break between remarks about the colors things have, about the shapes they take, and about their uses. Talking about a block we grew up in, suppose we want to write equally about ten houses. Ten tiny paragraphs would be too choppy; one paragraph would be two pages of solid print. Here, we can subdivide our houses by talking about one side of the block and then the other, or by making a division for three architectural styles, or different shades of paint, or lengths of time they had been occupied by their tenants.

Some paragraphs must be short. When we write dialogue, we show a change of speaker by indenting a new paragraph.

> "Did you go downtown after lunch?" He was tapping the arm of his chair with his index finger. Behind his glasses his eyes wandered.
> "Yes," she said. "I suppose I did."
> "Why?"

But that use of paragraphing is mechanical. In descriptive or expository or narrative writing—usual ingredients in essay or autobiography, and frequently in story— short paragraphs are choppy, a rash of blurts, like someone who talks in the manner of a machine gun. When we move from dialogue to description or narration, we should provide a change of pace by keeping the paragraphs relatively long. The long paragraph is a rest or relief after several short ones: here is a bed big enough to lie down on. We do not want:

> The room was large, the chairs comfortable. He sat down on the overstuffed sofa.

> All around him the ticking of clocks wove a mesh of sound.
> There was dust on the windowpane, and the rugs were shabby.
> Dark pictures hung on the walls, and the woodwork was dark.

It is too much like standing up and sitting down all the time. We want to relax and read the description straight.

> The room was large, the chairs comfortable. He sat down on the overstuffed sofa. All around him the ticking of clocks wove a mesh of sound. There was dust on the windowpane, and the rugs were shabby. Dark pictures hung on the walls, and the woodwork was dark.

And the paragraph should continue for another five or six lines. Sometimes when we chop our prose into too short paragraphs we may be deceiving ourselves with handwriting, which can make a few words into full-sized paragraphs, and think that we are writing a long paper when we are not. Or perhaps we find it difficult to move from one thing to another within the paragraph, and so we break the paragraph to indicate a switch to another topic. Often this break need not be made. And at times, short paragraphs reveal our laziness. We fail to collect and to develop our thoughts, and so write paragraphs that are little more than a sentence announcing a topic, paragraphs lacking detail, elaboration, and support. We need to think of further ideas to support arguments; details to make description carry feeling.

In narrative, the paragraph break is rather arbitrary. We could justify one after every sentence, we could justify none at all; but neither of these solutions would be tolerable. So we break for a rest when it is most nearly logical, as when the character turns a corner, or sees something new, or understands what is happening.

It is tempting to be dogmatic, and to say, "Outside of dialogue, keep your paragraphs between 200 and 250 words." Life would be more comfortable, and writing easier, if simple prescriptions solved our problems. Although a highly formal essay might follow some such rule, most good modern writing has much more variety to it. As it is hard to type the best contemporary stylists as formal or informal, so it is hard to put limits on paragraph size. Although formal writing leads toward a more uniform length of paragraph, sometimes it uses something as short as a one-line paragraph. A skillful writer may make a long statement in periodic sentences, a 350-word paragraph that concludes with a flourish, and follow it by a paragraph that reads, in its entirety,

> On the other hand, maybe this reasoning is haphazard.

Then he may write another long paragraph. The one-liner has been a change of pace—at the same time restful, offhand, and revivifying: it keeps us on our toes. We don't know what might come next, we are perpetually a little off balance. Look at this example from a student theme:

> When you approach the city from the East, you enter a down-trodden world with shabby filling stations, electric signs with letters missing, potholes, boarded-over houses, and bars which never close—dark holes of degradation and hopelessness. Next to them often you see old men asleep in gutters. No one looks young or happy or as if there is any future. The only thing you see which is bright and shiny and new is a police car.
>
> But that is only a part of the city.
>
> To the west and to the north, the lakes attract fine houses. To the south, past the new buildings of prosperous businesses, the farmlands spread in abundance. . . .

Here, the one-line paragraph—which makes a transition between the two longer paragraphs—could easily become a first sentence for the second paragraph, but the student has chosen this rhythmically shocking brevity to underline, to make even more emphatic, the totally changed scene that his prose begins to name.

On the other hand, look at these paragraphs of definition, more nearly equal in length:

> A classical understanding sees the world primarily as underlying form itself. A romantic understanding sees it primarily in terms of immediate appearance. If you were to show an engine or a mechanical drawing or electronic schematic to a romantic it is unlikely he would see much of interest in it. It has no appeal because the reality he sees is its surface. Dull, complex lists of names, lines and numbers. Nothing interesting. But if you were to show the same blueprint or schematic or give the same description to a classical person he might look at it and then become fascinated by it because he sees that within the lines and shapes and symbols is a tremendous richness of underlying form.
>
> The romantic mode is primarily inspirational, imaginative, creative, intuitive. Feelings rather than facts predominate. "Art" when it is opposed to "Science" is often romantic. It does not proceed by reason or by laws. It proceeds by feeling, intuition and esthetic conscience. In the northern European cultures the

romantic mode is usually associated with femininity, but this is certainly not a necessary association.

The classic mode, by contrast, proceeds by reason and by laws—which are themselves underlying forms of thought and behavior. In the European cultures it is primarily a masculine mode and the fields of science, law and medicine are unattractive to women largely for this reason. Although motorcycle riding is romantic, motorcycle maintenance is purely classic. The dirt, the grease, the mastery of underlying form required all give it such a negative romantic appeal that women never go near it.

Although surface ugliness is often found in the classic mode of understanding it is not inherent in it. There is a classic esthetic which romantics often miss because of its subtlety. The classic style is straightforward, unadorned, unemotional, economical and carefully proportioned. Its purpose is not to inspire emotionally, but to bring order out of chaos and make the unknown known. It is not an esthetically free and natural style. It is esthetically restrained. Everything is under control. Its value is measured in terms of the skill with which this control in maintained.

To a romantic this classic mode often appears dull, awkward and ugly, like mechanical maintenance itself. Everything is in terms of pieces and parts and components and relationships. Nothing is figured out until it's run through the computer a dozen times. Everything's got to be measured and proved. Oppressive. Heavy. Endlessly grey. The death force.

Within the classic mode, however, the romantic has some appearances of his own. Frivolous, irrational, erratic, untrustworthy, interested primarily in pleasure-seeking. Shallow. Of no substance. Often a parasite who cannot or will not carry his own weight. A real drag on society. By now these battle lines should sound a little familiar.

Robert M. Pirsig, *Zen and the Art of Motorcycle Maintenance*

These even, full, adequate paragraphs march in rank and in good order, helping to convince us—even by their shape itself—that they are calm, logical steps in a progressive statement of thought or opinion.

The variety and unity of the paragraph resemble the variety and unity of the sentence. The effective contrast, when the one-line paragraph follows the complex one, resembles the pleasure we take in a short, simple sentence after a long, complex sentence. One can mix a stew of variety without violating a unity that holds the essay together. The paragraph is one more ingredient of prose that the beginning writer can learn to use.

Development: Order and Clarity

If we do not want to irritate or confuse the reader, our information or argument must be orderly. Things must follow each other with a sense of purpose. Purpose makes clarity. We cannot say, "Oh, I forgot to say . . . ," or leave out steps in our progress. We must move in an orderly way, from earlier to later, or from less to more important, or from periphery to center, or from smaller to larger, or from larger to smaller. Sometimes we will want to move from center to periphery, from present to past. But we must not scatter our sequence—from larger to smaller to larger to larger to smaller to largest to larger to smallest to large. We may want A B C D E F. On occasion we may want Z Y X W V, but not A Q I X L D.

The order in this paragraph is fine; we move from generality in the topic sentence to particulars that describe and substantiate it:

> Winter is a catastrophe. Life on skid row is lived out of doors, and the cold and the snow bring with them intense suffering. The men often get drunk enough to lie in the streets in the midst of a storm. The first time one sees a body covered with a light blanket of snow, stretched out on the sidewalk, the sight comes as a shock and a dilemma. Is the man dead or just drunk? Or worse, the habitués are so obsessed and driven that stealing goes on in the dead of winter, and a man who needs a drink will take the shoes of a fellow alcoholic in the middle of January.
>
> Michael Harrington, *The Other America: Poverty in the United States*

The following paragraph, organized in a different way, moving from pieces of information to a general conclusion, is also well constructed:

> Last January as he was about to leave office, Lyndon Johnson sent his last report on the economic prospect to the Congress. It was assumed that, in one way or another, the Vietnam War, by which he and his Administration had been destroyed, would come gradually to an end. The question considered by his economists was whether this would bring an increase or a decrease in military spending. The military budget for fiscal 1969 was 78.4 billions; for the year following, including pay increases, it was

scheduled to be about three billions higher. Thereafter, assuming peace and a general withdrawal from Asia, there would be a reduction of some six or seven billions. But this was only on the assumption that the Pentagon did not get any major new weapons—that it was content with what had already been authorized. No one really thought this possible. The President's economists noted that plans already existed for "a package" consisting of new aircraft, modern naval vessels, defense installations, and "advanced strategic and general purpose weapons systems" which would cost many billions. This would wipe out any savings from getting out of Vietnam. Peace would now be far more expensive than war.

John Kenneth Galbraith, *How to Control the Military*

The organization in this paragraph, however, is not satisfactory:

The birds often flock in huge numbers on trees, sometimes breaking limbs off. They may bury a car parked below them in white dung. Starlings can be a terrible nuisance. The dark purplish-black pests may tear up a whole lawn in the process of searching for worms and insects, particularly as winter approaches and live food gets scarce. Their antics can drive a homeowner out of *his* tree. In large enough numbers, they can create a din of voices that blocks out all other sounds in the area. Their cries are strident and irritating.

The order is unclear. In this paragraph we move from specific to specific to general to specific to general to specific to specific, without meaningful progression. It would make much better organizational sense to begin "Starlings can be a terrible nuisance" and to end "Their antics can drive a homeowner out of *his* tree."

In writing a paragraph we usually have to settle on some controlling principle of order or sequence and then keep to it. An earlier section on methods of developing paragraphs offers some examples for exposition. Two of the simplest and clearest means of ordering—appropriate for all sorts of writing—are simple chronology and spatial proximity, discussed briefly when we looked into transitions. Here we see chronological order in exposition.

Then the Phillips staff compiled descriptions of about a hundred pieces of legislation that the Department had proposed or intended to propose to Congress, along with a list of the likeliest clashes over issues when the Ninety-first Congress convened a few days later. Memoranda were also prepared on the Department's involvement in certain pressing urban problems and its responsibilities vis-à-vis the District of Columbia. Since most of the Department's business with Congress is conducted through the Senate and House Judiciary Committees, Phillips and his staff drew up biographies of their members, which included information about where each man stood on important issues and the relative influence of the chairmen and the ranking members of both parties, along with an assessment of the strength of the coalition between Southern Democrats and Northern Republicans, which was expected to be more influential than ever. Finally, Phillips prepared a paper describing the procedure to be followed in the confirmation hearing that Mitchell would have to attend before the Senate Judiciary Committee in a couple of weeks.

Richard Harris, *Justice*

Chronology is probably the easiest method for ordering the material in a paragraph, and perhaps the most common. At times, in narration and exposition, we want to leap ahead and then catch up. We must use this violation of chronological sequence, however, only when we are fully aware of what we are doing.

> In December, 1941, Congress declared war on Japan, Germany, and Italy. The declaration was an immediate result of the Japanese attack on Pearl Harbor, but earlier events had made such a move inevitable. Perhaps the Treaty of Versailles. . . .

Here, the opening sentence states an ultimate topic, an event to be reached by way of causation, and the paragraph develops by reverse chronology. Presumably, the writer will turn around and advance through the twenties and thirties in a conventional forward direction. If we had begun this essay referring to the earliest event mentioned—that is, if we had followed regular chronology—the reader might have expected, for a moment, that the Treaty of Versailles was the subject.

Development: Order and Forcefulness

Clarity is not our only consideration when we organize paragraphs; we must also organize for appropriateness and forceful effect. Look again at the paragraphs by Hutchins (page 183) and Woolf (page 184), as discussed for topic sentences. Look at the order of the paragraphs compared with the effects achieved. By their positions the topic sentences give *force* to these paragraphs.

Or take the method that lets us order according to spatial proximity. It can be more than a means to clarity; it can direct the reader's attention significantly, and achieve dramatic effect. Here is a passage from *Gandhi* by Louis Fischer quoted earlier.

> At Rajghat, a few hundred feet from the river, a fresh pyre had been built of stone, brick, and earth. It was eight feet square and about two feet high. Long, thin sandalwood logs sprinkled with incense were stacked on it. Mahatma Gandhi's body lay on the pyre with his head to the north. In that position Buddha met his end.

Notice how the paragraph moves gradually closer to its subject, like a camera that dollies in for a close-up in a film. We start from far back, and move gradually closer. If the author had described the body of Gandhi first, and then its surroundings, the passage would be less forceful.

When we consider how we organize our paragraphs, we must always consider our *purpose* in writing. In expository writing, we may want to be sure that the reader knows what we are doing at all times. We may want to avoid listing statistics before telling what they demonstrate. Imagine the other paragraph I quoted about Gandhi with the first sentence placed at the end.

> The province of Natal, in 1896, had 400,000 Negro inhabitants, 51,000 Indians, and 50,000 whites. The Cape of Good Hope Colony had 900,000 Negroes, 10,000 Indians, and 400,000 Europeans; the Transvaal Republic 650,000 Negroes, 5,000 Indians, and 120,000 whites. In 1914, the five million Negroes hopelessly outnumbered the million and a quarter whites. Gandhi recognized that the whites in South Africa thought they needed protection against a majority consisting of Negroes and Indians.

Revised as above, the paragraph's order—same words, same sentences—makes the paragraph confusing and pointless. The reader does not know what is going on until he finishes reading the paragraph. He will be confused, bored, and inattentive.

And yet if our purpose in writing is to create an ominous or tense atmosphere—in narrative, perhaps, either fictional or autobiographical—we might want to list unexplained details first, waiting for the end of the paragraph to offer an interpretation. This suspenseful order would give our paragraph *force.*

> The forest, all at once, had grown silent. The monkeys had stopped their chattering, and the birds darted their heads apprehensively. The wind in the trees became audible, and then, faintly, the sound of drumming rose from the village enclosure. It could only mean that Godzilla had awakened once more.

Imagine how anticlimactic it would be in a film to show the monster suddenly appearing, and then to pan around the trees. It wouldn't make emotional or dramatic sense.

Revising Paragraphs

Make sure that your paragraphing is useful, to the mind that understands and to the eye that reads. Consider your paragraphs for their unity and variety, coherence, adequacy of development, and their clarity and effective ordering. Consider their internal organization, and their transitions both internal and between paragraphs, both overt and implicit.

EXERCISES

1. These phrases might be notes for the paragraphs in an essay. Arrange them in a possible order of paragraphs.

> the 747 and airborne mass transit
> the modern airport
> ground transportation to and from airports
> the handling of baggage
> the start of commercial aviation
> the outlook for the future
> the SST
> the aerospace industry and the airlines
> competitive routes
> faster airlines
> the DC-3
> the 707
> the CAB
> midair collisions
> VTOL
> the declining railroads
> the trouble with buses
> youth fares
> charter flights

2. Here is a short essay on baseball, in which I have mixed up the paragraph order, and numbered them in the mixed-up order. See if you can restore them to their original sequence.

1. At any one point, there's anticipation, deliberation, preparation: "Now" is a building-up. "Now" is never only for itself. It's cumulative "progressing," in strife, to form the game's unfolding. Nor are any two games alike, any more than two art works that push themselves into being through the resistance of time, incident by incident, in head-on conflict by two complicated machines designed to win through accidents and opportunity. "What's happening" is contingent. There's a whole game to be gotten through.

2. This is to see baseball as an art-work-in-the-making affair, totally unrehearsed, improvised by more than eighteen men, who thrust in their various skills while the moving parts pass through innings, highlighted by crucial plays, to the conclusion being thereby created.

3. The game in progress is a structure-in-the-becoming; if you see it, through time, as a whole, all the separate episodes can come flashing together, and interlock, to shower aesthetic illumination on a drama of its own devising.

4. Like literature, music, opera, theater, and the dance, baseball takes place in time. (Architecture, sculpture, and painting don't—they're purely spatial.) The performer and the observer, while a game is in progress, look back and look ahead: the present action is laid out in a shifting, dramatic time field. A rhythm, of sorts, weaves its way through the "accidents" on the playing field. A current play, involving positioning and decisions, is affected by what was previous in the game, and is having its effect on what's to come later; the game may be seen as an organic unit. Every pitch has its place in there, somewhere.

Marvin Cohen, *Baseball the Beautiful*

3. Analyze these paragraphs for their unity. (a) Do any of these paragraphs have extraneous material? (b) Does each paragraph contain a topic sentence? Underline topic sentences, and discuss in class. (c) What does the position of each topic sentence accomplish, if anything?

a. The sea, autumn mildness, islands bathed in light, fine rain spreading a diaphanous veil over the immortal nakedness of Greece. Happy is the man, I thought, who, before dying, has the good fortune to sail the Aegean Sea.

Many are the joys of this world—women, fruit, ideas. But to cleave that sea in the gentle, autumnal season, murmuring the name of each islet, is to my mind the joy most apt to transport the heart of man into paradise. Nowhere else can one pass so easily and serenely from reality to dream. The frontiers dwindle, and from the masts of the most ancient ships spring branches and fruits. It is as if here in Greece necessity is the mother of miracles.

Towards noon the rain stopped. The sun parted the clouds and appeared gentle, tender, washed and fresh, and it caressed with its rays the beloved waters and lands. I stood at the prow and let myself be intoxicated with the miracle which was revealed as far as the eye could see.

Nikos Kazantzakis, Zorba the Greek

b. In Munch, the thinker, the poet and the painter are in equilibrium. He is no mere formalist. Art, as the realm of human imagination and creativity, found again in Munch that unity peculiar to the great artists of past ages: Georgione, Rembrandt, Tintoretto, Goya. No one can draw a distinction between the technique of their work and its content, between the content and the man. They are one.

Munch strove for the expression of new humanity. When he started out on his wanderings through Europe, he found the ground was already prepared by the conflict of ideas to receive his message. His personal fate, the sorrow he had experienced, the doubts with which he had wrestled, his attitude towards life gave a universal validity to what he had to impart to the world of his time.

J. P. Hodin, Edvard Munch

c. A philosopher—is a human being who constantly experiences, sees, hears, suspects, hopes, and dreams extraordinary things; who is struck by his own thoughts as from outside, as from above and below, as by *his* type of experiences and lightning bolts; who is perhaps himself a storm pregnant with new lightnings; a fatal human being around whom there are constant rumblings and growlings, crevices, and uncanny doings. A philosopher—alas, a being that often runs away from itself, often is afraid of itself—but too inquisitive not to "come to" again—always back to himself.

Friedrich Nietzsche, Beyond Good and Evil

d. Franco's reestablishment of the Catholic Church as a dominant force in Spanish life, through the restoration of religious education, of state financial support for the Church, and by the repeal of Republican anti-clerical laws, led in 1941 to a working arrangement with the Vatican that was finally formalized by a treaty in 1953.

These measures, however, did not serve to protect the Franco regime from the severe censure of the Allies after the Second World War. In July 1945, Spain found herself branded by the Potsdam Declaration as unfit to associate with the United Nations. In December 1946 the

United Nations formally ostracized the Spanish government and recommended that all its member nations withdraw their ambassadors
from Madrid. Thus Spain found itself practically friendless in the post-
war world, with only the dictatorships of Portugal and Argentina still
lending the Nationalist regime their support.

Robert Goldston, The Civil War in Spain

4. Here are some incoherent paragraphs. (a) Consider the different sorts of incoherence in each paragraph. Which paragraphs can
profit by reorganization? In class, reorganize them. (b) Which paragraphs need further development, in order to achieve coherence? In
class, speculate on the directions development might take.

a. The heavy wooden door was painted red, but the wood
showed through in many places where the paint was flaking off. Dan-
delions covered the lawn, but there were few weeds in the dark grass.
A white and black cat lay curled by the door. Three huge oaks threw
their shadows across the wide lawn. Far off, a deer was watching from
the edge of the woods. There was no knob on the door.

b. The days were unusually hot and humid, even for that part of
the state. Joe didn't want to go to the beach. His girlfriend, Linda, did.
She wasn't a good swimmer. She loved to swim. Joe was working on his
car. He was a fanatical sports enthusiast.

c. He had found that the wolves subsisted mainly on a diet of
mice. Farley had been dropped in the middle of the Canadian tundra.
He discovered that the hunters were lying, and that they themselves
were the insane murderers. Hunters had been complaining that the
wolves were slaughtering thousands of caribou for the sheer pleasure
of killing. He had made an astonishing discovery. He had been assigned to investigate the killing of caribou by timber wolves.

d. *Delivery* by Paul Jamesy is a story of the adventures of a
group of department store delivery boys sent on a mission into the
suburbs of a large metropolis. The journey is a revelation of the inner
world of modern man—the wanton violence of five-year-old foot-
ballers, the vast boredom of the swinging teens, the horrors of afternoon romance in respectable families. The author himself is a former
cheerleader and national frog-jumping champion. All but one of the
young men become trapped in a labyrinthine and nightmarish Kresge's
store. Only one, who wins the voluptuous blonde named Shirley, succeeds in making his big—*Delivery*.

5. Here are two coherent paragraphs, from the essay by E. B.
White in which he speaks of Simonizing his grandmother. Look at
these paragraphs for their unity and their coherence. (a) Which words

help White move his paragraphs along? (b) How does he accomplish transitions?

Communication by the written word is a subtler (and more beautiful) thing than Dr. Flesch or General Motors imagines. They contend that the "average reader" is capable of reading only what tests Easy, and that the writer should write at or below this level. This is a presumptuous and degrading idea. There is no average reader, and to reach down toward this mythical character is to deny that each of us is on the way up, is ascending. ("Ascending," by the way, is a word Dr. Flesch advises writers to stay away from. Too unusual.)

It is our belief that no writer can improve his work until he discards the dulcet notion that the reader is feeble-minded, for writing is an act of faith, not a trick of grammar. Ascent is at the heart of the matter. A country whose writers are following a calculating machine downstairs in not ascending—if you will pardon the expression—and a writer who questions the capacity of the person at the other end of the line is not a writer at all, merely a schemer. The movies long ago decided that a wider communication could be achieved by a deliberate descent to a lower level, and they walked proudly down until they reached the cellar. Now they are groping for the light switch, hoping to find the way out.

E. B. White, *The Second Tree from the Corner*

6. What is disorganized or incoherent about these examples?

a. Robert and Daniel crouched in the cave, listening for the sound of approaching footsteps. He thought the troops must have left the area by now. For the moment he was reassured by the silence, but he worried about the sharp pain in his knee, and he wondered if he would be able to walk on it if he had to. He was glad to have his old friend with him. He looked at him. Their gazes meeting, he felt tears come to his eyes from straining to see in the half-darkness, and from thinking where he and his friend had been just yesterday.

b. When the gate opens at last, four thousand music lovers push, crush, and shove each other forward in an immense mass. The sun glares down, the musicians struggle to tune their sweaty instruments, and the ice cream salesman exhausts his stores in twenty minutes. Finally the music started at 1:30.

7. A student writing a theme about a teachers' strike wanted to make these points in one paragraph:

1. Teachers have no legal right to strike.
2. The teachers' union claims the strike is their constitutional right.

3. Some school boards try to fire their striking teachers and hire new ones.

4. Striking teachers sometimes find judges who will issue injunctions against this firing and hiring.

5. Picketing disrupts the classes with new teachers.

Here is a first draft of the paragraph.

Of course it's against the law for teachers to strike anyway. Some teachers say that the law against striking is unconstitutional. So the school board fires the teachers who are striking and hires new teachers who are looking for work. The striking teachers get a judge to make an injunction against the school board. The picketing disrupts classes with the new teachers.

This first attempt was incoherent. Does the paragraph have a topic sentence? Does it have *a topic?* Can you see how one sentence follows from another? Does the last sentence appear to belong in the paragraph?

Here is the paragraph as it appeared in the final draft of the theme.

Although a state law forbids strikes by teachers, teachers still strike, claiming that the state law violates the U.S. Constitution. When a school board tries to break the strike, firing the old teachers and hiring new ones, some judge usually agrees with the strikers, and puts an injunction against the school board. Meantime, if one set of teachers is picketing another, whatever the argument between legislators and judges, the children in the classroom suffer.

(a) How does this paragraph improve over the previous one? (b) By what means does this student connect sentences to each other? (c) In the last sentence, why does the student write, "whatever the argument between legislators and judges . . ."?

8. Analyze these paragraphs for their transitions, both within the paragraphs and between them.

When Saint-Exupéry begins his second paragraph, which word especially links it to the end of the first paragraph? What binds the third paragraph to the second? When the fourth paragraph follows the third, an idea rather than a word makes the transition: underline the words that are intellectually related to each other.

Once again I had found myself in the presence of a truth and had failed to recognize it. Consider what had happened to me: I had thought myself lost, had touched the very bottom of despair; and then, when the spirit of renunciation had filled me, I had known peace. I know now what I was not conscious of at the time—that in such an hour a man feels that he has finally found himself and has become his own friend. An essential inner need has been satisfied, and against that satisfaction, that self-fulfillment, no external power can prevail. Bonnafous, I imagine, he who spent his life racing before the wind, was acquainted with this serenity of spirit. Guillaumet, too, in his snows. Never shall I forget that, lying buried to the chin in sand, strangled slowly to death by thirst, my heart was infinitely warm beneath the desert stars.

What can men do to make known to themselves this sense of deliverance? Everything about mankind is paradox. He who strives and conquers grows soft. The magnanimous man grown rich becomes mean. The creative artist for whom everything is made easy nods. Every doctrine swears that it can breed men, but none can tell us in advance what sort of men it will breed. Men are not cattle to be fattened for market. On the scales of life an indigent Newton weighs more than a parcel of prosperous nonentities. All of us have had the experience of a sudden joy that came when nothing in the world had forewarned us of its coming—a joy so thrilling that if it was born of misery we remembered even the misery with tenderness. All of us, on seeing old friends again, have remembered with happiness the trials we lived through with those friends. Of what can we be certain except this—that we are fertilized by mysterious circumstances? Where is man's truth to be found?

Truth is not that which can be demonstrated by the aid of logic. If orange-trees are hardy and rich in fruit in this bit of soil and not that, then this bit of soil is what is truth for orange-trees. If a particular religion, or culture, or scale of values, if one form of activity rather than another, brings self-fulfillment to a man, releases the prince asleep within him unknown to himself, then that scale of values, that culture, that form of activity, constitute his truth. Logic, you say? Let logic wangle its own explanation of life.

Because it is man and not flying that concerns me most, I shall close this book with the story of man's gropings towards self-fulfillment as I witnessed them in the early months of the civil war in Spain. One year after crashing in the desert I made a tour of the Catalan front in order to learn what happens to man when the scaffolding of his traditions suddenly collapses. To Madrid I went for an answer to another question: How does it happen that men are sometimes willing to die?

Antoine de Saint-Exupéry, *Wind, Sand and Stars*

9. In this passage from Thoreau, underline the topic sentence of the first paragraph. (a) How does the paragraph grow from this sentence? (b) Is every other sentence in this paragraph related to the topic sentence? (c) How do the sentences proceed? Underline transitions. (d) Do you find implicit transitions in this paragraph, and later between paragraphs? Find the basis for each implicit transition.

The mass of men serve the State thus, not as men mainly, but as machines, with their bodies. They are the standing army, and the militia, jailers, constables, "posse comitatus," &c. In most cases there is no free exercise whatever of the judgment or of the moral sense; but they put themselves on a level with wood and earth and stones; and wooden men can perhaps be manufactured that will serve the purpose as well. Such command no more respect than men of straw; or a lump of dirt. They have the same sort of worth only as horses and dogs. Yet such as these even are commonly esteemed good citizens. Others, as most legislators, politicians, lawyers, ministers, and office-holders, serve the State chiefly with their heads; and, as they rarely make any moral distinctions, they are as likely to serve the devil, without intending it, as God. A very few, as heroes, patriots, martyrs, reformers in the great sense, and *men*, serve the State with their consciences also, and so necessarily resist it for the most part; and they are commonly treated by it as enemies. A wise man will only be useful as a man, and will not submit to be "clay," and "stop a hole to keep the wind away," but leave that office to his dust at least:—

> "I am too high-born to be propertied,
>   To be a secondary at control,
>   Or useful serving-man and instrument
>   To any sovereign state throughout the world."

He who gives himself entirely to his fellow-men appears to them useless and selfish; but he who gives himself partially to them is pronounced a benefactor and philanthropist.

How does it become a man to behave toward this American government to-day? I answer that he cannot without disgrace be associated with it. I cannot for an instant recognize the political organization as my government which is the *slave's* government also.

All men recognize the right of revolution; that is, the right to refuse allegiance to and to resist the government, when its tyranny or its inefficiency are great and unendurable. But almost all say that such is not the case now. But such was the case, they think, in the Revolution of '75. If one were to tell me that this was a bad government because it taxed certain foreign commodities brought to its ports, it is most probable that I should not make an ado about it, for I can do without them: all machines have their friction; and possibly this does enough good to counterbalance the evil. At any rate, it is a great evil to make a stir about it. But when the friction comes to have its machine, and oppression and robbery are organized, I say, let us not have such a machine any longer. In other words, when a sixth of the population of a nation which has undertaken to be the refuge of liberty are slaves, and a whole country is unjustly overrun and conquered by a foreign army, and subjected to military law, I think that it is not too soon for honest men to rebel and revolutionize. What makes this duty the more urgent is the fact, that the country so overrun is not our own, but ours is the invading army.

Henry David Thoreau, "On the Duty of Civil Disobedience"

10. Read these paragraphs and classify them according to their methods of development. (See pages 195–200.)

a. It's sometimes argued that there's no real progress; that a civilization that kills multitudes in mass warfare, that pollutes the land and oceans with ever larger quantities of debris, that destroys the dignity of individuals by subjecting them to a forced mechanized existence can hardly be called an advance over the simpler hunting and gathering and agricultural existence of prehistoric times. But this argument, though romantically appealing, doesn't hold up. The primitive tribes permitted far less individual freedom than does modern society. Ancient wars were committed with far less moral justification than modern ones. A technology that produces debris can find, and is finding, ways of disposing of it without ecological upset. And the schoolbook pictures of primitive man sometimes omit some of the detractions of his primitive life—the pain, the disease, famine, the hard labor needed just to stay alive. From that agony of bare existence to modern life can be soberly described only as upward progress, and the sole agent for this progress is quite clearly reason itself.

Robert M. Pirsig, *Zen and the Art of Motorcycle Maintenance*

b. But there is an aspect of the crystal of our nature that eschews the harness, scorns sublimation, and demands to be seen in its raw nakedness, crying out to us for the sight and smell of blood. The vehemence with which we deny this obvious fact of our nature is matched only by our Victorian hysteria on the subject of sex. Yet, we deny it in vain. Whether we quench our thirst from the sight of a bleeding Jesus on the Cross, from the ritualized sacrifice in the elevation of the Host and the consecration of the Blood of the Son, or from bullfighting, cockfighting, dogfighting, wrestling, or boxing, spiced with our Occidental memory and heritage of the gladiators of Rome and the mass spectator sport of the time of feeding Christians and other enemies of society to the lions in the Coliseum—whatever the mask assumed by the impulse, the persistent beat of the drum over the years intones the chant: Though Dracula and Vampira must flee the scene with the rising of the sun and the coming of the light, night has its fixed hour and darkness must fall.

Eldridge Cleaver, *Soul on Ice*

c. For twins they are very dissimilar. Colin is tall and active and Johnny is short and middle-aged. Johnny doesn't kick off his shoes, he doesn't swallow beer caps or tear pages out of the telephone book. I don't think he ever draws pictures with my best lipstick. In fact, he has none of the charming, lighthearted "boy" qualities that precipitate so many scenes of violence in the home. On the other hand, he has a feeling for order and a passion for system that would be trying in a head nurse. If his pajamas are hung on the third hook in the closet instead of on the second hook, it causes him real pain. If one slat in a Venetian blind is tipped in the wrong direction he can't have a moment's peace until somebody fixes it. Indeed, if one of the beans on his plate is slightly longer than the others he can scarcely bear to eat it.

Jean Kerr, *Please Don't Eat the Daisies*

11. Here is a short essay by Hermann von Kreicke, a chapter from a book recounting his adventures and travels as an émigré. Analyze this essay for its use of the paragraph. Apply the standards of this chapter.

It is time, perhaps, to withdraw for the moment from this picaresque account of our wanderings, in order to examine the question of exile as a psychological condition forced upon vast numbers of Europeans in the 20th century. My own generation was victim of the demented Austrian posing as a German. White Russians formed the bulk of the emigrant population in Paris when Hermione and I, all unwitting what awaited us in a subsequent decade, wintered there in the 20's. Transfer of populations between Turkey and Greece had earlier exiled thousands under the cruel guise of repatriation. The Irish question repeatedly forced Irish and Anglo-Irish to France and to England. During and after the war in Spain, Spaniards fled their country, hoping to return, but all too often to die in squalid exile—in France, in Puerto Rico, in New York, and of course in Latin America.

But I need not multiply examples further.

In our travels, Hermione and I made acquaintance with exiles from every corner of the globe. I have spoken of the Bulgarian F—— S——, of the Nigerian tribal chieftain whom I have called Okomo, and the South African socialist R—— Mc A——, and of others. I have not yet attempted to name the common thread that wove through all our conversations. This universal fabric, we have come to understand, is a profound and extreme ambivalence relative to the homeland, a love-and-hate so thoroughly interwined that its dual structure can be discerned in the slightest utterance.

That ambivalence is the nature of human emotion, I have never doubted. One remembers the joke about elephants and national character. The American writes, "The Elephant and the Profit Motive." The Frenchman writes, "Les Amours des Eléphants." The Englishman writes, "The Imperial Elephant." The Pole writes, "The Elephant and the Polish

Question." All exiles are Poles, and if they drink wine they think of the wines of their youth; if they watch a magnificent sunset over the Pacific, they remember sunset over the Urals or the Austrian Alps or on the deserts of Africa. An item in a newspaper about a cabinet shift in Stockholm brings to mind the politics of change in their own country, and since they (I should say we) are all participants of loss, they remember with tenderness and rage the hopes and despairs of long ago.

We live in the twilight country of the remote past, and in a present country and present circumstance which is lit by dim light. We bump into the walls of the present, expecting to find an older wall, a window that is not there, and that looks over remembered landscape

But the internal landscape is loud with the alternation of laughter and of tears. Klaus K—— walks through the railway station in New Haven, Connecticut, returning from Manhattan to his position as curator of the art museum at a large university. But he is not there; he is walking through a railway station in a small Bavarian town in 1936. He hears an aggregation of local musicians, in the December cold outside, and smiles to hear the energetic tuba trying and failing to keep the correct time. For a moment he has forgotten the purpose of his journey, which is to revisit the family estate in the forlorn attempt to settle his affairs before he must flee his fatherland. He emerges from the station. On the arm of the tuba player a cloth band proclaims by its swastika the vicious omnipresence of National Socialism. He must not show his feelings. He ducks his head into the wind and snow, grinding his teeth. And now, although it is May in Connecticut, twenty years later, Klaus ducks his head into the wind and snow that surround him still. He grinds his teeth in the light breeze of Connecticut spring.

Herman von Kreicke, *The Migrant Swan*

(a) Can you find an abrupt and disturbing jump—a lack of transition—in the first paragraph? Or does an implicit transition work? (b) Is this paragraph adequately developed? Is it long enough? Does its order lead to clarity? Is its order forceful? (c) Could you suggest ways to improve this paragraph? to make it more coherent, more forceful, or more clear? (d) Is the one-line paragraph effective? (e) How is the third paragraph developed? Name the methods of development of the rest of the paragraphs.

12. Take these excerpts from the *Detroit Free Press*, tiny newspaper paragraphs, and copy them out into longer paragraphs, as you would organize paragraphs in a theme. Break the paragraphs logically and usefully.

He may have been the greatest golfer who ever lived—or so the legend says, and legends are hard to dispute.

"The Phantom of the Links," he was called, and "The Garbo of Golf."

Some called him one of the world's strongest men. Others called him a con man. Police records called him an extortionist, and there was talk of robbery and smuggling.

Some knew him as John J. Montague, the man Grantland Rice called "the greatest golfer on earth," and Walter Hagen termed "the most amazing golfer in the world."

A few may have even known him, all 300 pounds of him, as Laverne Moore. Because that was his real name—or so the legend says.

The man known as Laverne Moore and John J. Montague—golfer, millionaire, mystery man—has died at the age of 67.

He palled around with famous names—Bing Crosby, Spencer Tracy, Bob Hope—but his own rang no bells outside his own circle and was rarely emblazoned in headlines with Palmer, Nicklaus, Snead and Hogan.

He might have beaten those famous golfers with a baseball bat. Or a tennis racket and a dead mackerel. A truck axle. Anything he could lay one of his big hands on and swing at a golf ball.

UPI

Here's what the historic arms limitation agreements signed here Friday night in the Kremlin mean.

What they do, essentially, is to freeze a "balance of terror" between the world's two nuclear superpowers.

Each side, in these agreements, retains the ability to kill millions of defenseless civilians on the other side.

Washington and Moscow will be defended from nuclear attack with anti-ballistic missile systems (ABMs).

But Detroit and every other major city in the U.S. will remain undefended. So will Leningrad and Kiev, and other major cities in the Soviet Union.

Thus each side, in a sense, will hold the civilian population of the other side hostage—as a means of discouraging the other side from launching nuclear war.

The fact is, as Henry Kissinger, White House national security adviser, has put it: "Both sides are now vulnerable to each other . . . this has been a fact now for five or six years."

The new SALT agreements seek to freeze the 25-year-old nuclear arms race at that point—on the theory that a "balance of terror" is the best guarantee either side has, in this terrifying age, of preventing war.

But what of other major questions?

How important are the agreements? Can they work? Can they be monitored? Don't the agreements give the Soviets a numerical advantage? What will they mean to the average citizen?

James McCartney

13. Look at paragraphing—especially the length of paragraphs—in these examples. Do the authors provide variety in length and type of paragraph? Are there moments when you would prefer that a long paragraph be broken up? Do any paragraphs seem choppy? Are transitions adequate? Make notes in the margin for class discussion.

a. What, in our human world, is this power to live? It is the ancient, lost reverence and passion for human personality, joined with the ancient, lost reverence and passion for the earth and its web of life.

This indivisible reverence and passion is what the American Indians almost universally had; and representative groups of them have it still.

They had and have this power for living which our modern world has lost—as world-view and self-view, as tradition and institution, as practical philosophy dominating their societies and as an art supreme among all the arts.

By virtue of this power, the densely populated Inca state, by universal agreement among its people, made the conservation and increase of the earth's resources its foundational national policy. Never before, never since has a nation done what the Inca state did.

By virtue of this same power, the little pueblo of Tesuque, in New Mexico, when threatened by the implacable destroying action of government some twenty-five years ago, starved and let no white friend know it was starving. It asked no help, determined only to defend its spiritual values and institutions and its remnant of land which was holy land.

If our modern world should be able to recapture this power, the earth's natural resources and web of life would not be irrevocably wasted within the twentieth century, which is the prospect now. True democracy, founded in neighborhoods and reaching over the world, would become the realized heaven on earth. And living peace—not just an interlude between wars—would be born and would last through ages.

John Collier, *Indians of the Americas*

b. When it comes to the so-called obscene words, I should say that hardly one person in a million escapes mob-reaction. The first reaction is almost sure to be mob-reaction, mob-indignation, mob-condemnation. And the mob gets no further. But the real individual has second thoughts and says: Am I really shocked? Do I *really* feel outraged and indignant? And the answer of any individual is bound to be: No, I am not shocked, not outraged, nor indignant. I know the word, and take it for what it is, and I am not going to be jockeyed into making a mountain our of a mole-hill, not for all the law in the world.

Now if the use of a few so-called obscene words will startle man or woman out of a mob-habit into an individual state, well and good. And word-prudery is so universal a mob-habit that it is time we were startled out of it.

But still we have only tackled obscenity, and the problem of pornography goes even deeper. When a man is startled into his individual self, he still may not be able to know, inside himself, whether Rabelais is or is not pornographic; and over Aretino or even Boccaccio he may perhaps puzzle in vain, torn between different emotions.

One essay on pornography, I remember, comes to the conclusion that pornography in art is that which is calculated to arouse sexual desire, or sexual excitement. And stress is laid on the fact, whether the author or artist intended to arouse sexual feelings. It is the old vexed question of intention, become so dull today, when we know how strong and influential our unconscious intentions are. And why a man should be held guilty of his conscious intentions, and innocent of his unconscious intentions, I don't know, since every man is more made up of unconscious intentions than of conscious ones. I am what I am, not merely what I think I am.

However! We take it, I assume, that *pornography* is something base, something unpleasant. In short, we don't like it. And why don't we like it? Because it arouses sexual feelings?

I think not. No matter how hard we may pretend otherwise, most of us rather like a moderate rousing of our sex. It warms us, stimulates us like sunshine on a gray day. After a century or two of Puritanism, this is still true of most people. Only the mob-habit of condemning any form of sex is too strong to let us admit it naturally. And there are, of course, many people who are genuinely repelled by the simplest and most natural stirrings of sexual feeling. But these people are perverts who have fallen into hatred of their fellow men: thwarted, disappointed, unfulfilled people, of whom, alas, our civilization contains so many. And they nearly always enjoy some unsimple and unnatural form of sexual excitement, secretly.

D. H. Lawrence, "Pornography and Obscenity"

VI

TYPES OF WRITING

In Chapter II, Writing a Paper, I talked about making a whole theme, using for examples Sharon Rustig's exposition about bicycles and cars, and Jim Beck's personal narrative. The chapters since then have dealt with matters common to all writing—with words, sentences, and paragraphs. Now we must move from parts of writing to types of writing.

The writer's purpose, each time he sets himself to write, puts a demand upon him. His purpose may require that he explain, or persuade, or narrate, or describe. Many essays make mixed demands: to explain we may need to describe, to persuade we may need to narrate. Fiction usually requires narration and description; so does biography or autobiography; writing research is exposition, after information has been gathered.

EXPOSITION

Expository writing explains. It does not argue—though exposition can form part of an argument. It does not tell a story—though it might explain something essential to telling a story.

Exposition also can take pure form, in whole essays of explanation. If you did an exchange year in England, you might feel called upon to write an essay explaining baseball or percolator coffee to your teacher and classmates. You could help to explain them by comparing them to

223

cricket or tea. If you tried to demonstrate the superiority of baseball or coffee, you would be adding argument to exposition. If you wrote a biography of Albert Einstein, you would certainly write a narrative of his life, you would probably use dialogue, and you would probably use description. Exposition would certainly be necessary also.

> But there was another consequence which Einstein now brought forward for the first time. If light is produced in a star or in the sun, an area of strong gravity, and then streams down on the earth, an area of weak gravity, its energy will not be dissipated by a reduction of speed, since this is impossible, light always having the same constant speed. What would happen, Einstein postulated, was something very different: the wavelength of the light would be shortened. This "Einstein shift," the assumption that "the spectral lines of sunlight, as compared with the corresponding spectral lines of terrestrial sources of light, must be somewhat displaced toward the red," was spelled out in some detail. However, he was careful to add the qualification that "as other influences (pressure, temperature) affect the position of the centers of the spectral lines, it is difficult to discover whether the enforced influence of the gravitational potential really exists." In fact the Döppler shift, produced by the motion of the stars relative to the solar system, was to provide an additional and even more important complication.
>
> Ronald W. Clark, *Einstein*

If you wrote a book about prose style, you would mostly write exposition.

Expository writing carries information. When we do research on a problem, we write our results mainly as exposition. Encyclopedia entries are expository. Exposition is usually the essay's foundation. The essayist will narrate and describe, and by contrasting passages of exposition he may argue. Argument lacking in exposition moves toward bombast or harangue.

Most writing assigned in college is exposition. So is almost all writing required in professional life—in business, in teaching, in science, in law, in medicine. When social workers deliver papers, when geologists make reports, when hospital directors release information on new diagnostic equipment—they write exposition.

The rules for exposition are clarity, conciseness, and vigor. Here are several passages that illustrate how we can vary exposition, and how we depend upon it. They also illustrate the clarity, vigor, and conciseness we should try for. Edmund Wilson begins a book about Canada:

> The relation of Canada to the United States has always been rather peculiar. The constant slight strain it involves is to be felt in the inveterate Canadian habit, always surprising to us, of referring to us as "the Americans," as if Canadians were not Americans, too. The reason for this is apparently that at the time of our 1776 revolution "the Americans" were seditious malcontents who rebelled against their status of British colonists and set up an anti-British republic. "The Americans," for a Tory like Samuel Johnson, were always to be referred to contemptuously because they had made trouble for the monarchy. The Canadians remained British, so were never in this sense Americans, and we were for long and are sometimes still disapprovingly regarded as a society founded on disloyalty to the sovereign and the destruction of ancient traditions, and devoted to the exploits of a vulgar success which are impious in both their mutinous origins and their insolence in surpassing the mother country.
>
> Edmund Wilson, *O Canada*

Wilson starts with a mild topic sentence, gives as evidence a detail from speech usage, explains usage by details from history, and rises to emotional force at the end. The paragraph develops by contrasting two nations, a contrast first stated in the topic sentence. The force he gives the conclusion depends upon charged words—"vulgar," "impious," "mutinous," "insolence"—in a context constructed to support them with historical fact.

Bergen Evans writes on the double negative:

> In English, two negatives in the same sentence generally reinforce one another. *I didn't say nothing* is an emphatic denial and no one who speaks English can misunderstand it. This is the normal way of strengthening a negative in all Teutonic languages, of which ours is one. In the past, double, triple, quadruple negatives were quite acceptable; Sir Launcelot was speaking the purest English when he said, *I never treacherously slew no man.*
>
> Today, this repeated negative is considered a shocking vulgarism. Negative pronouns (such as *no one* and *nothing*), negative adverbs (such as *hardly* and *scarcely*), and negative conjunctions (such as *neither* and *nor*), when used with a negative verb put a

man beyond the pale, provided the sentence is short enough. No
one who values public opinion can afford to say *I didn't hardly
hear you* or *you didn't hear me, neither.*

Bergen Evans, *A Dictionary of
Contemporary American Usage*

Again the subject combines usage and history. Evans begins with the
old usage—knowing that is sounds incorrect to educated ears—and
allows historical information to undermine our gentility. Evans' exposition debunks conventional wisdom.

Simone de Beauvoir gives information about abortion:

> Moreover, the law—which dooms many young women to
> death, sterility, invalidism—is quite powerless to assure an in-
> crease in the number of births. One thing that friends and en-
> emies of legal abortions agree on is the radical failure of repres-
> sive legislation. In France, according to good authorities,
> abortions have averaged about one million per year in recent
> times. And of these about two thirds are attributed to married
> women. An unknown but large number of deaths and injuries
> result from these clandestine and often improperly performed
> operations.

Simone de Beauvoir, *The Second Sex*

Arguing for abortion, in a book published in 1949, the author uses
exposition as a step in argument, citing details and statistics to support
her position.

The philosopher Charles S. Peirce makes distinctions and definitions:

> And what, then, is belief? It is the demi-cadence which closes
> a musical phrase in the symphony of our intellectual life. We
> have seen that it has just three properties: first, it is something
> that we are aware of, second, it appeases the irritation of doubt;
> and, third, it involves the establishment in our nature of a rule of
> action, or, say for short, a *habit.* As it appeases the irritation of
> doubt, which is the motive for thinking, thought relaxes, and
> comes to rest for a moment when belief is reached. But, since
> belief is a rule for action, the application of which involves fur-
> ther doubt and further thought, at the same time that it is a
> stopping-place, it is also a new starting-place for thought. That is
> why I have permitted myself to call it thought at rest, although

thought is essentially an action. The *final* upshot of thinking is
the exercise of volition, and of this thought no longer forms a
part; but belief is only a stadium of mental action, an effect upon
our nature due to thought, which will influence future thinking.
Charles S. Peirce, Values in a Universe of Change

Peirce uses analogies to define belief, and to explain the relationship
between thought and belief. First he compares belief to music. A little
later, when it "appeases" an "irritation," he compares it to some sort
of balm, like an unguent that relieves sunburn. When he defines habit,
he explains the word before he names it—"a rule of action, or, say for
short, a *habit*"—so that we accept the idea before we put a familiar
name to it. Later, speaking of thought and action, he uses metaphors of
stopping and starting. The final metaphor of place defines belief as "a
stadium of mental action." It may be quite far from a "demi-cadence"
to a "stadium," but Peirce has led us over this distance gently, in this
most difficult form of discourse: the exposition of abstract ideas.
     A literary critic begins to define a word:

> A myth, in its simplest meaning, is a story about a god, or some
> being comparable to a god. Hence myths usually grow up in
> close association with religions, but, because they are stories,
> they also belong to literature, especially to narrative, fictional
> and dramatic literature with internal characters. It makes no dif-
> ference to its relation to literature whether a myth is believed to
> be true or false. Classical mythology became purely literary after
> the religions associated with it died, but from a literary point of
> view we may speak of Christian or Hindu mythology even when
> the attitude towards it is also one of religious acceptance.
> Northrop Frye, "Myth and Poetry"

Frye's topic sentence defines "myth" simply, and then he extrapolates
on words used in the definition—"god" and "story." Finally, he dis-
misses any question about the myth's truth or falsehood. He sets out his
distinctions in a prose both admirably simple and thoroughly sophisticated.
     A novelist has his character think about another character:

> First, I assumed that the man who had shot Drew knew that he
> had shot him. That was a beginning. I also assumed that he knew
> we hadn't all been killed in the rapids. What then? He might be
> waiting above the calm where Bobby and Lewis were—where I

was, more or less—planning to draw down on them when they started out. If that were the case he would kill them both, though if Bobby gauged the change in the light well enough and set out when there was enough visibility to use the canoe but not enough to shoot by, they might have a chance to get past him, through the next stretch of rapids—the ones now a little downstream from me—and on down. Our whole hope rested on our being able to second-guess the man, and, now that I was on top of the gorge, it seemed to me that we had guessed right, or as right as it was possible for us to do. If Bobby moved out in the very early half-light, the chances of making a good shot down onto the water would be greatly reduced, and big gaps in the upper part of the wall, small deep ravines such as the one I had come up, would keep him from getting downstream at anything like the speed the canoe could make. I counted on his knowing this, and on the idea that he would try to solve the problem by setting up his shots downstream at calm water, where the target would be moving at a more constant speed and not leaping and bobbing. Below me, except for one rush of whiteness cramped between two big hedges of stone, the rapids seemed comparatively gentle, in places—so far as I could tell—scarcely more than a heavy-twilled rippling. But even this would be disconcerting for a marksman because of the bobbing it would cause. If I were going to kill somebody from this distance and this angle I would want to draw a long bead. Under those conditions, and if he was a good shot, there was no reason he couldn't get Bobby and Lewis both, and within a few seconds of each other, if he took his time and dropped the first one cleanly. That would take calm water, as slow as possible, and it would have to be downstream, out of sight around the next turn.

James Dickey, *Deliverance*

The "I" of the novel tries to think itself into another mind, following that mind's track as it would probably proceed through assumptions to actions. The writing describes landscape as it explains motives, since landscape helps to determine action.

ARGUMENT AND PERSUASION

In writing expository prose, we assemble details—facts, anecdotes, descriptions—to understand and to explain, not to take a position and defend it. Much of our writing is expository: we investigate the parliamentary system of government, or an innovation in psychotherapy, or a school of artists, or a sport. On occasion, we might seem to argue that something is superior to something else—say, the Cubist painters to the Impressionists—when we are really only giving reasons for personal preference. If we are explaining our own likes and dislikes, we are writing exposition; we are not arguing that anyone else should feel as we do. Exposing our preference is valid exposition. When I read someone's praise of crocheting, I can enjoy and understand it, without feeling any pressure to make an afghan.

On the other hand, sometimes we write arguments, in which we try to persuade the reader of a thesis, to convince him. In an argument, we will use exposition, narrative, and description, but we will also have a thesis to defend, and we will try to argue and persuade by means of clear thinking, reasonableness, and taking account of the opposition.

Most of the time, in writing an argument, we are dealing with debatable material. We cannot *prove* our thesis, as a mathematician or a philosophical logician can, by manipulating his own terms. We cannot measure our results in a cyclotron like a physicist. We are dealing with probabilities and persuasions, not certainties or proofs. Or say that we are dealing with an old-fashioned sense of the word "proof," an inexactness that we might call "the agreement of reasonable men." We have an opinion; we may feel it strongly; we may believe it is true. But we must recognize that other people have other opinions, and respect their differences, if we are going to try to persuade them.

The honest writer avoids some forms of persuasion, or attempted persuasion. "The rhetorician would deceive his neighbors./The sentimentalist himself"—as I quoted before from W. B. Yeats—and in much dishonest writing the writer is both sentimentalist and, in Yeats's sense, rhetorician. The loaded word—when the dictator's police shoot "unarmed civilians" or "a traitorous rabble"—or loaded syntax—when the beer company asks, "As a lawyer, what do you think of Fitz's?"—can combine to make a whole essay into loaded argument, or propaganda. Arguments, ideas, or phrases seem to say one thing, and really say another. In good writing, we must avoid such subterfuge.

Clarity in Argument

To avoid fooling ourselves, and trying to fool others, we must apply to our arguments all the standards for clarity and forcefulness that we have discussed in talking about words and sentences. Misusing the passive verb can help us avoid responsibility, and confuse an argument. Abstract nouns are misused often by the writer reluctant to *see* what he is talking about; this reluctance makes a vagueness, which fuzzes over a reality that might do damage to an argument. To argue well, you must be wary of misusing conjunctions in the complex sentence, by which you may imply cause or sequence or another relationship that the evidence you offer will not support. Most first drafts leave us with problems in verb forms, abstract nouns, and askew syntax; but in arguments, these errors often attempt to defend us against understanding what we are saying. These errors are not merely mechanical; they are *learned* errors by which we fool ourselves. Here is some hasty thinking from an impromptu.

> Last night Blood Sweat and Tears played at the gym. I started thinking about Mr. Williams back in Harbor Springs (my counselor). Because he was forty or fifty, he hated the new music, and once a terrific trick was played on him. He was acting principle and some guys got the key to the p.a. and hooked up a two hour tape of rock and turned the p.a. up loud and jammed the lock and split. (Blood Sweat and Tears was part of the tape.) People like him should never be in high schools. They hate kids. They never remember that they were kids and they've got no sense of humor at all. In fact, middle aged people should never be allowed to teach teen-aged kids. They don't understand. This fact was true in my whole school except for Miss Casey since she never grew up anyway. Nobody at school ever heard of revelance.

Mr. Williams may well have been annoying, and the practical joke amusing, but we cannot take an argument seriously when it is so one-sided.

Reasonableness in Argument

Most of the time, we persuade by being reasonable—and also by seeming so. The *being* is clear thinking; the *seeming* is tone. We will *be* reasonable by writing with clarity, and by avoiding typical errors of thinking that I will mention later. We will *seem* reasonable by refusing to be dogmatic, by allowing time to opposing points of view, and by modesty that distinguishes between fact and opinion. It is not that we should continually qualify our remarks by tagging them with phrases like "in my opinion"; it is more the attitude we take. If it is factually raining, it will not be dogmatic to assert that the grass is wet. But if we look at a girl and call her pretty, obviously we are uttering a feeling of our own; nothing *necessarily* follows except within ourselves.

Of course fact and opinion are mixed; the mixture is humane and necessary. It is only obligatory for the sake of honest writing that the writer know what he is doing. A fact is information that can be documented from historical and scientific sources. ("Truth" is elusive; the scientific "facts" of one century may be illusion to the next; a "fact" is what we can reasonably accept as true.) It is also a statement of personal experience that can be accepted as reasonable. "It rained all day, July 5th, 1971" can be fact; "Hester looked pretty" is opinion, or surmise, and not fact. When we quote someone else's documented opinion—"her minister thought that Hester looked pretty"—we are on the border between fact and opinion. It is a pity that human life is so full of twilights; day and night are so easily distinguishable; but everything human seems to flourish in twilight.

When we quote the minister, we have quoted an outside source, which makes us appear objective, yet we have quoted only an opinion. With this sort of reference, we can write as if the reference were fact if we do not lean on it too heavily. If we make the minister's opinion the fulcrum in our essay ("But contrary to her doctor's statement, we know from her minister that Hester looked pretty. Therefore . . .") the opinion will crumble and the essay collapse. We have let ourselves seem to be unreasonable.

For persuasive argument, we must discover a tone that uses fact when it is relevant, inserts opinion modestly and reasonably, allows time and space to doubts, and builds a sequent argument by paragraph steps that the reader can follow. Here is a typical argument, from a book about "the corporate oligarch," in which the author finds a new type of businessman. It mingles fact and opinion with clarity and without loss of energy.

> That he is a major figure in the contemporary world few will deny. Contrary to popular belief, however, it is not a simple matter to identify him precisely, to define his powers, to describe his methods or to explain his motives. A massive literature exists on the subject of management, most of it published in the last fifty years. The lives of men at the top of the corporate hierarchy have been treated in novels, motion pictures, biographies and television programs. Yet the subject remains confusing and overburdened with generalizations.
>
> The problem begins with definitions.
>
> Underlying the most widely accepted definition is a belief that "the motive of business is pecuniary gain, the method is essen-

tially purchase and sale. The aim and usual outcome is the accumulation of wealth. Men whose aim is not increase of possession
do not go into business. . . ." So wrote Thorstein Veblen. This
seeking after wealth would make the corporation no more than
"a legal device," as A. A. Berle and Gardner Means put it,
"through which private business transactions may be carried on."

If this were the whole story, the subject of this book would
be the men who have become rich through successful business
ventures which are set up as corporations. Many of the top
executives of the 1,323,180 corporations in existence in the
United States at the beginning of the 1960s would consider
this definition of their role correct. But observers of the modern
corporation differ. To most of them corporations have become
what Reinhold Niebuhr called "quasi-sovereignties," what Earl
Latham called "a rationalized system for the accumulation,
control, and administration of power," what others have called
plutocracies or oligarchies.

This suggests that the lives of the men who head corporations have changed in ways that have not been fully ac-
knowledged. How much they have changed is unclear. For instance, it is generally agreed that the older type of businessman
was an entrepreneur and that the new type of businessman is a
professional manager. But the distinction between the two is
not a sharp one. No one man is all entrepreneur, none all
professional manager. Every executive of modern corporations
is an entrepreneur as well as a manager, since he assumes the
risks of his business very much as he would if he owned it.
And some of the great fortune makers, or moguls, or robber
barons, of yesteryear were conscientious managers as well as
entrepreneurs, since they were extremely efficient in the way
they conducted their business. The change has only been one
of emphasis in this respect. Many contemporary business men
tend to give a higher priority to running a well-organized company than to making a lot of money. And it is only to dramatize
the difference in emphasis that the generalizations "entrepreneur" and "professional manager" have been useful.

David Finn, *The Corporate Oligarch*

Here, exposition helps to begin a thesis about social change that is in
itself an opinion—but an opinion that the author will defend with facts
and with reasoning.

For a purer example of argument, we might go to the editorial page.

Studded tires are definitely out of season in July and they may be out of season permanently if legislation banning tire studs gets to the governor's desk, as now seems likely.

The News supports this legislation, not because it doubts the margin of safety that studded tire users claim is increased but because the case against their continued usage in Michigan is stronger and more economically defensible.

Even the safety factor of studded tires may be overrated, In applying the studs ban, enough senators accepted the contention that studs cut grooves in highways which, when filled with water during rainstorms, set up conditions for hydroplaning.

Hydroplaning may occur when a cushion of water builds up between the pavement and the tires, causing the driver to lose control.

Studding tears up highways, there doesn't seem to be any question about that. Road repair programs are accelerated under the pounding of stud wear. Instead of getting a 20-year life expectancy out of concrete highways, Michigan motorists may get only half that, when studded tires are permitted.

.   .   .

All this means is that state taxpayers will be paying more and more to keep their highways in decent shape. Snow tires already provide some safety without the disadvantage of chewing up roads. And of course, winter-time driving requires special care and restraint on the part of drivers anyway.

Studded tires are best on glare ice, a condition that occurs only a few times during winter. With or without studded tires, glare ice conditions or sleet requires the utmost in driver caution. In fact, drivers are urged not to take to the roads in these conditions.

Continued use of studded tires is not warranted for the few occasions in which they work best. Do they save lives? Their supporters say they do. But caution and restraint save lives without the disadvantages studded tires have. Highways are for the pleasure and utilization of all motorists, not just those who believe in studded tires.

"Highways Are for Everyone, Not Just Studded Tire Users,"
The Ann Arbor News

This editorial is pure in the sense that it contains little exposition, little explaining, and much advocacy. Still, to advocate its points, it must stop to explain what "hydroplaning" is, and it must refer to facts like life expectancy for highways.

Also, it must try, at least, to account for the opposition's arguments.

Time for the Opposition

When we hope to persuade, we should pay court to the opposition. We should seek to imagine all possible rebuttals to our position, and answer them. We should be both sides of the debating team, like any good debater. Then in our argument we should deal with the most important objections. Sometimes we can take on the objections directly. Suppose we are arguing that football is superior to baseball, presenting not merely a personal preference, which would be exposition, but an argument or a persuasion of general superiority. Recognizing a common objection to football, we might say, "People have argued that football glorifies violence, and baseball skill, but. . . ." Then we could adduce contradictions by anecdote, by appeal to a hypothesis, or whatever. And we could do the same for other objections.

Thinking of opposing arguments is a natural system for multiplying ideas. Put yourself on the other side. Gather evidence and argument against your thesis. Counter every notion of your own, and by this means gather material. But when you write it, don't arrange it like a dialogue between disputants. A pro-con structure jerks the head from right to left to right, as if we were watching a ping-pong ball. You don't need to give equal time. You need not say:

> It has been argued that middle-aged people have more experience than the young, because they have lived longer.
> But mere time does not give understanding. In fact, age seems to diminish understanding. . . .

Brainstorming the opposition's argument, you can accept it and counter it in the flow of one sentence.

> Although middle-aged people obviously have more experience than the young, they don't seem to profit from it.

Similarly, you find positive ideas because you have thought up answers to negative ones. Suppose you are attacking the SST. Trying to gather arguments, you think of a proponent saying, "Time to cross the Pacific will be cut by a third." You turn this to your own purposes by saying,

"Surely we do not need to spend billions of dollars in order to give businessmen three fewer hours to drink Scotch in the lounge of a 747." Of course on some occasions, the opposition's voice, droning in the Senate of your head, may come to sound more and more reasonable. If it happens, you might as well take a deep breath, cross out your old title, and begin again: "The Necessity for Studded Tires."

Our most persuasive argument, in the long run, will be positive praise, and not attack on the opposition. We persuade by praising football more than we do by attacking baseball. If we record straightforwardly too many opposing arguments, we lose focus; we are spending most of our time dealing with the contrary to our thesis, even suggesting ways in which the reader might disagree with us, and our statement will become fuzzy. We lose not only unity but argument as well. Often, it is wise to deal with opposing arguments obliquely, raising them in dependent clauses, while the main clauses carry the argument, as we did in the argument above about the middle-aged and the young. This device raises the issues that the opposition would raise, but keeps clear direction. We might say, "Although football is violent, there is a skill to its violence that is greater and more subtle than the skill of baseball."

Time for the opposition is part of tone, and is part of the honesty in openness. We do not win many arguments by asserting that *no* other point of view is possible, and that anybody who disagrees with us is stupid. *Admit* that football is violent, that studded tires may stop a skid on glare ice, or that middle-aged people sometimes understand the young. If you don't admit these facts, you are telling lies and leaving your valid argument unsupported. Also, you are losing your reader, especially if he is the one you want to reach—the idiot who disagrees with you.

The Order of Argument

When you have gathered valid arguments, you must organize them. In your catalogue of argumentative points and details of evidence, some entries will make a stronger case than others, and some will be more interesting. The general rule is to save the best for last. Where narration is primarily ordered by time, and description by space, argument or persuasion is ordered by increasing intensity. We can start with the arguments in which we have to concede most to our opponents, or the arguments to which we hear our mental adversary objecting, "But . . . but. . . ." Then while he is still spluttering, we pin him to the ground with our best points. The persuasive effect derives from the crescendo. Suppose we are arguing that a national educational television network should be set up, parallel in budget to NBC, CBS, and ABC. We might list:

> success of BBC
> annoyance of advertisements
> higher cultural level
> pressure of advertisers
> guards against government control
> expense small compared to other expenses of govt.
> public service broadcasts
> service for minorities

Of course the relative weight carried by each item, in this limited list, would depend on the evidence and argument the writer could adduce in support. Another writer might find a different order more persuasive.

But for an example, let us speculate on what we have here. Two of the arguments are rebuttals of the imagined adversary, who tells us, "Government television will be the mouthpiece of the state," and, "All this money should go to more worthwhile uses." Perhaps the essay could begin by generally affirming the thesis, and then proceed by acknowledging that, of course, laws should provide a certainty that government could not interfere with programming. In answering the objection about cost of the enterprise, we might be able to turn it in the opposite direction, and use it to further the thesis. Money spent on a national network, we could say, could be used for minority representation, and for educational programs; the network would *serve* social welfare, not *starve* it. For many an essay, this point might be strong enough for a conclusion.

We might give examples of the annoyance that advertising causes; anecdote could supply detail, Anecdote from research might also indicate pressure from advertisers, and this topic might lead to the content in commercial television, contrasted to the content possible on public television. In one writer's scheme, the final point might be the BBC example. "You say it will never work? Here it is, and it works."

My point is not that there is only one way of doing it. Each of us has a way to order our argument *best*, according to our best material. In general, the crescendo is the right kind of noise. In the essay imagined above, an alternative conclusion might be to talk about the network's high cost;—as if we were giving away a point—and then turn it around and say that, despite the cost, the social effects would be so great that the network is cheap at any price. We would certainly *not* end it, after the BBC example or the argument about social effects, by remarking that, of course, it would be essential to avoid government interference.

We should organize the arguments in ascending form. But one kind of exception might come up. Our opening—our zinger—ought to be *interesting,* and not merely our least effective argument. We might open with an anecdote about a BBC program, and not mention that institution again until the end, when we reap the crop that grew from the seed we planted. Or we might start with an anecdote about a tasteless commercial, one that annoys everybody, and will not only catch the reader's attention but engage his sympathy. In the beginning, we are most interested in holding readers so that we can persuade them later. At the end, we are interested in convincing them once and for all.

A relay team in track has four runners. Usually the fastest one runs last. The second fastest runs first, second is slowest, and third is third: 2, 4, 3, 1. It is a good arrangement for arguments, also.

Logic and Emotionalism

If we wish to persuade, we must avoid illogic. Logic is not the only mode of persuasion, goodness knows; poems and stories convince us; although they are sometimes logical in form, they usually convince by embodying feeling in character and image. Arguments embody feeling also, usually in anecdote and detail. But when we think publicly, and preferably when we think privately, we must understand logic in order not to think badly. We all know some logic without perhaps calling it that; it is common sense. Suppose I told you an anecdote about a man with long hair who hijacked a schoolbus. Suppose I told it well, embodying feelings of fright and outrage. But suppose then I added, "Therefore, people with long hair are dangerous criminals." You would laugh at my thinking; and you would be right. I would have committed logical error, generalizing from insufficient evidence. If I had been more modest in my declaration, I could at least have shown you my opinion without raising laughter; if I had said, for instance, "I know it is dangerous to generalize from a particular, but this sort of news item seems to me to characterize what is wrong with the United States today. At least to my prejudiced eyes, someone with long hair is always making the trouble." Here, the anecdote is used not for pseudo-argument, but as a device to introduce an opinion. There is no false logic, because there is no claim to logic.

When we decry "emotionalism" we are blaming not feelings but

misuse of them, or misunderstanding of how to use them. Emotionalism uses an appeal to feelings to disguise a defect in thought. If we say:

> I love this country, its history and its landscape, and I would die
> to defend it against an invader. I don't believe that anyone who
> refuses to defend his country should enjoy the rights of citizen-
> ship.

we are taking a rather extreme position, based on emotion, but we are
not covering bad thinking with camouflage made of feeling. We are
openly displaying our patriotism and our prejudice. We do not say that
the second sentence follows *logically* from the first. It certainly depends upon it *emotionally*. But if we write,

> Cowards who run away to Canada to keep from getting a scratch
> in defense of their great country ought to be jailed for life be-
> cause of all the brave men who have died for freedom.

we write loaded words, we beg questions, and we state an illogical
cause. The errors in writing and thinking are manifold, but we may
lump them under a general label, "emotionalism pretending to argue."
We find this kind of bad writing on any heavily charged issue: busing,
abortion, amnesty, legalizing of marijuana.

Common Fallacies in Thinking

If we wish to study logic seriously, we should go to the philosophy
department. The philosophical study of logic resembles composition-
course logic as a 747 resembles a balsawood glider. Yet knowing a little
about common errors in thinking is essential, if we are to make arguments for our essays that are likely to persuade a reasonable reader.

Many common fallacies in thinking are misuses of induction or
deduction.

To begin with, here are two quick definitions. *Inductive reasoning,*
or *induction,* draws general conclusions from particular examples or
evidence.

> As a result of these experiments we conclude that if the temper-
> ature of water falls below 32 degrees it will freeze.

Deductive reasoning, or *deduction,* applies a general truth to a specific
instance.

> All men are mortal. My editor is a man. My editor is mortal.

Here are some fallacies that most of us fall into, from time to time.

Generalizing from a Particular. Arriving at a general statement from a single supporting fact, or from too narrow a range of particulars, is a common error of induction. We do not collect enough evidence, and we seem to assume that because we have evidence that X is repeated twice, X will always happen. Because the one Eskimo in our circle of friends likes to read Trollope, we may generalize that Eskimos enjoy Trollope. Clearly, such an assumption is illogical. We need a greater sample, we need to spread the net wider for evidence; if we cannot support a generalization, we must abandon it, or admit its worthlessness as proof.

This advice is not to be construed as advice to avoid the particular. Often an argument takes on persuasive power because a specific bit of evidence is taken as *typical* of the generalization. The argument's effectiveness depends upon the validity of the assertion. In the essay on public television, if one began by describing a nauseatingly boring commerical, and then said, "Therefore, we must have at least one national network without advertising," one would be illogical. If, after the particular, one listed other offensive commercials, and perhaps gave statistics on the time devoted to commercials, one would be ready for a generalization without having relied on a single particular.

The Overinclusive Premise. In the furnace of argument, many logical errors are forged from flawed metal like the overinclusive premise. All of us are guilty. "Everybody who goes to medical school is out for money." "All people who act like that are communists/fascists." These statements are generalizations (possibly from a limited sample), which common sense will not tolerate. If we say "some" instead of "all," we are more sensible—and we have admitted that our charge is not inclusive.

Guilt by Association. Guilt by association (or holiness by association, for that matter) is another common form of faulty thinking. The Mafia, we believe, is an Italian organization. Whenever we identify someone as Italian, the Mafia may cross our minds. Everyone *knows* this sort of thing is absurd; yet if we do not keep constant scrutiny over ourselves, we fall into it again and again. Politics thrives on guilt by association. Because socialists believe in free medicine, anyone who believes in free medicine is a socialist. If we attach an emotional negative to the word "socialist," we can think that we have just argued free medicine down. We have just associated emotively; we have not *argued* at all.

Begging the Question. In this error the arguer assumes the premise of an argument that readers may question. The arguer could try to prove the assumption, but does not. Someone might say, "The rising incidence of mongolism proves that early advocates of a test-ban treaty were correct." The writer neither demonstrates that mongolism *is* rising, nor shows that nuclear testing causes mongolism. Causation asserted but unsupported is common in sloppy thinking. In an earlier example, we quoted, "Cowards who run away to Canada. . . ." Here the reader hears the assumption that anyone who went to Canada to avoid the draft is a coward. The question is not raised and explained or argued. A questionable idea is asserted. Sometimes misused conjunctions beg the question: "Although middle-aged, he wore levis."

Evading the Issue. Cleverly avoiding facing an issue is another favorite tactic of politicians, usually introduced by an assertion that they will *not* evade this issue: "I'm glad you asked that question." Sometimes a politician will say something like, "I believe in freedom of assembly, and the freedom of all Americans regardless of race, creed, or color to assemble with people of their own choice." If we look at the context, we may see that the speaker is not defending freedom but segregation, the rights of associations to exclude members on account of race. "Right to work" laws are laws against forms of union organizing. "Freedom of the press" is sometimes an umbrella for pornographers. Ignoring the question is frequently a deliberate illogic, an attempt to deceive the public by diverting attention from a real goal, which might seem disreputable, to a substitute goal, of which anyone might approve. Evading the issue is euphemism in paragraph form. The gap between expression and meaning is large enough to power the buses of Cincinnati for twelve years and six months.

Nonsequitur. "Non sequitur" is Latin for "it does not follow." We use the term for a statement or idea that *apears* to grow out of an earlier one (by causation, by chronology, by logic, or whatever), but which upon examination fails to make the trip.

> He was a doctor, and therefore an all-around man.
> She left an hour ago, although her car wouldn't move.

Nonsequiturs sometimes afflict us when we are trying to make complex sentences for conciseness.

Sequence as Cause. Post hoc ergo propter hoc, literally "after this, therefore because of this," is a form of the nonsequitur. The assumption is that if B follows A, A is the cause of B. This assumption is not logical. The philosopher David Hume argued that we cannot *know* cause at all. Because we saw one billiard ball hit another, and the second ball move, we *assume* cause and effect, but we cannot see it.

Again, the politics of paranoia adopts sequence as cause for its argument. "Rudolph Blast was in Newark the day before a bomb went off; therefore. . . ." Such evidence is not even circumstantial, and it does not hold up in court. If a hurricane comes after a bomb test, we are not safe to assume that the bomb test caused it. Sequence is not causation, and is inadequate evidence for it.

The Argument ad Hominem. The argument ad hominem—the Latin means "at the man"—rises in us frequently when we lose our tempers. The ad hominem argument diverts attention from issue to personality, and thus it is a refinement of evading the issue, and of the nonsequitur. We ignore the issue and attack the person defending the issue or symbolizing it. When someone defends destroying trees to make a parking lot, we attack him for wearing white socks. A friend says, "I believe in a socialist form of government, because the profit motive, which is basic to a capitalist system, robs us of our humanity and corrupts our intelligence to serve materialism." We rebut him, "Your cousin sells lipstick."

Analogy as Fact. Analogies in argument are most useful. They illustrate the sense in which we mean a statement that might otherwise be too tenuous to be understood. They embody attitude and feeling, and they persuade by being exact carriers of feeling. But we can fall into another common form of illogic by arguing from analogy as if it were fact. Suppose we want to write about different civilizations, which seem to have features in common—like beginning, developing, fulfillment, and decay. To carry this idea to a reader, we invent an analogy; each civilization is like an organism: it is born, it grows up, it matures, it becomes old, and it dies. So far so good. We follow the abstract thought by associating it with concrete things. But many writers become so accustomed to a dominant analogy that they begin to take it literally. Arguing later that our own civilization must end, we say, "Like all organisms, our society must come to death." The argument is invalid because a civilization is not literally an organism and therefore we have not proved that what is true of an organism will be true of civilization. The analogy is not the thing itself.

The General Fallacy: Imprecision. These common fallacies are not exclusive. An issue is often evaded by a nonsequitur, or by an argument ad hominem. Our terms overlap, as our errors do. Common to all these errors is the general fallacy, imprecision.

Ambiguity is a general term that can apply to various imprecisions, to misplaced modifiers, to pronouns with uncertain antecedents, and to words used carelessly for position and for meaning. Clarity is essential to argument. One of the commonest flaws in argument is using one word in several senses. We can fool ourselves into thinking that we have said something profound when we are really just playing with words. Abstractions lend themselves to ambiguity more readily than specific words. Watch out for prose like this, from a theme about campus politics:

> Jerry was liberal, but not so liberal as Mary Huncher. Some of the professors, even the most liberal, were conservative when it came to Mary Huncher, who claimed that they weren't liberal at all.

With ambiguity, or question begging, or whatever, we fall into fallacies unless we examine ourselves. By self-serving, or laziness, or in anger, we commit sloppy thinking, and when we think carelessly we lose the argument, if our reader is thinking well. We must discipline ourselves to honest clarity in thought, or we lose not only arguments but much more. The careless thinker is a liar, and will never learn to be clear.

DESCRIPTION

In description we gather sensuous detail. Description may occur within other forms of writing—exposition, narration, argument—or by itself. Expository description may explain a process, for instance, by listing actions as we would perceive them visually; or it may define the species of a whale by naming its physical properties. Narrative description may recount a river's habits, like the passage from *Deliverance.* Description in argument may persuade us to like or dislike the object described; we might support an argument by telling of roads gouged by studded tires.

Description by itself *evokes* place, scene, or time of day; we feel that we are there. Evocative description, of course, forms a frequent part of fiction and autobiography.

The order we give to details, in description, is usually *spatial.* But words follow each other—they are not simultaneous in the way a picture seems to be—and we necessarily move in words from point to point in a sequence that has to be chronological. So in description we talk about space in a temporal way. In describing a scene, we can begin from the periphery and move to the center, or move from the center to the periphery. The order is not crucial: it is crucial that there *be* an order; that we do not move from center to periphery to center to periphery to periphery.

Some writers seem to think of description as filler, or padding. Not only beginning writers, but professional ones who write the less skillful stories in adventure or confession magazines—and are paid by the word. In these places, we will see description used to delay information, to tantalize.

> Rhonda turned from the window, her eyes wet. "Belinda," she said to me, "I could forgive you for Ron. I could forgive you for Bruce. I could even forgive you for Althea. But there is one thing I can never forgive you for!"
>
> She turned back to the window, her eyes flooded with tears. My cheeks suffused with shame. Over her shoulders, I could see the sweet meadows of home, adeck with lilacs and daisies. their sleepy heads waving in the soft breezes of June, while above, storm clouds gathered to chase away the white puff-ball clouds of early morning.
>
> "They Had a Name for Me," *Real Romance*

Description's main function here seems to be suspense, as a daytime television serial uses an advertisement. To be sure, it also shows a heavy-handed attempt to use description as a good writer does, *for the meaning and the feeling that images carry.* This anonymous writer has her protagonist look at the fields in an attempt to symbolize her past innocence, contrasted to the torment (storm clouds) of the sinful present.

When you write well, your description cannot seem to approach pure symbolism because then it will not seem to be real description.

But there is room for invention, especially when we use comparisons (simile, metaphor, analogy) that carry feeling. Remember the girl writing about her grandfather's funeral. "The sky turned dark" was boring. "Storm clouds gathered" would have been a pathetic and trite attempt to appeal to our emotions. But the new comparison would have worked.

In *Ulysses,* James Joyce has Stephen Dedalus look at the sea when he is feeling depressed. "The ring of bog and skyline held a dull green mass of liquid." Though the description is literal enough, it expresses Stephen's emotions. Here is a passage from a book by a doctor who spent a year in Vietnam. He describes finding some bodies washed up on a riverbank.

> Four nude, markedly swollen, water-logged bodies lay side by side on their backs. Each had a massively swollen face. Eyes seemed to try to bulge out of sockets whose contents were as big as apples. Their lips were three times normal size and each mouth was open and round like that of a fish, with a massive splitting tongue protruding skyward. A thin, bloody fluid trickled from their nostrils.
>
> Massive edema and rigor mortis held their arms up and out in front of them with fat fingers reaching toward the clouds. Their scrota were the size of softballs, and their swollen penises stood as if erect. Their knees were bent in identical frog-leg positions. The smell was overwhelming and hundreds of flies circled around those which were already busy inspecting the mouths and nostrils. There was not a mark on the front of their bodies.
>
> John A. Parrish, M.D., *12, 20, & 5*

The accurate description has modifiers that come from observation, not from the worn tracks: *fat* fingers, *frog-leg* positions, *massively swollen;* it has statements of fact and measurement, like "massive edema" and "three times normal size"; it has comparisons that embody feeling, like "scrota . . . the size of softballs," "mouth . . . open and round like that of a fish," and ". . . as big as apples."

Statistical accuracy in description must never be confused with emotional accuracy. Again, sometimes we must lie, to tell the truth. A contemporary poem ends with a sudden vision: a hundred cows in a field. Reviewing this poem, a hostile critic (carried away by his anger into absurdity) asked *how* the poet could tell that exactly one hundred cows were in the field. He received a postcard from the poet: "I counted the teats and divided by four." The pseudo-particular has a long tradition. It does not lie, because we know it is not intended to be statistically accurate. When Wordsworth says of daffodils, "Ten thousand saw I at a glance," we do not suspect him of counting. If we write, "The sandwich was as thick as the toe of Italy," we are saying that it was "very thick"—so thick that it astounded and delighted us. If we say, "The sandwich was two-and-five-eighths inches thick," we are being pedestrian, and expressing little astonishment. Mere accuracy is all right, but the exaggeration is a lie that is truer to the feeling than accuracy is. Sometimes in writing, you can be accurate in both ways at once; maybe a list of ingredients could be literally true, and also carry an astonished reaction to abundance: "salami, bologna, ham, roast beef, corned beef, Swiss cheese, provolone, onions, lettuce, red peppers, olive oil, vinegar, and, I believe, oregano."

NARRATIVE

At its simplest, narrative is telling a story. At its broadest, it is any development—in sentence, paragraph, or paper—by chronological order. Narrative can belong to exposition, as we describe the phases of the moon, or the stages of a rocket ship in flight. Narration may help us in argument, where we need anecdote or exposition. And obviously we use narrative in autobiography and in fiction.

Narrative must find its way between two extremes. It must have enough detail so that the reader knows what is happening. It must not have so much detail that the reader gets bogged down. The detail must be appropriate; it must have the right quality, as well as the right quantity. Here is a fragment from a theme.

> When I heard the doorbell, I stood immediately, my heart pounding. I knew it was her. I didn't answer it quickly, and heard the door opening toward me. I must have forgotten to lock it! I looked around for a second. Then I picked up my suitcase and climbed through the open window.

The first version had been:

> When I heard the doorbell, I placed my hands against the arms of the chair and pushed myself upright immediately. My heart pounded in my chest. I knew it was her. For some reason, I didn't

move toward the door right away. I just stood there and stared, my heart pounding, my legs shaking. Then I heard a sound like the doorknob turning, and a creaky noise as she must have started to push the door open. I realized that I had forgotten to lock it when I came in from the drug store. I looked all around to see if there was any way to escape. I saw the window open beside me. Without thinking of what I was doing, I picked up my suitcase, checked the fasteners on it, set it on the windowsill and lowered it to the ground, which was only about 2½ feet down. Then I sat down on the sill myself, swinging my legs through, and pulled the rest of my body after me.

This student was commendably rich in detail; but total recall is boring. We need the essential narrative, and nothing more. The revision does it. If the writer had gone further in cutting, and written,

When I heard the doorbell, I climbed out the window.

we would have missed some crucial information.

Here is a passage from the book about Vietnam from which I quoted earlier. It begins with exposition and ends with narrative.

The western perimeter of the camp bordered on a "free-fire zone." Anyone or anything that moves in that area is free game and can be shot, mortared, or bombed. All of the military maps had it marked as such and supposedly all civilians in the area had been informed.

The camp dump was in this "free-fire zone." Each morning at the same time a truck drove out to the dump and all of the tin cans, cardboard containers, wrappers, and garbage from the camp was dumped about fifty meters inside the zone. Within minutes, the dump was filled with Vietnamese from nearby villes [hamlets] gathering cans and garbage. The marines in the watchtower would fire close to them to frighten them away. A few days earlier, an eight-year-old Vietnamese boy had been wounded by these warning shots and was brought to the aid station where he was kept until his wounds were healed. One day he stole an orange soda from a marine who shot and killed him as he tried to run away.

John A. Parrish, M.D., *12, 20 & 5*

This is a good example of narrative used in exposition, and ultimately, as you can see, in an argument that does not need stating.

Dialogue and Quotation

Dialogue belongs with narrative, in fiction and autobiography. In exposition or argument we may use *quotation,* repeating conversations to explain or to persuade; and in writing up research it sometimes lends verisimilitude to quote directly from an interview, or from a source of speeches like the *Congressional Record.*

Dialogue moves best with fewest direction markers. Here are two passages for contrast.

> The door opened. Nancy stood there, wearing a white coat.
> "What do you want?" inquired Jim quizzically.
> "I want my ring and my record player," she spat. Her eyes flashed.
> "Get out!" he exclaimed.
> "Don't you care at all, any more?" she beseeched him tearfully.
> "Shut up!" he shouted, slamming the door.

Let us revise this passage by cutting it.

> The door opened. Nancy stood, wearing a white coat.
> "What do you want?" said Jim.
> "I want my ring and my record player."
> "Get out."
> "Don't you care at all, any more?"
> "Shut up!" He slammed the door.

Maybe the second example is too sparse, but it is better than the first. Beginning writers often explain things too much, telling us twice what we know the first time. (It is like speaking of "white snow.") And in dialogue, it is usually better to use varieties of "say," or to use nothing, than it is to use verbs like "growled" and "whimpered." (See H. W. Fowler, in *Modern English Usage,* on "Elegant Variation"; he says fine things about substitutes for "say.") In other contexts, we prefer the particular because it is more expressive, but these dialogue-verbs have been overused, and if the dialogue is adequate, the verb usually overexplains what we know from the speech itself. Sometimes, we might want to know that "he whispered," because we need the information that he was trying not to be overheard. When you can, omit this information. The writer of dialogue should try to convey the speaker's tone *within* his speech, and avoid the stage directions.

AUTOBIOGRAPHY

In the Vietnam book quoted earlier, Dr. Parrish was writing autobiography; not a book about his whole life, but about a bad year of it. We are all authors of a continual autobiography. In letters we tell what we have been doing and thinking; we confide to a diary or a journal; in conversation we tell anecdotes about experiences lived through or observed. We may even tell an old friend what we did last summer; the traditional theme is only as far away as paper and ball-point pen.

Your own life is your greatest source for writing. Even when you are explaining, arguing, doing research, or writing fiction, your own experiences—eating, reading, loving, being tired, playing checkers—are what you think with and what you argue by. Analogy and metaphor derive from experience. The problem is reaching the source, and bringing the experiences back for use, so that a reader can understand them. In writing out of your own life, you confront that mass of experience directly. The exercise we furnish the imagination in recovering the past for autobiography is an aid to other writing. The same spirit that floats to recall the old summers, in autobiography, will float to discover the precise analogy, in argument.

Memories of childhood make good subjects. Many writers seem to need the distance years give—the long mellowing in the mind—before they can write fully and with feeling. Everyone alive has the material to fill a thousand books. Our minds are huge storehouses of material— the look and smell of a room on an afternoon in May, five years ago, the sun making stripes on the wood floor, the sounds of the mother in the kitchen, and the newspaper hitting the door. Nothing fully understood is trivial. Any difficulty lies in a heaviness in our spirits that will not float. We must recover in order to make new. Sometimes it helps to close the outward eyes to let the light reach the inward eyes of memory; to feel, see, hear, and taste the vivid past. Then if we hold the mental image close, we can describe it in original words, and the words will release other memories, and by soft explosions we remake an old world in new words. From description we can move to action, and bring narrative into our autobiographical writing. Remembering the people we know, we hear them talk the way they talked. We write dialogue, in autobiographical prose, not as a word-for-word transcript of ancient conversations, but as imitated style joined to remembered content. We write dialogue by ventriloquism.

In the first chapter of this book, I talked about "getting ideas." I have just been talking about it again. Of course our own experience should be our happiest source in writing. *It is all there.* But many young people are curiously alien to their own pasts. They write more easily about Egypt than they do about Shaker Heights. I suspect that this happens when writing is entirely mental, and is even subsumed by the intellect. By daily writing, and by deliberate brainstorm—*by cultivating daydream*—we can learn to recover the past, and to reconstitute it by means of style. Here is a passage of reminiscence, which the author has organized by place.

The first I heard of Runkel's Saw Mill was when the oldest Johnson boy, Dave, who was working there at one dollar a day, came home from the doctor with his arm in a sling. When the doctor looked at the arm hanging like a rope with every bone crushed into fine splinters, he told Dave he would have to cut it off up close to his shoulder and Dave said, "You cut off my arm and some day I'll kill you. You put those bones back in place." Dave had noticed that a wide leather belt was running a bit to one side of its pulley and tried to push it back in place with his hand while it was running, and his whole arm had been pulled around the pulley. The doctor had done his best to put the bone splinters together, but he told the boy that he had no hope that he would ever have any more use of that arm. There were days and weeks when everybody thought the doctor was right, but Dave's healthy body and fine spirit fooled them all. His elbow was always stiff and bent so he appeared to be wanting to shake hands with you, but within a year he was able to do a man's work again.

My next contact with Runkel's Mill was when I dropped my new jackknife into the mill race. One of my brothers and I were fishing above the race, and I caught a small bass that had swallowed the hook so far down that I had to use my knife to cut it out. Just as I did that I dropped both the fish and my knife into water moving rapidly towards the mill wheel. When my brother saw how quickly both fish and knife disappeared he said, "Let's get away from here. If we ever fell in we'd be ground to pieces by that wheel."

It wasn't the water wheel but one of the circular saw blades that killed the mill owner. And it wasn't the big seven-foot blade used to rip lengthwise through the logs, turning them into boards and planks, but a small eighteen-inch blade used to cut boards into various lengths. Mr. Runkel had left the saw running and had gone some distance from it when the lock nut turned off and then the blade went spinning through the air, striking him across his back as he was bending down. It cut his body nearly in half and went on to embed itself in a beam on the side of the mill. It was said that his death must have been instantaneous. After that the family operated the mill a few years with hired help, but its usefulness was about at an end.

When the creek left the mill and pond it flowed on through a wide valley. About once a year, in the spring rains, it overflowed its banks and the whole valley became a shallow river. . . .

Tracy Redding, *Hoosier Farm Boy*

And the author goes on about the creek, *remembering.*

WRITING FICTION

Writing fiction is writing out of your life with imagination added. It is autobiography to write about what happened last summer. It is fiction to write about what happened next summer. Really, we are most apt to write fiction by using last summer, but revising it in our imaginations. Sometimes we write what we *wish* had happened last summer. Sometimes we write what we *fear* might have happened last summer. Suppose in reality we went swimming, were frightened by undertow, but made it safely to shore. We could write it autobiographically. Or we could "make up" a story: a character ("he") drowns trying to make it to shore; or he saves a pig from drowning/discovers a cache of perfume bottles/meets a grandmother who flies balloons. Starting from real experience, the daydream can take us anywhere. And wherever we go, we must ultimately take care that our story is formal, economical, and makes its point—just as we do in other forms of writing.

Daydream can take off from next to nothing. You are in a store, and you have an impulse to shoplift. You resist the impulse, but walking home you dramatize in a daydream what might have happened. Perhaps you get away with it and feel guilty. Then what do you do? You return the stolen goods surreptitiously. And are accused of shoplifting! Or you mail them back. Or you give them to someone who needs them, and relieve your guilt, but then wonder further about your action. On the other hand, perhaps you daydream that you are caught: police, trials, disgrace. The daydream can lead to a story in the third person. "She" does some shoplifting. You describe her, her feelings, her actions, her responses to actions by others, and the end of her story. It all started from your own impulse and your subsequent daydream. Or the daydream can be a happy one, a wish fulfillment. You do the impossible feat, and everyone loves you. But make it "he" or "she." When the daydream is glorious, the word "I" is self-glorifying. For that matter, sometimes "he" or "she" sounds narcissistic, when the character shares obvious background with the author. Beware of writing about a noble freshman. Scrutinize your daydreams for dealing with the wholeness of a feeling. In fiction as in autobiography, we often omit a discreditable feeling because we don't want to admit it to ourselves.

Fiction by definition is a lie. But more profoundly, good fiction is telling the truth, because fiction embodies an emotional truth. The wishes and the fears in daydream are as real as tables or days of the week. Fiction *can* lie badly, and often does, when it distorts human nature to flatter the author's or reader's ego, or when it gives the reader or the author an easy way out of a real dilemma, or when it substitutes comfort for anxiety by turning birth and death into something like cotton candy. Situation comedies on television—those endless hours of cute children, cranky husbands, and kooky wives: the television family—distort our lives wholly, to manufacture a light narcotic that induces the passive consumer to buy products. We have all been nurtured on these lies; they are big as mountains inside us, and we must be wary, or we will spend our lives reciting lies under the impression that we are speaking the gospel of observation. Truth to feeling requires vigilant scrutiny.

A good deal of fiction, in fact, is more autobiography than invention. Only the names are changed to protect the guilty. Good fiction is seldom written out of daydream widely detached from the author's experience. In good historical fiction, and in good science fiction, the authors are able to daydream feelings from their own experience into situations they imagine. But historical novelists know history, and science fiction writers know science. Writers do well to stick close to their own background. Northern liberals write bad fiction about southern racists *or* the black world of northern cities. Farm girls write badly about the jet set, and boys from expensive prep schools write badly about camps of migrant laborers.

We make up stories, and we use our experience as the starting point and as the continuing reference point. Making up stories is an acquired ability. If we write much fiction, we develop a story-making facility. If we see a stop sign punctuated with bullet holes, we begin to imagine the hunters who used it for target practice. We see them, we hear their dialogue, we imagine or create their motives. Imagination depends upon experience, upon understanding ourselves and the people we have known. The story-maker creates a world of strangers based upon a lifetime of friends and acquaintances.

Description, narrative, and dialogue are ingredients of fiction, but the most important ingredient is the formal imagination. The same instincts for shape that lead you to cut irrelevances in autobiography, and to distort the real for the sake of the whole and the probable, work in fiction. Many writers find it necessary, in fiction as in autobiography, to write big and to cut small. In the first draft they cannot be sure which details are going to be expressive, and which not. They float to gather. It is important for many writers not to adhere too closely to a plan. If you start to write a story about shoplifting, and then find yourself getting more and more interested in the storekeeper's character, let it happen. You may find that you have written a story about the day of a shopkeeper, and in rewriting you can shift your attention to accord with what you find you have written. Let the characters have a life of their own. Let your imagination take over from your planning intellect. Let it ride. Then revise to make a whole.

One of the most useful ways to keep a story whole is to stay with one viewpoint: either your own, viewing all your characters' minds as if you were God; or one of your characters, a "he" or an "I," whose mind you read. Point of view helps unity and focus, which are as important to fiction as they are to essay.

As there are clichés of adjective/noun, and of dead metaphor and of analogy, so there are clichés of plot. Though we write from experience, we must be sure that it is our experience of people we have observed in real life, and not our experience of that television family. Formula plots fill television, movies, confession magazines, and bestsellers. Boy meets girl, boy loses girl, boy gets girl. Good man appears evil, usually by his own nobility; good man is vindicated and keeps his ranch. Be wary of pat resolutions, problems solved along commonplace lines. As with all writing—from single words to trilogies—originality is honesty/is knowing yourself/is hard-headed scrutiny *as well as* the loose invocation of dream. We arrive again at the paradox of the miserly spendthrift.

WRITING ABOUT WRITING

Often we are asked to write about something we have read. Sometimes we write to investigate something about writing; we may analyze the argument of an essay, or the paragraph structure, or the use of narrative and description. But here, I want to deal briefly with the kind of writing we usually call "criticism," essays that talk about the content, the form, and the value in other essays, in stories, and in poems.

When we write an essay on an essay, we judge its clarity, its persuasiveness, its unity, its interest—and we attempt to apply appropriate standards. If the essay is wholly expository—say, a disquisition on constructing golf courses—we are silly if we blame it for its lack of persuasiveness. If we read a polemic between a feminist and a male chauvinist, we miss the point if we don't deal with the argument. It is sensible to draw a line between explaining and evaluating. Though the two activities are not wholly separable, we should try for clarity to know what we are up to. It is perfectly possible to explain without evaluating. It is not possible to make an understandable evaluation without giving some concrete reasons for your position—without quoting or paraphrasing, examining, and explaining.

In looking at an essay—or even, sometimes, at a story or a poem—it is sensible to check three questions. It helps you to avoid mistakes in reading. First, consider the purpose, moment, or occasion behind the writing. Is this a reminiscence or an editorial? A recipe or a denunciation? You must ask: *What is it for?* Second, you must ask: *Who is it talking to?* Is it addressed to friends or strangers, to initiates or adversaries, to Kiwanis or the Hell's Angels? Third, *What is its tone,* or assumed vantage point? Is it the humble investigator or the omniscient intelligence? Is it sharing a discovery, piece by piece, or is it handing out results from a discovery already consummated?

For more guidance in criticism, look at a book like Sylvan Barnet's *A Short Guide to Writing about Literature.* Here, we must be content to name two general ways of dealing with literature, to look at two common fallacies in dealing with literature, and to present a few examples of criticism from the classroom and from printed sources.

One way to deal with poems and stories is to analyze them, to separate the qualities in the work of art—a mental act of taking stock by stepping back inside your mind and looking—and report on them separately. In dealing with a story or a novel, for instance, you can analyze the author's characterization, use of setting, and development of plot. Also, you can analyze *within* these categories. The writer will show character by dialogue, by description, by action, and by other characters' reactions. In analyzing poetry, we may of course deal with character, setting, and plot (and speaker and occasion) also. Or with sound, or imagery, or metaphor.

In analysis we dig into the methods a writer uses, to explain what he has done. Never worry, as so many beginning critics do, that analysis will destroy a work of art. Ten million words have been written about *Hamlet. Hamlet* still sits on the top shelf, looking down at all the books written about it, smiling a little.

Remember as in all essays to narrow your topic. You cannot write a six-hundred-word essay called *Hamlet* and approach your topic. If you are going to write about *Hamlet,* or *Huckleberry Finn,* or "The Love Song of J. Alfred Prufrock," find a tiny topic and be adequate about it. Write about "Mark Twain's Use of the River in *Huckleberry Finn,*" or "Hamlet's Puns," or "Eliot on Prufrock's Character."

Another kind of critical paper is explication, analyzing line-by-line a short poem or a passage from a longer poem or a work of fiction. We use explication more with poems than with prose. Explication and analysis both deal with similar problems, like character and metaphor. Analysis means attempting to deal with larger units, and must be more summary. Explication is more narrow and more thorough, dealing with the words as they come—somewhat as Chapter III of this book deals with words—and therefore lacking the overview. In a paper of explication on *Hamlet,* you might take the Queen's lines about Ophelia's death.

> There, on the pendent boughs her coronet weeds
> Clambering to hang, an envious sliver broke;
> When down her weedy trophies and herself
> Fell in the weeping brook. Her clothes spread wide;
> And, mermaid-like, awhile they bore her up:
> Which time she chanted snatches of old tunes;
> As one incapable of her own distress,
> Or like a creature native and indued
> Unto that element: but long it could not be
> Till that her garments, heavy with their drink,
> Pull'd the poor wretch from her melodious lay
> To muddy death.

and go through them line by line; you find the *use* of flowers, as a parallel to Ophelia and as a value put upon her; you also find the vivid imagery that carries the action—those floating clothes!—and the metaphor of drunkenness. And more.

Of course a million pitfalls await anyone writing criticism. One of the greatest is the reader's sense of the author. Too often in reading we ask ourselves silly questions: "Did T. S. Eliot really mean all these hidden meanings?" The whole notion of "hidden" meanings begs the question: who is supposed to be hiding what from whom? And to suggest intention is naïve. With anything complicated in our own lives, are we ever really certain of our own intentions? Then how are we able to know Eliot's intention in 1909, or Shakespeare's in 1601? We must keep our eyes on the text, not on the imagined "idea of the author." If something is *there* in the text, if we can show that it is *there,* then it's *there*—no matter if the author rises before us in ectoplasm and denies it. The only qualification we need make is historical, and governs the meanings words had at the time they were used. "King" meant something to Shakespeare it cannot mean to us. The OED is especially helpful in reading old books.

Avoid *the biographical fallacy.* First, avoid arguing from intentions, which are always unknowable. Second, avoid using the work of literature to illuminate the author's life. Of course if you are writing a biography, write a biography—and use the literature as you will. But do not write biography that pretends to be criticism, as so many critics have done. People writing about a novelist try to explain the novels by referring to his first marriage, his depressions, and his isolation. But novels are novels—if they are any good—and we learn nothing about them by learning what experience *may* have informed them. Critics writing about W. B. Yeats's poems seem to run from the poems to the life as fast as they can. When a poem is about a woman, they cry "Maud Gonne!"—the name of a woman whom Yeats loved, unhappily and unrequitedly—and lift their eyes from the page. They have said nothing about the poem. Therefore keep your eyes on the words in front of you, when you write criticism. If you love an author's work, it is fascinating to know something about his life, and nothing is wrong with this knowledge. But when you write about the work, write about the work.

The beginning critic should avoid the biographical fallacy, even if it seems artificial to avoid using what he knows. Probably it is more difficult to avoid *the autobiographical fallacy.* This kind of criticism is not really about the poem; it is about the reader's response to it. At the extreme, it can read like this passage from an examination:

> I like this poem. When I first read it I felt scary, and then when I read it over again I felt good. I like the images and the sounds and the ideas. The poem is *right on!*

There is no need to quote the poem that the student is writing about—it could be any poem. All he talks about is himself.

This kind of paper often comes from enthusiasm, and is an understandable excess. We *respond* to something! We want to tell people.

We want to copy our response in our prose, making it equivalent to a printout of our heartbeat, body temperature, and brain waves. We try to name our feelings. But in our enthusiasm, we have forgotten the object about which we are supposed to be enthusiastic. Our subject, instead, is I, I, I. Unwittingly, we have fallen into egotism, and we praise the poem because it was able to create such a response in us. Remember two things especially, when you write criticism: *The poem is important, not the poet,* And equally, *The poem is important, not the reader.*

Robert Frost has a poem called "Acquainted with the Night."

> I have been one acquainted with the night.
> I have walked out in rain—and back in rain.
> I have outwalked the furthest city light.
>
> I have looked down the saddest city lane.
> I have passed by the watchman on his beat
> And dropped my eyes, unwilling to explain.
>
> I have stood still and stopped the sound of feet
> When far away an interrupted cry
> Came over houses from another street,
>
> But not to call me back or say good-by;
> And further still at an unearthly height
> One luminary clock against the sky
>
> Proclaimed the time was neither wrong nor right.
> I have been one acquainted with the night.

One student on a final examination began an "analysis" of this poem:

> I really love this poem. I chose to write about it because I know just the feeling that Frost is writing about. It reminds me especially of one night at home last summer. All afternoon I had been feeling depressed, listless. I turned on the television and turned it off. After supper I helped my mother with the dishes but then I didn't want to hang around with my brothers the way I usually did but I felt like taking a walk. It was really funny, because I never take walks, but that night I really wanted to.
>
> I didn't walk outside town, so that part isn't the same. But it rained! When I read the poem it all came back to me, so clearly! . . .

.   .   .

The poem is excellent because it is so realistic and so moving. Reading it, my whole body felt just what was happening. It made me remember the strangest feeling of my life, when I too was one acquainted with the night.

This reader, partly because of coincidence, will not let herself see the poem itself. Another student wrote about the same poem.

Robert Frost's "Acquainted with the Night" recounts an experience of loneliness and of restlessness. Frost—or the man who says "I" in the poem—is all alone. He listens as if somebody might be calling for him but it is never him. It seems as if it couldn't be him, or even as if he wanted to be alone. Why does he walk back and forth in the night if he doesn't want to be alone? He is *sad* (a lane isn't sad unless you are) and he is guilty or shameful about something ("dropped my eyes, unwilling to explain")—maybe about wanting to be alone? When you come to the clock at the end of the poem, at first it seems to be some sort of symbol of what he is looking for. It is "luminary," which can just mean that it was lighted up, but which sounds mysterious and grand. And it was "at an unearthly height." What does this mean? Well, it could just mean that it was really separated from the earth a lot—as Frost (the walker) isn't, concerned with street and lanes and feet. But it is *sort* of a hint of God or some mystery too. But just when he thinks he's going to get an answer, it turns out that the time of day isn't what matters. It's "neither wrong nor right" so the walker must be worried about right and wrong, or about not being able to tell them apart. Maybe that's why he wants to be alone?

The poem has fourteen lines. It is some sort of a sonnet. It doesn't have much colorful language in it. It's mostly just what happens, but there are words (like the ones at the end I mentioned) which are really well used. "Acquainted" is a funny word, like an "acquaintanceship" not a "friendship." It sounds as if Frost knew the night *very well* but didn't like it very much. And the part I like best is when he says

> stopped the sound of feet
> When far away an interrupted cry
> Came over houses from another street.

It's so *cold,* that way of referring to your own walking by hearing it.

> The poem is a good one. It's more complicated than it looks. It gives a feeling—of desolateness—and a reason for it.

This sensitive examination answer, pondered over and revised into an essay, would make a good piece of criticism.

Here is an example of polished criticism. The paragraph is from a book about Thomas Hardy, and introduces a discussion of *Tess of the d'Urbervilles.*

> With *Tess of the d'Urbervilles* we come to one of the most contentious novels in the language. Once again the theme is preposterous human suffering, an ill-starred individual, fighting the good but lonely fight against invincible odds. But this time the sufferer is an attractive peasant girl, "a pure woman" who, although she had "passed the Sixth Standard in a National School," was still a child, still a country innocent, when she was sordidly raped. Yet in *Tess,* a Transcendental purity of spirit, embracing all that is charitably humble and devotedly unselfish, survived long enough to enthrone humanity in a brief splendour. The book, too, is a commentary not only on Victorian morality but on the complexity of sexual morality as a whole. Despite the martyrdom and literary canonisation of Tess, there is no vindication of unchastity, and this is a factor not necessarily forced by the magazine-readers. All Hardy's heroines are chaste.
>
> George Wing, *Hardy*

Because this is a paragraph from a book, I do not print it as a model for a theme, but as an example of a writer beginning to cope with fiction and fictional character. It is easier to find explications and analyses of short poems or parts of poems. Here is R. P. Blackmur going to work on a few lines by a poet named Hart Crane.

> To illustrate the uniformity of approach, a few examples are presented, some that succeed and some that fail. In "Lachrymae Christi" consider the line
>
> Thy Nazarene and tinder eyes.
>
> (Note, from the title, that we are here again concerned with tears as the vehicle-image of insight, and that, in the end, Christ is identified with Dionysus.) Nazarene, the epithet for Christ, is here used as an adjective of quality in conjunction with the noun tinder also used as an adjective; an arrangement which will

seem baffling only to those who underestimate the seriousness
with which Crane remodelled words. The first three lines of the
poem read:

> Whitely, while benzine
> Rinsings from the moon
> Dissolve all but the windows of the mills.

Benzine is a fluid, cleansing and solvent, has a characteristic tang
and smart to it, and is here associated with the light of the moon,
which, through the word "rinsings," is itself modified by it. It is, I
think, the carried-over influence of benzine which gives startling
aptness to Nazarene. It is, if I am correct for any reader but
myself, an example of suspended association, or telekinesis; and
it is, too, an example of syllabic interpenetration or internal
punning as habitually practiced in the later prose of Joyce. The
influence of one word on the other reminds us that Christ the
Saviour cleanses and solves and has, too, the quality of light.
"Tinder" is a simpler instance of how Crane could at once isolate
a word and bind it in, impregnating it with new meaning. Tinder
is used to kindle fire, powder, and light; a word incipient and
bristling with the action proper to its being. The association is
completed when it is remembered that tinder is very nearly a
homonym for tender and, *in this setting,* puns upon it.

R. P. Blackmur, "New Thresholds, New Anatomies"

You don't have to know all the references Blackmur makes to see his
method. And you don't have to write with such references to write
criticism.

By and large, I suspect that it is good policy, when you are about to
write a critical essay, to avoid reading critics—especially critics of the
work you are writing about. (Sometimes it is useful to write a research
paper on the criticism of a work of art, to sample the range of opinion.
But this is another matter.) If we are going to write on Huck Finn, we
can easily drown ourselves in the contradictory criticism of Huck Finn,
and end by being too frightened to have an opinion of our own. I think
we do better, once we have found out what we need to know about the
vocabulary in a work, if it is old, to deal intensively with the work
itself, and avoid the secondary material that comes from biographers
and critics.

For writing criticism is a matter, not of knowing about criticism, but
of knowing about the work criticized. Committing ourselves, in our

own words, to interpret and evaluate a literary work, we may find that we have read more deeply than we have read before, and think more deeply about what we have read. Criticism helps us learn to read, while we are learning to write.

WRITING RESEARCH

Although research can support an argument, the research paper differs from an argumentative paper by paying most of its attention to assembling information. Sometimes a research paper has no thesis at all. It sets out to answer a question—by what means did the United States acquire Alaska?—and not to prove a point. Research is a way of learning, important in formal study, which we can use the rest of our lives: we can research voting records of members of Congress, recipes, genealogy, precedents in zoning for the neighborhood, or types of schooling for information to give the PTA. Research is a method. The research paper is a particular embodiment of the general method. It applies findings from library research, or other investigation, to the aims and forms that make the essay.

First you must choose a subject. Choosing a subject often resembles discovering Chinese boxes, starting with a large box, moving to the smaller one inside it, then to a smaller one inside *that*, until finally we arrive at something of suitable size. We must, as always, *limit the topic*. Often—maybe *usually*—the hardest part of a research paper is finding a suitable topic, and then limiting it. (On pages 35–36, I talked about focus, and about narrowing a topic.) Broadness however is not the only problem that can afflict a topic. In fact, broadness need not be a grievous problem; one can almost always whittle a broad topic down. "Vegetable Gardening" can become "Raising Organic Tomatoes," and "Voting in a Democracy" can become "Absentee Balloting: Its Effects on the Two Parties."

When a subject is too scientific or too technical, on the other hand, only years of specialized study will prepare a student to write about it, and "Genetics," for all its breadth, is no more difficult than "The Effects of Gamma Rays on Drosophila." Here, we must abandon our desired topic and look for something less technical. Other subjects prove impossible because research material is unavailable, or insufficiently available. "Vampires in Brazil" sounds fascinating enough, but the library is unlikely to provide the reading necessary. Still another kind of problem is the subject about which there is little to say—a subject adequately covered by an encyclopedia entry, like the history of basketball.

In writing a research paper, the most important decision is choosing a manageable topic—a topic neither too large nor too small to be handled in the assigned number of pages, and a topic neither too technical for a lay audience, nor too specialized for the facilities of a university library.

Since the library is essential to the research paper, let us look at ways to use it.

Using the Library

Libraries hold the past of the species. Large university libraries, with microfilm vaults that collect old books and manuscripts, as well as current periodicals, can satisfy the most special inquiries. But even the smallest library contains more than we are likely to learn and to retain in a lifetime. When we walk into a reference room, or among the stacks of coded volumes, we walk in a universe of possibilities. Everything thought and done in human history surrounds us. The first sight of a big library can be a terrifying vision. All these books! How do I find my way? Many a student, entering the largest library he has yet seen, has wanted to flee in terror, and perhaps to settle down in front of the television set, with a bag of potato chips.

But the road maps are there, and people to help. In the next few pages I will talk about card catalogues and reference collections, but first, I want to mention the most obvious things—things sometimes overlooked. Many colleges offer library orientation, and you should never ignore such help. Many also provide a small guide to their facilities, printed or mimeographed, which you can keep and consult when you need to. Finally, there are the librarians—at a desk labeled Information, or at the reference desk, or wherever, who sit there in order to help you out, to advise you, and to acquaint you with the resources stockpiled around you. *Never be afraid to ask a librarian a question.* Whatever you ask, the librarian has probably heard it before: Where do I find out about vampires? What do you have on blue whales? How do you spell "drosophila"?

The librarian will not find the answer for you, but will tell you where to start looking.

The Card Catalogue

The card catalogue records everything that is in the library. Thousands of 3-by-5-inch cards, in long trays, are alphabetized by author, title, and subject. Every book is represented by at least three cards. One card is alphabetized under the author's last name; to find Georges

Blond, you look under B and not under G. Another card is alphabetized under the first major word of the title; *The Great Story of Whales* will be found under G, not under T. A third card is alphabetized under the subject, like Whales. Naturally enough, most books are listed under more than one subject; three cards is only the minimum that will represent each book.

Each card gathers all sorts of information, including a *call number* that, in conjunction with the library's own map of its collection, tells us where to find the volume. The cards list publisher, edition (if other than the first), the number of pages and illustrations, and usually the author's dates and the subjects covered in the book.

Here are the subject, title, and author cards for a single book.

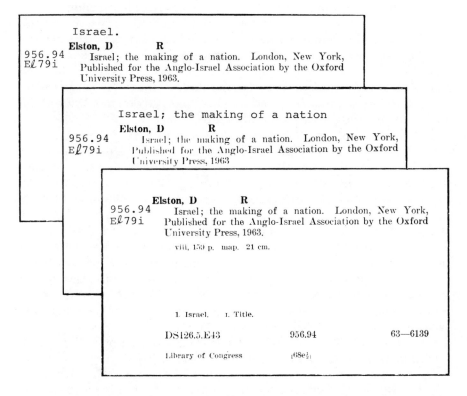

When we do research, we find the subject cards especially helpful. Under Whales, and Whaling, are more than a hundred and fifty cards in one large university library. But the other listings, of author and of title, are essential also. Sometimes in our background reading we will find a title but no author; then we require the title index. Sometimes we will find a person quoted, but not know whether he has collected his thoughts into a book. Perhaps he has published a book recently. Such speculations will lead us back to the card catalogue, to see if there are books under his name that we should consult.

Here are some things to remember about the organization of a card catalogue.

Subjects are not always listed under the names we choose for them. Therefore the library cross-references for us. If we look up Farming, as a subject in the card catalogue, we will be told to See Agriculture. If there is no entry, under the word you have chosen for your subject, try to think of near-synonyms. Or ask a librarian.

Abbreviated words are alphabetized as if they were spelled out. "St."—for "Saint"—is alphabetically ahead of "seraglio." Names beginning with "Mc," "M'," and "Mac" are alphabetized as if they were spelled "Mac." When names with prefixes like "de" and "von" are alphabetized, the prefixes are ignored; "de Kruif" comes under K.

A writer is an author before he is a subject. Books *by* W. H. Auden will appear before books *about* W. H. Auden.

Reference Works

First let me mention a reference book about reference books, appropriately titled *Reference Books*, by Saul Galin and Peter Spielberg. Most libraries have this book, and it is worth looking at; the table of contents indicates the material available in a good library reference room. The authors list encyclopedias first and then dictionaries. The *Encyclopaedia Britannica* remains the best general encyclopedia. Its newest edition divides itself into two multi-volumed works. The Micropaedia of ten volumes provides short entries for most topics, and gives bibliographies and also cross references to the detailed, nineteen-volume Macropaedia, which has immense articles—as long as a book—on the history of China, for instance. The bibliographies of course lead you straight to the card catalogue in your library.

The various dictionaries include the massive *Oxford English Dictionary* (see pages 65–66). (When you consult British dictionaries, beware of British spelling.) There are also, as Galin and Spielberg show, numerous dictionaries that come to our aid when research leads us in special linguistic directions: dictionaries of slang, of the American idiom, and even *A Dictionary of Clichés.*

Biographical dictionaries run from the common *Who's Who* through the *Dictionary of American Biography,* and into biographical diction- aries that cover all countries and all times. Invaluable to anyone re- searching contemporary problems are the indexes to periodicals and newspapers, from the *Readers' Guide to Periodical Literature* to the equally useful *New York Times Index.* Then there are bibliographies, catalogues of printed books by which we can discover books our library lacks—and can perhaps acquire by interlibrary loan. The *United States Catalogue* and *Cumulative Book Index* are important, as is the *Pub- lishers' Trade List Annual,* of which most libraries keep back copies.

Then, still dealing with general material, there are all the almanacs and yearbooks, like the *World Almanac* and *Facts on File.* Here we find statistics. Even the *Guinness Book of Records* may be useful in a research paper, at least in a lighter moment. Of course there are atlases and gazetteers with much social and historical information, coded according to geography.

When we leave general categories and become specific, we find that there are reference books *within* all disciplines. There are *Who's Who*'s that are scientific and medical. There are encyclopedias of music and of architecture, of archaeology and of anthropology. There are indexes to works of art. Many of these special reference books can be found in the card catalogue under the subject name of the discipline itself. And do not forget to consult the kindly librarian.

Under the subject Literature are innumerable reference works, from histories of the literatures of various languages, to dictionaries—like the *Oxford Companion to English Literature* and another to American literature, and the *Oxford Classical Dictionary. Twentieth Century Authors* has been useful to at least a million students. Some of these books, like the last mentioned, quote criticism of the authors discussed, and most of them include bibliographies of works by the authors, and of works written about them.

In almost all fields of study are works of reference that can help us with research. I cannot list everything that might come in handy. (Galin and Spielberg, attempting to list only the *most* useful books, filled more than three hundred pages.) A few titles may hint at the range that you can expect. There is Grove's *Dictionary of Music and Musicians;* the *Congressional Record;* the *New Catholic Encyclopedia;* the *McGraw-Hill Encyclopedia of Russia and the Soviet Union;* the *Bibliography of Comparative Literature; Anthropology Today: An En- cyclopedic Inventory;* the *Mental Health Book Review Index;* the *In-*

ternational Bibliography of Political Science; the *Nuclear Science Abstracts;* Chambers' *Technical Dictionary; Chemical Abstracts; Mathematical Reviews;* the *Encyclopaedic Dictionary of Physics*—and on and on and on.

Whether you find usable material or not, you will need to take a note for every book consulted, for your own bibliography. And when you find a fact or a notion that you might want for your paper, you need to record it. A 3-by-5-inch card is most useful. Any time you make a note, be sure to write down the information that you will need for a footnote. But to deal with this subject, we need another section.

Bibliography

A bibliography is a list of books or other printed sources that the writer has consulted in order to write a paper. Research papers depend especially on outside resources, but even an argument or a book review frequently takes the writer to the library. See the bibliography on page 280, at the end of "The Protector Unprotected." At the end of any paper for which you have done reading, list your sources alphabetically by author. If you quote or paraphrase anything without naming your source, you are plagiarizing. Bibliography and footnotes are your acknowledgment of indebtedness, your statement of research done, and your contract of honesty.

For a thorough summary of the manners to use in a bibliography, consult the *MLA Style Sheet,* second edition. Here is a brief outline.

Underline the titles of books, and enclose the titles of articles from newspapers and magazines in quotation marks. Include page numbers when you refer to periodicals, but omit them when you list a book. List publishers of books, cities of publication, number of edition when there is one, and date of publication. When you refer to a magazine, include the date and volume number, and underline the name of the magazine. When an article or book is anonymous, list it alphabetically by title, using the first word that is not "a," "an," or "the." Here are some of the possible varieties of bibliographical entry; notice punctuation.

A periodical article with an author:

> Mumford, Lewis. "The Cult of Anti-Life." *The Virginia Quarterly Review,* 46, No. 2 (Spring 1970), 198–20*.*

An anonymous article from a periodical:

> "Freud on Death." *Time,* 100, No. 3, 17 July, 1972, p. 33.

A book with one author:

> Graves, Robert. *Wife to Mr. Milton.* New York: Creative Age Press, 1944.

A book with more than one author:
> Cordell, Richard A., and Lowell Matson. *The Off-Broadway Theatre.* New York: Random House, 1959.

An edited book.
> *Page 2.* Edited by Francis Brown. New York: Holt, Rinehart & Winston, 1967.

An article from an edited book:
> Vonnegut, Kurt, Jr. "Science Fiction." *Page 2.* Edited by Francis Brown. New York: Holt, Rinehart & Winston, 1967.

A translated book:
> Chuang T'zu, *Basic Writings,* tr. Burton Watson. New York and London: Columbia University Press, 1964.

A book in several volumes:
> Johnson, Edgar. *Charles Dickens: His Tragedy and Triumph.* 2 vols. New York: Simon & Schuster, 1952.

Remember to list the edition of the book consulted.

Footnotes

Footnotes name the source of a quotation you use in the text, or the source of information used, or on occasion qualify or elaborate a portion of the text. The last use is the least common; it can detract from the flow of a text; we use it only when some information is half-pertinent.

Footnote what you must, but omit footnotes if you feel that the material you are using is obvious. Telling us that whales are mammals, you need not footnote the *Encyclopaedia Britannica;* the information is readily available.

Footnote at the bottom of each page, rather than in a clump at the end, for the reader's convenience. To save the proper space for the appropriate footnotes takes planning ahead when you are typing. When you start a new page, in typing up your draft, estimate how many lines of manuscript you will cover, and how much space the footnotes to those lines will occupy.

For meticulous advice on footnoting, covering multitudinous contingencies, consult the *MLA Style Sheet,* second edition.

Single-space your footnotes at the bottom of each page. If a page has more than one footnote, double-space between them.

Number footnotes consecutively throughout the paper; do not start each page with 1.

The number for the footnote is placed at the end of the material footnoted, and slightly above the line of the text, thus.[5]

If the name of the book or the author is given in the text, do not repeat the information in the footnote.

You can abbreviate long titles of periodicals and supply the full name in the bibliography. *The Review of Analytic Psychology* can be *RAP* in a footnote.

Here are some sample footnotes, followed by a list of short cuts and abbreviations frequently used in footnoting.

An article from a periodical:

> ¹Leslie Raddatz, "Actress-Equestrienne with a Problem," *TV Guide,* 20, No. 30 (1972), 16.
>
> ²Audrey F. Borenstein, "Reflections on Woman's Identity," *The Georgia Review,* XXVI, No. 2 (1972),156–158.

When a periodical has no volume number or issue number, give the exact date and indicate the page number as "p.," or "pp." if you refer to more than one page.

A book with one author:

> ³Germaine Greer, *The Female Eunuch* (New York: McGraw-Hill, 1971), p. 57.

It is possible to omit the publisher's name and give just the city of publication, If no author is named, begin the footnote with the book title and proceed as above. If no date is given, write "n.d." where you would have put the date. With no publisher listed, write "n.p."

A book with two or three authors:

> ⁴Frederick J. Hoffman, Charles Allen, and Carolyn F. Ulrich, *The Little Magazine* (Princeton: Princeton University Press, 1946), pp. 64–66.

When a book has more than three authors, use the first name and "et al.," which means "and others" in Latin. Or use "and others."

A book with an editor:

> ⁵*Poets on Street Corners,* ed. Olga Carlisle (and so on).

A book with a translator:

> ⁶Chuang T'zu, *Basic Writings,* tr. Burton Watson (New York and London: Columbia University Press, 1964), p. 33.

An encyclopedia article:

> ⁷"Nicaraguan Relations," *Encyclopedia of American History,* Updated and Revised Edition, 1965, p. 323.

An essay in a collection:

> ⁸Ned Rorem, "The Music of the Beatles," in Jonathan Eisen, ed., *The Age of Rock* (New York: Random House, 1969), p. 150.

An interview:
> ⁹Russell Fraser, personal interview on teaching Shakespeare, Nantucket, Mass., July 30, 1972.

A newspaper item:
> ¹⁰*The Ann Arbor News,* May 12, 1959, Section B, p. 1.

A quotation cited in a secondary source:
> ¹¹Stanislaus Joyce, *My Brother's Keeper,* as quoted in Richard Ellmann, *James Joyce* (New York: Oxford University Press, 1959), p. 12.

A review:
> ¹²A. Alvarez, rev. of *Delusions, Etc.,* by John Berryman, *The New York Times Book Review,* June 25, 1972, p. 1.

In the last example we might have called the periodical *NYTBR* and referred the reader to the bibliography. Use initials, however, only if you footnote the periodical more than once.

Here are some short cuts and abbreviations used in footnoting.

When you have been quoting from a book earlier in your paper, you need not repeat the whole citation of book and author after the first time you give it. If a footnote refers to the book cited in the footnote immediately previous, write:
> ²Ibid. ("in the same place"), p. 20.

If you refer later in the paper to a book previously cited, and you refer to only one book by the author, you can repeat his name only:
> ³Green, pp. 72–74.

Under the same circumstances, but with the author's name mentioned in the text, write:
> ⁴op. cit. ("in the work mentioned"), p. 84.

Abbreviations that are frequently used and not previously explained include:

cf. (compare)
ch.,chs. (chapters)
e.g. (for example)
ff. (the following pages or lines)
i.e. (that is)
il. (illustrated)
ll. (lines)
loc. cit. (in the place mentioned)

Notice that *loc. cit.* resembles *op. cit.* Usually it refers to a source further back in the text than *op. cit.* does.

ms., mss. (manuscript)
n. (note)
pass. (see mentions further in text)
q.v. (see for confirmation)
rev. (revised)
v. (see)
viz. (namely)

A Research Project

A student named Jennifer Case decided she wanted to write her research paper about ecology.

> "Fine. Come back in twenty years with thirty volumes. What *about* ecology?"
>
> "I think I would like to write about animals that become extinct because of what men do."
>
> "Fine. What animals?"
>
> "I don't know. There are birds and wild animals I could do. Some are extinct and some are going to be. But I like whales best."
>
> "Fine. *What* whales?"
>
> "I don't know."
>
> "Go to the library and find out."

This dialogue, between the student and her instructor (which can happen inside the student's head, too, between student-student and intructor-student) did the preliminary narrowing of the topic. To move from "ecology" to one species of whale is to move from thirty volumes to a possible research paper. But more preliminary work remained. Jennifer Case needed to read loosely among the whale books, looking for two things. One was a thesis or an argument; but the general tone of her argument was clear before she chose whales as a species to investigate. It was the specifics that remained, to flesh out the thesis using a special whale. The first necessity was to find the whale to write about.

The *Encyclopaedia Britannica* seemed a good place to start, because it gave a brief and factual overlook at this large subject, like a map of a whole country. Jennifer read the Britannica article, which talked about different types of whales, and was most attracted to two—the blue whale because it is the largest mammal of all time, and the humpbacked whale. Thinking about it later, she said that the humpback reached her because of the record, "Songs of the Humpback Whale," which she had first heard Judy Collins mention on the old Dick Cavett Show, and which she had later listened to; and also because, when she saw a picture of the humpback, she was drawn to it because of its ludicrous shape; it was an ugly duckling among the graceful whales. These last details—Dick Cavett, and maternal feeling toward an underdog—are examples of the reasons we choose to write about specific subjects, reasons that are eventually irrelevant to our argument and therefore extraneous to our paper, but human feelings that are originally pertinent to the choices we make.

Jennifer went to the card catalogue in the library and looked up Whales, and Whaling. She found a hundred and fifty library cards. Libraries cross-index by subject, and usually store the books in the stacks by subject. If your library has open stacks, you can find from the card catalogue which shelves in the library contain most of the books on any subject, and then browse in this section. In the University of Michigan library, SH 381 turned out to have the most cards on whales and whaling. A 11 was also helpful, and QL.

Jennifer checked out seven books, and began reading in order to make a choice. She took few notes at this stage, writing something down only when she couldn't resist it. But for every book that she consulted, she made a bibliography card: call number, author, title, publisher, city, year. Then if she took a note from a book—either paraphrases or quotations—she wrote down the author's name in order to clue her to the bibliography card, and she wrote down the page number for her quote or reference. By this means, she saved herself time; when she needed later to check a fact or a quotation, she could refer herself back to the bibliography card and find the address of the book in the library. When she came to make her bibliography, she needed only to alphabetize her bibliography cards and type them up without the call numbers.

Jennifer read loosely for eight or ten hours, gradually acquiring familiarity with the humpback. She also read much of *The Year of the Whale*, a good book about the blue whale, but could not use it because her choice was the humpback. She followed her humpback through various sources, taking notes frequently now, on 3-by-5-inch cards. *Whales*, by a Dutch author named E. J. Slijper, was particularly useful. At the back of books, and in footnotes, she found references to other sources of information, periodicals and government pamphlets and books. She consulted periodicals in the library, and discovered with a

librarian's help how to use microfilm. She consulted the *Readers'
Guide to Periodical Literature* for the latest publications. She built a
collection of cards. Here are a few of them.

Bibliography cards for two books:

Sci. Lib.
SH
381
.A57

Andrews, R. C. <u>Whale Hunting</u>.
New York: Appleton, 1916.

Sci. Lib.
QL
737
.64
I622
1963

Norris, K. S. <u>Whales, Dolphins &</u>
<u>Porpoises</u>. Berkeley: U. of Cal.
Press, 1966.
     (proceedings of a symposium in
Wash. D.C. held in 1963, ed. by
Norris)

A bibliography card for a periodical:

Hickel, W. J. "When a Race Breathes
No More; Extinction of 47 Species
of U.S. Wild Life"
<u>Sports Illustrated</u>, December 14, 1970

Three cards with information on them:

Matthews

p. 59
    highly dev. sense of hearing
in whales

Sanderson

    p. 311

       modern industry based first on
fin whales, then humpbacks, then
blues

Sliper

    p. 378

       maternal ties and "aunts"

After another ten hours of disciplined reading and note-taking, Jennifer Case was ready to organize and begin writing.

In the meantime, she had developed respect for libraries. The card catalogue, the subject index, the microfilm machine, and the reference room were added to her experience. She had learned the beginnings of

research in high school, but the high school library had limited resources. In the college library's reference room were the encyclopedias, the *Who's Who's*, the dictionaries of biography, indexes to the
Congressional Record and to *The New York Times*, yearbooks on all
sorts of subjects—and a reference librarian who helped her. At first, the
walls of books in the stacks were threatening; how could she ever cope
with such multiplicity? But gradually the library grew familiar, and
she accepted the fact that she was not writing a Ph.D. thesis, and that
her knowledge would remain limited.

In organizing the paper, she had only to try different orders for the
3-by-5-inch cards that held her notes. A stack of 3-by-5's is an instantly
changeable outline. You can place them in piles according to topic,
order them in each pile according to the best arrangement of facts, and
then order the piles in the best sequence for the essay. Because each
piece of information is a unit that might go anywhere in the paper—we
cannot organize our information until we have collected all of it; when
we start, we don't know where our facts will best fit our argument—it is
wise to keep the notes short, to write on one side of the card only, and
to make a series of 3-by-5's even when we are finding several things on
one page in a book, rather than lumping different facts on one card.
Later, organization will be easier.

Jennifer tried different orders. She found that she worked best by
starting with general information, apparently objective but gathered
around ideas about maternity and protection, and then moving onward
to opinion, argument, and exhortation at the end. She worried about
her beginning. She had read that a prehistoric mammal, ancestor to
prehistoric whales, had a long horn protruding from its head, and
might be the source of our myth about the unicorn. She played with
the idea of suggesting that the humpback whale might one day be as
extinct as the unicorn. But it seemed elaborate and strained.

She tried beginning with an analogy.

> The great whales graze on plankton floating in the sea as the
> bison once grazed in oceans of prairie grass. [That certainly takes
> itself seriously.] As the American bison was hunted to near ex
> tinction during the last few centuries, so is the number of whales
> now seriously and permanently reduced.

The bracketed aside (her own, in a draft) dismissed this attempt. Then
she decided to begin abruptly, without a conventional introductory
paragraph, and let the title do the introducing. The cards were in

order and she was ready to begin. The first draft felt nearly right, because she had prepared and organized well. A few facts that interested her did not fit; she put the cards aside, to see if later she could find a place for them. She set the manuscript aside for a day, corrected it for style, inserted one new paragraph, drafted her footnotes, consulted *Writing Well* for the mechanics of footnoting and bibliography, and typed her paper.

The Protector Unprotected
Jennifer Case

Humpbacks are mammals, as all whales are; they breathe into huge lungs, bear live young, which they nurse for the better part of a year, and have vestiges of hair which scientists believe once covered the bodies of terrestrial ancestors. The shape of the humpback's body, when compared to the other great whales, is comical—rotund, with long knobby flippers, and bumps, like freckles, all over the head and snout. The dorsal fin is small, sticking out slightly from its back. Behind this fin are several more small, irregular bumps—probably the source of the humpback's name. The upper part of the body is black while the underside is usually whitish. The average length of a mature humpback is forty-five feet.

Unlike a toothed whale, like the sperm whale, which uses its teeth to catch and devour its food, the humpback is a filter-feeder, subsisting mainly on plankton, but also on any small fish unfortunate enough to be in the way. Even birds sometimes fly into the huge mouth. The humpback is a baleen whale; as it swims through the water, mouth open, tiny organisms catch in a mesh of hairy bristles called baleen, which run the length of the whale's palate.

The migration of humpbacks relates directly to their feeding habits. They feed mostly in Arctic or Antarctic waters, areas particularly rich in plankton. But when winter comes to the poles, the whales are driven toward tropical waters which are, oddly, nearly barren of the humpback's food. So while "... 90 per cent of captured humpback whales had their stomachs filled to capacity ..."[1] when taken in the Antarctic (in a study done in 1942), "... only one out of 2,000 humpbacks (taken in waters off Australia) was found to have food in its stomach."[2] The tagging of

[1] E. J. Slijper, *Whales* (New York: Basic Books, 1962), p. 257.
[2] Slijper, p. 316.

humpbacks has shown that they migrate along the coasts of the continents and that there are several rather distinct populations, one of these feeding in the Arctic, the other feeding in the Antarctic. There seems to be little intermixture between the two groups.

Although humpbacks are slow swimmers, they are famous for their playful behavior. They often jump completely out of the water, unlike most of the larger whales. Christopher Ash has suggested that humpbacks jump and splash to shake off the barnacles that inevitably attach themselves to the flippers and tail of the whales.[3] According to E. J. Slijper, the humpback also:

> likes to roll on the surface, slapping the water with its flukes and wing-shaped pectoral fins as he does so. The slaps can often be heard many miles away. Moreover, humpbacks like to swim on their backs for a while and to display their white bellies. They often turn whole series of somersaults both above and under the water.[4]

Sometime during their fourth year the humpbacks mate in the warm waters of the tropics. After a long period of love-play, they swim at each other, picking up speed. At the last instant they turn toward the surface and, belly to belly, jump out of the water. Probably they copulate at this moment, although some scientists maintain that this jumping behavior does not include copulation, but is rather an elaborate part of the whale's love-play. Humpbacks also copulate while lying on the surface of the water on their sides. In this case, they glide past each other before mating, stroking and slapping with their long , wing-like flippers. While the love-play is rather long in duration, it seems that copulation lasts only a short period of time—from ten to thirty seconds. How many times the same pair of whales mates is unknown.

Eleven to twelve months later the baby whales are born, usually one calf to a mother, although there are records of multiple births among humpbacks. Humpback babies are born, like most whale babies, tail first, and large in proportion to the size of the mother. The average mature female is forty-five feet long

[3] Christopher Ash, *Whaler's Eye* (New York: Macmillan, 1962), p. 61.
[4] Slijper, p. 97.

while the average calf is fourteen feet long at birth—nearly one-third the size of its parent. Almost immediately after the birth of the calf, the mother and perhaps one other mature female from the herd (called the "aunt") nose the baby gently toward the surface of the water where it will take its first breath.

Maternal ties are strong in whales; the mother stays very close to her calf for months after it is born often allowing no other whale but the aunt to swim between her and her offspring. In its earlier stages, the American whaling industry capitalized upon this instinct. Whalers harpooned suckling calves knowing that the mothers would stay by their young and be easy prey. There is now an international agreement which protects calves and nursing or pregnant females.

The humpback's protectiveness is called "epimeletic" behavior. When this protectiveness is maternal, or the act of any older whale on the part of any younger whale, it is specifically called "nurturant." An article called "Epimeletic Behavior in Cetacea" includes descriptions of strong maternal affection in humpbacks. There is a report by a whaling captain of female humpbacks buoying up dead young for hours.[5] In the same article, "succorant" behavior is described. This is care-giving behavior between mature whales: remaining in the area of an injured companion, or supporting it so it can breathe, or even attacking the source of the injury. Male humpbacks display succorant behavior more often than females. but there are reports of "standing-by" in both sexes.

The most highly developed of the whale's senses is its hearing. There is no particular reason for a whale's sight to be highly developed since it often feeds at depths which are dark. The humpback's sense of hearing is used to locate food and to locate other whales.

Dr. Roger Payne has done considerable research on the sounds made by humpback whales. He believes whale songs like bird songs make contact with other members of the species. *Newsweek* (June 8, 1970) quoted Dr. Payne as saying that, ". . . in certain layers of the ocean, known as sound channels, hump-

---

[5] Kenneth Norris, *Whales, Dolphins, and Porpoises* (Berkeley: University of California Press, 1966), p. 77.

back songs can travel thousands of miles without losing much power." Dr. Payne's recording, "Songs of the Humpback Whale," is available commercially. In the notes on the record jacket he explains that,

> Humpback whale songs are far longer than bird songs. The shortest humpback song recorded lasts 6 minutes and the longest is more than 30 minutes.

It is difficult to describe the sounds humpbacks make. Sometimes their noises are like incredible belches. Sometimes the humpbacks sound like cows bellowing or jungle birds screeching far away. The pitch and the duration vary enormously. When my cats heard the record for the first time, they paced nervously back and forth in front of the speakers and then ran out of the room to hide under a bed.

For many years the humpback was of basic importance to the American whaling industry, partly because of the whale's habit of migrating close to shore, making him easy to catch, and partly because humpbacks yield a good amount of oil for their size. In a Congressional Hearing on the Conservation of Whales (1931), Dr. A. B. Howell had this to say: "For all practical purposes it may be said that the existing whaling industry is dependent upon the Blue Whale, Finback, and Humpback. . . . But at present all three species have been almost exterminated commercially in all but the most inaccessible portions of their ranges." (p. 3) The latest figure I could find on the number of remaining humpbacks is "a few thousand" (*Newsweek,* Jan. 25, 1971), down from hundreds of thousands.

Until 1963, humpbacks were only partially protected by the International Whaling Commission. In that year, the Commission forbade even the limited four-day take of humpbacks due to the near extinction of the species. As reassuring as this sounds, the humpback is still the victim of whalers not belonging to the member nations of the Commission and even, occasionally, of whalers from member nations—sometimes out of simple error and sometimes because of inadequate enforcement of the regulations. (Victor Scheffer, author of *The Year of the Whale,* would like to see enforcement of whaling regulations by the United Nations.) Another discouraging fact is that the whaling industries of various nations have turned to other endangered species, especially the fin whale, to take their quotas.

Given modern processing techniques, many products can be made from the body of a whale. Not only oil and meat come from the carcass, but cattle-feed, fertilizer, glue, glycerin, and insulin. In 1955, Georges Blond estimated the commercial value of an Antarctic blue at four to six thousand dollars.[6] I should mention that the blue whale is the largest of the great whales, in fact, the largest mammal known to inhabit the earth, now or ever.

The problem is this: either we continue whaling policies as they now exist in order to acquire what the whale affords, until we have killed off all whales, or, we develop alternative sources for the products now supplied by the whaling industry. Since we would have to find alternatives eventually, it seems sensible to look for them now, and preserve the declining population of whales in our oceans. In previous centuries, it was fashionable for women to cinch their waists with corsets stayed by whale-bone. That practice is no longer "essential." It never was. Science could make whale oil as obsolete a source of lubricants as whale-bone is obsolete in women's corsets. The same goes for cattle-feed and glue and all the rest. With proper application of the brain-power in this world we can find other means to satisfy our wants. We need not exterminate one species of animal after another.

If we should find ourselves unable to make alternatives in the laboratory, perhaps we should question how badly we need the products in the first place. Perhaps, to preserve a species, we could learn to do without things like ambergris (which comes from the sperm whale and is used in making perfume) and whale meat for cattle-feed. A T-Bone steak is an incredible waste of matter and energy if it comes from a steer that ate a whale that ate a herring that ate some plankton that ate. . . . In the portion of a poem that follows, Gary Snyder embodies the interconnected-ness of all living things. He is talking about eating shark meat but it could as well be whale steak:

[6] Georges Blond, *The Great Story of Whales* (Garden Coty, N.Y.: Hanover House, 1955), 16.

Sweet miso sauce on a big boiled cube
as I lift a flake
to my lips,
Miles of water, Black current,
Thousands of days
re-crossing his own paths
to tangle our net
to be part of
this loom.[7]

So far it seems that every generation thinks the next generation is the one that will have to stop the destruction of the ecosystem. That kind of thinking can't go on. We must protect our brother the humpback, as the humpback protects his brother. The movement toward protection of humpbacks by international agreement is a small move in the right direction.

[7]Gary Snyder, *Regarding Wave* (New York: New Directions, 1970), p. 29.

Bibliography

Ash, Christopher. *Whaler's Eye.* New York: Macmillan, 1962.

"Battle of the Whales." *Newsweek,* 25 Jan., 1971.

Blond, Georges. *The Great Story of Whales.* Garden City, N.Y.: Hanover House, 1955.

Norris, Kenneth. *Whales, Dolphins, and Porpoises.* Berkeley: University of California Press, 1966.

Slijper, E. J. *Whales.* New York: Basic Books, 1962.

Snyder, Gary. *Regarding Wave.* New York: New Directions, 1970.

U.S. Congress. Special Commitee on Conservation of Wildlife Resources. *Whales.* Washington: Gov't Printing Office, 1931.

"Whale of a Singer." *Newsweek,* 8 June, 1970.

Jennifer Case wisely limited her paper, and it works well within its limits. She has a fine eye for detail, and embodies her ideas and feelings in the facts that fascinate her. As a result, she is able to interest the reader.

Perhaps this account of Jennifer's paper is misleading, because she found her topic rather easily, and no major problems got in her way when she proceeded to work. She narrowed her topic without a struggle, and she found her way through a large library without getting lost with a librarian helping. Also, she gave enough time to the paper to write it well.

Many students fall into bear traps, and find themselves in trouble. But each trouble is particular; there is no *general* bear trap, once an adequate subject is found. Student X is intimidated by the library, and does research that is inadequately documented; Y gets involved in a technical side issue, fascinating to him but destructive to the paper's shape and purpose; Z becomes tied up in a Gilbert and Sullivan production, and does not take the time to do his research or write his paper, and tries to complete his paper in twelve hours, midnight to noon, on the day it is due. Maybe Jennifer Case's good luck has partly to do with being *sensible*.

Competent writing is the final ingredient in her paper. But we should not allow our pleasure in her writing to obscure the *basic* ingredients of research and organization. Reading and note-taking, hours and hours of them, supply us with the details we find ourselves using. We must be willing to put in the time and the thought to *accumulate* detail. Then we must use our shaping intelligence to set the right details in the right order, and *eliminate* the useless, even when it is amusing or intriguing. Then we must work over our words, sentences, and paragraphs for style. It is worth it.

EXERCISES

1. If you have used an anthology of essays in your composition course, discuss in class the types of writing you have recently read. Which essays—and which parts of essays—might best be classified as expository? Argumentative? Descriptive? Narrative?

2. Here are some argumentative passages. Analyze them for their logic, order, reasonableness, and for their fallacies if they have any. Remember that these passages are excerpts.

a. A realistic discussion of the place of athletics in our educational program is long overdue. There is in both our schools and colleges today a vicious overemphasis on competitive athletics. Such overemphasis is seriously destructive of our entire educational system.

A short while ago, many Americans were disturbed because unofficial team scores showed that the Soviet Union had clearly taken first place, the United States second, in the Olympic games in Rome. These Americans were ready to argue that we must step up our concern with athletics in school and college as part of our struggle against communism. This line of reasoning needs to be examined. To understand my point, imagine that our independence as a free nation turned solely on the outcome of the next Olympic games—analogous to the ancient trial by combat between selected champions of opposing forces. Under such conditions, we would be forced to modify all our educational practices with the single aim of producing the greatest number of prize athletes.

This is pure fantasy, of course. One hardly needs to argue that we are engaged in a cold war—and in all probablity, a long one. What we must have to win this real struggle are more and better scientists, engineers, doctors, lawyers, teachers, technicians. In short, we must improve the academic output of our educational system. Such being the case, overconcern with the development of prize athletes might well jeopardize our future.

That we need to have concern with the physical development of our youth goes without saying. Our society is heavily industrialized and urbanized. Our children and young people need to devote more time to effective body building and physical exercise. This problem was recognized nationally when, in 1956, President Eisenhower by executive order established the Council on Youth Fitness at the Cabinet level and the Citizens Advisory Committee. I have come to believe that all public-school pupils should devote a period every school day to developing their muscles and body coordination. This means that each school needs a gymnasium of ample size. It also means, in many schools, drastic changes in the content of the physical-education courses. However, in many junior and senior high schools, there is not room enough in the gymnasium to allow my recommendations to be adopted. Too often, physical-education programs are scheduled for all pupils only two or three days a week.

Yet, in some of these same schools, the facilities and instruction are excellent for the relatively few on the basketball or football team that competes in interscholastic contests. Why? Because the community demands public entertainment in the form of winning teams. Fuzzy thinking attempts to relate athletic spectacles to the physical well-being of all our citizens. But there is little real concern for what is of prime importance, namely, the physical fitness of all youth, both boys and girls. . . .

James B. Conant, "Athletics: The Poison Ivy in Our Schools"

b. It should be obvious that even with schools of equal quality a poor child can seldom catch up with a rich one. Even if they attend equal schools and begin at the same age, poor children lack most of the educational opportunities which are casually available to the middle-class child. These advantages range from conversation and books in the home to vacation travel and a different sense of oneself, and apply, for the child who enjoys them, both in and out of school. So the poorer student will generally fall behind so long as he depends on school for advancement or learning. The poor need funds to enable them to learn, not to get certified for the treatment of their alleged disproportionate deficiencies.

All this is true in poor nations as well as in rich ones, but there it appears under a different guise. Modernized poverty in poor nations affects more people more visibly but also—for the moment—more superficially. Two-thirds of all children in Latin America leave school before finishing the fifth grade, but these "desertores" are not therefore as badly off as they would be in the United States.

Few countries today remain victims of classical poverty, which was stable and less disabling. Most countries in Latin America have reached the "take-off" point toward economic development and competitive consumption, and thereby toward modernized poverty: their citizens have learned to think rich and live poor. Their laws make six to ten years of school obligatory. Not only in Argentina but also in Mexico or Brazil the average citizen defines an adequate education by North American standards, even though the chance of getting such prolonged schooling is limited to a tiny minority. In these countries the majority is already hooked on school, that is, they are schooled in a sense of inferiority toward the better-schooled. Their fanaticism in favor of school makes it possible to exploit them doubly: it permits increasing allocation of public funds for the education of a few and increasing acceptance of social control by the many.

Ivan Illich, *Deschooling Society*

c. Women are contoured by their conditioning to abandon autonomy and seek guidance. It ought to be a priori evidence of the synthetic nature of our concept of womanhood that it is so often expounded. The number of women who resort to the paternal guidance of the psychoanalyst is indicative of the same fact. The existence of continual strain in the feminine situation cannot be concealed so it must be explained; in explaining it, traditional psychology, like the Captain in Strindberg's *The Father,* assumes as arbitrarily as he did that women have been subjected to conditioning which is improper to their biological function, which is the breeding of children and supportive work in the home. The woman who seeks academic guidance from psychologists might indeed find that some of the more galling conflicts are lessened as a result although this is a dubious conclusion. What she actually discovers is that the conditions against which she chafes are sanctioned by a massive structure of data and theory which she can only adapt to for there is no hope of shifting it. It takes another psychiatrist to explain to her the function of observer bias, and the essential conservatism of psychology. As far as the woman is concerned, psychiatry is an extraordinary confidence trick: the unsuspecting creature seeks aid because she feels unhappy, anxious and confused, and psychology persuades her to seek the cause in *herself.* The person is easier to change than the status quo which represents a higher value in the psychologists' optimistic philosophy. If all else fails, largactil, shock treatment, hypnosis and other forms of "therapy" will buttress the claim of society. Psychologists cannot fix the world so they fix women. Actually they don't even manage that: one Eysenck study (1952) reported that of patients treated by psychoanalysis, 44 percent improved; of those who were treated by other methods (drugs, shock, etc.), 64 percent improved; and of those who received no treatment at all, 72 percent improved. The subsequent reports of Barron and Leary, Bergin, Cartwright and Vogel and Truax bear out these negative results.

So much for the authority of psychoanalysis and the theory of personality. For the woman who accepts psychoanalytic descriptions of herself and of her problems there are specific perils far greater than the effects of personality prejudices on the other half of the community.

Freud is the father of psychoanalysis. It had no mother. He is not its only begetter, and subsequent structures of theory have challenged as well as reinforced his system. Probably the best way to treat it is as a sort of metaphysic but usually it is revered as a science. Freud himself lamented his inability to understand women, and became progressively humbler in his pronouncements about them. The best approach to Freud's assumptions about women is probably the one adopted by Dr. Ian Suttie, that of psychoanalyzing Freud himself. The cornerstone of the Freudian theory of womanhood is the masculine conviction that a woman is a castrated man. It is assumed that she considers herself to be thus deprived and that much of her motivation stems either from the attempt to pretend that this is not so, typical of the immature female who indulges in clitoral sexuality, or from the attempt to compensate herself for this lack by having children. Basically the argument is a tautology which cannot proceed beyond its own terms, so that it is neither demonstrable nor refutable. Ernest Jones, himself a devout Freudian, began to suspect that something was wrong with the basic hypothesis because he took the trouble to observe the sexuality of female children:

> There is an unhealthy suspicion growing that men analysts have been led to adopt an unduly phallocentric view of the problem in question, the importance of the female organs being correspondingly underestimated.

Unfortunately, the suspicion must have remained unhealthy, for it never flourished into a new theory. Psychoanalysts went on believing in the genital trauma despite evidence. Faith is not after all dependent upon evidence.

Germaine Greer, *The Female Eunuch*

d. In all previous consideration of class warfare there had been at least the assumption that the design of human beings was adequate, unbiased, functional, and not particularly in need of alteration. It was assumed that if the working class took over the functions of the ruling class, they would still be able to act with the conventional organs of men. But the ultimate logic of the sexual revolution required women to stand equal to the male body in every aspect—how could this equality prevail if women in competition with the other sex for the role of artist, executive, bureaucrat, surgeon, auto mechanic, politician, or masterful lover should have to cry quits every now and again for months of pregnancy plus years of uneasy accommodation between their career and their child, or else choose to have no children and so be obsessed with the possibility of biological harm, worse, the possibility of some unnameable harm to that inner space of creation their bodies would enclose?

One could speak of men and women as the poles of the universe, the universal Yang and Yin, offer views of the Creation in such abstract lands as seed and womb, vision and firmament, fire up a skyworks of sermon and poem to the incontestable mystery that women are flesh of the Mystery more than men—it would not diminish by a coulomb those electrics of wrath in the eyes of those women whose revolutionary principles are Jacobin. It was as if the High Grand *Geist* of the Jacobins had returned to state, "It was never enough to sever the heads of the aristocrats. The time is now come to get the first Aristocrat of them all. Since He designed women at a disadvantage, such Work must be overthrown!"

What a job! Men were by comparison to women as simple meat; men were merely human beings equipped to travel through space at a variety of speeds, but women were human beings traveling through the same variety of space in full possession of a mysterious space within. In that purse of flesh were psychic tendrils, waves of communication to some conceivable source of life, some manifest of life come into human beings from a beyond which persisted in remaining most stubbornly beyond.Women, like men, were human beings, but they were a step, or a stage, or a move or a leap nearer the creation of existence, they were—given man's powerful sense of the present—his indispensable and only connection to the future; how could a woman compete if she contained the future as well as the present and so lived a physical life on the edge of the divide? What punishment traveled into the future with the pile driver's clang? Whose unborn ear heard the loss of a note in the squawk of the static? The womb was a damnable disadvantage in the struggle with the men, a cranky fouled-up bag of horrors for any woman who would stand equal to man on modern jobs, for technology was the domain of number, of machines and electronic circuits, of plastic surfaces, static, vibrations, and contemporary noise. Yet through all such disturbance, technology was still built on conformity of practice. If it could adjust to rhythm, tide, the ebb of mood, and the phasing in and phasing out of energy in the men and women who worked its machines, nonetheless such adjustments were dear to technology, for each departure from a uniform beat demanded a new expensive control. The best operator was the uniform operator, and women had that unmentionable womb, that spongy pool, that time machine with a curse, dam for an ongoing river of blood whose rhythm seemed to obey some private compact with the moon. How this womb, unaccountable liaison with the beyond, disrupted every attempt at uniform behavior!

Did women get into automobile accidents? Count on it, more than half their accidents came on a particular week of the month—just before and during menstruation was the time of that week. So, too, were almost half of the female admissions to mental hospitals in that week, and more than half of their attempted suicides, half the crimes committed by women prisoners. . . .

Norman Mailer, *The Prisoner of Sex*

3. Discern and describe the flaws in these arguments:

a. You're stupid! That's why I'm right.

b. In 1971, Paul McCartney announced that he was no longer associated with the Beatles. When he decided to destroy the association, McCartney gave no convincing reasons.

c. When Luke hit the first pitch of the game into the left-field stands, it was obvious that Mitchell could no longer pitch.

d. When we consider the question of aid to underdeveloped nations, we should always consider first that we, too, are an underdeveloped nation.

e. Since democracy died in France with the elevation of De Gaulle, one can no longer go to the French for lessons in the democratic process.

f. No one who dresses like that could possibly know Mozart from Montovani.

g. Warmongers who masquerade as friends of Egypt or Israel attempt to deceive the gullible.

h. Everybody who votes for Wallace is a racist.

4. Take a subject in which you have some interest. Meteorology, for instance. Set up an argumentative thesis for a paper, like "Long-range weather forecasts are futile." Collect notes for arguments. Then take the opposite tack, and try to establish arguments against your original position, like "Long-range weather forecasts are useful."

5. Make up examples for each of the common fallacies of thinking listed in this chapter. Read aloud in class.

6. In books or magazines, find a passage of description, another of narrative, and a third of dialogue. Analyze the authors' use of these devices.

7. Take notes on a poem or a story and arrange them as you would if you were going to write a paper. Use these notes as a start for class discussion.

8. Here is a list of general subjects that you might wish to investigate, pursuing a topic for a research paper. In class, discuss what sorts of reference books you might consult in your investigation. Under what subjects would you look in the card catalogue?

coal mining
modern dance
the American labor movement
coinage in the ancient world
the history of hats
raising sheep
the geography of sport

9. In class discussion, consider the possibilities of limiting the topics listed above.

10. Looking at Jennifer Case's essay, "The Protector Unprotected," answer these questions: (a) Does she beg the question anywhere in the paper? (b) Might you have organized the material differently? Make alternative suggestions. (c) Does she use clichés? Are the sentences varied enough? Are the paragraphs well constructed? (d) Do you find any ambiguity of language in this paper? Does information seem to be lacking in some places? (e) Are there errors in logic in this paper? (f) Is the footnoting consistent? Is everything footnoted that ought to be? (g) Is the bibliography consistent? Is everything listed that ought to be? (h) Can you see when the author has omitted

connectives and transitions she might have been expected to supply? Are the omissions stylish? Are they obscure? (i) Are some details not sufficiently integrated into the whole? (j) What fundamental attitude toward the humpback whale supplies the structure of this paper? (k) Is this paper constructed more upon intellectual or emotional premises?

SOME COMMON PROBLEMS

A Brief Review of Grammar, Punctuation, and Mechanics

This book is mostly about style and structure, about making writing lively, honest, energetic, and clear. As you move through the text, you find grammar when you need it. Here, I want to make a concentrated review of the most common errors of grammar, punctuation, and mechanics, so that the beginning writer who feels confused—what *is* a whole sentence? when *do* I use a colon?—will have a place to come for answers to questions.

If your grammar is loose and shabby, your punctuation random, and your mechanics haphazard, you will lose your audience. We must put sentences together by rules, because rules describe the readers' expectations. If your language ignores these rules—if you substitute commas for periods, or neglect to match parts of sentences to each other—readers will be confused and bored; they will not follow where you want to lead them, even if your ideas are profound and your information fascinating.

When things go wrong in mechanics and grammar, for an inexperienced writer, they go wrong usually because of a few mistakes. If you can remember six general rules, you will avoid most of the errors beginners fall into.

289

1. Make whole, clear sentences.
2. Match the parts of sentences that need matching.
3. Connect modifiers with what they modify.
4. Keep the sentence consistent.
5. Keep punctuation clear.
6. Keep mechanics conventional.

These rules will only become useful if I do some explaining and give examples. Almost everything mentioned here is repeated from the first five chapters; this appendix is repetitious, but it ought to be useful. It differs from the text in how it approaches writing. In the text I talk mostly about the choices a writer can make, to express meaning with vigor and clarity. Here, you can read about the swamps that you as a writer can sink into, which keep you from beginning to reach your goal.

Many inexperienced writers have trouble with only one or two of the problems I list, and not with the rest of them. People sitting next to each other in class may have opposite, persistent troubles in writing. *A* writes sentence fragments, *B* uses commas for periods, *C* mixes up pronouns, and *D* dangles modifiers. None of them has the problem the other has, and each is thoroughly confused by his own problem. With this appendix, they can go directly to the problems that confuse them; I hope it can help the whole alphabet of writers.

MAKE WHOLE, CLEAR SENTENCES
Sentence Fragments

Beginning writers commonly make sentences—groups of words beginning with a capital letter and ending with a period—which don't complete an action. In a theme a student wrote

> The effects of World War II.

as if the phrase told us something. But the sentence is incomplete, a sentence fragment. What *about* World War II? We might want to say,

> Hungary suffered the effects of World War II.

or

> The effects of World War II brought prosperity.

or what? In this theme, the writer had said:

> The economy began picking up finally in 1939. The effects of World War II.

The writer needed to connect the sentence fragment to the sentence, making something like this:

> The economy began picking up in 1939 because of World War II.

The best writers sometimes put sentence fragments to good use (see pages 124–126), but when you are inexperienced, you should avoid them entirely. Wait until you have developed a firm and exact feel for the whole sentence's shape. Do not write:

> He was a good teacher. Being sympathetic with students and fascinated by his subject.

Instead, write something like,

> He was a good teacher, sympathetic with students and fascinated by his subject.

Do not write:

> The pumpkins froze. When the blizzard arrived unexpectedly in October.

Instead, write something like,

> When the blizzard arrived unexpectedly in October, the pumpkins froze.

Here are some inadvertent sentence fragments.

> *After the sun finally sank behind the hills.* It was dark and we were ready.

> *Seeing the Buick with all its tires flat and rusted out in the grass, with no license plates on it.*

> The principal of my high school was a nice person. *Believing that every kid was potentially all right.*

> The people at the fair stared at the twins and began to talk about them. *Because they looked different, I guess.*

> Graduate students in my opinion do not have the right to strike and miss their classes. *When students have already paid their tuition.*

Inadvertent sentence fragments are mainly of two kinds.

Many fragments are subordinate clauses treated as if they were whole sentences. In the last two examples above, the sentence fragments begin with *because* and *when*. These words—like *although, since, while,* and *after*—mean that the clauses they introduce depend, or hang from, a main clause; they are dependent or subordinate clauses. In the examples above, the main clauses (not in italics) make whole sentences by themselves. The sentence fragments could make subordinate clauses in complex sentences.

> Graduate students in my opinion do not have the right to strike and miss their classes, *when students have already paid their tuition.*

The other category is the fragment that modifies the main clause, and ought to be separated from it by a comma—not by a period and a capital letter.

> The principal of my high school is a nice person, *believing that every kid is potentially all right.*

Watch out for sentence fragments that begin with an *-ing* word, just as you watch for fragments beginning with *when* or *because.*

You can correct sentence fragments in several ways. But first, let me mention one way *not* to correct them. Do *not* substitute a semicolon for a period.

> The people at the fair stared at the twins and began to talk about them; *because they looked different, I guess.*

> Graduate students in my opinion do not have the right to strike and miss their classes; *when students have already paid their tuition.*

The semicolon fragment is just as confusing as the sentence fragment. A semicolon is closer to a period than it is to a comma; when we fall into the semicolon fragment, we separate a dependent clause from the main clause it depends on. In both of these examples, a comma would make a whole, clear sentence.

You can correct *many* sentence fragments simply by using a comma instead of a period. Or you can add a verb to the fragment and make it a whole sentence, equal to the other. Or you can sometimes use the dash—things seem to move faster. (Use the dash with caution. See pages 313–314.)

Here are some alternate repairs for sentence fragments used earlier.

> He was a good teacher. He was sympathetic with students, and fascinated by his subject.

He was a good teacher because he was sympathetic with his students and fascinated by his subject.

The blizzard arrived unexpectedly in October, freezing the pumpkins.

The blizzard arrived unexpectedly in October, and the pumpkins froze.

Because the blizzard arrived unexpectedly in October, the pumpkins froze.

After the sun finally sank behind the hills, it was dark and we were ready.

The sun finally sank behind the hills. It was dark and we were ready.

We saw the Buick with all its tires flat, rusted out in the grass, no license plates on it.

The principal of my high school was a nice person. He believed that every kid was potentially all right.

The people at the fair stared at the twins and began to talk about them; they looked different, I guess.

Notice that frequently a sentence fragment can become a whole clear sentence when we remove the subordinating word, like *because,* or change the modifying participle into a verb—like *we saw* for *seen.*

Comma Splices

Comma splices (or comma faults, and run-on sentences) are the opposites of sentence fragments. In the comma splice, a comma is forced into the work a period is meant for; in the sentence fragment, a period is pressed into the service a comma is designed to do. Here is a typical comma splice from a theme, two whole sentences incorrectly joined by a comma.

The Union stands back from the street about a hundred feet, it was built when land was still cheap.

Substitute a period for the comma, capitalize the next word, and you have two real, whole sentences.

Often the same writer makes sentence fragments and comma splices, because both errors depend upon an insecure grasp of how the sentence is made. Reading aloud, with pauses appropriate to the punctuation, we can sometimes discover these errors in time to revise them.

The comma splice is confusing to the reader, because two whole ideas are connected (spliced) as if they were not each whole and separate. The writer gives a signal by the comma but the sentence denies the message that the comma carries. The comma gives us the information that we are reading one continuous idea, which conflicts with the wholeness of the two spliced sentences. The best writers can sometimes use the comma splice to good effect (see pages 136–137), but the beginning writer should avoid the device entirely, until he has developed a firm sense of the sentence. Here are comma splices taken from themes.

> The port of New York has minimum safety requirements, some vessels have to dock in Hoboken.

> The inevitability of war became obvious to even the most casual observer, maneuvers were constantly being held.

> My father grew up on a potato farm in Idaho, he never saw a movie until he was twenty-two years old.

> She walked through the door into the dining room, she wore nothing but a bikini.

> When they were little, they liked to play in the empty warehouse down the block, it was a spooky and exciting place.

> I didn't know where the arboretum was, somebody had to show me.

> Never eat vegetables from a can which looks puffed up like a balloon, that's something I learned at camp.

> Whoever saw the man running away saw the burglar, that's the only possible explanation.

> Making a sweater from acrylic gets you into other problems, wool is better when you are beginning.

> The canoe started tipping as I approached the falls, I was terrified that I would lose all my gear.

When you correct a comma splice, you have four alternatives. Two of them require only a change in punctuation; two of them need another word.

Substituting a semicolon for a comma repairs most comma splices. Making a comma splice often means you want to show a close connection between two whole sentences. You try to move quickly from the one to the other, without the long pause implied by a period and a capital letter. The semicolon was invented for just this purpose: to show that two whole sentences follow quickly upon each other, and are closely related.

Here are comma splices repaired by semicolons.

> The Port of New York has minimum safety requirements; some vessels have to dock in Hoboken.

> The inevitability of war became obvious to even the most casual observer; maneuvers were constantly being held.

> When they were little, they liked to play in the empty warehouse down the block; it was a spooky and exciting place.

Or you can use the period and a capital letter; it will always be correct.

> My father grew up on a potato farm in Idaho. He never saw a movie until he was twenty-two years old.

> Never eat vegetables from a can which looks puffed up like a balloon. That's something I learned at camp.

On the other hand, you can make a complex sentence, if you find that one sentence can depend on the other, by using a subordinating conjunction.

> When the canoe started tipping as I approached the falls, I was terrified that I would lose all my gear.

Or you can connect the two sentences into one compound sentence with *and, but, or, nor, yet,* or *so;* the two clauses will be equally strong, or coordinate.

> I didn't know where the arboretum was, so somebody had to show me.

> The port of New York has minimum safety requirements, and some vessels have to dock in Hoboken.

> She walked through the door into the dining room, but she wore nothing but a bikini.

Each of these four solutions makes a slight difference in tone or meaning. In your context, one of the four will be best.

MATCH THE PARTS OF SENTENCES THAT NEED MATCHING
Matching Subjects with Verbs

When the subject of a sentence is one thing (singular), the verb must be singular also. When the subject is more than one thing (plural), the verb must be plural also. In standard English, we say, "the newspaper covers the waterfront murders," not "the newspaper *cover* the waterfront murders"; or we say: "the newspapers cover the waterfront murders," not "the newspapers *covers* the waterfront murders."

Here are some frequent pitfalls, and how to avoid them.

Sometimes we get into trouble because a phrase comes between the subject and the verb, and confuses us. We may have a single subject followed by a prepositional phrase that ends with a plural, and we make the verb plural because the plural phrase rings in our ears. "The newspaper of the six northern suburbs" is a singular subject. We should say,

> The newspaper of the six northern suburbs covers the waterfront murders.

not

> The newspaper of the six northern suburbs cover the waterfront murders.

We should say,

> The newspaper with four ace reporters covers the waterfront murders.

not

> The newspaper with four ace reporters cover the waterfront murders.

With words like *anyone, each,* and *everybody* (indefinite pronouns) we should use a singular verb. It's confusing: *everybody* refers to many people, but it's a single thing, a single "body"—as single as the *one* in *anyone* or *everyone*. We must say, "everyone hurts this morning"; not "everyone hurt. . . ."

None can be either singular or plural, agreeing with a singular or plural noun elsewhere in the sentence.

None is so happy as a cow in spring.
None are so happy as Venusians at a fly-by.

Do not say:

Everybody in town run down to the circus.

Each of the forty-seven students howl like wolves.

Many a humanoid, accompanied by slime and mist, step from the craft.

When you write a sentence that uses *either . . . or, neither . . . nor,* or *not . . . but,* use a singular verb if both subjects are singular.

Either the red-haired witch or her broomstick was on fire.

If one subject is plural, and the other singular, put the plural subject nearer the verb, and use a plural verb. Say

Either the red-haired witch or her two broomsticks were on fire.

Do not say,

Either her two broomsticks or the red-haired witch were on fire.

or

Either the red-haired witch or her two broomsticks was on fire.

Do not say,

Neither the father nor the son want to follow the witch's track.

It should be *wants,* a singular verb. Do not say,

Not the Prime Minister but the Members of his Cabinet believes in amnesty.

It should be *believe,* a plural verb matching the plural *members.* These sentences are incorrect:

Neither Hitler nor Ghengis Khan were conspicuous for humanitarianism.

Not the first potato but the second and the fourth contains the microfilm.

Either the roof or the shingling over the sheds were giving off a putrescent odor.

When your sentence uses a verb like *is* or *are* (a linking verb, a form of *to be*), make sure that the verb matches with the subject of the sentence, and not with a noun that comes afterward. Say

> The best part of the team was its outfielders.

not

> The best part of the team were its outfielders.

Say

> The outfielders were the best part of the team.

not

> The outfielders was the best part of the team.

These sentences are incorrect:

> The middle chapters was the section in the book I liked best.

> The best section of the book were the middle chapters.

Matching Pronouns with the Words They Refer to

Words called pronouns (*he, she, it, this, that, you, we*) take their identity from a noun which comes before them, and which they refer to, called their antecedent. The noun can come before them in the same sentence, or from a slightly earlier sentence. Pronouns must match their nouns both in number (singular or plural) and in gender (male or female).

Mostly, we match pronouns to their antecedents without trouble. Here are a few troublesome exceptions.

In formal writing, we use a singular pronoun with an indefinite pronoun like *anybody, everybody, each, none,* and so forth. We say,

> Everybody carried his tennis racket.

not

> Everybody carried their tennis racket.

This is a rule of formal writing. To avoid *his* as sexist, or to avoid *his or her* as awkward, we sometimes use the incorrect or informal *their.* If you do it, know that you are doing it. It is also possible, at times, to avoid gender entirely.

> Everyone carried a tennis racket.

Words like *team, committee, jury, class,* and *orchestra* are collective nouns. They are singular words that refer to plural collections of people. Use a singular verb when you describe the whole group; use a plural verb when you describe the many members. Say

> The team climbed on its bus.
> The team dispersed to their lockers.

Don't say:

> The jury went to ~~its~~ their separate rooms.
>
> The committee voted to disband themselves.
>
> The team voted to distribute their winnings among twenty-four ballplayers.
>
> The group destroyed their petition to remove the governor.

When a pronoun matches two or more nouns joined by *and,* it is always plural.

> When the boy and his dog wanted supper, they went to the tavern.
>
> Susan and Margaret prefer lamb stew.

When a pronoun matches nouns joined by *or, nor, either . . . or,* or *neither . . . nor,* and one of the nouns is plural, the pronoun matches the nearer of the two. When you use such a pair of nouns, the sentence sounds better if the second of the two nouns is the plural. Say

> Although Margaret and the Hamiltons are elderly, they run to the chopping block.

Don't say,

> Although Margaret and the Hamiltons are elderly, she runs. . . .

or

> Although the Hamiltons and Margaret are elderly, they run. . . .

Never use a pronoun when it could refer to either of two words before it. We must use pronouns so that we are always *certain* which previous noun they refer to. Uncertainty is intolerable. Don't say:

> When Wilhelmina declared herself to Bertha, she was aghast.

> Leaving his father's house and the dry valley, he was happy to see the last of it.

Both of these sentences lack a clear antecedent to the pronoun. Which of the ladies was aghast? Was he happy to see the last of the house, or of the valley, or of both?

Don't use the pronouns *this* or *that* or *it* to refer to general ideas in a previous sentence, or to an antecedent that is not there. Watch out for *this* or *that* when you use them as pronouns. Don't say:

> I couldn't find my way home because of the darkness and the strangeness of the streets. That's why I was late.

That lacks a clear antecedent, and the sentence drowns in imprecision. Here are more examples from themes.

> The state legislature never got around to getting the bill out of committee until October, and it was the reason the scholarships were never funded.

> Susan's brother is in his third year at Harvard Medical School, and this is the profession she wants to enter.

> The next thing that happened was that the screen door got stuck open and the mosquitoes could get in and the dog would get out whenever he wanted. My mother started crying about this.

> Preferential voting is fair because it gives the voter a chance to give a graded opinion of the different candidates, and therefore opens the way to third parties. That is the real justification for preferential voting.

> Down the block from me there was a family that had three cats. One of them was a big red tom named Mio, the biggest cat I ever saw—thirty-four inches long not counting his tail, and twenty-eight pounds. The kids in the neighborhood couldn't get over this.

We make another common error when we use a pronoun far removed from its antecedent. The result is more ambiguity, vagueness, and imprecision. Here are two examples.

> The partnership of Hudnut and Greenall was breaking up; business had declined, Hudnut's wife was ill, and Greenall's son had run off to Tibet. One Tuesday, they suddenly stopped speaking to each other.

When Sharon looked across the classroom, Bill winked and Larry looked away. Outside the window the clouds gathered for rain, and students were beginning to drive off for lunch, many of them carrying no books at all. Suddenly two girls ran toward a car that had stopped to pick them up. She saw that it was Matt.

CONNECT MODIFIERS WITH WHAT THEY MODIFY

In most sentences, we write phrases that describe (modify) other things in the sentence. We use prepositional phrases as modifiers (to define, to limit).

> the barn *with the red paint*
> the girl *in the corner*
> the chapter *about grammar*

For similar purposes, we use clauses beginning with words like *that, who, since,* and *because.*

> the barn *that was burning*
> Herbert *who tipped his hat*

And we use phrases beginning with *-ing* words (participles), which also modify.

> the chapter *containing the examples*
> *hanging from the skylight,* the plumber . . .

Most of the time we have no trouble controlling these phrases or clauses. We will find no trouble at all if we avoid two common errors.

Make sure that modifiers beginning a sentence really modify what the sentence claims that they modify. If we start a sentence, "Hanging from the skylight," we tell the reader something; we guarantee that the noun which will begin the main clause is what is hanging.

> Hanging from the skylight, the plumber screamed that he had climbed up there to escape a bear.

Too often, we are careless, and make a sentence like this next one— which starts to seem like the sentence above, and then changes its mind.

> Hanging from the skylight, the plumber looked at the huge spider's web.

Common sense can untangle the mess. The reader will eventually understand that the spider's web is hanging, and not the plumber. In the meantime, the reader has been first confused and then annoyed, by the misdirection a careless sentence gave.

Here are more examples of dangling modifiers.

> *Being a wreck with no gears at all,* she got the bicycle free.

> *Riding in a new car,* the beagle chased me half a mile.

> *Driven by his desire to succeed,* the test was easy.

> *Before making a reservation,* my roommate recommended a travel agent to me.

> *Humbled by circumstances,* the town looked better to him now than it had looked before.

Make sure that your word order says what you want it to say, when you place modifiers in a sentence. This advice applies to adverbs and adjectives, as well as to phrases or clauses that modify. The wrong word order can alter your meaning.

> I tell myself frequently to practice.

means one thing.

> I tell myself to practice frequently.

means something else. It is the writer's job to know the meaning and to say it. Here are some examples from themes in which mistakes in word order made sentences that are ambiguous, misleading, or silly.

> Hattie is the cousin who gave me the present in a housecoat.

> Joseph borrowed an egg from a neighbor that was rotten.

> The autobiography tells the exciting life of the man who lived it quickly and modestly.

> The lecturer told us about the problem of alcoholism in auditorium A.

KEEP THE SENTENCE CONSISTENT

Once we start a sentence, we commit ourselves to continue it as we started it. In the second and third sections of this Review, we discussed the commitments to match tense and number and gender, and to connect a modifier with what it modifies. We also commit ourselves to other consistencies.

When we write parallelisms, or parallel constructions, as in a series of clauses, we must keep the words grammatically parallel, for the sake of consistency. Otherwise, we find our sentences beginning to come apart, to veer off the road and into incoherence. We list adjectives or we list nouns, but we do not list three adjectives followed by one noun. Don't say,

> He was tall, rich, funny, and a bank robber.

Say something like,

> He was tall, rich, funny, and fond of robbing banks.

When one phrase is constructed by one grammatical formula, its parallel phrase must be constructed in the same way. Don't say,

> The dog had a long nose, a black tail, and barked loudly.

Instead, talk about the dog's *loud bark*. Don't say,

> The cities are deserted, the countryside parched, the government paralyzed, and the economy not healthy.

Instead, say something like,

> The cities are deserted, the countryside parched, the government paralyzed, and the economy diseased.

Here, the sentence must continue its phrases ending in *-ed* words (past participle), or it will be inconsistent.

Consistency is the rule. If you start a sentence—or a linked group of sentences—with one subject or person, be consistent. Don't say,

> When you get a good grade, one should be proud.

Say either *you* or *one*, and stick to it.

Don't use the active voice in one part of a sentence, and shift to the passive in another, when you could perfectly well use the same subject.

> We could hear raucous sounds from the party as the house was approached.

Be consistent in using the past or present of verbs. Don't say,

> He went into the room, closed the door, opened the window, and goes to bed.

Remember that we need consistency within related sentences, as well as within the sentence. Here is an inconsistent paragraph.

The median tax on houses in Centerville is $852 a year. You could appeal to the city assessor if you wanted to. But one is well advised not to; he can always hit you for more tax, and you are punished for asking.

KEEP PUNCTUATION CLEAR

Learning to punctuate correctly, we learn the conventions that an experienced reader expects of us. No one can argue that the conventions of English punctuation are ideal. But they are clear, and for the most part they are sensible.

End Punctuation

At the end of a sentence, we use a period, an exclamation point, or a question mark.

Period. Periods end sentences.

Periods indicate abbreviations (Mr., no., st., St., etc., i.e., Mass., U.S.A.). See pages 314–315.

Periods indicate omissions. See pages 317–318.

Exclamation Point. Use exclamation points only for a proper exclamation,

> Oh! Zap!

or for a remark almost shouted,

> It's Godzilla!

Avoid using them frequently, or they diminish in effect, like a vague intensifier.

> I could not make out the face! Then I saw. It was Algernon!

Question Mark. At the end of a sentence asking a direct question, we use a question mark.

> Did you ask Fernando?

> Have you bought the paper, the pins, and the manila envelopes?

Do not use a question mark to end a sentence that includes a question but does not ask it (an indirect question). These sentences are incorrectly punctuated:

> He asked what time it was?
> I waited to find out where the carnival was?

They should end with periods.

Commas

The most common mark of punctuation—and the most commonly misused—is the comma. I will not talk here about the comma splice, because I discussed it on pages 293–296. Here are some of the main uses of the comma.

We use commas to separate whole clauses.

In the compound sentence, where two or more whole clauses are connected by *and, or, nor, for,* or *but,* we use a comma just before the connective.

> The faculty senate debated for three hours, but no one could resolve the issue of the blind pig.

When the main clauses are short, the comma is optional. The pause is shorter, and therefore the rhythm different. We can decide whether we prefer,

> The wine was old, and we drank it slowly.

or

> The wine was old and we drank it slowly.

On the other hand, we can also opt to use the semicolon instead of the comma. It creates a longer pause. Sometimes we want this extra pause when the main clauses are especially long, when they themselves contain commas, or when we make strong contrast between the two parts of the sentence.

> The cliff was red, solid, and perpendicular; and the car disappeared into the face of it.

We use commas to separate items in a series,

> The dress was black, green, and purple.

to separate phrases in a series,

> She wore it to parties, in the bathtub, and at work.

and to separate subordinate clauses in a series,

> She explained that it was warm, that it needed washing, that it was comfortable, and that it was in good taste.

or whole clauses in a series,

> She shook her head, she stood up, and she left the room.

When we use "and" with each item of a series, we do not use the comma.

> He touched first and second and third.

It is possible to omit the comma before the "and," in a series of words or short phrases,

> He touched first, second and third.

but it can sometimes seem ambiguous, as if the baserunner were able to straddle, and touch second and third at the same time.

We use commas to set off introductory phrases.

Adverb clauses, transitional phrases, and phrases introduced by verbals or prepositions, when they come at the beginning of the sentence, usually require a comma to set them off from the main clause. These adverb clauses need a comma:

> *If a dunce applies himself thoroughly,* he can dream of becoming President.

> *When I turned to the left at the end of the lane,* I found the old house intact.

Omitting these commas would leave the sentence hopelessly awkward and confusing. If the order of clauses is reversed, a comma, though possible, is no longer necessary.

> A dunce can dream of becoming President if he applies himself thoroughly.

> I found the old house intact when I turned to the left at the end of the lane.

An introductory adverbial clause, if it is short, need not always carry a comma. A comma is optional in,

> *If I lead* he will follow.

Introductory phrases of transition, like *on the other hand,* usually need a comma.

> On the other hand, sometimes they don't.
> In fact they are optional.
> In fact, they are optional.

Retaining the comma is appropriate in formal writing and is acceptable in all writing. Omitting the comma is rhythmically more colloquial. Interjections like *Oh,* or *shucks,* however, almost always take the comma.

> Gosh, that's not what you said the last time.

We use a comma frequently when the sentence begins with a long phrase governed by a preposition, or with any phrase that begins with a verbal.

> *In the century after the Civil War,* progress in Civil Rights was minuscule.

> *Being tall,* he was able to reach the highest shelf.

The comma is optional, and often omitted, when the introductory prepositional or verbal phrase is short.

> *At twelve* she was full-grown.
> *Having won* they adjourned to a saloon.

We use commas to avoid ambiguity. Sometimes we need a comma to indicate a pause which the voice would make, in speech, for clarity, but which is not otherwise necessary.

> Outside the fields spread to the river.

is clearer with a pause:

> Outside, the fields spread to the river.

To find such potential ambiguities in your prose, sometimes it is helpful to say it aloud, pronouncing it as it is written—which means pausing when there is a comma, and *not* pausing when there is *not* a comma.

We use commas to set off nonrestrictive, or parenthetical, clauses.
It is useful to know the difference between a restrictive and a nonrestrictive clause. A restrictive clause describes or limits its subject.

> The knight who was dressed in black won all the events in the tourney.

Here, "who was dressed in black" defines the knight, as if we were pointing a finger. Also, see

> The building that overlooked the river was the most popular of all.

In such restrictive clauses as these, no comma separates the clause from the rest of the sentence.

Nonrestrictive clauses, on the other hand, do not define; they could become separate sentences or coordinate clauses, and unless they are very short, they take commas at both ends. It is possible to use both clauses above in sentences in which they become nonrestrictive.

> Sir Galahad, who was dressed in black, won all the events in the tourney.

This sentence, as opposed to the restrictive example above, could be broken into two sentences with no violence done to the meaning.

> Sir Galahad was dressed in black. He won all the events in the tourney.

Or, using the clause from the other example, we could have the sentence,

> The house, which overlooked the river, was built in 1975.

We use commas to enclose other words, phrases, or clauses that are like a parenthesis.

Quotations are common parenthetical elements. So are phrases and words like *of course, naturally,* and *heavens to Betsy.* When asides or parenthetical expressions appear at the beginning of sentences, place a comma after them. When they appear at the end of sentences, put a comma just before them.

> God knows, the situation is desperate.
> The situation is desperate, God knows.
> Fellow Americans, I speak to you as a concerned citizen.
> I am a representative of the people, of course.

Omitting commas in these examples would make the sentence ambiguous or hard to read.

> God knows the situation is desperate.

Does He?

At times the commas can be omitted with *no* awkwardness or confusion, and the omission becomes optional. Short sentences in which word order precludes ambiguity give us this option.

> The situation was of course desperate.

On occasion one can take stylistic advantage of the rhythmic speed offered by this option.

Use a comma before and after parenthetical expressions within a sentence.

> I think you're tired, Fred, and hungry.
>
> The student worked, in a manner of speaking, for three whole days.
>
> I heard him calling, "There's my bubble gum," to the audience.

We use commas around appositives, which are nouns or noun substitutes placed next to another noun which explain or define it.

> Peter, *the flying dwarf,* escorted Tarquinia, *his good fairy.*

In many of our first drafts, we use too many commas, or put them where they do not belong. Beginning writers often feel that something is going wrong if they haven't used a comma lately, and so they shake commas over their prose like salt. Here are some sentences, taken from themes, which have commas they either don't need, or should not have.

> But, it was not too late.
> Clarke came by, later.
> When I left she, followed me.
> The dimensions were, approximately three by five.
> I quickly saw Ed, and Sara.
> He thought she was sickly, and studious.
> The old barn was painted, red.
> A runner, who likes to win, has to train, every day.
> The agency sold, life, fire, and theft, insurance.

Semicolons

Semicolons between Whole Clauses. Semicolons separate whole clauses, making a pause longer or more emphatic than a comma, but shorter and less definite than a period. The semicolon shows a close connection between the clauses.

It may be used between two (or more) balanced and equal clauses.

> The sun rose; the sky lightened; day had come.

Or it can be used between clauses of unequal length and different construction.

> The sun rose; instantly, the air was alive with birds singing so happily that anyone who heard them could not help but smile.

These sentences are compound, the semicolon replacing the conjunction.

Semicolons with Series. A semicolon used with a conjunction shows more separation or pause between clauses than the comma would show.

> He flew to Denver that night; and we were glad he did.

Adverbs acting as conjunctions in compound sentences *(besides, nevertheless, also, however, indeed, furthermore, still, then)* take a semicolon. Transitional phrases in mid-sentence *(on the other hand, in fact, in other words, on the contrary)* do the same.

> Let us take the matter in hand; however, we must not be foolhardy.

> The sun rose in a clear sky; in fact, the sky was painfully bright.

Semicolons with Adverbs as Conjunctions. Sometimes, in a long sentence, semicolons separate series or divisions, making the divisions clearer than commas would, particularly if commas are already within the divisions.

> There were three sorts of students waiting on table at the Inn: fraternity boys who were dating expensive girls; girls from Detroit whose Daddies cut off their allowances because they had moved in with their boy friends; and street people, boys and girls, working for a week or two until they got tired of it.

Semicolons with Incomplete Clauses. Semicolons also separate incomplete clauses when a verb in one of the clauses is omitted but understood.

> Poetry is one thing; verse another.

Apostrophes

Possessives. We use the apostrophe to show the possessive, with singular words:

> The bag was Sara's.
> It was the weather's fault.

and with plural words:

> the hens' feed
> Mr. and Mrs. Jones's automobile
> the women's club

Contractions. We use the apostrophe to show contractions. Use an apostrophe to show that you have omitted one or more letters in a phrase, commonly a combination of a pronoun and a verb. *I'm, she's, he's, we've, you've, they're,* etc.; *we'd, you'd, he'd, she'd; he'll, she'll, who'll, who's.*

Three of these contractions become problems. *They're* sounds like *their* and *there,* and we may spell one when we mean another. "*Their* out working" is as incorrect as "*there* work" and "working *their.*" (Correct: "*They're* out working"; "*their* work"; "working *there.*")

It's always means *it is.* It is not possessive, like "*its* shadow." Whenever you write or see the apostrophe with these letters—*it's*—remember that the *'s must* stand for *is.* Or memorize the phrase,

> *It's* afraid of *its* shadow.

Who's is another common contraction and once again there is a confusion. *Whose* gets mixed up with *who's.* Again, the *'s* means *is,* and *who's* always stands for *who is,* whereas *whose* is a possessive pronoun.

> *Who's* drinking *whose* soup?

Other common contractions involve the verb and the negative: *isn't, aren't, doesn't, don't, can't, haven't, won't.*

Plural of Numbers. We use the apostrophe to form the plurals of typographic symbols, words referred to as words, letters, and figures.

> The 7's on the new office typewriter are black as e's, 8's are unreadable, and half the time simple the's are obscure.

Notice that an apostrophe does not form part of the possessive of a pronoun.

Her book.
The book was *hers*.

Quotation Marks, and Punctuating Quotations

The exact words of a speaker or writer, included in a paragraph, are set off by quotation marks. Put a comma at the end of the quotation before the quotation mark, or a period if the quotation ends the sentence. If the quotation ends with a question mark or an exclamation point, these marks of punctuation take the place of the comma and occur inside the quotation marks.

Al asked Wayne, "Didn't you?"

On the other hand, sometimes we quote in order to exclaim about the quotation, or inquire about the quotation. In such a sentence, the exclamation point or question mark occurs after the quotation marks.

What did he mean when he said, "Good morning"?
She had the nerve to say "Hello"!

When we quote a passage longer than fifty words, in a research paper for instance, we can use a colon to introduce the quotation and detach the quotation from the text by indenting it. Ellipses can help you avoid long, detached quotations.

See Indirect quotation in the Glossary, and Colon and Ellipses below.

Other Marks of Punctuation

Brackets. Brackets are useful in prose especially in three places, all within or close to quotations. We use them when we add to a quotation material which was not in the original but which is needed for clarity. Sometimes a bracketed word supplies the antecedent to a pronoun.

"He [O'Toole] smashed his fist through the window of the bar."

And it can supply other information lacking in the quotation but available in the context from which the quotation comes.

"It was in mid-June [1976] that the storm began."

Sometimes, in quoting the spoken word, we use brackets to enclose an indication of action, like a stage direction.

"... and, finally, I want to ask you willingly and cheerfully to share the huge burden of responsibility which the age has thrust upon us all." [Boos.].

Sometimes we use brackets to correct a quotation.

> "It all happened in the early hours of September 20th [actually September 21] when the sun began [to] rise over the board-walk."

Colons. Colons direct our attention to what comes after them. Usually they follow an introductory statement that leads us to expect a follow-up, though sometimes the introduction is implicit, or the colon itself reveals that the clause preceding it was introductory. Here are some explicit introductions.

To a long quotation, either included in the text in quotation marks, or indented without quotation marks,

> E. B. White wrote of his old Professor: "In the days when I was sitting in his class he omitted so many needless words, and omitted them so forcibly and with such eagerness and obvious relish, that. . . ."

To a list,

> He narrowed his choices to three: Mary, Elizabeth, or Karen.

Less elegantly, to an appositive at the end of a sentence,

> He narrowed the field until he arrived at one name: Zona.

A comma, here, would be just as correct, and perhaps less prone to melodrama.

Sometimes we put a colon between two main clauses, like a semi-colon; it implies that the second clause is a result of the first.

> The hands of the clock seemed never to move: she had never been late before.

Here the colon adds a meaning that the semicolon would lack. The semicolon would present the two statements as closely connected, but without the implication that the second clause derived from the first.

Dashes. Use dashes with caution—but use them. Make them on your typewriter by putting two hyphens next to each other.

In the sentence above, the dash shows a hesitation in the voice, followed with a rush by something that seems almost an afterthought. Dashes are informal. For some careless writers, dashes become substi-tutes for all other forms of punctuation; they not only lose any special meaning dashes may contribute, they also rob other punctuation of its meaning. For instance:

> Yet many people use them too often—they become substitutes for all other forms of punctuation—and thus lose their special meaning—at the same time they rob other punctuation of its meaning—

Two legitimate uses for the dash are the implied afterthought, as in the first sentence above, and the informal parenthesis. Marks of parenthesis ( ) look more formal; dashes give a sense of speech. These two sentences illustrate a slight, characteristic difference:

> The myth of connotative and denotative meanings was destroyed by Carnap (the logician who taught at the University of Chicago) some twenty-five years ago.

> The myth of connotative and denotative meanings was destroyed by a logician and philosopher—I think it was Carnap—about twenty-five years ago.

Ellipses. A line of three dots . . . indicates that you have omitted something from a quotation. Use four dots if the words left out were at the end of a sentence: three to indicate the omission, a fourth for the period.

Ellipses are useful in research papers or arguments using references. Much of a paragraph may be irrelevant to our point. To include the whole paragraph in our text would slow the pace and violate the unity in our argument. Therefore we piece-cut the quotation, and make it blend smoothly with our essay. Instead of writing:

> Marlowe was more direct than Shakespeare, and more vigorous. As Professor William Wanger puts it:
>
> > If the *Jew of Malta* is Marlowe's *Merchant of Venice*, it is at the same time better and worse than Shakespeare's famous comedy. The lesser-known play has fewer quotable passages, perhaps, and certainly fewer that are quoted; but we must acknowledge that Marlowe's play has more energy than Shakespeare's. What it lacks in finesse it makes up in vigor, and the character of the Jew is surely more complex, and more thoughtfully observed, than the character of the Merchant.
>
> What Professor Wanger says of two plays, we can say of all. . . .

we can write:

> Marlowe was more direct than Shakespeare and more vigorous.
> Comparing comedies by the two men, Professor William
> Wanger found Marlowe "better and worse than Shake-
> speare . . . ," lacking "in finesse" but superior in "vigor" and "en-
> ergy." He found Marlowe's characterization, in one comparison,
> "more complex, and more thoughtfully observed" than Shake-
> speare's.

When we are obviously making excerpts, as with single words like
energy and detached phrases like the last quotation, we do not need
ellipses, because ellipses provide information: if we already know that
quotations are excerpted, we do not need rows of dots to tell us so. But
after *Shakespeare,* earlier in the paragraph, when we cut between a
noun and an apostrophe indicating possession, we need the ellipses.

Hyphens. We use hyphens to break a word at the right-hand margin. Dictionaries usually indicate the syllables that make up a word by
placing a dot between them (com • pound • ed.). Hyphenate only at
the syllable break. Write com-/pounded, never comp-/ounded. When
the syllable to be isolated is only one or two letters long, avoid division
(a-long; man-y, compound-ed).

We use the hyphen on occasion to join two adjectives, or words,
serving as adjectives, modifying a noun. They make a temporary compound word.

> *blood-red* hair
> *mile-long* avenue

Avoid the temptation to multiply hyphenated phrases, which can become a virulent form of adjectivitis.

> The *purple-green cloud-forms sweep-crawl.* . . .

We use hyphens with some common temporary compounds. Before
wheel and *barrow* became the compound word *wheelbarrow,* there
may have been a stage at which men wrote *wheel-barrow.* Consult
your dictionary when you are in doubt. Hyphens in compounds are a
matter of spelling.

We use hyphens in compound numbers from twenty-one through
ninety-nine.

We hyphenate fractions used as adjectives and placed before the noun modified,

> a *two-thirds* majority

but not otherwise.

> *three quarters* of the population

We use the hyphen to avoid ambiguity. We must spell the word *re-creation* to avoid confusing it with *recreation*.

We use the hyphen with some prefixes and suffixes.

> governor-*elect*
> *ex*-wife
> *self*-determined

We use the hyphen as a typographic device to indicate a manner of speaking, when we indicate that someone is spelling a word by writing it *w-o-r-d*, or when we indicate a stammer, *w-w-word*.

Italics. When we type, or write by hand, we show italics by underlining the word, <u>italics</u>. It comes out in type, *italics*.

Use italics for the names of ships: the *Niña;* for the titles of books, films, and plays: *War and Peace;* for the titles of magazines: *Sports Illustrated;* and for foreign expressions: *faute de mieux, in medias res.*

Also, we use them to indicate a special use of a word.

> We might call the directory an *encyclopedia* of has-beens.

We use them, from time to time, to indicate emphasis.

> Do you really *mean* that?

Using italics for emphasis is tricky, however. Italics are a vague gesture, an attempt to register a tone of voice that often fails because it cannot indicate a *specific* tone of voice. A writer who relies on emphatic italics often is being lazy; a more careful choice of words, a more precise context, and the emphasis will be clear without italics.

Parentheses. Use parentheses to enclose material which digresses or interrupts the main idea of the writing, or which explains something but remains a detachable unit.

> The minister continued to pace up and down (though he normally slept through the night) and to stare out the window into the darkness.

De Marque points out (not only in the Treatise, but in the Harmonics as well) that Jolnay was ignorant of Graf.

Fred Papsdorf (Charles Laughton bought his paintings) lives on Jane Street, near East Detroit, in a small bungalow.

She complained that she weighed ten stone (140 lbs.; a stone, an English measure of avoirdupois, is fourteen pounds) and had been seven stone a year ago.

Also, use parentheses for numbers or letters that divide.

There are three reasons, (1) . . . , (2) . . . , and (3). . . .

KEEP MECHANICS CONVENTIONAL

Like punctuation marks, the mechanics of English prose are conventions that make life easier. We can argue that the rules of spelling or manuscript form are irrational, and we can make a good case. But if we all agree to abide by the same mechanical conventions—irrational or not—we can more easily understand each other. Here are some remarks about abbreviations, capital letters, manuscript form, numerals, and spelling.

Abbreviation

For the use of abbreviations in footnotes and bibliography, see pages 267–271.

In formal writing, we abbreviate only some words that go with names, like: *Mr., Mrs., Ms., Dr., St.* (for *Saint,* not *street*), *Jr., Sr.;* degrees, like *Ph.D.* or *M.A.;* and indications of era or time like A.D., B.C., A.M. and P.M. (We use the latter initials only with actual time indicated; we speak of "4 P.M.," not "it was the P.M.") We do not abbreviate Monday or August or street or road or volume or chemistry, in ordinary writing.

Some writers use no. as an abbreviation for number, but it looks out of place in formal prose. So does *USA* instead of *the United States,* and *Penna.* or *Pa.* instead of *Pennsylvania, lb.* instead of *pound,* and *oz.* instead of *ounce.*

Some institutions are so commonly called by their initials that it is overly formal to spell them out. *Federal Bureau of Investigation* seems a pompous way to talk about the *FBI.* On the other hand, consider your audience; many people will need to be told that *SEATO* is the *South-East Asia Treaty Organization.*

In conjunction with a figure, *mph* and *rpm* are used in formal writing. We write of *50 mph* and *1,000 rpms*. But if we write without figures, we spell them out.

> It is difficult to assess the speed of a space capsule, when it is told in *miles per hour.*

Titles like Governor can be spelled out or shortened. Frequently, we shorten it when we give a whole name,

> *Gov.* William Milliken

and spell it out with a last name alone,

> *Governor* Milliken

The abbreviation is not appropriate to the most formal prose.

Capital Letters

Capitalize people's names, the names of cities and countries, titles of people, books, plays, names of religious or national groups, languages, days of the week, the months, holidays, organizations and their abbreviations, names of events in history and important documents, and names of specific structures like buildings and airplanes and ships. In titles of books, plays, and movies, capitalize the first word and all subsequent words *except* articles and prepositions.

John Doe	June
Great Britain	Memorial Day
Berlin	General Motors
Mayor Abe Beame	G.M.
Moby Dick	Marathon Oil Company
The Importance of Being Earnest	Declaration of Independence
Methodist	Empire State Building
Polish or European or Bostonian	the Winnie Mae
Monday	the *Titanic*

Do not capitalize the seasons, the names of college classes (*freshman, senior*), or general groups like *the lower classes* or *the jet set.*

Adjectives are capitalized when they derive from proper nouns and still refer to them, like *Shakespearean*. Other nouns or adjectives, which derive from names but no longer refer to the person, lose their capitals:

> boycott
> quisling

The title that is capitalized before the proper noun

> *Mayor* Hermann Garsich

loses its capital when it is used outside of its titling function, as a descriptive word placed after the proper noun.

> Hermann Garsich, *mayor* of our town.

Sections of a country may take capitals,

> the *West*
> the *South*

but the same words take the lower case when they are directions.

> Go *west,* young man.

Sentences begin with capitals.

Manuscript Form

Type if you can.

Double-space on one side of white 8½-by-11-inch twenty-pound bond paper. Never use erasable paper; it won't take inked corrections, it smudges, it sticks together, and it is altogether unpleasant to read. Instead, use Correct-O-Type or a similar easy device for corrections.

Always make a carbon or a photocopy. The most careful graders occasionally lose a paper. The corporations providing stolen papers for rich students make off with manuscripts when they can. Keep a copy to protect yourself.

Make margins of 1 inch to 1½ inches at top, bottom, and sides.

Number pages consecutively, including notes, appendixes, and bibliography.

Put your name in the upper left-hand corner of the first page.

Type the title, capitalizing the first letter of the first word and of all other words except articles and prepositions, two or three inches down from the top of the first page. Do not underline or add a period to your title.

If quoted material is short—up to fifty words of prose, or two lines of poetry—place it within the paragraph, and use quotation marks. With lines of poetry, use a slash mark (/) to indicate line breaks, and follow the capitalization of the poem.

> Of man's first disobedience, and the fruit/Of that forbidden tree. . . .

If quoted material is longer than fifty words or two lines of poetry, detach it from the text. Indent the quotation half an inch to the right of the place where you begin paragraphs, and single-space the quotation. Do not use quotation marks.

Numeral

In dealing with decimal points and highly precise or technical figures, it is wise to use numerals.

> 69.7 decibels

It is acceptable to print dates in numerals also.

> June 14, 1971

The same goes for population figures and addresses.

> 104,000 inhabitants
> 1715 South University Avenue

Print out the figures except when they are long to the point of being ridiculous. If you can write that a town has *one hundred and four thousand inhabitants,* write it. If necessity requires precision, *104,627* will do, and *one hundred and four thousand, six hundred and twenty-seven* might look precious.

Never begin a sentence with a numeral.

> 97.6 mph showed on the speedometer.

Here you can turn it around to

> The speedometer showed 97.6 mph.
> 30 people stood up

should certainly be spelled out as

> Thirty people stood up.

It is unnecessary, unless you are a lawyer, to include both spelled-out numbers and figures. Do not write,

> The building was at least twenty (20) stories tall.

Either will do—preferably the written-out word—but both together belong only to legal or business documents.

Spelling

Spelling is irregular and irrational in English. There are a few rules of thumb, but the rules always have exceptions. We memorize to learn to spell. By memory we write *there* when it is fitting and *their* when it is fitting. By memory we spell *plough, although, enough,* and *slough.*

Here are some problems in spelling, and some suggestions about overcoming them.

Each of us has problems of his own, and sometimes we can make up our own ways to remember the correct spelling. Suppose you have trouble with the *ite/ate* ending: *Definate* is a common mistake for *definite.* Maybe you can remember that it resembles the word *finite;* or the third *i* in *infinity* will help you. Or maybe you write *infinate* by mistake. Remember the antonym *finite* and remember *separate,* as in "*separate* rooms," and not *separite.*

I/e, e/i. People mistakenly write *concieve* instead of *conceive,* and *beleive* instead of *believe.* The old recipe

> I before E
> Except after C

is useful. Examples, both ways: *achieve, niece, piece; receipt, ceiling, receive.* Exceptions: *either, seize, weird, leisure, species.*

Variant plurals. Some words change spelling in moving from singular to plural: *wife/wives* (like *knife, life, calf,* and *half*); *man/men* (like *woman, milkman,* etc.); *hero/heroes* (like *tomato, potato*).

Dropping a final -e before a vowel. Most words ending with a silent *-e* drop it when we change them to a participle or other form that begins with a vowel. We spell the verb *move,* and we spell the participle *moving.* The silent *-e* usually remains when the added form begins with a consonant. Exceptions to both generalizations occur (*argue/argument; mile/mileage*), but they are infrequent and the rule is an unusually safe one.

The final -y. When *y* is a final vowel after a consonant (*dry*) it turns to *-ie* before *-s,* and to *-i* before other letters, except when the ending is *-ing,* in which case the *y* remains: *dries, drier, drying. Beauty/beautiful.* When the *y* follows another vowel, it generally remains *-y,* as in *joys* and *grayer,* with occasional exceptions, as in *lay/laid.*

Doubling consonants. Usually we double a final consonant before *-ed, -ing, -er,* or *-est.* We do this when the original verb or noun ended with a short vowel followed by a single consonant. *Hop* becomes *hopping.* When the vowel is long or a diphthong, we usually show it by a silent *-e* after the single consonant, and a single consonant with the suffix. *Hope* becomes *hoping.* Notice the difference between *plan/ planning, plane/planing, slip/slipping, sleep/sleeping.*

Here are some words frequently misspelled.

accept	embarrass	professor
accommodate	exaggerate	precede
acknowledgment	explanation	proceed
advice	existence	quantity
advise	friend	quite
all right	fulfillment	receive
allusion	grammar	referred
a lot	height	separate
annual	hypocrisy	shining
argument	irritable	similar
arrangement	its	succeed
beginning	it's	surprise
believe	library	than
business	lonely	then
capital	lonliness	their
capitol	necessary	there
coming	nuclear	they're
committee	obstacle	to, two, too
complement	occurred	villain
compliment	piece	who's
decide	possession	whose
definite	principal	writing
desert	principle	written
dessert	privilege	
divide	probably	

A GLOSSARY OF USAGE AND GRAMMATICAL TERMS

The entries are of two kinds:

1. Words frequently misused—clichés, commonly confused pairs of words, and words or phrases that should be avoided.
2. Grammatical and rhetorical terms, and the names of figures of speech. These appear often in the discussion of writing.

A, an
  See **Article.**

Abbreviation
  See pages 317–318.

Absolute element
  An absolute element is a word or a group of words which is grammatically independent of the rest of the sentence, and which is not joined to it by a relative pronoun or a conjunction.

  > Come hell or high water, I'll get to Dallas by Thursday.
  > Neither twin was there, to tell the truth.

323

Abstract, abstraction

An abstraction is a noun referring to the idea or quality of a thing, and not to a thing itself: *redness, courage.*

We use the word *abstract* relatively, referring to more general and less particular words. *Enclosure* is more general, say, than *room* or *cage* or *zoo.*

For remarks on abstractions and prose style, see pages 84–87.

Accept, except

These words sound alike but mean different things. *Accept* means to receive something voluntarily.

> I *accept* the compliment.

Except as a verb means to exclude.

> I *excepted* Jones from the goup I wished to congratulate.

Acronym

An acronym is an abbreviation, pronounced as a word, which is composed of the first letters of the words in the title or phrase abbreviated.

> *SAC* (Strategic Air Command)
> *snafu* (situation normal, all fouled up)

Active voice

Verbs are in the active voice when the subject of the sentence does the action the verb describes.

> Bob *hit* the spider.

When the subject is acted upon, we do not have the active voice.

> The spider *was hit* by Bob.

See **Passive voice.**

Adjective

Adjectives describe or limit a noun or a noun substitute. These adjectives describe:

> *green* onions
> *happiest* year
> The man was *old.*

These adjectives limit in a variety of ways:

indefinite:

> *Some* men walked in the road.

demonstrative:

> *Those* men walked in the road.

possessive:

> *Their* men walked in the road.

numerical:

> *Twelve* men walked in the road.

interrogative:

> *Which* men walked in the road?

relative:

> The men *who* walked in the road kept coming onward.

Nouns can be used as adjectives.

> *university* professor

But the writer should beware of using several nouns as adjectives in a row.

For the formation of comparatives, see **Comparison of adjectives and adverbs.** For a stylistic approach to adjectives, see pages 93–102.

Adjective clause

An adjective clause is a dependent clause used as an adjective.

> The man *whose nose is purple* will stand out in a crowd.

Adjectives frequently misused

Try to avoid the adjective used vaguely. These words once meant specific things. *Terror* once inhabited *terrific;* now it can mean "unusually pleasant."

> What a *terrific* summer day!

Some other adjectives are frequently used as vague praise, vague blame, or vague intensives.

terrible	nice	cute	real
funny	unique	wonderful	fantastic
awful	interesting	incredible	

That *terrible* man with the *cute* name was *awful* to the *nice* girl.

Adverb

Adverbs describe or limit any words except nouns and pronouns. Adverbs work with verbs, adjectives, other adverbs, verbals, and entire clauses.

Adverbs commonly show degree:

extremely hungry

or manner:

ran *slowly*

or place:

hurried *here*

or time:

she *then* left

For stylistic advice on the adverb, see pages 93–102.

Adverb clause

An adverb clause is a dependent clause used as an adverb.

I'll be gone *before she starts spraying.*

The adverb clause, *before she starts spraying,* modifies the verb *will be gone.*

Adverbs frequently misused

Most of the adjectives frequently misused become misused adverbs, with a *-ly* added. *Terrible* becomes *terribly,* as in "*terribly* comfortable." Strictly adverbial adjectives are misused also.

terrifically	actually	wonderfully	literally
certainly	very	rather	hopefully
absolutely	virtually	practically	really

It *certainly* was a *very* hot day and I was *practically* done at the *absolutely* last minute when *actually* a *rather* large man *virtually* beheaded me.

Advice, advise
　　The first word is a noun; the second, a verb.

　　　　I was *advised* to ignore your *advice.*

Affect, effect
　　The two words are commonly confused. These examples illustrate proper uses of them:

　　　　Bob *affected* (influenced) the writing of Wright.

　　　　Sarah *affected* (assumed) the manner of a Greek tragedian.

　　　　The harder spray was *effected* (brought about) by an adjustment of the hose's nozzle.

　　　　The *effect* (result) of the new style was unpleasant.

Agreement
　　The formal correspondence between one word and another. This correspondence indicates singular or plural number; first, second, or third person; and masculine, feminine, or neuter gender.

　　　　He is so evil.
　　　　They are so evil.
　　　　Tom took *his* crocodile down to the river.
　　　　Tom and Maria took *their* crocodiles down to the river.
　　　　The *car* and *its* trailer rounded the corner.

　　See pages 296–301.

Agree to, agree with
　　One *agrees to* a proposal or an action, one *agrees with* a person.

All ready, already
　　The words differ in meaning. To say that someone is *all ready* is to say that he is prepared; the word *already* means beforehand in time, as in

　　　　He was *already* there.

All right, alright
　　All right is the correct form. *Alright* means the same thing, but is a recent creation based on the old word *already.* In formal writing, stay away from *alright.*

Along with

Avoid this wordy and useless phrase, as we use it in sentences like

Along with tennis, big game hunting is my favorite sport.

MacDowell is my candidate for the presidency, *along with* Ellis and Giusti.

Instead, say something like

Big game hunting and tennis are my favorite sports.
For the presidency, I favor MacDowell, Ellis, or Giusti.

A lot

Many people have taken to spelling *a lot*

A lot of policemen showed up.

as one word, *alot*. *A lot* is two words, like *all right*.

Although, though

Although is preferable in formal writing.

Altogether, all together

The two do not have the same meaning. *Altogether* means *wholly* or *entirely*. *All together* combines two commonly understood words.

Xavier, Abby, Frank, and Al were *all together* at the table.
Guy Woodhouse was *altogether* disgusting.

Ambiguity

Writing is ambiguous when it has more than one possible meaning or interpretation.

Amid, amidst

Avoid these words, which are not common to the American language, and which sound stuffy and bookish.

Among, amongst

Among is preferable. *Amongst* is bookish.

Among, between

Use *between* when you are dealing with two things, *among* for more than two.

between you and me
among the three of us

In highly informal writing, this distinction is often ignored.

Amoral, immoral, unmoral

Amoral means outside morality, neither moral nor immoral.

> Beauty is *amoral.*

Immoral is contrary to codes of morality.

> Benedict Arnold was *immoral.*

Unmoral is a near-synonym for *amoral,* and is seldom used. *Amoral* is often used when the assertion is contentious, *unmoral* when the statement is merely factual.

> Dogs and cats are *unmoral.*

It would sound pretentious or silly to accuse dogs and cats of being amoral.

Amount, number

Amount refers to a quantity of things viewed as a whole, or to the quantity of one item; *number* describes the separate units of a group.

> The *amount* of money in his bank account was staggering.
> The *number* of dollar bills on the floor was small.
> He took a large *amount* of salt a *number* of times.

Analogy

An analogy is an extended comparison, used for illustration and argument. For examples and stylistic uses, see pages 110–111.

And/or

This legalism frequently occurs in nonlegal prose where *or* would do just as well.

> Cooking with pots *and/or* skillets requires nothing more than a hotplate.

Omit the unnecessary word.

Antecedent

An antecedent is a word or group of words to which a pronoun refers.

> As *Kevin* and *Quentin* ran in, *they* dropped the gas pellets.

Kevin and *Quentin* are the antecedents of the personal pronoun *they.*

Antonym

An antonym means the opposite of another word. *Bad* is the antonym of *good*.

As there are no exact synonyms, so we must not expect antonyms to be precisely opposite.

Any, any other

Be careful to use these words properly. If you say,

> *"King Lear* is more moving than *any other* play in the English language."

you are probably saying what you intend. If you say, however, that

> *"King Lear* is more moving than *any* play in the English language."

you imply that *Lear* is not in English—or that *Lear* is better than itself, which would be nonsensical. If you say that

> "Sophia is sexier than *any* woman in Italy."

you imply that she is not in Italy.

Anybody, anyone

The words are singular, not plural. They take singular pronouns, like *every, everyone, everybody.*

> *Everyone* charges *his* meal at Alice's.

is formally correct, and not

> *Everyone* charges *their* meal at Alice's.

But an exception to this rule could make the second example the preferable form of the sentence. When a pronoun has *anybody* (etc.) as an antecedent, we may wish to use forms of the plural *they* in order to avoid deciding between *he* and *she,* because *they* does not indicate gender.

> Did *anybody* call? What did *they* say?

Anyways

This form of *anyway* belongs to speech, not to writing.

Apostrophe

See pages 311–312.

Appositive

An appositive is a noun, or a noun substitute, which is placed next to another noun, and which explains or defines it.

> Peter, *the flying dwarf,* escorted Tarquina, his *good fairy.*

Flying dwarf is the appositive of *Peter,* and *good fairy* is the appositive of *Tarquina.*

Article

The definite article is *the,* the indefinite *a* or *an.* They are adjectives, always indicating that a noun or a noun substitute will follow.

The names an individual:

> *the* table
> *the* abstraction

A and *an* are indefinite articles, naming the member of a class:

> *a* table
> *an* abstraction

The difference in meaning is small but indispensable.

The article *a* is used before words beginning with a consonant sound (even if the letter is a vowel):

> *a* train
> *a* unit

An is used before words beginning with a vowel sound:

> *an* interesting idea
> *an* herb

As, like

In formal writing, we avoid using *like* as a conjunction. We use *as* instead. Instead of saying,

> I write *like* I talk.

we say

> I write *as* I talk.

At

Don't use the redundancy, "Where are you *at?*" *Where* means "at which place?"

Auxiliaries

Auxiliaries in verb phrases indicate distinctions in tense and person. Common auxiliaries are: *will, would, shall, should, be, have, do, can, could, may, might,* and *must.*

> We *are* eating the chocolate.
> You *would have* done the same.

Awful, awfully

Literally, if we are *awful,* we are "full of *awe.*" We no longer use the word to mean what it means. It is a vague intensive like *terrific, wonderful,* and *horrible.*

Bad, badly

When we use *bad* as a predicate adjective, in an expression like "I felt *bad* yesterday," we sometimes confuse it with the adverb *badly.* If you claim that you "felt *badly,*" your words mean that your sensory apparatus did not function correctly. Saying *badly* for *bad* as a predicate adjective affects gentility but reveals ignorance. It is correct to say,

> She looked *bad* when she came up to bat.

and incorrect to say,

> She looked *badly* when she came up to bat.

The latter sentence denigrates her vision. It is correct to say,

> They seemed *bad* this morning, after the ocean voyage.

referring to the appearance of illness. Do not say,

> They seemed *badly* this morning after the ocean voyage.

Other constructions require the adverb, *badly.*

> She played *badly,* the first seven innings.

Here,

> She played *bad* the first seven innings.

is incorrect.

Badly has another sense, which is "very much." It is colloquial or informal.

> They wanted *badly* to be elected.
> She was *badly* in need of a drink.

If you mean to employ this colloquialism, be careful of your word order. If you say, "She needed to sing very *badly*," you appear to say something quite different from "She needed very *badly* to sing." If in doubt, be more formal; say,

> She needed *very much* to sing.

or

> She needed to sing *very much*.

Balanced sentences
See pages 151–158, where I discuss balance and parallelism.

Beside, besides
Each word has several meanings of its own.

> She stood *beside* (by the side of) the bureau.
> Matt was *beside* himself (almost overwhelmed) with anger.
> It's *beside* (not connected with) the point.
> No one was awake *besides* (other than) him.
> *Besides* (furthermore), it's in questionable taste.

Between
See **Among, between.**

Bibliography
See pages 267–268.

Big words
Never use a big word where a little word will do. Never say *domicile* where you could say *house*. Never say *individual* where you could say *person*. Never say *utilize* where you could say *use*.
   See **Genteel words** and **-ize verbs.**

Bracket
See page 312.

Can, may
Both words express possibility, but *can (could)* expresses physical possibility.

> He *can* go to market because he has the car.
> She *could* eat the potato salad but she doesn't want to.

May (or *might*) implies that something is a chance, and often implies volition.

> He *may* go to Alaska (or he may not).
> She *might* be the last of the clan (or she might not).

Often we can hesitate between the two, and choose the one over the other for the precise shade of meaning. "He *could* take the exam" and "He *might* take the exam" offer different possibilities.

In conversation, and in the most informal writing, *may* often disappears in favor of *can,* and a distinction disappears, which is a loss. Instead of saying, "She *may* read Shakespeare, or Julia Child, or *Young Lust,*" we substitute the wordier, "She *can* read Shakespeare, or Julia Child, or *Young Lust,* depending on what she feels like." The final clause supplies the chanciness and the volition implied in *may.*

In asking or granting permission, genteel prose uses *may.*

> May I enter?
> Randolph, you *may* not.

But *may* in this usage almost invariably sounds like an effort to be refined.

Cannot, can not

These arrangements are equally acceptable. *Can not* looks more formal.

Can't hardly

Because *hardly,* as Bergen Evans says, "has the force of a negation," *can't hardly* functions as a double negative, or at least as an ambiguity. Does "I *can't hardly* hear you" mean "I *can't* hear you" or "I *can* hear you well" or "I *can hardly* hear you?" Logically, the double negative should make it mean the second, but it means the last. We should save a word, and increase the efficiency of our language, by saying simply, "I *can hardly* hear you." The same advice applies to *"can't scarcely."*

Capital letters

See page 318.

Case

See **Inflection.**

Cf.

We often find this abbreviation in footnotes, and sometimes in parentheses. It tells us to "compare," as in

> *(Cf. Toothe v. Carey.)*

Circumlocution

Circumlocution is taking the long way to say something, using clichés, verbs combined with other parts of speech instead of simple verbs, and filler words and phrases. In

> *Notwithstanding the case of* the seamstress, it is *going to be* obvious that *in general, in a manner of speaking, we do well to remember the observation that a man who* is always in a hurry will lose *something or other in the long run.*

the circumlocution is general, and phrases typical in circumlocution are in italic. Notice that the last seventeen words might be rendered

> Haste makes waste.

Cite, sight, site

Cite means to quote or to refer to.

> They *cited* the constructive things they'd done.

A *sight* is a view,

> a moving *sight*

or vision itself.

A *site* is a location.

> a building *site*

Clause

A clause is part of a sentence with a subject and a predicate. It may be principal (or main or independent) or it may be subordinate (dependent on a whole clause).

> *The year ended* and *the year began.*

In this sentence, two whole clauses are made into a compound sentence by *and.*

> The year ended *when it had just begun.*

In this sentence, the italic clause is subordinate or dependent.

Cliché

A cliché is a much used combination of words. *Writing Well* uses and defines this word several times. See pages 3–6, for instance.

Collective noun

See **Noun.**

Colon

See page 313.

Comma

See pages 305–309.

Comma splice

See pages 293–296.

Common nouns

See **Noun.**

Compare to, compare with

To compare *to* shows similarities between things that are obviously different.

>   He *compared* the sparrow *to* a ten-ton truck.

(Of course by showing similarity, it reveals difference as well.) To compare *with* shows differences between things that are obviously similar.

>   She *compared* lunch *with* dinner.

(Of course it reveals similarities at the same time.)

Comparison of adjectives and adverbs

The comparison of adjectives and adverbs indicates relative degree. The three degrees are: positive, comparative, and superlative.

Positive	Comparative	Superlative
good	better	best
obnoxious	more obnoxious	most obnoxious
quick	quicker	quickest
quickly	more quickly	most quickly

Comparisons

For a discussion of simile, metaphor, and analogy, see pages 108–111.

Complement

A complement is one or more words that completes the meaning of a verb, or an object. A subject complement:

> Phyllis is a wicked *girl.*

The predicate noun—*girl*—completes the sense of *Phyllis,* which it refers to. An object complement:

> The dog chewed the bone *raw.*

Raw modifies and completes *bone.*

Complement, compliment

A *complement* makes something whole or complete.

> Work is the *complement* of play.

A *compliment* is praise.

> I paid you a *compliment.*

There is also an archaic meaning, in which *compliments* means something like formal politeness, and which survives in the phrase, "*compliments* of the season."

Complex sentence

A complex sentence contains a main clause and a subordinate clause. Here the subordinate is a relative:

> I whistled at the boy who hung from the cliff.

See pages 123, 131–135, and 147–149.

Compound sentence

A compound sentence includes two or more main clauses and no subordinate clauses.

> The moon rose at 10:35 P.M. and the stars appeared to recede into the darkness.

Compound-complex sentence

This sentence type combines, as you might expect, the complex and the compound sentence. It has two main clauses, and at least one subordinate clause.

> The snow stopped falling when the sun rose, but the temperature stayed below 10°.

See page 124.

Compound word

Compound words are two or more words commonly used together as a single word.

> brother-in-law
> blackbird
> wheelbarrow
> handwriting

See a dictionary for current spelling. See **Hyphens,** on page 315.

Conjugation

See **Inflection.**

Conjunction

Conjunctions connect or coordinate (*and, but, for, or,* and occasionally *yet* or *so*), or they subordinate (*after, because, while, when, where, since*). With coordinate conjunctions be careful to preserve unity by keeping the coordinate phrases or clauses parallel (see pp. 151–158). With subordinate conjunctions, remain aware of the habits of complex sentences (pp. 123, 131–135, and 147–149). Contrary to the old rule, the best contemporary writing uses conjunctions at the beginnings of sentences.

Conjunctive adverb

A conjunctive adverb can be used to connect main clauses: *then, besides, however, therefore, otherwise.* Use a semicolon between the main clauses.

Consider . . . as

Writers frequently misuse the verb *consider* by adding an unnecessary preposition, *as.* Say

> She *considered* him handsome.

not

> She *considered* him *as* handsome.

Another use of the verb takes *as* appropriately. In the example above, *consider* means "believe to be." In the example below, *consider* means "think about" or "talk about":

> She *considered* him *as* an administrator and *as* a scholar.

Consist in, consist of

Consist of refers to the parts that make a whole:

The government *consists of* legislative, executive, and judicial divisions.

Consist in refers to inherent qualities:

The value of democracy *consists in* the responsibility with which it endows the citizen.

Continual, continous

The two words have slightly different meanings. *Continual* describes an action that is repeated frequently.

He called her *continually* throughout the day.

Continuous describes an action done without stopping.

The bleeding was *continuous* for three hours.

Coordinates

Coordinate means equal in rank. Two infinitives are coordinate, for instance, or two main clauses, as in a compound sentence.
See pages 122–123.

Correlative conjunctions

Both . . . and, either . . . or, neither . . . nor, and *not only . . . but also* are coordinating conjunctions, and require parallel forms in the coordinated phrases or clauses.

Could have, could of

The phrase is *could have. Could of* is a mistake. Don't say,

She *could of* been a great actress.

but say,

She *could have* been a great actress.

Counsel, council, consul

Counsel is advice, or a lawyer, or someone acting as a lawyer. Though it would be a confusing sentence, one could say,

The court-appointed *counsel* gave his client *counsel.*

A different spelling, with the same pronunciation, gives us the word *council,* which is a legislative group.

Harris for City *Council!*

A *consul* represents his government in another country where he keeps residence.

The vice-*consul* was out to lunch.

Couple
In the idiomatic sense of *a few,* the word is extremely informal, and in your writing you ought to try to substitute *two,* or *a few,* or *several.*

Cutting words from quotations
See pages 314–315.

Dangling constructions
A phrase loosely placed in a sentence dangles. Modifiers dangle frequently, and disastrously.
See pages 301–302.

Dashes
See pages 313–314.

Data
In the most formal prose, we recognize the etymology of *data* as a Latin plural, and therefore use the word with a plural verb form. It is correct—if highly formal—to say,

These *data* convince us.

rather than,

This *data* convinces us.

The singular, rarely used, is *datum.*

Declension
See **Inflection.**

Deductive reasoning
In this form of thinking we apply a general truth to a specific instance. Thus, if it is true that going through a time-warp causes pain, we may *deduce* that if Quasimodo goes through a time-warp he will feel pain.

Demonstratives
Demonstratives are adjectives like *this, that, these,* and *those,* used to point the finger.

This is the man who took it; *that's* my basketball.

They can be pronouns, and should have clear antecedents.

You said you couldn't read. I could not believe *that.*

Different from, different than
Different from is usually preferable, especially in formal prose. When a clause follows, *different than* is acceptable.

> This place is *different than* I expected it to be.

Direct address
A noun or pronoun used to direct a remark to a specific person.

> I was thinking, *Ron,* that you'd like to go up in a balloon.
> *Irving,* close that closet.
> Hey *you!*

Direct object
See **Object.**

Direct quotation
See page 312.

Discreet, discrete
The two words have different meanings. *Discreet* means "prudent in one's conduct or speech."

> She would never reveal it; she was exceptionally *discreet.*

Discrete means "distinct" or "separate."

> The words are different; they have *discrete* meanings.

Disinterested, uninterested
These words are frequently confused. To be *uninterested* is to lack fascination about something, even to be bored by it.

> I tried to arouse his enthusiasm for a game of golf, but he was *uninterested* in such a pastime.

Disinterested is the condition of being impartial or neutral, or of having no stake in an issue. Frequently the word is used positively as a precondition for fairness, as in the phrase "*disinterested* party."

> The judge declared his *disinterest* in the matter.

This judge is proclaiming his ability to judge the case fairly. If he had claimed to be "*uninterested* in the matter," he would have been rejecting the appeal.

Doesn't
See **Don't.**

Don't

Goes with *I, you, we,* and *they.* It doesn't go with *it, he,* or *she.* It contracts *do not.* It does not contract *does not; doesn't* does.

Double negative

A double negative occurs in a sentence that uses two negative terms when only one is needed.

> He *didn't* say *nothing.*
> You *shouldn't never* do that to a bird.

In earlier English such doubling was thought to give emphasis, as in "I never treacherously slew no man" (Bergen Evans' example). But today such double negatives are regarded as unacceptable and illogical. If I should *not* never-do something, then by implication I should (positively) do it sometime.

See **Can't hardly.**

Doubt but

Omit *but.* Also omit *but* in *help but.*

> They couldn't *doubt* but that the Racquet Club was best.

becomes

> They couldn't *doubt* that the Racquet Club was best.
> They couldn't *help but* know the worst.

becomes

> They couldn't *help* knowing the worst.

And always avoid "They couldn't *doubt but* what. . . ."

Due to

Never use *due to* for *because of* in adverbial phrases. "She won the race *due to* her long legs" sounds unnatural. It is probably best to reserve the word for finance. Sometimes people multiply error by writing, "due to the fact that . . . ."

E.g.

This is the abbreviation for a Latin expression that means *for example.* It is usually best to use the English, but on occasion we will find these initials, often in scientific or legal prose.

> The review board overlooked significant evidence, e.g., *Baxter* v. *Baxter.*

Each, every

 Each is a pronoun,

   Each went his own way.

and an adjective.

   Each package of bubble gum has five pieces.

Each means the individual units of a conglomerate,

   Each of the Boy Scouts

but *every* means the conglomerate itself.

   Every Boy Scout

In the Boy Scout examples above, *each* is a pronoun, *every* an adjective.

 When the adjective *each* modifies a singular noun, the following verb and pronouns are singular.

   Each player lifts *his* bat.

When *each* modifies a plural noun or pronoun, and comes before the verb, the pronoun and verb are plural.

   They *each go their* own way.

When *each* works as a pronoun, it is usually singular.

   Each goes his own way.

There are exceptions. In the example just above, if the pronoun referred to men and women, we might have written,

   Each go their own way.

When *each* refers to two or more singular words, or when a plural word comes between *each* and the verb, the number of the verb is optional. We may say,

   Each of the players *is*

or

   Each of the players *are*

We may say,

   When *Mark and Linda* speak, each of them *says*

or

   When *Mark and Linda* speak, each of them *say*

The negative of *each* is *neither.* Do not write *each* with a negative,

> *Each* did not speak.

but write,

> *Neither* spoke.

Egoism, egotism

Egoism has the connotation of a philosophy, *egotism* of a neurosis. *Egoism* is the other side of *altruism,* and is a belief in the value of self-interest. *Egotism* is the necessity to use the word *I* all the time. In the argot of the day, *egotism* is an ego-trip.

Either

Either, like *each,* can be pronoun or adjective.

> *Either* Bob or Jane . . .
> *Either* of the twins . . .

When *either* means more than one, it takes a plural verb.

> *Either* of you are qualified.

When it means one or the other it takes the singular.

> *Either* Rick or Chris is lying.

Negative statements, and the pronoun *you,* make *either* take a plural verb, even if the sense is singular.

> He did not report that *either* of them were qualified.
> When *either* of you are finished, let me know.

Either takes *or* and does not take *nor. Nor* belongs to *neither.*
See page 151.

Elicit, illicit

Elicit means "to bring out."

> We could *elicit* no further response from the members.

Illicit means "not permitted."

> They were having an *illicit* love affair.

Ellipses

See pages 314–315.

Eminent, immanent, imminent
Eminent means outstanding.

> The *eminent* philosopher...

Immanent means inherent.

> ...will discuss *immanent* ideas...

Imminent means impending.

> ...*imminently.*

Enormity, enormousness
An *enormity* is a moral outrage. *Enormousness* is hugeness.

Etc.
This *and so forth*, from the Latin et cetera, is out of place in formal prose. In whatever prose, it often trails off the end of a sentence into vagueness, and avoids extending the brain. Stay away from it in formal prose. Think before you use it in any context.

Etymology
Etymology is the study specializing in the origins and histories of words.

Euphemism
Euphemisms are fancy or abstract substitutes for plain words. We use them for social elevation, as when an undertaker becomes a mortician, or to avoid facing something frightening, as when we say that someone passed away, instead of saying that he died.
See pages 62–64.

Everybody, everyone
Everybody and *everyone* take a singular verb.

> *Everybody goes* to church.

The words can take a singular pronoun, especially in a formal context,

> *Everyone* finds *his* seat and waits for the minister.

or a plural pronoun, especially when it refers to men and women and we wish to avoid the prejudice of picking either *his* or *her*.

> *Everybody* waited until *they* caught *their* breath.

See pages 298–299.

Exclamation point
See page 304.

Expletives
When *it* and *there* fill space in a sentence without contributing to its meaning, we call them expletives.

> *There are* men who cultivate sand to grow elephants.
> *It is* understood that the rain was falling.

Fact
Avoid the phrase *the fact that*, which is wordy and unnecessary.

Famous, notorious
To be *famous* is to be well known or celebrated. To be *notorious* is to be well known for something shady.

> He was a *famous* movie star, musician, and second baseman.

> He was a *notorious* pirate, extortionist, and linguist.

Farther, further
As "distance to go" the two are interchangeable. Where *further* means "more," *farther* is not a possible alternative.

> We have no *further* use for him.

Few
See **Less.**

Field
Don't say, *in the field of.* . . . It is a dead metaphor, and means little.

Figure
See **Numeral.**

Fine
This word is vague and overused.

Finite verb
A finite verb is complete, a predicate in itself.

> The house *collapsed.*

Gerunds, infinitives, and participles are not finite verbs but *verbals.*

Footnote
See pages 268–271.

Foreign words and phrases

Foreign words and phrases often look pretentious in our writing. In dialogue, they can be useful to characterize someone, as foreign or as pretentious. Occasionally nothing in English seems quite so apt as a foreign phrase. But look hard before you give up. If you must use one, italicize it by underlining it.

Foreword, forward

The two have different meanings. A *foreword* is a preface, the introductory statement at the beginning of a book. *Forward* is usually a direction. On occasion, *forward* means "bold" or "presumptuous."

> She stuck her tongue out at him; she was very *forward.*

Gender

Gender is a grammatical indication of sex. English nouns lack gender except as their own sense indicates. That is, *sister* is feminine, *brother* masculine, and *sibling* can be either. Some pronouns have gender *(he, she)* and most do not, *(I, they, you, we).* In some languages, all nouns are assigned a gender. In French, *grass* is feminine, and *time* is masculine. In English both are neuter.

Genteel words

Some words act as euphemisms by seeming socially preferable to plainer alternatives. People who use them seem to be *trying* to be genteel. Avoid them unless you are making a genuine distinction. For instance:

Genteel	Ordinary
perspire	sweat
wealthy	rich
home	house
luncheon	lunch

Gerund

See **Verbal.**

Get

We multiply this little word in our speech; it has small place in our writing. "I went down to *get* some wallpaper" is passable but wordy. In writing, it would be better to *choose* or *buy* the wallpaper.

Good, well

It is common and incorrect to use *good* as if it were an adverb.

> He ran *good.*

When referring to an action *well* is the right word.

> He ran *well.*

Be careful with the word *feels;* to say that a person *feels good* is to say that he is in a pleasant frame of mind; to say that a person *feels well* is to say either that he feels healthy or that his sense of touch is functioning efficiently.

Grammar

Grammar describes how words function in a language.

Guerrilla, gorilla

A *guerrilla* is an irregular soldier. A *gorilla* is an animal. *Guerrilla* is also used as an adjective, and has recently been used adjectivally to indicate activity in the service of revolution: *guerrilla* theater, *guerrilla* television.

Had ought

This combination is clumsy. Instead of writing,

> We knew he *ought* to come.

write

> We knew he *ought* to come.

Hanged, hung

Hanged pertains to the execution of human beings, *hung* to the suspension of objects.

> Sam Hall was *hanged* in October.
> We *hung* the portraits in the hall.

He, him

See **Pronoun.**

He or she

This locution is awkward and clumsy. Sometimes we wish to use it to avoid sexism.

See the note on page 150.

Help but
　　See **Doubt but.**

Homonym
　　Homonyms are words that, although pronounced the same, are
　　spelled differently and mean different things.

　　　　to, too, two　　　　heir, air
　　　　through, threw　　　bare, bear
　　　　blew, blue

Hopefully
　　Hopefully is an adverb frequently misused as a dangling modifier.
　　We say,

　　　　Hopefully, the plane will be on time.

　　when we do not mean to imply that the plane is full of hope. We
　　could say,

　　　　Hopefully, I will meet her at the gate.

　　We come to use *hopefully* as if it meant "I hope." The first example,
　　above, is meant to say,

　　　　I hope the plane will be on time.

Hyperbole
　　Hyperbole is extreme exaggeration to make a point.

　　　　That cat *weighs a ton.*

　　Use it with discretion.

Hyphen
　　See page 315.

I, me
　　See **Pronoun.**

I.e.
　　i.e. abbreviates the Latin *id est,* or *that is.* We use it sometimes to
　　introduce an explanation or definition of a word or phrase.

　　　　She was nonessential, *i.e.,* they didn't need to employ her any
　　　　more.

　　Usually, the expression seems overprecise, and too much like legal or scientific writing. The sentence above can omit the Latinism, and use instead a colon or a semicolon.

> She was nonessential: they didn't need to employ her any more.

Immigrant, emigrant
An *immigrant* is someone who enters a country; an *emigrant* leaves one. Obviously our forefathers had to emigrate before they could immigrate.

Incredible, unbelievable
In theory, these words are synonymous. In practice, *unbelievable* holds up better.

> The charges were *unbelievable*.

states rather straightforwardly the disbelief.

> The charges were *incredible*.

suffers from the use of *incredible* as a vague intensive.

> Those hamburgers were *incredible*.

simply praises the hamburgers in hyperbole from which constant use has drawn the strength. *Unbelievable* undergoes some of the same diminishment:

> . . . *unbelievably* rare

and may also lose its utility in time.

Indefinite pronoun
See **Pronoun,** and pages 296–297.

Independent clause
See **Clause.**

Indirect object
See **Object.**

Indirect quotation
We use indirect quotations when we attribute a remark without claiming to use exact words, and without using quotation marks.

> The Congressman from Ohio then claimed that he had heard enough.

> She said that Herbert was the nicest boy she had ever met.

When we indirectly quote information taken from a source, we should footnote it just as we would a direct quotation.

Inductive reasoning

This form of thought draws general conclusions from particular examples or evidence.

> As a result of these experiments we conclude that if the temperature of water falls below 32 degrees it will freeze.

Infer, imply

We *infer* or understand from what a speaker or writer *implies* to us. We cannot say that another person *inferred* something to us. He *implied* it, and we *inferred* a meaning in his implication.

Inferior to, inferior than

Inferior than is incorrect. Say either *inferior to* or *worse than*.

Infinitive

See **Verbal.**

Inflection

Inflection is the change in the form of a word to indicate a change in meaning or grammatical relationship. The inflection of nouns and pronouns is called *declension;* of verbs *conjugation;* and of adjectives and adverbs *comparison.*

Inflection of nouns indicates *number* and *case.*

> aardvark, aardvarks; aardvark's, aardvarks'; man, men; man's, men's

Inflection of pronouns indicates *case, person,* and *number.*

> she, her, her, hers; who, whom, whose

Inflection of verbs indicates *tense, person,* and *mood.*

> bore, boring, bores, bored
> spring, springing, springs, sprung

Inflection of modifiers indicates *comparison* and *number.*

> thin, thinner, thinnest
> this dog, that dog, these dogs, those dogs

In regard to, in regards to

In regard to is preferable, but when both can be avoided, they ought to be.

Intensive pronoun

See **Pronoun.**

Intransitive verb

An intransitive verb neither has an object nor is passive in form.

> I *was* at Annette's house in Santa Fe at the time.
> Quaker *has been waiting* on the flagpole for hours.

Irony

Intentional irony, in our language, is the conscious statement of an untruth, intended to convey the opposite of what it seems to say. We can say that the weather is marvelous when we are standing in a downpour. Our irony is obvious. When Jonathan Swift wrote his satirical "Modest Proposal," he suggested that Irish babies be slaughtered and eaten, as a convenience to the English. He did not intend the suggestion literally. Most of his readers perceived his irony.

Irregardless

Use *regardless. Irregardless* is a redundancy, made in error on the model of *irrespective.*

Italics

See page 316.

Its, it's

It's always stands for *it is. Its* is possessive.

> *It's* eating *its* supper.

See page 311.

-ize verbs

Avoid making new verbs ending in -ize, like "tomato-ize the spaghetti." Avoid using some recent coinages too: "utilize" (say "use"); "personalize," "finalize."

Jargon

Jargon is the argot of a profession, or a peer group, like educationists' jargon, or astronauts', or rock musicians'. Businessmen fall into a jargon frequently. Sometimes they "firm up" a deal before they "finalize" it. Sometimes two negotiators are "not in the same ballpark."

Slang makes jargon too. The hip-revolutionary talk of the late sixties was jargon.

Right on, man. Split, the fuzz. Do you dig it? Heavy.

Jargon is a language by which we attempt to prove that *we* are the initiated, and to keep noninitiates in confusion and befuddlement. It is language, not to communicate, but to exclude.

Jargon has a real purpose when it is the precise shorthand of a science. But for most of us most of the time, jargon has a tendency to be considerably vaguer than the larger language we share.

Kind of

This phrase is misused, and even used properly is often not helpful. When we say *"kind of* big" we are qualifying "big," as if we said *"rather* big." It is a misuse of the word, in speech and in writing. In correct use, *kind* means species.

It is a *kind* of pine tree.

This usage works, but we often slide into vague species-making.

She is a *kind of* blonde I can't stand.

The sentence cannot be rewritten; it must be rethought. What exactly is it that you cannot stand? Name it.

I do not like a blonde who has red eyebrows.

The same remarks apply to *sort of.*

Lay, lie

Lay/laid/laying applies to: she is *laying* an egg; you *laid* the book on the table; I *lay* my pen on this pad. *Lay* takes a direct object. The past tense is *laid.*

He *laid* the pool on the lawn.

Lie takes the past tense *lay,* which is a source of confusion. *Lie/lay/ lying* applies to: I *lie* on the grass; she *lay* on the bed all day; we were *lying* in the sun. *Lie* never takes a direct object.

Lead, led

Lead is present tense, *led* is past, and *lead*—when pronounced like *led*—is the metal.

Yesterday I *led* the class.
Today I *lead* the escape.

Leave, let

Leave means "to go away"; *let* means "to allow."

> Leave me (Go away from me.)
> Let me. (Allow me to.)
> Leave me out. (Don't include me.)
> Let me out. (Allow me to go.)

Less

This word is frequently misused where *fewer* would be correct.

> There are *less* flowers in the vase today.

should be

> There are *fewer* flowers in the vase today.

Fewer refers to actual numbers; *less* refers to quantity in general.

> The powerful nations are *fewer* than they used to be.
> Nations have *less* power.

Like, as

See **As, like.**

Likewise

This expression is a clumsy transition, almost always a piece of bone in the hamburger.

Linking verb

A linking verb expresses the relationship between the subject and the predicate noun or predicate adjective. The principal linking verbs are *appear, be, become, seem,* and verbs used for sensations.

> Lorca *is* magnificent.
> Rose *became* a mother.
> Joe *looks* sick.
> The steak *smells* rotten.

Literally

We often say *literally* when we mean the opposite: *figuratively*. We use a metaphor, but we realize that it is dead and we play Dr. Frankenstein to the monster by applying the cathodes of *literally* (or *literal*).

> She was *literally* big as a house.
> He was a *literal* man of straw.
> He hit the ball *literally* a thousand miles.

The monster never walks.

Literal means "according to the letter" or "as it actually appears." Never use it unless you mean it *literally*. When you find yourself misusing it for the purposes above, you can either omit it and settle for the corpse of your metaphor, or you can make a new metaphor. "She was as big as. . . ."

Litotes

Litotes is understatement. "It's not a beauty" may mean "It's ugly."

Little

Often we misuse this word—which is necessary to common speech in its literal meaning—as a vague qualifier.

> He's a *little* late.

We misuse *pretty* in the same way, without considering its meaning. James Thurber tormented his editor on *The New Yorker* by writing that something was "a little big" and "pretty ugly."

Logic

See **Deductive reasoning** and **Inductive reasoning.**

See pages 230–244 for some remarks about persuasion, and an account of some common errors in thinking.

For further reading, consult Manuel Bilsky's *Patterns of Argument.*

Loose, lose

Different spellings make different words.

> The dog is *loose.*
> I *lose* the dog.
> The *loose* rope *loses* the dog.

Luxuriant, luxurious

Luxuriant means "abundant in growth"; *luxurious* means "seeking the pleasures of the senses" or providing such pleasure.

> Her *luxuriant* hair was golden red.
> It was done in a *luxurious* gold and leather edition.

Main clause

A *main clause* can stand by itself. It can be a whole, simple sentence.

> They built an armadillo.

Two *main clauses* can make a compound sentence.

> They built an armadillo and they traded it for a VW.

In a complex sentence, a *main clause* (in italics) governs a subordinate clause.

> When night fell, *they built an armadillo.*

Manuscript form
See pages 319–320.

Man who . . .
A common circumlocution uses a noun (like *man* or *woman* or *person* or *senator* or *typist*) in a relative clause when the extra words serve no function.

> He was *a man who* drank half a bottle of Scotch before breakfast.
>
> She was *a woman who* knew better.
>
> She was a *Senator who* always filibustered.

If this last sentence gave us the information that she was a senator, it would be justified.

> He was a *typist who* never typed more than twenty-seven words a minute.

These sentences can become:

> He drank half a bottle of Scotch before breakfast.
> She knew better.
> She always filibustered.
> He never typed more than twenty-seven words a minute.

May, can
See **Can, may.**

Metaphor
See pages 108–109.

Modifier
Any word or group of words that describes or qualifies another word or group of words is a modifier.

Momentary, momentous
Momentary has to do with time. It means something that lasts only a moment, or happens at any moment. *Momentous* means of extraordinary importance, as in the cliché, "a *momentous* occasion."

> The affliction was *momentous.*
> She looked West, awaiting his *momentary* arrival.

Mood

The mood (or mode) of the verb indicates an attitude on the part of the writer. The mood may be indicative, imperative, or subjunctive. The indicative mood states a fact or asks a question.

> Fred Lynn *is* here.
> *Was* Bob Lanier there?

The imperative mood gives a command, gives directions, or makes a request.

> *Beware* of darkness.
> *Turn* right at Golgotha.
> *Mend* my parachute, please.

The subjunctive mood may express uncertainty, contradiction, wishfulness, regret, or speculation.

> I would feel better if Bizarre *were* there.
> If I *had* my way, I would tear this building down.

Morale, moral

Moral is a matter of ethics, *morale* of high or low spirits.

> Their *morals* were low, but their *morale* was high.
> Murder is not a *moral* act, usually.

Ms.

A recently invented title, on the analogy of *Mr., Mrs.,* and *Miss, Ms.* reveals female gender while it conceals marital status.

N.b.

This common abbreviation means, "notice well!," and serves to draw our attention to something.

Neither

See **Either.**

Neologism

A neologism is a made-up word, used out of laziness or affectation when an old word would do. *Finalize* is a neologism; *end* or *finish* are the old words.

None

None can be either singular or plural, but is singular in more formal writing.

> *None* of the other guys *were* going to the game.

> *None* of his fellow senators *was* likely to take so strong a stand on the war.

Nonrestrictive modifier

A nonrestrictive modifier is a parenthetical expression that does not limit the noun or pronoun modified. It can be a nonrestrictive clause,

> The Buick, *which was a car new to my neighborhood,* was the object of fascination.

or a phrase,

> The banana, *a fruit new to our taste,* was divided evenly.

See pages 307–308.

No one, nobody

These words take a singular verb. Third person pronouns, singular and plural, can refer to them: *he, his, him, she, hers, her, they, them.* We use *they* and *them* when we feel that the gender of the pronoun would be invidious.

Not un-

Eschew the habit of writing *not un-'s.*

> A *not un*distinguished gentleman, in a *not un*elegant dinner jacket, *not un*gracefully strode past the *not un*chic lady.

Noun

There are several types of nouns. *Common* nouns belong to one of a class of people, places, or things (woman, country, table). *Proper* nouns are names of specific people, places, or things (Max von Sydow, Liv Ullman, Casablanca, Ann Arbor, *The New York Times*). *Concrete* nouns name something that can be perceived by the senses (acid, trees, eggs, horses). *Abstract* nouns name a general idea or quality (terror, love, harshness, agony). *Collective* nouns refer to a group as a unit (band, tea, council, league). These categories are not mutually exclusive; a word like *tree* is both common and concrete.

Nouns, whatever their functions in a sentence, retain their form, varying it only in forming the plural and the possessive. The plural in most nouns is formed by adding *-s* to the singular, the possessive by adding an apostrophe and an *-s* to the singular, or an apostrophe after the *-s* of the plural: hen, hens, hen's, hens'; house, houses, house's. Some nouns add *-es* for the plural: hero, heroes, hero's, heroes'. A few nouns change their internal spelling: man, men; woman, women; here, the possessive is formed by an apostrophe and an *-s*, in singular and in plural. Other nouns with an irregular plural are listed on page 321.

For stylistic advice about nouns, see pages 82–90.

Nouns commonly used as blanks

Many nouns, which are perfectly useful when spoken with care, are frequently used imprecisely, wordily, and without utility—nouns used as blanks: *aspect, case, character, factor, fact, element, effect, nature, manner, respect,* and *feature.*

> Some *aspects* in the *case* of Rumpelstiltskin have the *character* of *elements* that seem sinister in *nature*. The *fact* that the enraged dwarf was a *factor* in the *nature* of the King's *manner* is a *feature* with *respect* to which we can not distinguish the *effect*.

This paragraph has the consistency of mud or an annual report.

Noun substitute

A noun substitute, clause or phrase or pronoun, functions as a noun.

Number

See **Inflection.**

Numeral

See page 320.

Object

A complete sentence needs a subject and a verb; it need not have an object.

> The cat screeched.

is a complete sentence.

> The cat clawed *Herbert.*

includes an object. An object is something a verb acts upon.

Objects are direct and indirect. *Direct object:* Any noun (or noun substitute) that answers the question *What?* or *Whom?* after a transitive verb. Direct objects are the objects of the verb's action.

> She toppled *the giant.*
> He knows *what she wants.*

Indirect object: A noun or noun substitute which is indirectly affected by the verb's action and which tells *to whom* or *for whom* the action is done.

> She gave *him* a karate chop.

Him is the indirect object, *karate chop* the direct object.

Object complement
See **Complement.**

Of
We often use *of* when we don't have to.

> outside *of* the house
> off *of* the ground
> inside *of* the room

The phrases read more stylishly as:

> outside the house
> off the ground
> inside the room

Exceptions occur when the extra preposition changes meaning. "Outside *of*" can mean "to the exclusion *of*," and we are correct to say, "Outside *of* scientific speculation, there is no use for such calibration." "Inside *of*" can mean "in less than." "Inside *of* an hour, he had finished the work."

One, you
Be careful not to use *one* in place of *you* so much that it sounds awkward or pretentious.

> Should *one* be careful to avoid the use of the word "one" when *one* is speaking to a woman whom *one* loves?

As suggested by this example, context is important when you consider using *one*. It is useful at times, but it has a way of seeming affected. Never use it as an obvious disguise for the word *I*.

> *One* took an amusing jaunt to Cedar Point last summer.

One of the most . . .
This cliché is drained of meaning.

> She is *one of the most* lovable people in the world.

> The rodeo last summer was *one of the most* exciting experiences of my life.

Parallelism
See pages 151–155 on Parallelism.

Parentheses
See pages 316–317.

Participle
See **Verbal.**

Passive voice
A verb is in the passive voice when it *acts upon* the subject.

Kaline *was hit* by the wild pitch.

Period
See page 304.

Person
In grammar, the person of a verb or a pronoun shows that someone is speaking (in *first person*), or is spoken to *(second person),* or is spoken about *(third person).* In "I see, you see, he sees," the person of the pronoun changes each time; the verb form for the first person and the second person happens to be the same, but the verb form changes to indicate the third person.

Phrase
Phrases function as a part of speech, and do not have a subject and a predicate.
An *infinitive* phrase:

I studied *to learn Greek.*

A *prepositional* phrase:

The flower grows *in the mountain.*

A *verb* phrase:

The zebra *is catching up.*

A *participle* phrase:

Sliding into second, Zarido tore a ligament.

Plagiarism
Plagiarism is using other people's work, whether it is a published source used without acknowledgment or a friend's old paper or a term paper bought from an entrepreneur.

Possessive
For the possessive of nouns, see **Noun.** For the possessive of pronouns, see **Pronoun.**

Precede, proceed
  To precede is to go before or in front of.

> The Pirates *preceded* the Reds onto the field.

  To proceed is to continue, or to begin again.

> After the game, they *proceeded* to the airport.

Predicate
  A predicate is the part of the sentence *about* the subject. It includes verbs, and, on occasion, objects, indirect objects, and clauses attached to the predicate.
  See pages 119–120.

Predicate adjective
  See **Complement.**

Predicate noun
  See **Complement.**

Preposition
  Prepositions show the relationship between a noun or noun equivalent and another word in the sentence. Some of the most commonly used prepositions are: *across, after, at, behind, between, by, for, from, of, on, over, to, under,* and *with.*

> Tom hid *in* the attic.

  The preposition *in* relates the noun *attic* to the verb *hid.*

Presently
  This word means "in a little while," and not "now" or "currently." Say,

> He is *at present* a milkman.

  not

> He is *presently* a milkman.

  But say,

> He will come back to Chicago *presently.*

Pretty
  See **Little.**

Principal, principle
  Principle is a noun meaning a general truth (the *principles* of physics) or moral ideas (she had the highest *principles*). The adjective *principal* means the foremost. One could speak of the *principal principle* of a science or a philosophy. The noun *principal* means the chief officer, as in "the *principal* of a school."

Pronoun
  A pronoun is a word used in place of a noun.

  > *Personal pronouns:* I, you, he, she, we, etc.

  > *Relative pronouns:* who, which, that.

  > *Demonstrative pronouns:* this, that, these, those.

  > *Indefinite pronouns:* each, either, any, some, someone, all, etc.

  > *Reciprocal pronouns:* each other, one another.

  > *Reflexive, or intensive, pronouns:* myself, yourself, etc.

Proper noun
  See **Noun.**

Prophesy, prophecy
  The word with the *s* is the verb, the word with the *c* the noun.

  > The priest *prophesied* doom.
  > It was an accurate *prophecy.*

Punctuation
  See pages 304–317.

Quotation marks
  See page 312.

Rational, rationale
  Rational means reasonable and sensible. It is an adjective. *Rationale* is a noun meaning the whole system of reasons behind an idea, a position, or an action.

  > His arguments were *rational.*
  > Her *rationale* for the program was easy to discern.

Real, really

Conversational usage accepts *real* as an adverb, but it will not do in writing. Write:

> The boat was *really* handsome!
> Josephine seemed to be a *really* happy girl.

Don't write:

> The boat was *real* handsome.
> Josephine seemed to be a *real* happy girl.

Real as an adjective survives.

> It was a *real* boat.

Reason is because

Don't use this construction. If you must use "reason is," have it be "reason is that. . . ."

Relative clause

See **Subordinate clause.**

Relative pronoun

See **Pronoun.**

Respectfully, respectively

Respectfully is an adverb that modifies an action full of respect.

> I remain, yours *respectfully,*

Respectively pertains to each of a number, in an order.

> He swore that he saw Ted and Joan wearing a flower and a bowler, *respectively.*

Therefore to end a letter "Yours *respectively*" makes little sense.

Restrictive clause or modifier

A restrictive modifier is a clause or a phrase essential to the identity of what is modified.

> Everybody *who wants* can get to the top.

See **Nonrestrictive modifier** for contrast.

Rhetorical question

The rhetorical question is a frequent device of argument or persuasion. One asks a question, not to be answered, but to affect the listener or reader.

> Are we born, to suffer and to die, only to satisfy the whims of rich warmongers?

> Must we write themes forever?

Run-on sentence

A run-on sentence fuses two sentences.

> I was eight my brother was ten.

is a run-on or fused sentence. It should read:

> I was eight. My brother was ten.

Satire

Satire is a form of literature, either prose or poetry, which uses ridicule to expose and to judge behavior or ideas that the satirist finds foolish, or wicked, or both.

Seldom ever

This phrase is redundant. *Seldom* will do. Instead of,

> He *seldom ever* brushed his hair.

say

> He *seldom* brushed his hair.

Semantics

The study of the meanings and associations of words. See S. I. Hayakawa, *Language in Thought and Action.*

Semicolon

See pages 309–310.

Sensual, sensuous

The two words have different meanings. *Sensual* has unfavorable connotations and means "preoccupied with or inclined to the gratification of the senses or appetites."

> He was wholly *sensual* in his priorities; his gluttony came before all else.

Sensuous has complimentary connotations and describes things that give pleasure to the senses.

The passage is one of the most *sensuous* in all literature.

Sentence fragment
See pages 124–126, and 290–293.

Sentence types
See **Compound-complex sentence, Compound sentence, Complex sentence,** and **Simple sentence.**

Shall, will
In common speech and most writing, we make small distinction between the words.
Formally, *I shall* expresses a person's belief about his future.

I *shall* be twenty-one in December.

I will expresses his willpower, his wish.

I *will* get to Japan before I die!

Should, would
Should can express obligation.

You *should* be ashamed.

It is confused with *would* when it is used in other senses.

I *should* not have reached Chicago without your loan.

Also, when we use the past of *shall* in an indirect quotation, formal prose requires *should* instead of *would.*

I said that you *should* be ready before eight.

Would commonly expresses habitual activities.

He *would* visit the lake and fish from dawn to dusk.

When another phrase (like "every summer," if it were added to the last sentence) expresses habit, we can drop the *would* and use the past tense alone.

He visited the lake every summer, and fished from dawn to dusk.

Should have, should of
The words are *should have,* which can be pronounced *should've. Should of* does not make sense.

Sic

Pronounced "sick," this Latin word is used in brackets to signify that an error was made in the source material, not by the writer copying the quotation.

> Studebaker writes, "I would rather be Thoreu [*sic*] unhappy than a contented pig."

Simple sentence

A simple sentence has one main clause and no subordinate clauses.

> She barked at the full moon.

See pages 121–122.

So

This word is a stylistic pitfall for many beginning writers.

As a coordinating conjunction, *so* is often boring and repetitious, leading the writer into dull compound sentences.

> She was tall *so* he asked her how she liked the weather up there.
> She was tired of hearing that question *so* she knocked him flat.

As a vague intensive, *so* is as useless as *wonderful* and *terrible*, though it occupies less space.

> The building was *so* tall.
> I am *so* glad to see you!

Sort of

See **Kind of.**

Spelling

See pages 320–322.

Split infinitive

An infinitive is the form of the verb that uses *to* as in *to run, to think, to scratch.* When we place another word (commonly an adverb) in the middle of an infinitive, we are splitting the infinitive.

> *to quickly run*
> *to occasionally think*
> *to from time to time scratch*

Grammarians used to insist that the infinitive never be split. People split them anyway.

> Remember *to never split* the infinitive!

Now, most grammarians consider a prohibition against split infinitives fussy. But careful writers rarely split them.

Stationary, stationery

Stationary is an adjective that means "standing still." *Stationery* means "writing materials."

Style

See Chapters I to V. See also Strunk and White, *The Elements of Style;* and Bergen Evans, *A Dictionary of Contemporary American Usage;* and *A Dictionary of Modern English Usage* by H. W. Fowler, rev. and ed. by Sir Ernest Gowers. See also *The Modern Stylists,* ed. Donald Hall, a collection of some of these writers with essays and excerpts by George Orwell, Ernest Hemingway, Ezra Pound, Edmund Wilson, James Thurber, and others.

Subject

A subject is a noun, or a noun substitute, about which something is stated or questioned. The subject usually comes before the predicate. The complete subject is the subject and all the words (modifiers, etc.) that belong to it.

> The grinning barbarian, *his teeth clenched,* looked into the barnyard.

Barbarian is the simple subject; the first six words make the complete subject.

Subjunctive

See **Mood.**

Subordinate clause

A subordinate (or dependent) clause cannot stand by itself and make a whole clause or sentence. It depends upon a main clause.

> I cannot see *who it is.*
> The claws are not lethal, *because he was de-clawed.*

Substantive

A substantive is a word or group of words used as a noun; they may be *nouns, pronouns, phrases,* or *noun clauses.*

Suppose, supposed

The past tense often disappears, and meaning disappears with it. See **Used to, use to.**

Syntax

Syntax is the way in which words are put together to form larger units, *phrases, clauses,* or *sentences.* Or it is that part of grammar which describes this putting together.

Tense

The tense of a verb shows the time it takes place in. In the last sentence, *shows* is in the present tense. In

> I *showed* you.

showed is in the past tense.

> I *will show* you.

uses the future tense.

Than, then

Notice that these words are different in spelling, meaning, and function. *Then* refers to time, and *than* makes a comparison.

> We were nice *then*.
> She was taller *than* he was.

That, which

We use the word *that* in a number of ways.

It is a demonstrative, as in "*that* cat."

Many writers are confused about when to use *that* and when to use *which* in introducing clauses. Nonrestrictive (nondefining) clauses take *which*.

> The old car, *which* was struggling through the winter, seemed younger when spring arrived.

When the clause is restrictive or defining, we use *that* when it is possible, which is most of the time.

> The old car *that* Mr. Hornback owned was struggling up the hill.

Which is possible in this last sentence, but seems overprecise or rigid, and is stylistically inferior. However, when a sentence requires several restrictive clauses in a row, *that* can become confusing, and we had better revert to *which*.

> The old car *which* Mr. Hornback owned, *which* had one head-light dangling loose, and *which* smelled perpetually of gasoline, chugged struggling up the hill.

Remember that *who* applies to people, whether the clause is restrictive or nonrestrictive, and *which* never applies to people.

> The folks *which* lived next door.

is incorrect. Some writers, informally, substitute *that* for *who* on occasions when the person is seen as if from a distance.

> The man *that* stood outside the door was tall and fortyish.

Their, there, they're
  See page 311.

Through, thru
  Thru is incorrect, merely a labor-saving device adopted by sign painters, advertisers, and the fabricators of headlines.

Toward, towards
  Either is possible. *Toward* is more American.

Transitive verb
  A transitive verb *must* have a direct object to fill out its meaning.

> He *put* the book down.

Try and
  Like *take and.*

> *Try and see* if she's home.

  is a long way to say,

> See if she's home.

Type
  Type is another word to stay away from. Even used grammatically, it is usually filler.

> It was a strange *type* of animal.

  boils down nicely to

> It was a strange animal.

  Occasionally, as with *sort* or *kind*, we actually mean something by the word.
  Never use it next to a noun, without the preposition *of* coming between. It is useless to say:

> a new *type* soft drink
> a long *type* Buick
> their *type* business
> that *type* handsomeness

  In all these examples, an *of* would make the phrases more acceptable; but in the first three, omission of *type* would be the better solution. We save a word. In the fourth example, the idea of *type* (or *sort* or *kind*) has more meaning.

Unthinkable, inconceivable

Something that is literally *unthinkable* is probably literally unmentionable. We use *unthinkable* as hyperbole, usually to describe something that we deplore.

His conduct was *unthinkable*.

Inconceivable seems to mean the same thing. In use, it means "impossible to imagine or explain."

Her absence was *inconceivable*.

Until, till

We say *till*, but we write *until*. *Till* looks stilted and literary on the page.

Used to, use to

The correct form is *used to*.

I *used to* see her every morning at 9 o'clock.

Probably because of our slovenly pronunciation, we sometimes drift into,

I *use to* see her every morning at 9 o'clock.

when we write it down. We should use the correct form, to make temporal sense.

Verb

For advice on style and the verb, see pages 72–79. In this glossary, see **Mood, Object, Passive voice,** and **Predicate.**

Verbal

Verbals are words derived from verbs but used as nouns or adjectives, and sometimes as adverbs. Verbals are *gerunds, participles,* and *infinitives.*

Gerunds always end in -ing and are used as nouns.

Flying is fun.
Running is good exercise.
Neal and Liz have benefited from their *running*.

Participles are used as adjectives.

This *flying* manual is essential.
His *shattered* hip was mending slowly.
"The *rising* cost of living" is a common phrase.

Infinitives are used primarily as nouns, but sometimes as adjectives or adverbs. They are composed of *to* and a verb, but in use the *to* can occasionally be omitted.

> We started *to run* from Godzilla.
> *To fail* is a pleasure he can't afford.
> He dropped out *to begin* his career as a clown.
> They helped [to] *eat* the submarine.

Vocative

See **Direct address.**

When

Don't use *when* as an introduction to definitions.

> Loneliness is *when* you play the radio just to hear the announcer's voice.

This usage is corny and unacceptable.

Where

See **When.** The same injunction applies.

Which, that

See **That, which.**

While

The word means "at the same time" or "during the time that." Sometimes writers use it in place of *although,* and it can work.

> *While* John is large, his stomach is not excessive.

But this usage is prone to ambiguity.

> Winter is warm in the southern hemisphere, *while* summer is cold.

Think about this sentence for a moment, and it is absurd.

Who, whom

Who is a subject, *whom* an object.

> *Who's* on first?
> To *whom* should I deliver the testimony?

In the last sentence, *whom* is the object of the preposition *to.* In formal writing, always say *whom* when it is an object—of a verb or of a preposition.

Sometimes position leads us into error. When a pronoun precedes a verb, it sounds as if it were a subject; it isn't always. We may be tempted to write,

> From *who* is the noise coming?

but the phrase is *from whom,* and *the noise* (not *who*) is the subject of *is.* We should write,

> From *whom* is the noise coming?

Sometimes a clause separates the subject *who* from its verb, and we misuse *whom* for *who.* We write,

> Herbert, *whom* she said would be here at 6:30, strolled in at 8:00.

In this sentence the three noun-verb combinations make a box within a box within a box. "Herbert . . . strolled" is the outside box, "who . . . would be here" is the middle box, and "she said" the inside box. When *whom* comes before a preposition of which it is the object, it is correct but highly formal.

> *Whom* am I looking at?

Here, we always write *who* in informal writing. Frequently, *whom* will sound *too* formal even in an essay that is mostly formal. Use your judgment. The position of the pronoun makes the problem, which comes up when it is the object of a verb as well as when it is the object of a preposition.

> *Whom* do I see?
> *Who* do I see?

The first is correct and the second incorrect—technically—but it would take a highly formal context to accept the "correct" formulation without creating a moment of stuffiness.

Whose, who's

See page 311.

-wise

Stylewise, avoid this syllable in combination with words with which it has not been combined before. *Clockwise* and *otherwise* are parts of the language. Avoid literarywise, poetrywise, intelligence quotientwise, Septemberwise, costwise, Sallywise, ecologywise—and anything similar.

Woman, women

People seem to forget that the two spellings show a difference in number. *Woman* is singular, *women* plural.

AUTHOR AND TITLE INDEX

"Acquainted with the Night," Frost, Robert, 256

Addams, Jane
Twenty Years at Hull House, 60–61

Adventures of Ideas, Whitehead, A. N., 38

Agee, James
"A Mother's Tale," 103
"Southeast of the Island: Travel Notes," 113

American Nuclear Society
Nuclear Power and the Environment: Questions and Answers, 103–104

"America the Beautiful," McCarthy, Mary, 128, 145

Angelou, Maya
I Know Why the Caged Bird Sings, 82

Ann Arbor News, 130, 233

Armies of the Night, Mailer, Norman, 139–140

As You Like It, Shakespeare, William, 175

"Athletics: The Poison Ivy in Our Schools," Conant, James B., 281–282

Auden, W. H.
The Enchafed Flood, 134

Baldwin, James
Nobody Knows My Name, 92–93

Baraka, Imamu Amiri. *See* Jones, Leroi

Baseball the Beautiful, Cohen, Marvin, 210

Beauvoir, Simone de
The Second Sex, 226

Beck, Jim
"How I Came to College" (impromptu), 7; (free theme), 8–10

Beggar in Jerusalem, A, Wiesel, Elie, 126

Benedict, Ruth
Patterns of Culture, 91

Bergman, Ingmar
Four Screenplays of Ingmar Bergman, 172

Beyond Good and Evil, Nietzsche, Friedrich, 211

Bible, The, 161, 175

"Big Two-Hearted River," Hemingway, Ernest, 104

Black Arts, The, Cavendish, Richard, 144

Blackberry Winter, Mead, Margaret, 24

Blackmur, R. P.
"New Threshold, New Anatomies," 258–259

Brandeis Reader, The, Pollock, Irwin H., 198–199

Brinnin, John Malcolm
The Sway of the Grand Saloon, 48–49

Brown, Norman O.
Life Against Death, 91

"Building Fermi-2," in *The Nuclear Way,* 71–72

Camus, Albert
"Encounters with André Gide," 192
The Stranger, 145–146

Cancer Ward, Solzhenitsyn, Alexander, 38

Carson, Rachel
The Sea Around Us, 69

Case, Jennifer
"The Protector Unprotected," 275–280

Cather, Willa
The Professor's House, 115–116

Cavendish, Richard
The Black Arts, 144

375

Childhood and Society, Erikson, Erik, 177
Chisholm, Shirley
  Unbought and Unsold, 144
Churchill, Sir Winston
  in *The War in the Air,* 144
Civil War in Spain, The, Goldston, Robert, 211–212
Clark, Ronald W.
  Einstein, 224
Cleaver, Eldridge
  Soul on Ice, 176, 217
Closing Circle, The, Commoner, Barry, 72
Cohen, Marvin
  Baseball the Beautiful, 210
Collier, John
  Indians of the Americas, 221
Commoner, Barry
  The Closing Circle, 72
Company Manners, Kronenberger, Louis, 50
Conant, James B.
  "Athletics: The Poison Ivy in Our Schools," 281–282
Confessions of a Disloyal European, Myrdal, Jan, 192
Conroy, Frank
  Stop-Time, 14–15, 144
Corporate Oligarch, The, Finn, David, 231–232
Cousteau, Jacques
  The Silent World, 104
Creating a Role, Stanislavski, Constantin, 172
"Crow in the Wood, The," Updike, John, 55

"Death in Venice," Mann, Thomas, 190
Defeat of the Spanish Armada, The, Mattingly, Garrett, 135
Deliverance, Dickey, James, 227–228
Deschooling Society, Illich, Ivan, 282–283
Detroit Free Press, 219–220
Dickey, James
  Deliverance, 227–228
Dictionary of Contemporary American Usage, A, Evans, Bergen, 225–226
"Dilemma of Determinism, The," James, William, 171–172
Dillard, Annie
  Pilgrim at Tinker Creek, 128–129
Don't Fall off the Mountain, MacLaine, Shirley, 68
"Duende, The: Theory and Divertissement," Lorca, Federico Garcia, 197–198

Ecclesiastes, 161, 175

Eckhart, Meister, 157
Economics and the Public Purpose, Galbraith, John Kenneth, 198
Edvard Munch, Hodin, J. P., 211
Einstein, Clark, Ronald W., 224
Elbow, Peter
  in *Uptaught,* Macrorie, Ken, 4
Elements of Style, The, White, E. B., 176
"Eli, the Fanatic," Roth, Philip, 145
Enchafed Flood, The, Auden, W. H., 134
"Encounters with André Gide," Camus, Albert, 192
Erikson, Erik
  Childhood and Society, 177
Evans, Bergen
  A Dictionary of Contemporary American Usage, 225–226

Family, The, Sanders, Ed, 116
Fanon, Frantz
  The Wretched of the Earth, 92
Female Eunuch, The, Greer, Germaine, 283–285
Films of Orson Welles, The, Higham, Charles, 196–197
Finn, David
  The Corporate Oligarch, 231–232
  "Modifying Opinions in the New Human Climate," in *Public Relations Quarterly,* 70
Fischer, Louis
  Gandhi: His Life and Message for the World, 196, 199, 208
Fitzgerald, F. Scott
  from a notebook, 19–20
  Tender is the Night, 134
"Flowering Judas," Porter, Katherine Anne, 105
Forster, E. M.
  "What I Believe," 45
Four Screenplays of Ingmar Bergman, Bergman, Ingmar, 172
Fowler, H. W.
  Modern English Usage, 178
Franklin, Ben A.
  "What Price Coal?," in *New York Times Magazine,* 71
Fraser, J. G.
  The Golden Bough, 38
Frost, Robert
  "Acquainted with the Night," 256
  Selected Prose of Robert Frost, 176
Frye, Northrop
  Myth and Poetry, 227

Galbraith, John Kenneth
    Economics and the Public Purpose, 198
    How to Control the Military, 205–206
Gandhi: His Life and Message for the World, Fischer, Louis, 196, 199, 208
General Motors Report, 70–71
General Psychopathology, Jaspers, Karl, 172
"Gent," in *The New Yorker*, Steiner, George, 117
"Gentleman from Cracow, The," Singer, Isaac Bashevis, 158
Gerassi, John
    The Great Fear in Latin America, 117
"Gettysburg Address, The," Lincoln, Abraham, 167
Golden Bough, The, Fraser, J. G., 38
Goldston, Robert
    The Civil War in Spain, 211–212
Gospel According to Thomas, The, 171
Great Fear in Latin America, The, Gerassi, John, 117
Greek Way, The, Hamilton, Edith, 143–144
Greer, Germaine
    The Female Eunuch, 283–285

Hamilton, Edith
    The Greek Way, 143–144
Hamlet, Shakespeare, William, 254
Hardy, Wing, George, 258
Harrington, Michael
    The Other America: Poverty in the United States, 205
Harris, Richard
    Justice, 206–207
Hart, Marian
    theme, 10–11
Hassler, Alfred
    Saigon, U.S.A., 172
Haunted Fifties, The, Stone, I. F., 172
Hayakawa, S. I., 84–85
Heilbroner, Robert, L.
    The Worldly Philosophers, 171
Hemingway, Ernest
    "Big Two-Hearted River," 104
    "In Another Country," 16, 99
Higham, Charles
    The Films of Orson Welles, 196–197
"Highways Are for Everyone: Not Just Studded Tire Users," in *Ann Arbor News*, 233
Hodin, J. P.
    Edvard Munch, 211
Home, Jones, Leroi, 177
Hoosier Farm Boy, Redding, Tracy, 249–250

"How Do You Know It's Good?," Mannes, Marya, 103
"How I Came to College," Beck, Jim, 7–10
"How Service Is Delivered," Official Tennis Rules, 82
"How Should a University Administrator Respond to Radical Action?" Hutchins, Robert M., 183
How to Control the Military, Galbraith, John Kenneth, 205–206
Hutchins, Robert M.
    "How Should a University Administrator Respond to Radical Action?," 183

I Know Why the Caged Bird Sings, Angelou, Maya, 82
Illich, Ivan
    Deschooling Society, 282–283
"In Another Country," Hemingway, Ernest, 16, 99
Indians of the Americas, Collier, John, 221
Island in the City, Wakefield, Dan, 92, 143

"Jackals and Arabs," Kafka, Franz, 104–105
James, William
    "The Dilemma of Determinism," 171–172
Jaspers, Karl
    General Psychopathology, 172
Jensen, Oliver
    parody of "The Gettysburg Address," 166–167
Jones, Leroi
    Home, 177
Justice, Harris, Richard, 201–207

Kafka, Franz
    "Jackals and Arabs," 104–105
Kazantzakis, Nikos
    Zorba the Greek, 210–211
Kerr, Jean
    Please Don't Eat the Daisies, 218
Kreicke, Hermann von
    The Migrant Swan, 49, 185, 218–219
Kronenberger, Louis
    Company Manners, 50

Lagerkvist, Pär
    The Sybil, 138–139
Laing, R. D.
    Self and Others, 81
Lao-Tzu, 171
Lawrence, D. H.
    "Pornography and Obscenity," 221–222
    The Rainbow, 81–82

Life Against Death, Brown, Norman O., 91

Lilly, John Cunningham
  The Mind of the Dolphin, 83–84

Lincoln, Abraham
  "The Gettysburg Address," 167

Lippard, Lucy R.
  Pop Art, 190

Lorca, Federico Garcia
  "The Duende: Theory and Divertissement," 197–198

Love and Will, May, Rollo, 197

McCarthy, Mary
  "America the Beautiful," 128, 145

McCartney, James
  in *Detroit Free Press,* 220

Machado, Antonio, 157

MacLaine, Shirley
  Don't Fall off the Mountain, 68

Macrorie, Ken
  Uptaught, 4

Mailer, Norman
  Armies of the Night, 139–140
  The Naked and the Dead, 82
  Of a Fire on the Moon, 54–55, 60
  The Prisoner of Sex, 285–286

Making of the President, The, 1960, White, Theodore, H., 196, 199–200

Male and Female, Mead, Margaret, 191

Mann, Thomas
  "Death in Venice," 190

Mannes, Marya
  "How Do You Know It's Good?," 103

Mattingly, Garrett
  The Defeat of the Spanish Armada, 135

May, Rollo
  Love and Will, 197

Mead, Margaret
  Blackberry Winter, 24
  Male and Female, 191

Mencken, H. L.
  The American Language, 62–63
  "Mr. Justice Holmes," 116

Merchants and Masterpieces, Tomkins, Calvin, 101

"Mexico," Ortiz, Sergio, in *Playgirl,* 69–70

Michigan Daily, 129

Migrant Swan, The, Kriecke, Hermann von, 49, 185, 218–219

Milford, Nancy
  Zelda, 49–50

Mind of the Dolphin, The, Lilly, John Cunningham, 83–84

"Mr. Justice Holmes," Mencken, H. L., 116

Modern English Usage, Fowler, H. W., 178

"Modifying Opinions in the New Human Climate," Finn, David, in *Public Relations Quarterly,* 70

Morris, Wright
  The Territory Ahead, 161, 175–176

"Mother's Tale, A," Agee, James, 103

"My Father's Place," Hart, Marian, 12–13

Myrdal, Jan
  Confessions of a Disloyal European, 192

Myth and Poetry, Frye, Northrop, 227

Naked and the Dead, The, Mailer, Norman, 82

"New Thresholds, New Anatomies," Blackmur, R. P., 258–259

New Yorker, The, 51–53, 117

New York Times Magazine, 71

Nietzsche, Friedrich
  Beyond Good and Evil, 211

Nobody Knows My Name, Baldwin, James, 92–93

Nuclear Power and the Environment: Questions and Answers, 72, 103–104

Nuclear Way, The, "Building Fermi-2," 71–72

O, Canada, Wilson, Edmund, 225

Of a Fire on the Moon, Mailer, Norman, 54–55, 60

"On the Duty of Civil Disobedience," Thoreau, Henry David, 91–92, 216–217

Ortiz, Sergio
  "Mexico," in *Playgirl,* 69–70

Orwell, George
  parody of Ecclesiastes, 163
  "Politics and the English Language," 63–64
  The Road to Wigan Pier, 115

Other America, The: Poverty in the United States, Harrington, Michael, 205

Our Polluted World, Perry, John, 71

Pacific Hawk, 92

Parody
  of Ecclesiastes, Orwell, George, 163
  of "The Gettysburg Address," Jensen, Oliver, 166–167
  of Hamlet's soliloquy, Quiller-Couch, Sir Arthur, 164

Parrish, John
  12, 20 & 5, 244, 246

Patterns of Culture, Benedict, Ruth, 91

Peirce, Charles S.
 Values in a Universe of Change, 226–227
Perry, John
 Our Polluted World, 71
Pilgrim at Tinker Creek, Dillard, Annie, 128–129
Pirsig, Robert M.
 Zen and the Art of Motorcycle Mainte-nance, 203–204, 217
Playgirl, "Mexico," 69–70
Please Don't Eat the Daisies, Kerr, Jean, 218
"Politics and the English Language," Or-well, George, 63–64
Pollock, Irwin H.
 The Brandeis Reader, 198–199
Pop Art, Lippard, Lucy, 190
"Pornography and Obscenity," Lawrence, D. H., 221–222
Porter, Katherine Anne
 "Flowering Judas," 105
Pound, Ezra
 "In a Station of the Metro," 34
Prisoner of Sex, The, Mailer, Norman, 285–286
Professor's House, The, Cather, Willa, 115–116
"Protector Unprotected, The," Case, Jen-nifer, 275–280
Proverb, Zen, 158, 171
Public Relations Quarterly, "Modifying Opinions in the New Human Climate," 70

Quiller-Couch, Sir Arthur
 parody of Hamlet's soliloquy, 164

Rainbow, The, Lawrence, D. H., 81–82
Real Romance, "They Had a Name for Me," 243
Redding, Tracy
 Hoosier Farm Boy, 249–250
Road to Wigan Pier, The, Orwell, George, 115
Roethke, Theodore
 from notebooks, 19
Roget's Thesaurus, 57
"Room of One's Own, A," Woolf, Virginia, 116
Roth, Philip
 "Eli, the Fanatic," 145
Rustig, Sharon
 "Two Wheels are Better Than Four," 47

Saigon, U.S.A., Hassler, Alfred, 172
Saint-Exupéry, Antoine de
 Wind, Sand and Stars, 214–215
Sanders, Ed
 The Family, 116
Sea Around Us, The, Carson, Rachel, 69
Second Sex, The, Beauvoir, Simone de, 226
Second Tree from the Corner, The, White, E. B., 213
Selected Prose of Robert Frost, Frost, Rob-ert, 176
Self and Others, Laing, R. D., 81
Shakespeare, William
 As You Like It, 175
 Hamlet, 254
Silent World, The, Cousteau, Jacques, 104
Singer, Isaac Bashevis
 "The Gentleman from Cracow," 158
Solzhenitsyn, Alexander
 Cancer Ward, 38
Soul on Ice, Cleaver, Eldridge, 176, 217
"Southeast of the Island: Travel Notes," Agee, James, 113
Stanislavski, Constantin
 Creating a Role, 172
Steiner, George
 "Gent," in *The New Yorker,* 117
Stone, I. F.
 The Haunted Fifties, 172
Stop-Time, Conroy, Frank, 14–15, 144
Stranger, The, Camus, Albert, 145–146
Sway of the Grand Saloon, The, Brinnin, John Malcolm, 48–49
Sybil, The, Lagerkvist, Pär, 138–139

Tender is the Night, Fitzgerald, F. Scott, 134
Territory Ahead, The, Morris, Wright, 161, 175–176
"They Had a Name for Me," in *Real Ro-mance,* 243
Thoreau, Henry David
 "On the Duty of Civil Disobedience," 91–92, 216–217
Three Guineas, Woolf, Virginia, 184
Thurber, James
 The Years with Ross, 38, 110, 162
Time, 37
Times (London) *Literary Supplement,* 111
Tomkins, Calvin
 Merchants and Masterpieces, 101
Town Burning, Williams, Thomas, 69
12, 20 & 5, Parrish, John, 244, 246
Twenty Years at Hull House, Addams, Jane, 60–61

"Two Wheels are Better Than Four," Rustig, Sharon, 47

Unbought and Unbossed, Chisholm, Shirley, 144
Updike, John
  "The Crow in the Wood," 55, 99
UPI, 219–220
Uptaught, Macrorie, Ken, 4

Values in a Universe of Change, Peirce, Charles, S., 226–227

Wakefield, Dan
  Island in the City, 92, 143
War in the Air, The, Churchill, Sir Winston in, 144
"What I Believe," Forster, E. M., 45
"What Price Coal?," Franklin, Ben A. in *New York Times Magazine,* 71
White, E. B., 169–170
  The Elements of Style, 176
  The Second Tree from the Corner, 213
White, Theodore H.
  The Making of the President, 1960, 196, 199–200

Whitehead, A. N.
  Adventures of Ideas, 38
Wiesel, Elie
  A Beggar in Jerusalem, 126
Williams, Thomas
  Town Burning, 69
Wilson, Edmund
  O, Canada, 225
Wind, Sand and Stars, Saint-Exupéry, Antoine de, 214–215
Wing, George
  Hardy, 258
Woolf, Virginia
  "A Room of One's Own," 116
  Three Guineas, 184
Worldly Philosophers, The, Heilbroner, Robert L., 171
Wretched of the Earth, The, Fanon, Frantz, 92

Years with Ross, The, Thurber, James, 38, 110, 162
Zelda, Milford, Nancy, 49–50
Zen and the Art of Motorcycle Maintenance, Pirsig, Robert M., 203–204, 217
Zen proverb, 158, 171
Zorba the Greek, Kazantzakis, Nikos, 210–211

SUBJECT INDEX

A, an, 323. *See also* Article
Abbreviation
    in footnotes, 368–369
    when to use, 317–318
Absolute construction, and saving words, 131
Absolute element, 323
Abstract, abstraction, 324
Abstract noun, 358
Abstraction
    in conceptual or argumentative prose, 86
    eliminating from beginnings and endings, 86–87
    and images, 61
    levels of, 84–85
Accept, except, 324
Acronym, 324
Active voice, 324
Ad hominem argument, 241. *See also* Thinking
Adjective
    avoiding the predictable, 93–94
    clause, 121, 325
    defined, 93, 324–325
    frequently misused, 325–326
    nouns used as, 325
    types of, 324–325
Adjectives and adverbs, comparison of (degree), 336
Adverb(s)
    clause, 121, 326
    dangling, 147
    defined, 93, 326
    frequently misused, 326
Advice, advise, 327

Affect, effect, 327
Agreement
    defined, 149, 327
    and indefinite pronouns, 150
    and style, 149–150
    See also Matching
Agree to, agree with, 327
All ready, already, 327
All right, alright, 327
Along with, 328
A lot, 328
Although, though, 328
Altogether, all together, 328
Ambiguity, 328
    and fallacies in thinking, 242
Amid, amidst, 328
Among, amongst, 328
Among, between, 328
Amoral, immoral, unmoral, 329
Amount, number, 329
Analogy
    comic effects with, 112–113
    defined, 110, 329
    as fact, 241–242
    looking for, 112
    in the negative, 112
    See also Comparison, Metaphor
Analysis of text, 253–254. *See also* Criticism
And/or, 329
Antecedent, 329
    unclear, 298–301
Antonym, 330
Any, any other, 330
Anybody, anyone, 330
Anyways, 330

381

Apostrophes, when to use, 311–312
Appositives, 131, 309, 331
Appropriateness, and style, 79
Argument
    and awareness of opposition, 234–235
    clarity in, 229–230
    defined, 229
    order of, 235–237
    and persuasion, 228–242
    reasonableness in, 230–234
    See also Thinking
Article
    definite, 331
    indefinite, 331
As, like, 331
Association, and meaning, 66–67
At, 331
Audience
    and subject, 168–169
    and vocabulary, 67–68
Autobiographical fallacy, 255–256
Autobiography, 248–250. *See also* Writing
Auxiliaries, in verb phrases, 332
Awful, awfully, 332

Bad, badly, 332–333
Balance
    contrasted with parallelism, 157
    in sentences, 156–158
Begging the question, 240. *See also* Thinking
Beginnings
    eliminating long, 39
    first sentence, 36–39
Beside, besides, 333
Bias, 61–62
Bibliography
    defined, 265
    form, 265–266
    for research paper, 265
Bibliography card, 270
    Examples of, 271
    See also Note cards
Big words, 333
Biographical fallacy, 255
Brackets, when to use, 312–313, 333
Brainstorming, in starting paper, 29–30

Can, may, 333–334
Can't hardly, 334
Cannot, can not, 334
Capital letter, when to use, 318–319
Card catalogue, how to use, 261–263
Case. *See* Inflection

Cf., 335
Circumlocution, 335, 356
Cite, sight, site, 335
Clarity
    and argument, 242
    and incomplete sentences, 125
    revising sentences for, 129–130
Clause(s)
    adjective, 121
    adverb, 121
    coordinate, 122–123
    defined, 120
    main (independent), 120, 335, 355–356
    noun, 121
    restrictive, 364
    subordinate (dependent), 120, 335, 368
Cliché
    in adjective-noun combinations, 86
    defined, 336
    and dishonesty, 3–4
    and mixed metaphor, 59
Coherence, in paragraph, 186–195
Collective noun, 358
Colon
    in long sentences, 135
    when to use, 313
Comma(s)
    in compound sentences, 135
    splices (faults), 293–296
    when to use, 305–309
Common noun, 358
Comparative (adjectives and adverbs), 336
Compare to, compare with, 336
Comparison, of adjectives and adverbs (degree), 336
Comparison
    appropriateness in, 109
    eliminating unintended, 111–112
    inflection, 351
    and originality, 105–109
    revising for, 114
    and simile, 59, 108
    See also Analogy, Metaphor
Complement
    object, 120, 337
    subject, 120, 337
Complement, compliment, 337
Complete subject, 119
Complex sentence, 123, 337
Compound-complex sentence, 124, 337
Compound sentence, 122–123, 337
Compound word, 338
Conclusion, resolution and completeness in, 45

Concrete noun, 358
Conjugation, 351
Conjunction(s)
  and complex sentences, 123
  coordinating, 338
  misusing, 147–149
  repeating, 153
  subordinating, 338
  and unity, 147–149
Conjunctive adverb, 338
Connectives, in compound sentences, 122
Connotation, and meaning, 56–57
Consider . . . as, 338
Consistency. *See* Parallelism
Consist in, consist of, 338–339
Context
  and choosing punctuation, 137
  and choosing words, 57–58
Continual, continuous, 339
Contractions, 311–312
Coordinate clauses, 123
Coordinates
  and agreement, 154
  defined, 339
Correlative conjunctions, 339
Could have, could of, 339
Counsel, council, consul, 339
Couple, 340
Criticism
  and autobiographical fallacy, 255–256
  and biographical fallacy, 255
  See also Writing
Cutting, revision by, 34–36

Daily writing, necessity of, 18–22
Dangling constructions, 340. *See also* Modifiers, misplaced
Dashes, when to use, 313–314
Data, 340
Daydreams, and originality, 106
Dead metaphors, detecting, 59
Declension, 351
Deductive reasoning, 238, 340
Demonstrative adjective, 325, 340
Demonstrative pronoun, 340, 363
Denotation, 56–57
Dependent clause. *See* Subordinate clause
Description, 243. *See also* Writing
Descriptive adjective, 324
Detail, accumulating and selecting, 29–34
Development, in paragraph, 195–209. *See also* Paper, middles
Dialogue, and quotation, 247–248

Diction
  comic effects with, 170
  mixing formal and informal, 169–170
Dictionaries, 57, 65–66
Dictionary synonyms, and insides of words, 58
Different from, different than, 341
Direct address, 341
Direct object, 119, 359
Discreet, discrete, 341
Disinterested, uninterested, 341
Don't, 342
Double negative, 334, 342
Doubt but, 342
Due to, 342

E.g., 342
Each, every, 343–344
Editorial, as pure argument, 233
Editorializing. *See* Bias
Egoism, egotism, 344
Either, 344
Elicit, illicit, 344
Ellipses, when to use, 314–315
Eminent, immanent, imminent, 345
Emotionalism, and logic, 237–238
Emphasis
  by contrast, 155
  by order, 156
  by repetition, 155
Endings
  concluding argument, 43–44
  eliminating long, 43–45
End punctuation, 304–305
Enormity, enormousness, 345
Etc., 345
Etymology, 255, 345
Euphemism
  defined, 11, 345
  and misusing words, 62–64
Evading issues, 240. *See also* Thinking
Everybody, everyone, 345
Exclamation point, 304
Experience, and ideas for writing, 248
Expletives, 346
Explication of text, 254. *See also* Criticism
Exposition, 223

Fact, 346
Fact, and opinion, 230–231
Famous, notorious, 346
Farther, further, 346
Feeling, honest and dishonest, 2–6
Fiction, 250. *See also* Writing

Field, 346
Figurative language, 60. *See also* Image
Fine, 346
Finite verb, 346
Focus
    in early drafts, 11
    and purpose, 35–36
    and shape, 33
Footnoting, rules for, 266–269
Foreign words and phrases, 347
Foreword, forward, 347
Formality
    and abbreviations, 317–318
    and commas, 307
    and complicated sentences, 162–163
    and conciseness, 152
    gone bad, 163–164
    and long paragraphs, 200
    and long sentences, 133–135
    and pronouns, 298
    and semicolons, 136
    See also Informality

Gender, 298, 347
Generalizing from particulars, 239. *See also* Thinking
Genteel words, 347
Gerund, 371
Gerund phrase, 120
Get, 347
Good, well, 348
Grammar, 348
    review of common problems, 289–304
Guerilla, gorilla, 348
Guilt by association, 239–240. *See also* Thinking

Had ought, 348
Hanged, hung, 348
He or she, 348
Homonym, 349
Hopefully, 349
Humor, and disunity, 161. *See also* Diction, comic effects with
Hyperbole, 349
Hyphens, when to use, 315–316

I.e., 349–350
Ideas
    getting, 27–28, 248
    order of, 40–41
Image, 59–61, 108
Immigrant, emigrant, 350
Imperative mood, 357

Incomplete sentence, 124–126. *See also* Sentence, fragments
Incredible, unbelievable, 350
Indefinite adjective, 325
Indefinite pronoun, 363
    and agreement, 150
Independent clause. *See* Main clause
Indicative mood, 357
Indirect object, 119, 359
Indirect quotation, 350–351
Inductive reasoning, 238, 351
Infer, imply, 351
Inferior to, inferior than, 351
Infinitive, 371–372
    phrase, 120, 361
    split, 367
Inflection, 351
Informality
    gone bad, 166–168
    and participles, 133
    and using dashes, 313–314
    versus formality, 160–170
    See also Formality
In regard to, in regards to, 351
Insides of words, 65–66
Intensive pronoun, 363
Interrogative adjective, 325
Intransitive verb, 352
Irony, 352
Irregardless, 352
Italics, when to use, 316
Its, it's, 352
-ize verbs, 352

Jargon, 3–4, 352–353
Journal, 18

Kind of, 353

Language, pompous, 164–165
Lay, lie, 353
Lead, led, 353
Leave, let, 354
Less, 354
Library, and research paper, 261–265
Like, as, 354
Likewise, 354
Linking verb, 354
Literally, 354–355
Literalness and metaphor, 59
Litotes, 355
Little, 355
Loaded words, 62
Logic, 237–242, 355. *See also* Thinking

Loose, lose, 355
Luxuriant, luxurious, 355

Made-up words. *See* Neologism
Main clause, 120, 335, 355–356
Manuscript form, 319–320
Man who . . . , 356
Matching
   pronouns and antecedents, 298–301
   subjects with verbs, 296–298
   See also Agreement
Material, running out of, 21, 22. *See also*
   Ideas
Meaning
   literal, 59
   private and general, 66–67
   and word order, 302
Mechanics, review of common problems,
   317–322. *See also* Abbreviation, Capital
   letter, Manuscript form, Numerals,
   Spelling
Metaphor
   contrasted with simile, 108
   defined, 59
   eliminating unintentional, 96–97
   and imagery, 108
   mixed, 59
   See also Analogy, Comparison
Middles (developing papers), 40–43
Modifiers
   adjectives, adverbs, and others, 93–102
   dangling, 301–302
   defined, 121, 356
   eliminating useless, 95–97
   in expository prose, 100
   misplaced, 146–147
   nouns as, 98
   restrictive, 364
   revising, 102
   some common problems with, 301–302
   that weaken nouns, 94–95
Momentary, momentous, 356
Mood (mode), 357
Morale, moral, 357
Ms., 357

N.b., 357
Narrative, 245. *See also* Writing
Neologism
   defined, 357
   and nouns, 88
   and verbs, 79
News magazines, and insides of words,
   61–62

None, 357
Nonrestrictive clause, 307–308
Nonrestrictive modifier, 358
Nonsequitur, 240–241. *See also* Thinking
No one, nobody, 358
Notebook, 18
Note cards, 274
   examples of, 272, 273
   See also Bibliography card
Notes, taking random, 29–30
Not un-, 358
Noun(s)
   abstract and particular, 84–86
   as blanks, 359
   clause, 121
   defined, 82
   fancy, 88
   invisible, 87
   made up from verbs, 88
   as modifiers, 98
   revising, 88–90
   substitute, 359
Numerals, 320
Numerical adjective, 325

Object(s)
   complementary, 120
   defined, 119, 359
   direct, 119, 359
   indirect, 119, 359
   of prepositions, 119–120
Of, 360
One, you, 360
One of the most . . . , 360
Opening sentences, examples, 37–38
Order
   chronological, 40
   and emphasis, 156
Originality
   finding images, 107–108
   and memory, 109
   overhearing your own, 106–107
   and skill, 56
Overinclusive premise, 239. *See also* Thinking
Overwriting, and false color, 78

Paper
   accumulating detail, 29–33
   beginnings, 36–39
   cutting, 34–36
   endings, 43
   focus, 11, 33–36
   getting ideas, 27–28, 248

Paper *(continued)*
 middles (development), 40–43
 narrowing the topic, 35–36
 order of ideas, 40–41
 and purpose, 33–34
 samples of. *See* Author and Title Index:
  Jim Beck, Marian Hart, Sharon Rustig,
  Jennifer Case
 selecting detail, 34
 shape, 33–48
 taking notes, 29–30
 topic sentences, 183
 unity in, 146–170
Paragraph(s)
 coherence in, 186–195
 deciding order of, 179–181
 defined, 178
 focusing with, 179–181
 formality of long, 200
 length and completeness of, 200–205
 revising, 209
 and topic sentence, 183–186
 transitions between, 189–195
 unity in, 181–186
 ways to develop, 195–209
Parallel constructions, as transitions, 191–
 192
Parallelism
 contrasted with balance, 157
 defined, 151
 as emphasis, 155
 and formality, 151–154
 and grammatical consistency, 303–304
Parentheses, when to use, 316–317
Parenthetical elements, and commas, 308–
 309
Parenthetical expression, 358
Parody
 defined, 17
 examples of, 17–18, 163–164, 166–167
Participle(s)
 dangling, 146
 defined, 132
 phrase, 120, 361
 present, 74
 used as adjectives, 371
Passive voice, 75–76, 361
Period, 304
Periodic sentence, defined, 156
Person, 361
Personal pronoun, 363
Phrases, types of, 120, 361
Plagiarism, 265, 361
Plural nouns, 358–359

Plural of numbers, and apostrophes, 311
Point of view, and unity in fiction, 252
Positive (adjectives and adverbs), 336
Possessive(s)
 adjectives, 325
 and apostrophes, 311–312
 nouns, forming, 358–359
Practice. *See* Daily writing
Precede, proceed, 362
Predicate
 complete, 119
 defined, 119, 362
 filler, 160
 simple, 119
Preposition, 362
Prepositional phrase, 120, 361
Presently, 362
Principal, principle, 363
Principal clause. *See* Main clause
Pronouns, types of, 363
Propaganda
 and dishonest argument, 229
 and insides of words, 61
Proper nouns, 358
Prophesy, prophecy, 363
Punctuation
 conventions of, 304–317
 in compound sentences, 135–138
 See also Apostrophes, Brackets, Colon,
  Comma(s), etc.
Puns
 and literal mindedness, 59
 and originality, 106
Purpose
 focus through, 33–34
 and organizing paragraphs, 208–209

Question mark, 304–305, 312
Quotation
 and dialogue, 247–248
 ellipses in, 314–315
 indirect, 350–351
 punctuating, 312
 when to detach from text, 319–320

Rational, rationale, 363
Reading and writing, 14
Real, really, 364
Reason is because, 364
Reciprocal pronoun, 363
Reference works, and research, 263–265
Reflexive pronoun, 363
Relative
 adjective, 325

clause, 123
    pronoun, 363
Repetition, and coherent transitions, 190–
    191
Research paper
    bibliography, 265–266
    footnote form, 266–269
    manuscript form, 319–320
    narrowing topics, 269–270
    note cards, 274
    and plagiarism, 265
    preparing and organizing materials, 269–
    275
    purpose of, 260
    quotations in, 312, 319–320
    sample of, 275–280
    using the library, 261–265
Resolution
    defined, 158
    and unity, 45, 146
Respectfully, respectively, 364
Restrictive
    clause, 307–308, 364
    modifier, 364
    See also Nonrestrictive clause, Nonre-
        strictive modifier
Revision
    checking for focus, 33–35
    importance of, 6–7
    of paragraphs, 209
    of sentences, 140–141, 170
Rhetorical question, 365
Rhythm, 158
Run-on sentence, 365. *See also* Comma(s),
    splices

Satire, 365
Seldom ever, 365
Self-deceit, avoiding, 64–65
Semantics, 365
Semicolon(s)
    in compound sentences, 135–137
    fragment, 292
    when to use, 309–310
Sense words, 59–61
Sensual, sensuous, 365–366
Sentence(s)
    balanced, 157
    complex, 123, 337
    compound, 122–123, 337
    compound-complex, 124, 337
    defined, 118
    fragments, 290–293
    incomplete, and informality, 124

long, and formality, 133–135
    mixing types of, 138–140
    parts of, 118–121
    periodic, 156
    and resolution, 159–160
    revising for unity, 170
    revising for variety and conciseness, 140–
    141
    run-on, 365. *See also* Comma(s), splices
    simple, 121–122, 367
Sentimentality, and language, 61
Sequence as cause (Post hoc ergo propter
    hoc), 241. *See also* Thinking
Sexism, and pronouns, 150, 298
Shall, will, 366
Shape (methods of shaping papers), 33–48
Should, would, 366
Should have, should of, 366
Showing, not telling, 14, 61
Sic, 367
Simile
    contrasted with metaphor, 108
    defined, 59, 108
    and imagery, 108
Simple sentence, 121–122, 367
Simple subject, 119
Sincerity, 4–5
Slang, 353
So, 367
Sort of, 353
Spelling, rules, 320–322
Split infinitive, 367
Stationary, stationery, 368
Structure, chronology and, 40
Style
    choosing, 93
    and meaning, 73, 83, 131
    readings on, 368
    and variety in sentence structure, 130–141
Subject
    complete, 119, 368
    simple, 119, 368
Subjective complement, 120
Subjunctive mood, 357
Subordinate clause, 120, 335, 368
Substantive, 368
Summary, concluding argument with, 43
Superlative, adjectives and adverbs, 336
Suppose, supposed, 368
Synonyms, 56–58
Syntax, 132, 368

Tact
    and audience, 67–68

Tact *(continued)*
  and transitions, 194
Tense
  consistency of, 150
  defined, 369
Than, then, 369
That, which, 369
Thesaurus, 57–58
Thesis, in argument, 229
Thinking, common fallacies in, 238–242
Through, thru, 370
Tone
  in argument, 231–232, 235
  in choosing punctuation, 137
  and levels of diction, 160
  revising to control, 141
Topic
  finding, 27–28
  narrowing, 35–36
Topic sentence
  in narrative and descriptive prose, 185–186
  and unity in paragraphs, 183
  varying location of, 183–186
Toward, towards, 370
Transition(s)
  developing multiple means of, 194
  implicit, 193–195
  overt, 189–190
  and parallel constructions, 191–192
  repeated words or phrases, 191–192
Transitional words and phrases, 192–193
Transitive verb, 370
Try and, 370
Type, 370

Underlining. *See* Italics
Understatement. *See* Litotes
Unity
  defined, 10
  grammatical, 146–151
  need for, 146
  revising for, 170
  structural, 151–170
  and topic sentence, 183
Unthinkable, inconceivable, 371
Until, till, 371
Used to, use to, 371

Verb(s)
  active forms of, 73
  and choice of style, 72–79
  consistency of tense, 150
  false color in, 78–79
  fancy, 79
  finite, 346
  intransitive, 352
  invisible, 77
  made-up, 79
  particular and general, 76–77
  passive, 75–76, 361
  phrase, 120, 361
  tense, 369
  transitive, 370
  weak, 73–76
Verbal, 346, 371–372. *See also* Gerund, Participle(s), Infinitive
Vocabulary, and tact, 67–68

When, 372
While, 372
Who, whom, 372–373
-wise, 373
Woman, women, 373
Words
  big, 333
  as blanks, 66
  collecting new, 65–66
  deceiving with, 61
  dividing, 315
  eliminating unnecessary, 131–132
  filler, 370
  foreign, 347
  frequently misspelled, 322
  genteel and ordinary, 347
  insides of, 54–68
  loaded, 62
  and meaning, 66–67
  originality in choosing, 105–106
Writing, types of, 223–281

Zingers
  in argument, 237
  defined, 37
  See also Paper, beginnings

To The Student

We, the author and publisher, would like your opinion of *Writing Well, Second Edition*. If we are to make a better book next time, we must know what students think of what we've already done. Please help us by filling out this questionnaire and returning it to us at: Little, Brown and Company, College English, 34 Beacon Street, Boston, Mass. 02106.

School: _____ Course Title: _____

Instructor's Name: _____

Other books assigned: _____

1. Did you like *Writing Well*? _____

2. Was it too easy? _____ Too difficult? _____

3. Which chapters were most useful to you? _____

   Why? _____

4. Which chapters were least useful? _____

   Why? _____

5. Were the exercises useful? _____ How might they be improved? _____

   _____

6. Were the examples useful? _____ How might they be improved? _____

   _____

7. Did you use Some Common Problems? _____ Any suggestions

   for changes or additions? _____

   _____

8. Did you use the Glossary? _____ Any suggestions for improve-

   ment? _____

   _____

9. Did you like the way the book was organized? _____

10. Did you like the book's physical appearance? _____

11. Do you feel your instructor should continue to assign this book next

    year? _____

12. Will you keep this book for your library? _____

13. Please add any general comments or suggestions. _____

    _____

    _____

    _____

14. May we quote you in our promotion efforts for this book?

    _____ Yes _____ No

_____   _____
date   signature

_____
address

                                        Thanks for your help.